Law, Governance and Technology Series

Volume 48

Series Editors

Pompeu Casanovas, UAB, Institute of Law and Technology UAB, Barcelona, Spain

Giovanni Sartor, University of Bologna and European University Institute of Florence, Florence, Italy

The *Law, Governance and Technology Series* is intended to attract manuscripts arising from an interdisciplinary approach in law, artificial intelligence and information technologies. The idea is to bridge the gap between research in IT law and IT-applications for lawyers developing a unifying techno-legal perspective. The series will welcome proposals that have a fairly specific focus on problems or projects that will lead to innovative research charting the course for new interdisciplinary developments in law, legal theory, and law and society research as well as in computer technologies, artificial intelligence and cognitive sciences. In broad strokes, manuscripts for this series may be mainly located in the fields of the Internet law (data protection, intellectual property, Internet rights, etc.), Computational models of the legal contents and legal reasoning, Legal Information Retrieval, Electronic Data Discovery, Collaborative Tools (e.g. Online Dispute Resolution platforms), Metadata and XML Technologies (for Semantic Web Services), Technologies in Courtrooms and Judicial Offices (E-Court), Technologies for Governments and Administrations (E-Government), Legal Multimedia, and Legal Electronic Institutions (Multi-Agent Systems and Artificial Societies).

Philippe Jougleux

Facebook and the (EU) Law

How the Social Network Reshaped the Legal Framework

 Springer

Philippe Jougleux
School of Law
European University Cyprus
Nicosia, Cyprus

ISSN 2352-1902   ISSN 2352-1910   (electronic)
Law, Governance and Technology Series
ISBN 978-3-031-06595-8   ISBN 978-3-031-06596-5   (eBook)
https://doi.org/10.1007/978-3-031-06596-5

This Springer imprint is published by the registered company Springer Nature Switzerland AG
The registered company address is: Gewerbestrasse 11, 6330 Cham, Switzerland

Contents

Chapter 1
Introduction to the "Facebook" Phenomenon

Once men turned their thinking over to machines in the hope that this would set them free.
But that only permitted other men with machines to enslave them.

— Frank Herbert (1965) Dune.

Discussing the legal impact of Facebook's (now Meta) numerous activities is a methodological challenge. Assuming that "an effort at unfolding the truth requires commitment to objectivity, and freedom from the undue influence of competing ideologies",[1] research on Facebook encounters a difficulty: by using it, the legal scholar experiences a series of personal feelings, both positive and negative, that could potentially affect his or her objectivity, but not using it would deprive him or her of an intimate knowledge of the functions of the famous social network. In practice, this question is not even pertinent anymore, as for personal, familial, or professional reasons, almost three billion individuals have adopted the social network as a core component of their everyday life. Consequently, this research on Facebook and EU law does not pretend to achieve an absolute objectivity. Nevertheless, it will present a varied panel of legal issues regarding the functioning of social media, with the purpose of conciliating clarity and completeness.

This book aims to propose a general overview of the most fundamental challenges surrounding Facebook. As it discusses very diverse fields of law, it would be impossible to be exhaustive. It was, in fact, a deliberate choice to focus on the specific issues that are more relevant to Facebook, proposing, this way, both a point of first access to the neophyte looking to learn more about Facebook's legal framework, and a more thorough discussion on how various legal reactions, through legislative initiatives or co-regulation techniques, have until now managed to work on this worldwide phenomenon.

---

[1] Ishwara Bhat (2019), p. 54.

In this introduction, we focus on Meta's background. First, a theory, or more correctly, a metaphor, is proposed, of the (seemingly) unique monopolistic power acquired by the company and a discussion follows on how this vast influence of Facebook on the Internet is reminiscent of the East India Company's situation, in the seventeenth century (Sect. 1.1). At stake is not only the economic power that the company has acquired through establishing its monopoly in this specific category of social networks (Sect. 1.2), but also how from an historical (Sect. 1.3) and societal perspective, it shaped the Internet, its content, and its usage (Sect. 1.4). Consequently, the legal issues that must be addressed in order to fully apprehend the tangled web of influences between the company, civil society, and the authorities are diverse but also connected (Sect. 1.5).

1.1   General Approach: Facebook's Influence on the Internet

1.1.1   From the East India Companies to the GAFAM

The subject matter of this book could be surprising at first sight for a legal scholar. The essence of the rule of law is that the law ought to be general and impersonal. This characteristic of the rule of law is related to the principle of equality before the law. It is not the function of the law to target specific individuals or legal entities. However, in some exceptional circumstances, it so happens that one range of activities is strongly associated with very few persons, either natural or legal. Although such situations are very specific, it must be underlined that this is not a new phenomenon. It may be useful to remember the precedent of the powerful East India Companies and specifically the British East India Company, which, at the apex of its power, possessed an army twice as large as that of Great Britain and controlled large parts of India.

To take the metaphor between the era of colonialism and our times a little further, the digital world has substantially transformed in the past two decades and it could be argued that we live in a time of digital colonialism. Certain protagonists of online activities have gradually emerged as dominant actors in the sector. An acronym has even been created to qualify this dominance of a few legal persons over the digital world: "GAFAM" (which stands for Google, Apple, Facebook—now called Meta, Amazon and Microsoft). Each one of them has, in its own way, not only shaped the technological landscape but also pushed the boundaries of the Internet's existing legal framework.

While Microsoft's empire is arguably built upon copyright law (Bill Gates famously negotiated with IBM to keep the rights in the DOS software and to license the software to IBM, while it was customary at the time to transfer ownership), it is also the source of a counter movement that led to development of open-source software and creative commons. Simultaneously, Apple's obsession with patent applications has led to a worldwide intellectual property war with Samsung and contributed to a debate on the subject matter of industrial property. Google's (now called Alphabet) perilous relationship with data privacy legislation, such as Google Street View's privacy issues, or with copyright law, with the Google Books' copyright law settlement for instance. Amazon has also provided an opportunity for some of the most fundamental cases on intermediaries' liability to be decided.

The multiple encounters that all members of the GAFAM have had with the judicial system, can be explained by the particularly dominant and innovative digital ecosystem they have created. It has been famously claimed that "[m]ore than 70% of all Internet traffic goes through sites owned or operated by Google or Facebook.".[2] This means that more than 70% of access to third-party content comes from Google and Facebook, while an analysis of the use of Internet bandwidth shows that the GAFAM monopolizes "only" around 31% of the Internet's connections.[3]

Therefore, in a strict technical sense, it is wrong to say that the GAFAM has a monopoly on the Internet. However, the GAFAM's dominance over the digital world should not be underestimated and is not to be reduced to mere connection numbers. In this context, Meta occupies a very specific place, different from the other members of the GAFAM's informal group. More than the others Meta's wealth is based on a main service, the Facebook platform, which defined a new genre of the digital ecosystem: online social media.

Furthermore, it is worth mentioning that the GAFAM's dominance is not limited to a digital empire only. On the contrary, it could be said that the private sector physically owns the Internet nowadays. Indeed, it is estimated that 95% of voice and data traffic travels through giant undersea cables.[4] This network of undersea cables preexisted the Internet, as they were already in place in the age of telephony, mostly on the initiative of a consortium comprising public and private interests. However, the everlasting need for more bandwidth and connection speed requires a replacement of this old network with a new network of fiber optic cables. In this context, online platforms have decided to ensure control over the infrastructure of their services and have massively invested in the cable industry (and sometimes also in the energy sector). This hold on the Internet's physical backbone has become substantial enough that there have been calls concerning the potential impact that both the privatization and the splintering of the Internet will have on citizens' digital rights.[5]

---

[2] Warren E. (2019) Here's how we can break up Big Tech. https://medium.com/@teamwarren/heres-how-we-can-break-up-big-tech-9ad9e0da324c.

[3] Stapp (2019).

[4] Internet Health Report (2019).

[5] Song (2018).

1.1.2   The Rise of Online Social Networks

Although the Internet is often described as a revolution, its history in fact shows a long series of small steps towards the network we know today. The creation of the Arpanet in 1967,[6] the decision in the 1990s by a consortium of universities to open the network to private companies, and the first graphic representation (the creation of html) of a website coincided with the development of what could retrospectively be called "Web 1.0". In other words, the Internet, as a network of networks, gave birth to a shared information space: the "Web".

However, this first generation of the Internet was limited for both technical and structural reasons. First, the speed—the bandwidth—was simply insufficient to support fast and massive audiovisual communications. In this respect, McLuhan's theory that "the medium is the message"[7] is even more applicable to the digital era. The speed of connection conditions the content available to the users, and, ultimately, the relevant legal framework. Second, Web 1.0 suffered from its own philosophy: as a decentralized network, it placed a burden on the average user to be in a position to learn and manage the basic requirements of a real interaction: knowledge of the html language, of the methods of communication (ftp for instance for any transfer to a server), and of a domain name and server's technical characteristics.

Web 2.0 was built on the simple idea that this burden hinders the network's potential. Using more advanced languages that allowed more complex interactions between the servers, its database, and the clients (the individuals' devices), some platforms began to offer Internet users hosting of their contents. This asymmetry between the author of the content and the owner of the medium nowadays constitutes the new backbone of the Internet and gave birth to the online social media phenomenon.

Social media is characterized by some fundamental elements: firstly, and obviously, the definition only concerns a web-based service. Moreover, the service allows individuals to build a public or semi-public profile within a delimited system, to articulate a list of other users with whom they share a connection, and, finally, to view and traverse their list of connections and those made by others with the system.[8]

Numerous new legal challenges appear in the context of Web 2.0 and online social media. While the control and legal framework of e-mails and the URL governed the period of Web 1.0, the notion of the "user's account" has become ubiquitous under Web 2.0. This evolution also correlates with the gradual rise of smartphones. The most intimate technological device in history, a companion of each moment and a vault of its owner's activities, thoughts, feelings and sentiments, the mobile phone fuses with social media in an exponential amplification of the

---

[6]Leiner et al. (2009), pp. 22–31.

[7]McLuhan (1964).

[8]Danah and Ellison (2008), pp. 210–230.

influence of social media in the everyday life of individuals. Web 2.0 feeds off user-generated content, and its rise not coincidentally corresponds to the parallel emergence of Facebook.

Nowadays, some arguments are made in favor of Web 3.0. Some scholars consider it a new characteristic of the web, which, through the deep interconnexion of smart devices, becomes a "web of everything".[9] Others extrapolate from the development of blockchain technology, mainly—but not exclusively—used nowadays as infrastructure for cryptocurrencies.[10] Another trend is to distinguish Web 3.0 from Web 2.0 by its artificial intelligence (AI) driven technology.[11] Finally, for other scholars, Web 3.0 is encapsulated in virtual reality (VR) technology. Web 4.0 is even predicted, that will regroup all these new technologies together.[12]

New trends and technological innovations are inevitable, and it would be futile to believe in the immutability of Web 2.0 as infrastructure. However, there has been no empirical sign of a regression of the influence of Web 2.0 on society. Social media are still in an early phase of their development, as their complex uses oblige them to consider the application of multiple new legal etiquettes in various EU legislative instruments: providers of online service, publishers, hosters, controllers, gatekeepers, traders, essential platforms of service or intermediaries, for instance, are various legal terms that appear in recent legislative initiatives and serve as definitions of the GAFAM. In other words, instead of investigating the decline of social media, the discussions on Web 3.0 only emphasize the expected transformation of social media. In this context, Meta plays a leading role and, to protect its ubiquity,[13] is very attentive to technological trends (such as VR) in order to maintain its position. For instance, it quickly acquired the company developing the Oculus VR system, invested heavily for more than a decade in AI's development, and is preparing its own blockchain-based currency, called Diem.

1.2 Economic Considerations Regarding the Facebook Phenomenon

It is important to differentiate Facebook as a service from the company first called Facebook Inc and now Meta. Indeed, the company's activities are not limited to the Facebook service anymore, as it has acquired some famous assets such as Instagram, (bought in 2012), WhatsApp and Oculus VR in 2014. It is however safe to say that the company's value continues to be based on the value of its main service: the social network Facebook. This clearly poses a lot of questions, but the first one is: how does

---

[9]Cook et al. (2020).

[10]Ragnedda and Destefanis (2019).

[11]Issa and Isaias (2015).

[12]Nath and Iswary (2015), pp. 337–341.

[13]Asur and Uberman (2010), pp. 492–499.

one determine the value of a social network? By definition, all the content is created by users, who can subscribe or unsubscribe anytime. When the company went public, its fast depreciation showed that there was an overvaluation of its value. In 2018, after the publication of disappointing results, another small stock market crash occurred. Nevertheless, the company is worth around EUR 531 billion and its president and founder, Mark Zuckerberg, is estimated to be the fourth richest man in the world.

The second question is: how do we calculate the value of this network, then? Some decades ago, Robert Metcalfe, the inventor of Ethernet, formulated a theory on the value of a network. He intuitively considered that the value V of a network is proportional to the square of the size n of the network ($V \propto n\,2$). In other words, once a network acquires a large number of users (and Facebook counts 2.6 billion active users who connect at least once a month) the network's value becomes enormous. Empirical research on Facebook's data shows that Metcalfe's law on a network's value is in practice the best formula to predict the capitalization of the network.[14]

If the company's capitalization is impressive, its revenues do not depend directly on the service itself, that is, the users do not pay to access and use the social network. On the contrary, the company primarily makes its money by selling advertising space. In this context, the more precise the profiling of the users, the more effective the advertising will be, which means that the advertising space (or maybe more accurately "time", as it is a matter of time spent watching advertisements on the social network) acquires more value. The cost of advertisements is measured through "impressions", that is the number of times that the adverts were on-screen.

Even if the sector of Internet service providers is extremely competitive, as Facebook competes with, amongst others, Alphabet (Google), Apple, Microsoft (LinkedIn) and Amazon, it operates in a de facto dominant position in the specific segment of social media. This obviously triggers some issues of competition (anti-trust) law each time Meta wants to acquire new assets.

Almost half of Meta's revenues come from the exploitation of the North America market and, more specifically, from US companies. This creates a certain form of dependency. In the summer of 2020, for instance, a movement from some big advertising companies was formed, boycotting the company's advertising offer for one month, as a protest against the company's inaction in combating hate speech and disinformation.

1.3   Facebook's History: A Series of Legal Controversies

The history of Facebook is littered with legal incidents. They start even before the creation of Facebook itself. In 2003, while Mark Zuckerberg was still a second-year student at Harvard University, he created an online service called "FaceMash",

---

[14]Zhang et al. (2015), pp. 246–251.

which compared the face of two students and asked users to choose the "hotter" person. The university's administration quickly shut down the project, arguing obvious violations of copyright law, individual privacy concerns and breach of security (it seems that the pictures were stolen by hacking the university's server).

But the idea was there, and something very valuable relating to students' connections and interactions was waiting to be created. The US movie "The Social Network"[15] depicted a romanticized version of the time period between Zuckerberg's first attempt at creating a social network and the final distribution of "The Facebook" (as Facebook was originally called). And here, it appears again that from a legal point of view, the process was highly problematic. Two twin brothers, Cameron and Tyler Winklevoss, hired Mark Zuckerberg to work on a project involving the creation of a social media platform called "ConnectU". Mark Zuckerberg was accused of having stolen the project idea and part of the actual source code in order to build his own project. The case was settled in 2008 for USD 65 million in damages, in favor of the brothers.[16]

In February 2004, Mark Zuckerberg launched a new online service, called "TheFacebook". It began as an exclusive tool for Harvard University students but one month later it was made available to other US universities. The "wall" functionality (which in 2010 became the "timeline" functionality), permitting public messages, was introduced in the same year, and by the end of 2004 the service already had one million users.[17] Meanwhile, as the legal conflict with the twin brothers was still in an early phase, Mark Zuckerberg was caught using Facebook's data (specifically, failed login attempts) in order to access the private e-mail accounts of some of the journalists working at the local newspaper (The Harvard Crimson) who were investigating the case.[18]

Following these early legal controversies, the company flourished for more than a decade. In 2005, the service became "Facebook", and the related domain name was acquired for USD 200,000. In 2006, the first privacy concerns arose, with the introduction of a new service called the "news feed", consisting of the display of a sequence of algorithmically selected content from other users, and with the change of policy to permit users to register from the age of 13. The iconic "like" button subsequently appeared in 2009. A golden age of unprecedented economic growth followed, and the acquisition of various companies added new features such as WhatsApp and Instagram.

In 2012, Yahoo sued Facebook for allegedly infringing various patents. The litigation was settled a few months later after Facebook counterattacked and accused Yahoo of infringing its own patents. Meanwhile, the company acquired more patents, probably in order to shield itself against future legal controversies in this field.

---

[15] The social media (2010) Director: David Fincher, screenwriter: Aaron Sorkin.

[16] Slater (2009).

[17] Greiner et al. (2019).

[18] Carlson (2010).

By the end of its first decade, the company had acquired its known shape and its dominant position, at the price of numerous legal battles. Most importantly, the platform had gained the trust of the public as a dynamic company and unmissable online experience. In its second decade of existence, the company underwent radical changes. It saw the rise of multiple new legal issues (see Sect. 1.5), and uncountable legal actions that the company did not foresee. Furthermore, its public image was gravely impacted, notably after the Cambridge Analytica scandal (see Chap. 2). Characteristically of this evolution, in 2020 Netflix released a documentary called "The Social Dilemma",[19] which won various awards. The documentary focuses on the societal consequences of Facebook's ever-growing influence on its users' everyday life, with potentially extreme consequences on a political level. In 2021, the company decided to change its name and Facebook Ltd became "Meta". In a founder's letter, Mark Zuckerberg describes this move as "a different approach" that would encompass the rise of metaverse and virtual reality technologies in social media.[20] The change of name could also be read as an attempt to accentuate the diversity of Meta's activities at a time when the Facebook platform is starting, for the first time in its history, to lose users.[21]

1.4   Facebook's Usage: Sociological and Psychological Aspects

By the beginning of its second decade, the social network had ceased to belong to the private sphere. As private stories and pictures mixed with news reports and political content, Facebook acquired a societal dimension. The role of the social network in the Arab revolutions (the "Arab Spring"), for instance in Egypt, is undeniable.[22]

The ambiguity of Facebook's purpose, which de facto functions simultaneously as a news aggregator, as a tool for developing and maintaining social relationships and as a forum for public debates, leads to the conclusion that the online service affects a wide range of persons and on a global scale. Two consequences of this societal ubiquity of the platform must be highlighted, on an individual and on a societal level.

On an individual level, research from 2012 discussed the addiction to online social media from a psychological perspective, reflecting on each of the six core elements of addiction (salience, mood modification, tolerance, withdrawal, conflict, and relapse).[23] A debate then began on the reality of addiction in a strict sense, which

---

[19]The Social Dilemma (2020) Director: Jeff Orlowski.

[20]Zuckerberg (2021).

[21]Dwoskin et al. (2022).

[22]Herrera (2014).

[23]Andreassen et al. (2012), pp. 501–517.

needs precise measurement of the effects of the online service on mental health.[24] This new field of research has already confirmed the existence of an addition to Facebook.[25] However, the overall time spent on Facebook (mostly through mobile devices) seems to have peaked. Indeed, a small decrease has even been noticed, as US adult Facebook users spent on average 0:38 hours on the social network.[26] The principal psychological consequence of this addiction seems to be a rise in narcissism.[27] At the same time, it could be argued that a rise in egoism in the population would have dire consequences on the political level. Specifically, it could interfere in current debates that typically discuss the balance between private and general interests, such as climate change, vaccinations during a pandemic, etc.

On a societal level, the initial enthusiasm of early political use of social networks to promote democratic values has gradually been replaced by a darker approach that has been dubbed "internet centrism" by philosophers and political analysts. A characteristic icon of this approach, Evgeny Morozov published his book "The Net Delusion: The Dark Side of Internet Freedom" in 2011.[28] Internet centrism demonstrates how online interactions have concrete consequences on the "offline world", or in other words "how the infosphere is reshaping human reality".[29] Internet centrism means, first, that some characteristics of the Internet (decentralization, networking) tend to affect more traditional, offline, societal mechanisms. For instance, a certain trend against science—an anti-science movement—gradually emerges on a global scale, as a consequence of the online approach that every opinion should be equally valued.

Secondly, Internet centrism describes a certain form of secular worship of the Internet that creates a blind spot as far as the Internet's, and more particularly social networks', adverse consequences on society are concerned. Specifically, Facebook's inner mechanism of friendship and blocking leads to a social "partitioning": users are mostly confronted with political views of their immediate social environment that will confirm their point of view and consequently, believe that their own opinions are right. For instance, a huge Flat Earther community (people who believe that the Earth is flat) has recently developed. Two major factors explain this community's expansion on the platform: firstly, the opportunity these small radical groups must be established and to get together, and secondly, the general positioning of social networks as an alternative to classic ways of distribution of knowledge (such as school, scientific publications, classic media).[30]

---

[24]Ryan et al. (2014), pp. 133–148.

[25]Biolcati et al. (2018), p. 118.

[26]He (2019).

[27]Brailovskaia et al. (2019), pp. 52–57.

[28]Morozov (2011).

[29]Floridi (2014).

[30]Dyer (2018).

1.5   Facebook Activities Entangled in a Web of Legal Issues

In the nineties, Internet law was basically limited to proving that law in general applies to an area that was quickly characterized as a digital wild west.[31] However, in parallel with the rise of Web 2.0, a new wave of regulations appeared in the 00s that specifically focused on the Internet. These regulations were not homogeneous, in the sense that they did not aim for or achieve the creation of an Internet Law as an autonomous and coherent field of law. However, they have the common aspect of exclusively applying on the Internet. Consequently, instead of Internet Law, there are Internet laws, a patchwork of various legal frameworks related to internet infrastructure, online media, or e-commerce.

The heavy intervention of the European Union (EU) is in this aspect welcomed, as it allows on a certain level a simplification of a complex web of legal frameworks. In a communication in 2014, the Commission characteristically considered that "[f] or over fifteen years, the EU has helped to sustain and develop the Internet: as an essential part of life and a fundamental pillar of the Digital Single Market, the Internet has fostered innovation, growth, trade, democracy and Human Rights".[32] It is possible to find in this sentence the main components of the EU legislator's intervention: an attempt to regulate the Internet with the aim to ensure both economic growth and protection of democratic values. The EU is entitled to intervene because of the cross-border nature of the Internet. The fundamental pillars of the EU, such as the freedom of movement of people, goods, and services, require a harmonized legal framework for digital activities. Furthermore, the EU tends to consider the freedom of movement of data itself to be a fifth pillar of the Union, as demonstrated by the recent enactment of a Regulation on the free flow of non-personal data.[33]

EU Internet law is therefore the result of a complex entanglement between media law regulations adapted or extended in order to apply to the online environment and specific regulations aimed at policing online behaviors. Applying this statement to Facebook, a clear conflict appears between EU law and the online platform's activities. Specifically, because of its business model, Facebook must apply the full force of the EU regulation on personal data (Chap. 2). However, this study will not limit its scope to data privacy protection only. The social network has greatly contributed to a liberalization and democratization of speech. In accordance with this, all classic media law principles need to be revisited, adapted, or just enforced in a proper way with respect to the platform. Intellectual property law governs what is owned by whom, either protected by copyright law informational goods (Chap. 3), or mere non-personal data (Chap. 4). Jurisprudence in relation to defamation is developing, considering the consequences of the simple "like" action (Chap. 5).

---

[31] Shipchandler (2000), p. 435.

[32] EU Commission (2014).

[33] Regulation (EU) 2018/1807 of the European Parliament and of the Council of 14 November 2018 on a framework for the free flow of non-personal data in the European Union, OJ L 303, 28.11.2018, pp. 59–68, ELI: http://data.europa.eu/eli/reg/2018/1807/oj.

Meanwhile, Facebook is trapped in a dilemma that is of substantial interest for society: does it act as an online intermediary (Chap. 6), that is a mere neutral and passive protagonist of the Internet, or is it transforming against its will into an editor? Hate speech and fake news frameworks are the result of co-regulation principles of governance and are the manifestation of the gradual erosion of the classic model of neutral online intermediary (Chap. 7). These issues force our society to rethink and redefine the fundamental principle of freedom of expression in the online environment (Chap. 8). In parallel, the role of social media in the digital single market, both as a marketplace and as a vector for the development of a multitude of e-commerce, is explored (Chap. 9).

References

Andreassen CS, Torsheim T, Brunborg GS, Pallesen S (2012) Development of a Facebook addiction scale. Psychol Rep 110(2):501–517

Asur S, Uberman BA (2010) Predicting the future with social media. EEE/WIC/ACM International Conference on Web Intelligence and Intelligent Agent Technology, 2010, pp 492–499. https://doi.org/10.1109/WI-IAT.2010.63

Biolcati R, Mancini G, Pupi V, Mugheddu V (2018) Facebook addiction: onset predictors. J Clin Med 7:118

Brailovskaia J, Margraf J, Köllner V (2019) Addicted to Facebook? Relationship between Facebook Addiction Disorder, duration of Facebook use and narcissism in an inpatient sample. Psychiatry Res 273:52–57

Carlson N (2010) In 2004, Mark Zuckerberg Broke Into A Facebook User's Private Email Account. Business Insider. https://www.businessinsider.com/how-mark-zuckerberg-hacked-into-the-harvard-crimson-2010-3

Cook A, Bechtel M, Anderon S, Novak D, Nodi N, Parekh J (2020) The Spatial Web and Web 3.0 What business leaders should know about the next era of computing. Deloitte Insights. https://www2.deloitte.com/us/en/insights/topics/digital-transformation/web-3-0-technologies-in-business.html

Danah B, Ellison N (2008) Social network sites: definition, history, and scholarship. J Comp Mediated Commun 13:210–230

Dwoskin E, Oremus W, Lerman R (2022) Facebook loses users for the first time in its history. The Washington Post. 2022. https://www.washingtonpost.com/technology/2022/02/02/facebook-earnings-meta/

Dyer HT (2018) Flat Earthers, Facebook and Foucault. The conversation. https://theconversation.com/i-watched-an-entire-flat-earth-convention-for-my-research-heres-what-i-learnt-95887

European Commission (2014) Communication to the European Parliament, the Council, The European Economic and Social Committee and the Committee of the Regions, Internet Policy and Governance Europe's role in shaping the future of Internet Governance, COM/2014/072

Floridi L (2014) The Fourth revolution: how the infosphere is reshaping human reality. Oxford University Press, Oxford

Greiner A, Fiegerman S, Sherman I, Baker T (2019) Facebook at 15: how a college experiment changed the world. CNN. https://edition.cnn.com/interactive/2019/02/business/facebook-history-timeline/index.html

He A (2019) Average Time Spent on Social Media Declines. EMarketer. https://www.emarketer.com/content/average-social-media-time-spentL

Herrera L (2014) Revolution in the age of social media: the Egyptian popular insurrection and the internet. Verso Editions, London

Internet Health Report (2019) The new investors in underwater sea cables. https://internethealthreport.org/2019/the-new-investors-in-underwater-sea-cables/

Ishwara Bhat P (2019) Idea and methods of legal research. Oxford University Press, Oxford, p 54. https://doi.org/10.1093/oso/9780199493098.001.0001

Issa T, Isaias P (2015) Artificial intelligence technologies and the evolution of Web 3.0. 1-422. https://doi.org/10.4018/978-1-4666-8147-7

Leiner BM, Cerf VG, Clark DD, Kahn RE, Kleinrock L, Lynch DC, Wolff S (2009) A brief history of the Internet. ACM SIGCOMM Comp Communication Rev 39(5):22–31

McLuhan M (1964) Understanding media: the extensions of man. McGraw-Hill, New York

Morozov E (2011) The net delusion: the dark side of internet freedom. Editions Public Affairs, New York

Nath K, Iswary R (2015) What comes after Web 3.0? Web 4.0 and the future. In: Proceedings of the International Conference and Communication System (I3CS'15), Shillong, India, pp 337–341

Ragnedda M, Destefanis G (eds) (2019) Blockchain and Web 3.0: social, economic, and technological challenges, 1st edn. Routledge, London. https://doi.org/10.4324/9780429029530

Ryan T, Chester A, Reece J, Xenos S (2014) The uses and abuses of Facebook: a review of facebook addiction. J Behav Addictions JBA 3(3):133–148

Shipchandler S (2000) The wild wild web: non-regulation as the answer to the regulatory question. Cornell Int Law J 33:435

Slater D (2009) Quinn Emanuel inadvertently discloses value of facebook settlement. The Wall Street Journal. https://www.wsj.com/articles/BL-LB-8749

Song S (2018) Internet drift: how the internet is likely to splinter and fracture. Digital Freedom Fund. https://digitalfreedomfund.org/internet-drift-how-the-internet-is-likely-to-splinter-and-fracture/

Stapp A (2019) Debunking Elizabeth Warren's Claim that "More Than 70% of All Internet Traffic Goes through Google or Facebook". https://truthonthemarket.com/2019/09/27/debunking-elizabeth-warrens-claim-that-more-than-70-of-all-internet-traffic-goes-through-google-or-facebook/

Zhang XZ, Liu JJ, Xu ZW (2015) Tencent and Facebook data validate Metcalfe's law. J Comp Sci Technol 30(2):246–251

Zuckerberg M (2021) Founder's letter 2021. About FB. https://about.fb.com/news/2021/10/founders-letter/

Chapter 2
Personal Data and Privacy Protection: Facebook and the Big Data Mountain

This chapter aims to address one of the most fundamental legal issues related to Facebook, which is its business model. Most of Facebook's economy is based on the exploitation of its users' personal data. It is true that data privacy legislation has a direct and fundamental impact on the organization of the social media platform. However, the EU's data privacy legislation, principle-driven and horizontal in its approach, is not as simple and homogeneous as expected (Sect. 2.1). Furthermore, the practical range of this legislation is often underestimated. The combination of, on the one hand, an overreaching piece of legislation (guided by a dynamic definition of personal data, an extensive interpretation of user's rights, etc.), and, on the other hand, an omniscient profiling activity (the huge "mountain" of data that belongs to Facebook) leads to a direct confrontation between EU law and this specific business model (Sect. 2.2). Characteristically, even the most fundamental matter of choosing the appropriate lawful basis for the processing of personal data becomes confused in the context of Facebook (Sect. 2.3). Not only do the data privacy legislation's core principles affect Facebook and are affected by the social media's management, but also specific issues, such as the protection of minors, acquire new dimensions in this context (Sect. 2.4). Finally, the chapter focuses on Facebook's accountability, mainly as regards the thorny question of the transfer of users' data outside the EU, specifically to Facebook's US servers (Sect. 2.5).

P. Jougleux, *Facebook and the (EU) Law*, Law, Governance and Technology Series 48, https://doi.org/10.1007/978-3-031-06596-5_2

2.1   Privacy and GDPR: A Two-Body Dilemma

2.1.1   *Personal Data Protection: The Multiplicity of Legal Sources in the EU*

2.1.1.1   The EU "Acquis"

To understand Facebook's challenges and difficulties in applying the EU data privacy legislation it is, first of all, necessary to analyze the EU acquis in this field. The General Data Protection Regulation (GDPR),[1] enacted in 2016, has become very familiar even to non-jurists. Its reach indeed extends to virtually all domains of the digital society and obviously concerns social media. However, it would be short-sighted to limit the discussion only to the application of the GDPR. The apparent simplicity of a single horizontal regulation applying to all personal data processing hides a complex web of interactions between different legal frameworks. Indeed, three instruments are relevant in EU law: the GDPR itself, the Directive adopted on the same day that concerns personal data treatment in the context of police investigations,[2] and the ePrivacy Directive.[3]

Furthermore, the Charter of Fundamental Rights of the EU[4] has a direct influence on the issue of personal data protection. Interestingly enough, the Charter recognizes privacy and personal data as two different, autonomous fundamental values that require protection. Article 7, entitled "Respect for private and family life", states that "[e]veryone has the right to respect for his or her private and family life, home and communications.", while Article 8, entitled "Protection of personal data" states that

> 1. Everyone has the right to the protection of personal data concerning him or her. 2. Such data must be processed fairly for specified purposes and on the basis of the consent of the person concerned or some other legitimate basis laid down by law. Everyone has the right of access to data which has been collected concerning him or her, and the right to have it rectified. 3. Compliance with these rules shall be subject to control by an independent authority.

---

[1] Regulation (EU) 2016/679 of the European Parliament and of the Council of 27 April 2016 on the protection of natural persons with regard to the processing of personal data and on the free movement of such data, and repealing Directive 95/46/EC (General Data Protection Regulation), OJ L 119, 4.5.2016, p. 1–88, ELI: http://data.europa.eu/eli/reg/2016/679/oj.

[2] Directive (EU) 2016/680 of the European Parliament and of the Council of 27 April 2016 on the protection of natural persons with regard to the processing of personal data by competent authorities for the purposes of the prevention, investigation, detection or prosecution of criminal offences or the execution of criminal penalties, and on the free movement of such data, and repealing Council Framework Decision 2008/977/JHA, ELI: http://data.europa.eu/eli/dir/2016/680/2016-05-04.

[3] Directive 2002/58/EC of the European Parliament and of the Council of 12 July 2002 concerning the processing of personal data and the protection of privacy in the electronic communications sector (Directive on privacy and electronic communications), OJ L 201, 31.7.2002, p. 37–47, ELI: http://data.europa.eu/eli/dir/2002/58/oj.

[4] Charter of Fundamental Rights of the European Union, OJ C 326, 26.10.2012, p. 391–407, ELI: http://data.europa.eu/eli/treaty/char_2012/oj.

The European Court of Justice (ECJ) had the opportunity to directly apply Articles 7 and 8 to personal data matters. One specific issue was to determine whether Article 8 possesses an autonomous legal nature or if the protection of personal data merely constitutes an extension of the right to privacy. The Volker und Markus Schecke case[5] concerned the online publication of data relating to the beneficiaries of agricultural aid from an EU funding scheme. The Court concluded in this case that the EU authorities should have made a "distinction based on relevant criteria such as the periods during which those persons have received such aid, the frequency of such aid or the nature and amount thereof", in order to justify the publication of the data. In its decision, the Court uses ambiguous language, sometimes using the singular (it refers to "the right to respect for private life with regard to the processing of personal data, recognised by Articles 7 and 8 of the Charter",[6] implicitly assuming that Article 8 is the digital complement of Article 7) but mostly using the plural form, mentioning "rights". In a subsequent case relating to the EU biometric passport,[7] the Court continued to apply this empirical approach. The Court explained that "[i]t follows from a joint reading of those articles that, as a general rule, any processing of personal data by a third party may constitute a threat to those rights".[8]

However, this contrived joint reading of the two articles is not mandatory. As the Advocate General pointed out in the digital rights case,[9] "Article 8 of the Charter enshrines the right to the protection of personal data as a right which is distinct from the right to privacy. Although data protection seeks to ensure respect for privacy, it is, in particular, subject to an autonomous regime".[10] Specifically, the Advocate General distinguishes between two kinds of data: personal data of a more neutral nature,[11] which are exclusively governed by Article 8, and more intimate personal data,[12] to which a combination of Articles 7 and 8 must be applied.

---

[5]ECJ (Grand Chamber), C-92/09, Volker und Markus Schecke GbR and C-93/09, Hartmut Eifert v. Land Hessen, 09/11/2010, ECLI:EU:C:2010:662.

[6]Par.52 of the decision.

[7]ECJ, C-291/12, Michael Schwarz v. Stadt Bochum, 17/10/2013, ECLI:EU:C:2013:670.

[8]Par.25 of the decision.

[9]Villalón C. (2013) Opinion of Advocate General on the case C-293/12, Digital Rights Ireland Ltd v. Minister for Communications, Marine and Natural Resources, Minister for Justice, Equality and Law Reform, Commissioner of the Garda Síochána Ireland and The Attorney General, 12/10/2013, ECLI:EU:C:2013:845.

[10]Par.55 of the Opinion.

[11]Par.64 of the Opinion:

> There are data that are personal as such, that is to say, in that they individually identify a person, such as data which, in the past, could appear on a safe-conduct, by way of example. Such data frequently have a certain permanence and are frequently somewhat neutral too. They are personal but no more than that and, in general, it could be said that they are those for which the structure and guarantees of Article 8 of the Charter are best suited.

[12]Par. 65 of the Opinion:

> There are, however, data which are in a sense more than personal. These are data which, qualitatively, relate essentially to private life, to the confidentiality of private life, including

Essentially, it means that

> [s]ince the 'private sphere' forms the core of the 'personal sphere', it cannot be ruled out that legislation limiting the right to the protection of personal data in compliance with Article 8 of the Charter may nevertheless be regarded as constituting a disproportionate interference with Article 7 of the Charter.[13]

2.1.1.2   The Influence of the European Convention Human Rights

EU legislation is not the only relevant legal source that affects the discussion on the legal framework concerning personal data. Even if the EU has not adopted the European Convention of Human Rights (ECHR) of the Council of Europe, all its members are de facto members of this Convention. While the concept of personal data is apparently absent from the text of the Convention, it is necessary to mention two relevant factors with respect to the Convention's influence on data protection.

First, the European Court of Human Rights (ECtHR) has a long tradition of broad interpretation of the notion of privacy as enshrined in Article 8 of the ECHR. There are many instances in jurisprudence where the line between privacy and personal data is blurred. Some decisions even specifically address the issue of personal data protection. In the Amann case,[14] the Court unanimously found a violation of Article 8 arising from the creation and storing of a "card" (information held in the national security card index) regarding an individual's behavior. The card stated that the applicant was a "contact with the Russian embassy" because of a phone call from the embassy he had received in the past. In this case, the Court remarked that the "storing of data relating to the "private life" of an individual falls within the application of Article 8 § 1" and "in this connection that the term "private life" must not be interpreted restrictively".[15] It is possible to find this broad interpretation elsewhere in the Court's jurisprudence, where it was held that

> information retrieved from banking documents undoubtedly amounts to personal data concerning an individual, irrespective of it being sensitive information or not. Moreover, such information may also concern professional dealings and there is no reason of principle to justify excluding activities of a professional or business nature from the notion of "private life".[16]

> intimacy. In such cases, the issue raised by personal data commences, so to speak, further 'upstream'. The issue which arises in such cases is not yet that of the guarantees relating to data processing but, at an earlier stage, that of the data as such, that is to say, the fact that it has been possible to record the circumstances of a person's private life in the form of data, data which can consequently be subject to information processing.

[13] Par.61 of the Opinion.

[14] ECtHR, Amann v. Switzerland, 16/02/2000, no. 27798/95.

[15] Par.65 of the Decision.

[16] ECtHR, M.N. v. San Marino, 7/7/2015, no. 28005/12, par.51.

In one more case, the Court decided that the transfer of banking data to the US fell within the scope of Article 8.[17] Specifically, it is noted in this case that "the Court has regard, in this sphere, to the essential role played by personal data protection in safeguarding the right to respect for private life as guaranteed by Article 8."[18]

It can be concluded that, from the point of view of the ECtHR, any personal data processing de facto triggers the protection of Article 8 of the ECHR. A personal data processing is therefore handled as an "interference" with the right of privacy, but it does not automatically mean that the data processing breaches Article 8. For instance, in the case L.B. v. Hungary,[19] the publication of data on the Tax Authority's website naming the applicant as a tax defaulter and subsequently a major tax evader, the applicant argued that this constituted an interference with his private life within the meaning of Article 8. In such a situation, the Court applies a three-step test and considers whether the interference is in accordance with the law, answers to a legitimate aim, and is necessary in a democratic society. This third criterion of necessity in a democratic society is the most fundamental, as it implies a test of proportionality between the extent of interference and the importance of the legitimate aim. For instance, in this case, the Court ultimately considered that the publication of tax evader information does not violate Article 8. The measure was proportionate, since publishing information on tax defaulters on the Internet was the most appropriate means of achieving the objective pursued, particularly in relation to providing easily accessible information for potential business partners.

Second, it should be noted that the influence of the Council of Europe is not limited to this jurisprudential interpretation of the ECHR. The Council of Europe had already in 1981 proposed to its members the adoption of "Convention 108",[20] a treaty that sets out the core principles of personal data protection. The said convention has been signed by all members of the EU. In addition, a modification called "Convention 108+" was adopted in 2018, as a result of the need to modernize the old legal instrument.[21] The Convention 108+ aims to adopt a technologically neutral approach and serves as a "universal standard"[22] in matters relating to personal data.

---

[17] ECtHR, G.S.B. v. Switzerland, 22/12/2015, no. 28601/11.

[18] Par.90 of the decision.

[19] ECtHR, M.B. v. Hungary, 12/01/2021, no. 36345/16.

[20] Council of Europe Convention for the Protection of Individuals with regard to Automatic Processing of Personal Data (ETSNo.108), 1981.

[21] Protocol amending the Convention for the Protection of Individuals with regard to Automatic Processing of Personal Data, CETS No.223, Strasbourg, 10/10/2018, p.1, https://rm.coe.int/cets-223-explanatory-report-to-the-protocol-amending-the-convention-fo/16808ac91a.

[22] Council of Europe (2018) Explanatory Report to the Protocol amending the Convention for the Protection of Individuals with regard to Automatic Processing of Personal Data.

2.1.1.3   The Bosphorus Doctrine

In conclusion, matters related to the data processing of Facebook's users must be discussed not only in the light of the GDPR and related legislation, but also through the prism of a number of other principles: the Charter of Fundamental Rights, the ECtHR's case-law on Article 8, and the core principles of Convention 108+.

However, the simultaneous application of EU law (GDPR and the Charter) and of the ECHR potentially poses a serious issue of compatibility of the two frameworks with each other. Since there is no unifying resolution mechanism for divergent interpretations on this matter, it is not theoretically impossible for a normative conflict to occur between these two independent bodies of law. However, it could be said there is a "gentlemen's agreement" between the two courts, described by scholars as the "Bosphorus doctrine".[23] This gives a prima facie presumption of legality and/or compatibility of rulings from one body with the jurisprudence of the other one.[24] From an EU law perspective, this presumption results from the fundamental texts of the Union, as Article 6 (3) of the Treaty of the European Union (TEU) states that the fundamental rights enshrined in the ECHR constitute general principles of EU law.

Nevertheless, it is methodologically correct to assume that the analysis of the compatibility of a personal data processing with the protection of human rights should take place first, before discussing GDPR enforcement. In this context, online personal data protection benefits from a special consideration by the ECtHR. Because of the far-reaching consequences of online publication, the Court has formulated well-established case-law holding that the risk of harm posed by content and communications on the Internet to the exercise and enjoyment of human rights and freedoms, particularly the right to respect for private life, is certainly higher than that posed by the press.[25] This finding influences the interpretation given to various principles of the GDPR applied to Facebook.

To complete the picture, it can be added that the Organisation for Economic Co-operation and Development (OECD) proposes guidelines on data protection.[26] These guidelines are generally considered to be heavily influenced by European standards on data privacy law.[27]

In conclusion, an analysis that aims to discuss the legality of a personal data processing cannot refer only to the GDPR. Both within the EU legal framework (the fundamental rights) and without (Article 8 of ECHR and Convention 108+), there are legal instruments that apply to personal data protection in conjunction with the EU Regulation.

---

[23] Hazelhorst (2017).

[24] Gragl (2017).

[25] See ECtHR, inter alia, Egill Einarsson v. Iceland, no. 24703/15, 7/11/2017, § 46.

[26] OECD (2013).

[27] Greenleaf (2012), pp. 68–92.

2.1.2 The GDPR: More an Evolution Than a Revolution

2.1.2.1 The Novelties of the GDPR

The adoption of the GDPR has been marked in public opinion as a landmark event in the field of personal data protection. One of the most manifest for the public changes introduced by the GDPR was that it led to massive compliance and consent activities on websites.[28] A survey taken only 1 year later showed that already more than two thirds of Europeans had heard of the GDPR, a clear majority had heard of most of the rights guaranteed by the GDPR, and almost six in ten had heard of a national authority protecting their data.[29] However, this achievement does not reflect the reality of personal data protection in the EU. Indeed, two decades ago, the Directive 95/46[30] already laid the foundations for a harmonized legal framework in the EU. The vast majority of the core elements of the Directive have been reused in the GDPR. Practically, it means that the prolific ECJ case-law under the influence of the Directive continues to be relevant nowadays in most situations.

The Directive was drafted and adopted before the Internet era and needed to be modernized. But at the same time, the same technological-neutral approach remains, which minimizes the importance of the changes. Even if some principles have been reformulated, extended, or added, the core elements remain the same, with one notable exception. The large and open definition of personal data, the nature of the protection articulated around six main principles and a closed list of six specific justifications of the treatment, the statement of user's rights as regards their personal data, the control of cross border transfer of data outside the EU, the existence of sanctions, the distinction between ordinary and "sensitive" personal data, the regulation of automatic decision making based on personal data and the creation of an administrative independent national authority had already been introduced in the 1995 Directive.

However, the philosophy of data management radically changes in the GDPR. While the Directive was in a sense somehow bureaucratic, imposing in some cases a priori control by the national authority, the GDPR placed an emphasis on self-regulation and a posteriori control. With the notions of the data protection officer (DPO) and data impact assessments, it adds some elasticity to the regime, that is appreciated in the Internet era. Moreover, the GDPR also adopted some innovations, as it adds new concepts to the legal framework of data protection, such as the mandatory breach notification mechanism, the one-stop-shop, the philosophy of privacy by design, and more user's rights (right to portability, right to be forgotten).

---

[28] Libert et al. (2018), pp. 1590–1600.

[29] EU (2019).

[30] Directive 95/46/EC of the European Parliament and of the Council of 24 October 1995 on the protection of individuals with regard to the processing of personal data and on the free movement of such data. ELI: http://data.europa.eu/eli/dir/1995/46/oj.

Without minimizing the importance of the new rights and of the modernization of the key concepts of the data privacy legislation, such as the notion of consent, it could be argued that the real strength of the GDPR, compared to the previous Directive, does not lie in substantive legal innovations but in its enforcement method. Indeed, the mechanism of fines has been modified in order to create a substantial deterrent effect. Independently of the right to compensation, the supervisory authority possesses the right to impose administrative fines in case of violation of the GDPR. Article 83 of the GDPR divides the obligations into two categories. In Article 83 (4), the infringement of some obligations[31] is subject to administrative fines up to EUR 10,000,000, or in the case of an undertaking, up to 2% of the total worldwide annual turnover of the preceding financial year of the infringer (whichever is higher). In Article 83 (5), the maximum limit is doubled (EUR 20,000,000, or in the case of an undertaking, up to 4% of the total worldwide annual turnover of the preceding financial year, whichever is higher). Article 83 (5) concerns the core elements of the GDPR (the basic principles for processing, the data subjects' rights, the transfers of personal data to a recipient in a third country or an international organization).

This modification could be rightfully seen as a "gamechanger". For instance, in 2017 the French data protection authority, the CNIL, fined Facebook for profiling website visitors through cookies without obtaining prior consent and without transparency.[32] The fine amounted to EUR 150,000 and it was the maximum authorized at that time. Nowadays, for the same behavior, Facebook would be at risk of paying millions of euros. It is worth mentioning that the company reported revenue of USD 26,17 billion for the first quarter of 2021.[33] It means that a fine for a serious violation of a core principle could potentially reach roughly EUR 900 million.

However, it must be noted that under the GDPR, only the lead supervisory authority, which is the data authority of Ireland in Facebook's case, is now competent to rule on the fine (see Sect. 2.5.1). Indeed, Facebook's operation is by nature a cross-border processing.[34] In the philosophy of the one-stop-shop system of the GDPR, complaints are still received at national level, but the national supervisory authority must collaborate with the lead supervisory authority.

---

[31] the obligations of the controller and the processor pursuant to Articles 8, 11, 25 to 39 and 42 and 43; the obligations of the certification body pursuant to Articles 42 and 43; the obligations of the monitoring body pursuant to Article 41(4).

[32] CNIL (May 16, 2017), Facebook Sanctioned for Several Breaches of the French Data Protection Act, https://www.cnil.fr/en/facebook-sanctioned-several-breaches-french-data-protection-act.

[33] Rodriguez (2021).

[34] See Article 56 (1) of GDPR.

2.1.2.2 The GDPR's Process and Facebook's Lobbying

European officials hailed the GDPR as a major victory for consumers,[35] but it could be argued that the GDPR is not as innovative and protective as it claims.[36] The question that is therefore worth asking: has some lobbying been involved in the process, and has it actually interfered with the GDPR's content? Its legislative process was long, difficult, and complicated. The text was voted in 2016 and entered into force in 2018 but the negotiations had already started long before.

Lobbying activities are not illegal if carried out whilst respecting the principle of transparency and it could even be argued that they contribute to the good functioning of democracy. Facebook Ireland is legally registered as a lobbyist.[37] Four employees have access to the EU Parliament and the company declares an annual budget of EUR 4,250,000—EIR 4,499,999 as annual costs for lobbying in the EU. Facebook was officially involved in the legislative process, as it was invited to contribute to the debate during the negotiations. For instance, Facebook's managing director participated in a session of the European Parliament on the reform of the EU Data Protection framework in 2012.[38]

However, based on a leak of internal documents, it has been revealed that Facebook lobbies outside of the official framework against data privacy laws around the world.[39] According to the leaked documents, the company considers European data protection legislation to be a "critical" threat to the company. The lobbying strategy mainly involved exerting pressure on the Irish Prime Minister and the President of the EU Commission during the legislative process. As Meta's EU headquarters are situated in Dublin, Ireland's data protection agency has the responsibility of overseeing Facebook's activities in the EU (see Sect. 2.5.2). It remains unknown if Meta's lobbying had practical effects on the text. It is fair nevertheless to concede that the European regulation is considered to be the most protective data privacy law in the world.

---

[35] Scott et al. (May 22, 2019).

[36] See recital 7 of the GDPR : "Those developments require a strong and more coherent data protection framework in the Union, backed by strong enforcement, given the importance of creating the trust that will allow the digital economy to develop across the internal market. Natural persons should have control of their own personal data. Legal and practical certainty for natural persons, economic operators and public authorities should be enhanced."

[37] The registration's information can be accessed on the EU's website : https://ec.europa.eu/transparencyregister/public/consultation/displaylobbyist.do?id=28666427835-74.

[38] European Parliament (2012).

[39] Fowler (2019).

2.2   The Facebook Data Mountain

2.2.1   *Which Data Is Personal?*

2.2.1.1   Direct and Indirect Personal Data

It is necessary to give the most careful attention to the definition of personal data in order to understand the magnitude of the conflict between the GDPR's core principles and Facebook's business model. This definition poses much more difficulty than it first appears, and it has even been proposed to reject this distinction between personal and non-personal data in favor of a holistic approach to the concept of data.[40] The GDPR continues the previous Directive's tradition of a broad approach to the concept of personal data. As stated in Article 2 (2) of the GDPR, personal data means

> any information relating to an identified or identifiable natural person ('data subject'); an identifiable natural person is one who can be identified, directly or indirectly, in particular by reference to an identifier such as a name, an identification number, location data, an online identifier or to one or more factors specific to the physical, physiological, genetic, mental, economic, cultural or social identity of that natural person;

In other words, two categories of personal data are identified. On the one hand, the data that directly identify a natural person are defined as personal data. In the context of Facebook, this category encompasses for instance the user's name, their e-mail, phone number, pictures if their face is identifiable, and their unique Facebook identifier tag. On the other hand, data that only indirectly identify a natural person are also considered to be personal data. In this sense, subjective data that are associated with the personality of the user may become personal data in the right context. Any post, comment, like, share, all information about hobbies and activities, subscriptions to pages and groups, viewing history, time and duration of connection to the platform, reflect a part of the data subject's personality. It should be noted that this distinction between direct and indirect personal data already existed in the Convention 108.[41] However, the exponential growth of technological means of identification through data mining continues to push the boundaries of the concept of indirect personal data. Data mining here is an automatic technique of correlation between data that apparently looked non-personal. For instance, even statistical data, if precise and numerous enough, may lead to the characterization of an individual. Because of this extremely broad approach, the GDPR has even been described as potentially being the "law of everything".[42] In this approach, every kind of interaction with the platform, even if it is apparently inoffensive (such as information on the

---

[40] Graef et al. (2018).

[41] Council of Europe (1981), available at https://rm.coe.int/16800ca434: "Identifiable persons» means a person who can be easily identified: it does not cover identification of persons by means of very sophisticated methods."

[42] Purtova (2018), pp. 40–81.

speed with which users scroll down on their news feed), is to be classified as personal data if recorded by Facebook.

Some guidelines and case-law exist and offer some help in the delimitation of the concept of indirect personal data. A test to differentiate between indirect personal and non-personal data can be found in Recital 26 of the GDPR, according to which

> [t]o determine whether a natural person is identifiable, account should be taken of all the means reasonably likely to be used, such as singling out, either by the controller or by another person to identify the natural person directly or indirectly. To ascertain whether means are reasonably likely to be used to identify the natural person, account should be taken of all objective factors, such as the costs of and the amount of time required for identification, taking into consideration the available technology at the time of the processing and technological developments.

Two opposing theories are relevant here. In the first one, which could be called the "absolute" theory of personal data, the test must be used in abstracto. That means that if the data could lead even a third party to identify the data subject, the data is personal. This theory is based on the fact that Recital 26 refers to identification either by the controller "or by another person". Examples of this theory can be found in some decisions that discuss the anonymity of data and consider that data are not anonymous if there is even a slight technological possibility to reverse the anonymization process.[43] Conversely, a "relativist" theory embraces an in concreto approach, which is also implied in Recital 26. Only in the case where the identification is not only possible but likely as regards the means and efforts needed, should the data be qualified as personal. This theory essentially adopts a risk-based approach to classify information.[44]

In this context, one specific guideline on the notion of personal data formulated by the predecessor of today's European Data Protection Board (EDPB), the Article 29 Working Party, is important. Opinion W136[45] breaks down the notion of personal data into four criteria: "any information", "relating to", "an identified or identifiable", "natural person", with the third criterion being the most controversial. It is stated that information may indirectly lead to identification through the combination of data. The Article 29 Working Party establishes a test comprising three factors, used as alternative conditions: the purpose, the content, and the result of the process.[46] In other words, in case where an uncertainty arises as regards the classification of data as indirect personal data or not, the controller's intent to establish a profile (purpose), the easy means of identification of the identity of the data subject by analyzing the data (content), or, the practical threats to privacy to the

---

[43] See in France the decision of the administrative supreme court Conseil d'État, 10ème – 9ème ch. réunies, 8 /02/2017, N° 393714.

[44] Finck and Pallas (2020), pp. 11–36.

[45] Article 29 Working Party (2017b).

[46] See p. 10 of the Opinion: "it could be pointed out that, in order to consider that the data "relate" to an individual, a "content" element OR a "purpose" element OR a "result" element should be present."

individual that the process implies (result) means that the data enters into the definition of personal data.

It could be therefore argued that this three-factor test constitutes a confirmation of the relativist theory, as the test imposes an in concreto approach; but it is fair to assume the Article 29 Working Party did not take an absolute position on this debate. However, the ECJ had the opportunity to interpret the notion and take position in the landmark decision Becker.[47] Mr. Breyer brought an action before the German administrative courts, seeking an order restraining the Federal Republic of Germany from storing, or arranging for third parties to store, the IP address of the applicant's host system, after consultation of the websites accessible to the public run by the German Federal institutions' online media services. Such an order could only be granted if it were assumed or found that the IP address constitutes personal data.

Dynamic IP addresses are unique identifiers attributed by the Internet service provider to their user and used by all connected devices in order to communicate between each other. Facebook's platform, like a multitude of other services on internet, collects this IP address for various purposes: geotracking of the user, security, etc. IP addresses constitute the paradigm of the practical consequences of the debate between the absolute and relativist notion of personal data. As the Internet service provider keeps a log of its users' connections to the Internet, in an absolute approach all IP addresses are personal data. Indeed, a technological measure is available to identify the individual. On the contrary, from a relativist point of view, the IP address, by itself, does not reveal anything of the user's identity. Even smart objects, such as a smart TV or smart fridge, receive an IP address.

The ECJ takes a position on this point and considers that

[t]he fact that the additional data necessary to identify the user of a website are held not by the online media services provider, but by that user's internet service provider does not appear to be such as to exclude that dynamic IP addresses registered by the online media services provider constitute personal data within the meaning of Article 2(a) of Directive 95/46. However, it must be determined whether the possibility to combine a dynamic IP address with the additional data held by the internet service provider constitutes a means likely reasonably to be used to identify the data subject. Thus, as the Advocate General stated essentially in point 68 of his Opinion, that would not be the case if the identification of the data subject was prohibited by law or practically impossible on account of the fact that it requires a disproportionate effort in terms of time, cost and manpower, so that the risk of identification appears in reality to be insignificant.[48]

Consequently, the relativist approach prevails in the ECJ's case-law: an IP address is not personal data in absolute. It becomes personal data when in concreto the identification of the data subject is likely, by estimating a wide range of factors such as the legal framework and the practical potentiality of the identification.

Indeed, the Article 29 Working Party placed more importance on the notion of purpose. Users' data are personal from the moment that Facebook aims to use them.

[47] ECJ, C-582/14, Patrick Breyer v. Bundesrepublik Deutschland, 19/10/2016, ECLI:EU:C:2016:779.
[48] Par.44, 45, and 46 of the Decision.

At the opposite, the ECJ's case-law seems to give priority to the practical effectivity of the identification. Users' data are personal from the moment that Facebook is in a position to exploit them. This difference practically does not really interfere with the classification of Facebook's activities of data processing, as in both cases, empirically, the conclusion will be that the vast majority of all small or big interactions of the users with the platform will be classified as personal data.

2.2.1.2   Public Data and Personal Data

The notion of personal data is closely related to the notion of privacy (see Sect. 2.1.1), which is classically the opposite of the notion of the public domain. Therefore, the following question is worth posing: should data made public by the initiative of the data subject continue to be treated as personal data? The issue is very sensitive on Facebook as most of the information collected by the platform comes from the users themselves. Taking this approach, by uploading their data, the users would be consciously opting out of the protection offered by data privacy legislation, as they would reasonably not expect privacy from their public or semi-public posts and comments.

Nevertheless, the ECJ's Satamedia decision[49] definitively closed the debate. In this case, a newspaper collected public data from the Finnish tax authorities for the purposes of publishing extracts from those data in its regional editions. The same company decided to propose a text-messaging service allowing mobile telephone users to receive information published in the newspaper. Did this constitute a processing of personal data? The Court applied an implacable logic: it is undeniable that the data identify a natural person, it is clear that none of the closed list of exceptions applies, therefore even if published, the data is still protected by data privacy legislation. The Court added that, incidentally, "a general derogation from the application of the directive in respect of published information would largely deprive the directive of its effect. It would be sufficient for the Member States to publish data in order for those data to cease to enjoy the protection afforded by the directive."[50]

It would be inaccurate to conclude that the public character of personal data plays no role at all in its protection. Article 9 of the GDPR refers to special categories of personal data, which were called "sensitive personal data" under the previous Directive. It institutes a stricter and more specific regime for personal data

> revealing racial or ethnic origin, political opinions, religious or philosophical beliefs, or trade union membership, and the processing of genetic data, biometric data for the purpose of uniquely identifying a natural person, data concerning health or data concerning a natural person's sex life or sexual orientation

---

[49]ECJ, C-73/07, Tietosuojavaltuutettu v. Satakunnan Markkinapörssi Oy, Satamedia, 16/12/2008, ECLI:EU:C:2008:727.

[50]Par.48 of the Decision.

As a principle, processing of this category of personal data is prohibited and the GDPR lists numerous exceptions where this prohibition is lifted. One specific exception is worth mentioning here: Article 9 (2) (e) states that the processing that relates to personal data "which are manifestly made public by the data subject" is authorized. This exception obviously refers only to the prohibition of the processing of sensitive personal data and not to the legal framework in its entirety. In other words, the GDPR's principles and obligations still are relevant, independently of the public character of the personal data, but the public character of the data partially influences the legal framework.

2.2.1.3   Facebook and the Household Exception

The GDPR recognizes some very narrow exceptions such as the use of personal data in criminal proceedings and one of them, called the "household processing exception"[51] suspends the application of data privacy law in cases where the processing belongs to the private sphere of the individual. The opposite approach would lead to Kafkaesque situations, such as considering smartphones' owners to be controllers with respect to the contact information they possess.

At first sight, this exception does not seem to be relevant in the context of social media. However, the dismissal of the household processing exception is not as simple as it seems. On the one hand, data published as public information are clearly outside the scope of this exception. On the other hand, much data may be produced in confidential or semi-confidential contexts: chats in secret groups, check-ins and various other actions set on "to me only" visibility settings, saving some posts for future reading, etc. The danger would be to think that the small number of persons having access to the data means the exception generally applies.

The situation is best explained by the GDPR itself. Recital 18 of the GDPR indicates that

> [t]his Regulation does not apply to the processing of personal data by a natural person in the course of a purely personal or household activity and thus with no connection to a professional or commercial activity. Personal or household activities could include correspondence and the holding of addresses, or social networking and online activity undertaken within the context of such activities. However, this Regulation applies to controllers or processors which provide the means for processing personal data for such personal or household activities.

This recital could be interpreted as stating the obvious: the data subject is not to be considered as a controller of personal data processing in the sense of the GDPR when he reveals information about himself, but, at the same time, when data are collected and potentially exploited for the purpose of profiling by Facebook, this does constitute data processing in the sense of the Regulation. According to Recital 18, therefore, the household exception could apply to Facebook, but only to protect

---

[51] Article 2 (2) (c) of GDPR.

the activities of the users, not the processing by the platform. This approach has seduced some national judges. For instance, in Greece, an individual kept publishing on Facebook personal data concerning another person, with whom he was currently involved in court proceedings (for a labor law dispute), until this person sued him for violation of the GDPR. The Court of Appeal held that the GDPR did not apply in this case, as the publications were covered by the household exception.[52]

However, this exception should be interpreted in light of the ECJ's case-law, which has adopted a very strict approach in this respect. First, in the landmark Bodil-Linqvist case[53] which concerns the data privacy aspects of a personal blog that described personal moments of the blog author's social environment, the ECJ stated that, as a principle, data uploaded on the Internet that was freely accessible could not be exempted from the GDPR, even if the purpose of the publication was purely personal. The logic is that the household exception should cover only information that are kept in the possession of the person, in the sense that only the data subject has access to the data.

Second, the more recent Rynes case[54] further established the strict interpretation of the household exception. In this case, after he had already been robbed several times, an individual decided to install a camera system under the eaves of his family home. The camera was installed in a fixed position and could not turn; it recorded the entrance to his home, the public footpath, and the entrance to the house opposite. As the video surveillance covered, even partially, a public space, the Court found that the household exception had no significance here. The ECJ explicitly endorsed this restrictive approach, noting that the exception that

> falls to be narrowly construed has its basis also in the very wording of that provision, under which the directive does not cover the processing of data where the activity in the course of which that processing is carried out is a 'purely' personal or household activity, that is to say, not simply a personal or household activity.[55]

Consequently, it is not enough that the individual keeps the data in its own control for the household exception to be triggered and to counteract the application of the GDPR. It is also necessary to demonstrate that the processing itself does not make possible, even potentially, a threat to others' privacy. In the light of these two cases, the application of the household's exception to cover personal posts on Facebook should be limited to very specific situations where the online publication of personal data does not constitute a threat to the data subject, because of its confidentiality, for instance.

---

[52] Cour of Appeal of Dodekanisiou (Greece), case 224/2020.

[53] ECJ, C-101/2001, Bodil- Linqvist, 6/11/2003, ECLI:EU:C:2003:596.

[54] ECJ, C-212/13, František Ryneš v. Úřad pro ochranu osobních údajů, 11/12/2014, ECLI:EU:C:2014:2428.

[55] Par.30 of the Decision.

2.2.2 The Curious Little "Like" Button

The "like" button, designed as a blue "thumbs up" icon on Facebook's platform, was introduced in 2009 as a way of quickly interacting with, categorizing, and evaluating content. The instrument quickly became very popular not only as a reaction tool but also as a method of sharing content, as one "like" will make the post show up on friends' news feeds. A study[56] shows that the button answers to various and independent needs of communication. First, it serves as way of acknowledging the gratifications obtained through Facebook (entertainment, information/discovery, bounding, and self-identification). Second, it is used as communication tool to share information with others (for the purposes of presentation of the self, presentation of the extended-self, and social obligations). Third, the "like" function serves as a tool for impression management.

The "like" button is not only about "liking" generated-user content anymore, as other reactions have been added. From a GDPR point of view, the most sensitive issue is related to the fact that the "like" button does not only appear on the platform. Third parties can incorporate a "like" button on their own pages, but this option has some unexpected consequences for the average user. Indeed, the button is not only a small icon, but its presence hides some lines of codes, a bridge between the visited website and Facebook's platform. The button works as a small "spy", automatically sending to the platform information about the user's activity, even if he does not click/activate the button. The company that incorporates the button on its website also obtains some advantages: each time the "like" button is activated, it works as a small advertisement for the company, published on the social network.

The fact that the "like" button's real action is unknown to the public affects its legitimacy. The ECHR has developed a specific concept in many privacy cases: the reasonable expectation of privacy.[57] The court considers that

> [s]ince there are occasions when people knowingly or intentionally involve themselves in activities which are or may be recorded or reported in a public manner, a person's reasonable expectations as to privacy may be a significant, although not necessarily conclusive, factor in this assessment.[58]

In the context of the "like" button installed on a third-party website, it is fair to consider that the visitor has a relatively high expectation of privacy (not necessarily towards the website itself, but as regards the relationship between the website and Facebook), in the sense that most people are unaware of the second, hidden function of the "like" button.

---

[56]Ozanne et al. (2017).

[57]ECHR Bărbulescu v. Romania, App. no. 61496/08, 05/09/2017 and Lopez Ribalda and others v. Spain, Applications nos. 1874/13 and 8567/13, 17/10/2019.

[58]Par.89 of Lopez Ribalda' decision.

Therefore, the "like" button represents a huge legal issue, which has already been addressed by the ECJ. In the Fashion ID case[59] an online clothing retailer embedded on its website the "Like" social plugin from Facebook. A consumer protection organization applied for an injunction against the website owner to force it to stop that practice. As this practice seems to violate several principles of the GDPR (as mentioned, the visitor is usually unaware that data are being collected by Facebook, in contravention of the principle of transparency), the issue was to determine whether the website's owner could be responsible for it. The GDPR distinguishes two forms of liability, one for the data processor, in some very limited circumstances, and one that concerns the data controller.

The ECJ extensively analyzed the meaning of a controller in this case (see Sect. 2.5.1 below). One specific issue was to accept that the notion of data controller can apply non-exhaustively not only to the main entity collecting the data and organizing the profiling (Meta) but also to the company at the initiative of which the data are collected and which decides the kind of data collected (the owner of the third-party website). The ECJ clearly states that access to the data is not mandatory to regard a person intervening in the process of data collection as a controller. Furthermore, the Court finds a shared purpose between Facebook and the third-party website: Facebook proposes a "like" button plugin for obvious reasons, as it will further increase the amount of data collected on its users, and the third-party website accepts this as it also pursues a commercial (though different) objective (which is to gain visibility on the social network).[60]

In conclusion, the Fashion ID decision establishes that a third-party website owner that installs a "like" button on its website is to be regarded as a joint controller. This decision has both practical and dogmatic-normative consequences. From a theoretical perspective, the ECJ mentions that the website owner has to be considered as a joint controller only as regards the collection of data, considered to be the first phase of the data processing. This way, a phase-oriented approach[61] of the data processing is adopted, which is absent from the text of the GDPR. However, this phase-oriented approach offers a sort of solution to the difficulty posed by the rigid and sometimes impractical distinction between controllers and processors.

Practically, the decision clearly puts an end to the uncontrolled use of "like" buttons. Assuming that consent is the legal basis of the data processing, consent from the visitor as a data subject must be obtained by the party initiating the data processing. Therefore, the plugin should be deactivated at first, and sufficient information should be given as to the consequences of activation. For instance, a contextual box that appears when the cursor hovers over the button should explain that clicking will activate the plugin and inform Facebook about the visitor's activity on the website. Alternatively, in case where legitimate interest is chosen as the legal

---

[59] ECJ, C-40/17, Fashion ID GmbH Co.KG v. Verbraucherzentrale NRW eV, 29/07/2019, ECLI: EU:C:2019:629.

[60] Specht-Riemenschneider and Schneider (2020), pp. 159–163.

[61] Mahieu and van Hoboken (2019).

basis of the data processing (see Sect. 2.3.4), the ECJ states that this legitimate interest must be identified and justified both by Facebook and the third-party website.

It should be noted that the "like" button is not the only way to collect data from a third-party website and it would be a mistake to interpret the Fashion ID case narrowly. Facebook has also developed a tool called "Facebook's advertising pixel" that is advertised as a "piece of code for your website that lets you measure, optimise and build audiences for your advertising campaigns."[62] The advertising pixel creates a bridge between the user's activity registered on Facebook's platform and his activity on the third-party website. For instance, it warns Facebook if the user buys something on the e-commerce platform that installed the advertising pixel tool. It is reasonable to assume that the Fashion ID case applies by extension to Facebook's pixel.

2.2.3 The Compatibility Between the GDPR's Core Principles and Facebook's Business Model

All data processing is regulated by six fundamental principles, expressed in Article 5 (1) of the GDPR: the principle of lawfulness, fairness and transparency, the principle of purpose limitation, the principle of data minimization, the principle of accuracy, the principle of storage limitation, and the principle of integrity and confidentiality. Not all of these principles pose the same difficulties to the platform but every one of them has (or should have) a certain legal impact on the functioning of the platform.

2.2.3.1 The Principle of Lawfulness, Fairness and Transparency

The principle of lawfulness, fairness and transparency mainly provides that the user acknowledges the existence of a data processing. At first sight, users should expect their data to be processed when visiting and interacting with the platform. However, as seen above with the example of the "like" button and the advertising pixel, the extent of the data collected can sometimes be unknown to the average user. In other words, there is a huge gap between the users' general awareness that their personal data are being collected when interacting with the platform and the specific awareness of the data mountain related to them that is being processed each instant.

For example, most users adopt a specific behavior while interacting with the platform, which could be characterized as "self-censorship".[63] While a first impulse leads us to react to some stimulus and to publish some text and/or picture, a second

---

[62] https://www.facebook.com/business/learn/facebook-ads-pixel.

[63] Das and Kramer (2013).

mechanism intervenes as an afterthought that allows us to apprehend the potential adverse consequences of this action. Consequently, the message ready to be published is deleted at the last moment. Nevertheless, this data is collected by the platform. It is fair to say that "Facebook users don't expect their unposted thoughts to be collected".[64]

Facebook's data policy mentions that

> [w]e collect information about how you use our Products, such as the types of content you view or engage with; the features you use; the actions you take; the people or accounts you interact with; and the time, frequency and duration of your activities.[65]

On the one hand, Facebook does declare that any kind of interaction with the platform is monitored. On the other hand, the specific monitoring of self-censorship actions is not explicitly explained.

2.2.3.2   The Principle of Purpose Limitation

The idea that no data processing shall occur without a specific purpose constitutes the cornerstone of the protection provided by the GDPR. The purpose will be the judge of the legitimacy of the processing, of its extent, and of its duration. Any kind of data processing that does not correspond to the declared purpose is considered to be a new data processing, the legality of which has to be examined independently.

The GDPR states three characteristics that the purpose should have: it has to be specified, explicit and legitimate.[66] A specified purpose implies that the data processor determines and express the purpose of the data processing. Explicit means that the purpose has to be announced to the data subject. A legitimate purpose indicates that not just any purpose is accepted, as the purpose should be in line with the fundamental rights of the data subject. For instance, in the Heinz Huber[67] case, the ECJ considered that a legitimate purpose could not distinguish between individuals in a way that violates the principle of non-discrimination between EU citizens.

Facebook's purpose could be summarized in two words: "direct marketing". All data processing is related to the objective of determining what kind of advertising will be more relevant to or more effective on the data subject. This purpose is presumably acceptable under the GDPR as it is even cited as a lawful basis of legitimate interest. Indeed, Recital 47 of the GDPR explicitly indicates that "[t]he processing of personal data for direct marketing purposes may be regarded as carried out for a legitimate interest".

---

[64] Golberk (2013).

[65] https://www.facebook.com/about/privacy/your-info.

[66] Article 5 (1) (b) of the GDPR.

[67] ECJ, C-524/06, Heinz Huber v. Bundesrepublik Deutschland, 16/12/2008, ECLI:EU:C:2008:724.

Facebook's terms and conditions are written in a user-friendly way, which indeed facilitate understanding,[68] but also at the same time diminish the formality of the commitment. No formal reference is made to the GDPR's obligation to state the purpose of the data processing. Instead, two references to the purpose can be found in the terms of the service. At the beginning of the document, it is declared that

> [w]e use your personal data to help determine which ads to show you. We don't sell your personal data to advertisers, and we don't share information that directly identifies you (such as your name, email address or other contact information) with advertisers unless you give us specific permission. Instead, advertisers can tell us things such as the kind of audience that they want to see their ads, and we show those ads to people who may be interested. We provide advertisers with reports about the performance of their ads that help them understand how people are interacting with their content.[69]

Also, in Sect. 2, it is repeated that

> [i]nstead of paying to use Facebook and the other products and services we offer, by using the Facebook Products covered by these Terms you agree that we can show you ads that business and organisations pay us to promote on and off the Facebook Company Products. We use your personal data, such as information about your activity and interests, to show you ads that are more relevant to you.

The terms therefore insist on the notion of data as currency being justified by the free access to the service.

It cannot be denied that direct marketing is a legitimate purpose, in the context of the e-economy. However, is this purpose specific enough? The issue here is that, by definition, the purpose of direct marketing is not really as limited as it should be, as it claims that any kind of information and any amount of information is needed in order to ensure the better profiling of the data subject (which also poses an issue as regards the principle of data minimization, see below). In this context, the Article 29 Working Party had already specified in 2013 that a general and vague reference to direct marketing is not sufficient for the purposes of this principle. Specifically, it noted that

> [t]he purpose of the collection must be clearly and specifically identified: it must be detailed enough to determine what kind of processing is and is not included within the specified purpose, and to allow that compliance with the law can be assessed and data protection safeguards applied. For these reasons, a purpose that is vague or general, such as for instance 'improving users' experience', 'marketing purposes', 'IT-security purposes' or 'future research' will-without more detail-usually not meet the criteria of being 'specific'.[70]

Put otherwise, according to the Article 29 Working Party , Facebook is not at liberty to hide all activities behind the general label of "direct marketing". On the contrary, a clear description of all data involved must be provided.

---

[68] Recital 39 of the GDPR explains that "The principle of transparency requires that any information and communication relating to the processing of those personal data be easily accessible and easy to understand, and that clear and plain language be used."

[69] Facebook (2020) Terms of Service. https://www.facebook.com/legal/terms/plain_text_terms.

[70] Article 29 Working Party (2013), p. 15.

2.2.3.3 The Principle of Data Minimization

The GDPR slightly modified one of the core principles already enshrined in the previous Directive. While before the GDPR's enactment the amount of data collected had to be proportionate to the purpose of the data processing (principle of proportionality), nowadays the data collection has to be strictly necessary (principle of data minimization). In this new paradigm, the processor is obliged to collect as little data as possible. This principle constitutes a major obstacle for Facebook. Indeed, it would be very naïve to restrict the understanding of the scale of the collected data to messages, pictures, and "likes" only. Once again, one needs to look at Facebook's data policy in order to understand the full scale of data collected. For instance, the data policy includes a section on device information.
It is stated that:

> Information that we obtain from these devices includes:Device attributes: information such as the operating system, hardware and software versions, battery level, signal strength, available storage space, browser type, app and file names and types, and plugins. Device operations: information about operations and behaviours performed on the device, such as whether a window is in the foreground or background, or mouse movements (which can help distinguish humans from bots). Identifiers: unique identifiers, device IDs and other identifiers, such as from games, apps or accounts that you use, and Family Device IDs (or other identifiers unique to Facebook Company Products associated with the same device or account). Device signals: Bluetooth signals, information about nearby Wi-Fi access points, beacons and mobile phone masts. Data from device settings: information you allow us to receive through device settings that you turn on, such as access to your GPS location, camera or photos. Network and connections: information such as the name of your mobile operator or ISP, language, time zone, mobile phone number, IP address, connection speed and, in some cases, information about other devices that are nearby or on your network, so we can do things such as help you stream a video from your phone to your TV. Cookie data: data from cookies stored on your device, including cookie IDs and settings. Learn more about how we use cookies in the Facebook Cookies Policy and Instagram Cookies Policy.

In contrast to the enormous amount of personal data that the company is technically in a position to collect, the principle of data minimization can be seen as one of the most important issues that Facebook's compliance teams have to solve in the post-GDPR era.[71] For instance, it is not explained clearly enough why the company needs to learn about all Wi-Fi networks in range to strengthen the user's profile. Also, the principle of data minimization should prohibit the collection of data that are not directly related to the user, such as for instance the user's contacts' e-mails. Arguably, information related to declined friend requests, removed friends, deleted posts, photos or messages should also not be recorded.

---

[71] Devergranne (2018).

2.2.3.4   The Principle of Accuracy

The platform has a duty to ensure that the collected data are correct. Nevertheless, the company has an obvious interest in obtaining data that is as accurate as possible and has installed a software to control the usernames used by users. It also actively hunts for fake accounts. In 2019, Facebook deleted more than three billion accounts for this reason.[72] However, its estimate that 5% of active accounts are fake is under scrutiny, as some believe that it is widely underestimated.[73] Per the terms of Service, it is the users' contractual obligation to use "the same name that they use in everyday life" and to provide "accurate information about themself".

This real-name user requirement policy has been often criticized. For instance, the Electronic Frontier Foundation (EFF) has alerted that this policy disproportionately affects LGBT communities.[74] The policy also affects individuals from communities where naming traditions differ from Western culture. For instance, Native Americans have had some problems with the policy.[75] Finally, the policy increases the risks that activists in non-democratic countries are exposed to.

The principle of accuracy is therefore an ambiguous one. Its justification lies in the idea that incorrect data processing is potentially harmful for the data subject. However, and ironically, the principle's enforcement leads to further threat to privacy. For instance, the user's age constitutes a vital piece of information. Under a certain age limit (see below), minors do not have the right to open an account. However, an obligation for Facebook to verify the real age of an individual could potentially lead to situations such as scanning or photographing ID cards, which is much more intrusive for privacy.

2.2.3.5   The Principle of Storage Limitation

How long will Facebook hold personal data for? To answer this question, it is first necessary to distinguish the situation of data subjects that are not users of the platform. Facebook, like many other websites, automatically collects some information about visitors, even if they do not have an account. These data subjects are known as "shadow profiles".[76] Facebook keeps browsing data from its non-users for 10 days. It may not really exploit and monetize them, but it still can use them to advertise the platform itself.

On the other hand, users' data related to browsing are held for 90 days. Data published on the platform, such as posts, comments, and profile information are not deleted for as long as the user's account remains active. This constitutes another

---

[72] Wong and Brown (2019).

[73] Nicas (2019).

[74] York and Kayyali (2014).

[75] Holpuch (2015).

[76] Wagner (2018).

issue as most users are not aware of the long-reaching effects of their interactions. For instance, it is sometimes required from a candidate for a work position to provide access to their social media account. Access to Facebook's personal information through the psychological coercion of a candidate therefore becomes an extremely invasive and effective tool in the hands of a jury. This practice is not in itself illegal, in the sense that in no law the EU explicitly prohibits this "snooping" activity. However, this activity falls within the definition of data processing, and all the principles, plus the duty to find a legal basis, must be respected.

In this context, the Article 29 Working Party states that

> the employer should -prior to the inspection of a social media profile- take into account whether the social media profile of the applicant is related to business or private purposes, as this can be an important indication for the legal admissibility of the data inspection. In addition, employers are only allowed to collect and process personal data relating to job applicants to the extent that the collection of those data is necessary and relevant to the performance of the job which is being applied for. Data collected during the recruitment process should generally be deleted as soon as it becomes clear that an offer of employment will not be made or is not accepted by the individual concerned. The individual must also be correctly informed of any such processing before they engage with the recruitment process.[77]

The principle links the duration of the processing to its purpose. However, Facebook's purpose is to create an accurate profiling of the individual's personality in order to find the most relevant advertisements. It is a matter of interpretation, but it could be reasonably argued that a personality evolves with the passing of time. As Meta is only concluding its second decade of existence, this issue has not yet been sufficiently explored. Nevertheless, it could be argued that information about the data subject's private life from 20 years ago, for instance, would not be of any use in order to establish the user's profile. In this respect and if this argument is accepted, the principle of storage limitation requires the deletion of data that is not pertinent anymore. Nowadays, Facebook holds account information even after the death of the individual, which poses a serious legal challenge known as "digital inheritance" (see Sect. 4.2.1).

2.2.3.6   The Principle of Integrity and Confidentiality, Cambridge Analytica, and the Data Breach Notification System

When approaching the enforcement of the principle of integrity and confidentiality applied to Facebook, a name immediately comes to mind: Cambridge Analytica. This huge scandal marked a new era for Facebook. In 2013, a researcher working for the Cambridge Analytica firm Kogan built a Facebook app that comprised a quiz.[78] The quiz used a loophole in the Facebook app's API that allowed it to spy on the users. Through the game, the app collected data not only on the users that played it,

---

[77] Article 29 Data Protection Working Party (2017b), p. 11.

[78] Cadwalladr and Graham-Harrison (2018), p. 22.

but also on their "Facebook friends". Consequently, the firm managed to collect data related to 87 million users. The collected information was subsequently exploited by political parties in the US elections and during the Brexit vote, harvesting the data to create personalized profiles that targeted and influenced the users' most sensitive issues.

This data breach constitutes a violation of the principle of integrity. Even if it is probable (but not certain) that the company was unaware of the issue, the breach itself indicates a large degree of negligence in the creation and the management of the Facebook app's API. The UK Information Commissioner's Office (ICO) in 2018 fined Facebook GBP 500,000 (EUR 580,000) as a consequence of the scandal. Marc Zuckerberg characteristically wrote in response to the scandal: "We have a responsibility to protect your data, and if we can't then we don't deserve to serve you.".[79] At the same time, two class action lawsuits were filed in the UK by users believing their data were part of the data breach.[80]

The Cambridge Analytica scandal occurred just before the GDPR entered into force. It clearly shows the limits of the protection of the principle of integrity in case of massive scale data breach. However, the GDPR generalizes an already known mechanism (but with very limited range in the past): the data breach notification. From now on, in the case of a massive data breach, the controller is bound to immediately take some measures (alert his DPO, identify the damages, then alert the competent supervisory authority). Depending on the risk to privacy posed by the data breach (for instance, were the data encrypted or not? Were there sensitive data?), the supervisory authority may decide to compel the company to notify all concerned users or even all the public about the breach. This mechanism does not only have an informative function. With the wide publicity related to the communication to the public, the mechanism is bound to have a deterrent effect.[81] It is seen in practice as a form of reputational sanction.[82]

The Cambridge Analytica scandal is not the only case of data breach (see Sect. 2.4.2) concerning Facebook, but its magnitude and its relation with the very sensitive issue of the growing political power of the platform, that is the power to manipulate and influence its users (see Sect. 8.2.2), meant that it had deep consequences on the public image of the company and, eventually, on its legal framework.

---

[79]Zuckerberg (2018).

[80]Ridley (2021).

[81]Tang and Whinston (2020), pp. 410–427.

[82]Schwartz and Janger (2007), pp. 913–984.

2.2.4   User's Rights to the Data and the Theoretical Portability

2.2.4.1   The Right to Access

The third chapter of the GDPR is dedicated to the rights of the data subject. All these rights are relevant to Facebook, but in practice it is extremely difficult to exercise some of them. Articles 12, 13 and 14 refer to the right to be informed, which is de facto more an obligation that a user's right, as it has to be exercised automatically. The GDPR innovates with a very exhaustive list of information that has to be accessible the moment the data are collected, and this function is accomplished by Facebook's data policy.

The right of the data subject to have access to his data is fundamental for the good functioning of the regime, as it allows the data subject to control the extent of the data collection. This right is provided by Article 15 of the GDPR. In the context of Facebook, it is worth mentioning that this right was the starting point of a litigation that deeply affected Facebook's legal regime. Indeed, Max Schrems, still a law student in 2011, decided for the needs of his dissertation to exercise his right to access and wrote a formal letter to Facebook.[83] The company sent him a CD containing over 1,200 pages of data. The various findings in these data and the questions raised by some gaps in the database led the activist to sue the company and to start an awareness campaign. Later, all experts on privacy law came to learn about the landmark Schrems I and Schrems II decisions of the ECJ (see Sect. 2.5.3). Since then, Facebook has made it easy for the user to export data, as the platform offers a service that allows users to download the archive.

2.2.4.2   The Right to Rectification

The right to rectification presupposes a veracity in the information. It aims to correct the false data, by replacing it with accurate data. This right's usefulness is obvious when the information concerned is mere identification data, such as the name, address, or phone number. However, it is more challenging to apply it to behavior-related data. When the combination of big data and AI permits acute identification of behavioral patterns, the right to rectification becomes more difficult to exercise because, firstly, the data subject is not aware of it. For instance, Facebook classifies its users into various categories such as "currently away from family", "back from travel recently", etc. While this information is accessible through the right to access, the average users do not think of exercising it on a daily basis and thus verifying that the AI correctly understood that they have recently travelled, for instance.

Therefore, it has been proposed that the GDPR is lacking a new right that would complete the rights to access and rectification, namely the right "to reasonable

---

[83] Hill (2012).

inferences".[84] Indeed, it could be argued that in case of inferences, the data is neither collected from the data subject nor from a third party. This right would include a right to know about the inference and a right to rectify it. The closest user's prerogative to this right could be a general right to explanation in the case of AI-based profiling, but this right's practical range is debated (see Sect. 8.3.2).

2.2.4.3   The Rights to Erasure and to Object, the Right to Restriction and the Right to Oppose: The Problem of Account Deletion

Facebook's terms of service state that

> [y]ou also have the right to object to and restrict certain processing of your data. This includes: the right to object to our processing of your data for direct marketing, which you can exercise by using the "unsubscribe" link in such marketing communications, and the right to object to our processing of your data where we are performing a task in the public interest or pursuing our legitimate interests or those of a third party. You can exercise this right on Facebook and on Instagram.

Obviously, the ultimate expression of the user's right to object is the discretionary faculty for the user to terminate its contract with Facebook at any time. The right to erasure and to be forgotten is allowed when the data subject withdraws consent.[85] However, in this context, the principle of storage limitation[86] has notably been violated in the past, as regards the serious difficulties encountered by users who wanted to terminate their account on Facebook. Indeed, the company only deactivated the account instead of deleting it. In 2012, when Facebook filed its initial public offering in the US with the Securities and Exchange Commission, the company had to disclose that only about half of the 800 million subscribers they were claiming to have at the time were active daily users, implying that the number of "sleeping accounts" was grossly underestimated.

Even today, the steps required to delete an account make the process difficult.[87] The user has to find the "Account" option, choose "Settings and privacy", "Settings", "Privacy", "Your Facebook information", and, finally, "deactivation and deletion". The users are then asked for a reason for deleting the account, then a new warning is shown about the deleted data and, eventually, they have to confirm their password for security reasons. A new pop-up appears and explains then that the decision can be revoked for 30 days and asks for confirmation. Consequently, nine steps are needed to achieve the deletion and the option to delete is located in a misleading category (deletion is not always related to a privacy issue). This situation

---

[84] Wachter and Mittelstadt (2019), p. 494.

[85] Article 17 (1) (b) of GDPR.

[86] Article 5 (1) (e) of the GDPR, that states that personal data shall not be kept in a form which permits identification of data subjects for no longer than is necessary for the purposes for which the personal data are processed.

[87] Rodriguez Martinez and Abellan-Matamoros (2018).

exploits a loophole in the GDPR's protection, as it is not explicitly stated that the user should be able to exercise his or her rights with reasonable ease. This practice belongs to a general technique known as a "dark pattern": using design techniques in order to manipulate the user's behavior (see Sect. 2.4.4).

The right to erasure shall be exercised without undue delay, according to the GDPR. It is a matter of interpretation whether the Facebook's current practice of keeping the data up to 90 days is compatible with this principle. The company justifies this delay as some servers create backups of the data and the deletion request has to be notified to all servers.

As an alternative to the right to erasure, the GDPR also offers to the data subject the "right to restriction of processing".[88] This right allows the user to block further processing while there exists a dispute as regards the accuracy of the data, if unlawful processing has taken place, or if the user needs it to establish, exercise or defend legal claims. The restriction also enters into force if the legitimacy of the exercise of the right to object to the processing is being examined. In practice, the right to restriction freezes each activity related to the data, and only allows their storage.

Finally, where personal data are processed for the purposes of direct marketing, the data subject should have the right to object to such processing—including profiling—to the extent that it is related to such direct marketing, whether with regard to initial or further processing, at any time and free of charge. That right should be explicitly brought to the data subject's attention and presented clearly and separately from any other information. Even though Meta has made a lot of efforts in this field lately, it could be argued that, once again, the effective use of the right to object is hindered by dark patterns (see Sect. 2.4.4). For instance, with advertisements, the user has to choose the "Why you're seeing this ad" option, then "Hide all ads from this advertiser", which is a really simple and effective way to block a specific source. However , to oppose the profiling itself that led to this source, the user has to continue and choose "make changes to your ad preferences", then, in the left menu, "Ad settings" (it is also possible to arrive here by clicking on Profile/Settings and Privacy/Settings/Ads), then "Categories used to reach you", then "Interest categories and at last there appears a list of interests, that may be extremely long (depending on the user), with button on each individual interest to "remove" it. At each step, Facebook takes great care to remind the user that opting out of the data processing will not reduce the number of advertisements published, only their pertinence. In the same section, it is possible to deactivate use of data collected from Facebook's partners for advertisements.

---

[88] Article 18 of the GDPR.

2.2.4.4   The Right to Portability: A Chimera?

The right to portability is already an acquis in some sectors of the digital economy.[89] For some decades now, users expect to be able to keep their phone number when they change provider. However, before the GDPR entered into force, no general and horizontal right was recognized for the data subject to move personal data from one company to another. This new right differs from most of the other GDPR rights as it is not only justified by privacy matters, but also by reference to the principles of competition law. When a service has stored a user's profile, graphic preferences, history, and favorite topics, it possesses a digital identity of this person. Without the right to portability, users may feel "trapped" in a service, as the transfer to a new one would mean that they would lose the entire digital identity they had gradually built over time. In other words, the specific market would create a dominant position which would choke any kind of competition. In addition, a right to portability aims to foster a more competitive market environment, by allowing customers to switch providers more easily.[90]

This right to portability is even more necessary in the specific case of Facebook, as the company does not only profit from a somehow classic position of dominance in its market, but is also protected by a principle known as "the network effect".[91] Roughly, the network effect shows that the more people use Facebook, the more valuable the network becomes to each person using it and the more difficult it is to leave it. The presence on the platform becomes for the average users a necessary aspect of their professional life, in order to defend their reputation or just by fear of missing news, a potential client, or a life opportunity. The service "Facebook connect", which appeared in 2008, further complicates the process to leave the platform and further reinforces the network effect. Nowadays, multiple third-party services use the Facebook Login tool to facilitate login. The Facebook account therefore becomes a universal key to accessing multiple online services. This general lock-in of the users can be empirically ascertained by Facebook's statistics: even after multiple scandals and a general mistrust of the population against the various (sometimes real, but also often imaginary) modifications of the level of privacy protection on the platform, no decline in its use is perceptible.[92]

Under the GDPR, the users' right to portability of their data consists of two separate rights, the combination of which offers the possibility of data portability. The data subject has the right

> to receive the personal data concerning him or her, which he or she has provided to a
> controller, in a structured, commonly used and machine-readable format and have the right

---

[89] See the "Universal Service Directive" in 2002, now Directive (EU) 2018/1972 of the European Parliament and of the Council of 11 December 2018 establishing the European Electronic Communications Code (Recast) ELI: http://data.europa.eu/eli/dir/2018/1972/2018-12-17.

[90] Article 29 Working Party (2017a).

[91] Øverby (2018), pp. 37–40.

[92] Graef (2013), pp. 502–514.

to transmit those data to another controller without hindrance from the controller to which the personal data have been provided[93]

but also the right to "have the personal data transmitted directly from one controller to another, where technically feasible."[94]

This right only concerns processing carried out by automated means based on consent. Two more conditions are encapsulated in the definition of the right: the data must be in a "structured, commonly used and machine-readable format" and the transfer must be "technically feasible". Furthermore, paragraph 4 of Article 20 specifies that "[t]he right referred to in paragraph 1 shall not adversely affect the rights and freedoms of others." Indeed, during the process to transfer one user's personal data, a second user's personal data might be compromised. For instance, discussion logs, contacts, reactions to other posts, etc. imply interrelation with other persons and the portability has to take into consideration the risk involved to these persons.

Some major obstacles practically block the exercise of the right to portability as regards social media. The first one, of a hybrid nature, concerns the need to find an open access standard for the data. Portability presupposes interoperability. However, Facebook does not use a standard format for its database. On the contrary, it could even be argued that its database's structure is protected as a trade secret (see Sect. 4. 1.2).

It is a thorny issue: on the one hand, imposing open standards on all sectors would not only adversely affect intellectual property rights but also kill diversity and innovation. On the other hand, the lack of such a mandatory mechanism constitutes a huge loophole in the right to portability. The GDPR only provides that "[d]ata controllers should be encouraged to develop interoperable formats that enable data portability."[95] However, this encouragement is not followed by precise rules enforcing the use of interoperable formats where possible. Furthermore, the right only concerns data that are provided by the users, not all the personal data processed. For instance, is the activity log personal data provided by the user? It could be argued that this is data automatically created by the platform and not provided by the user. In conclusion, the final version of the right to portability in the GDPR is a lot "more prudent"[96] than the version first proposed by the Commission at the start of the negotiations.

Practically, Facebook is far from being the only social network in the market. For instance, other platforms such as Reddit work as content aggregators and offer similar systems of content evaluation. However, Reddit (for instance) offers anonymity. The specific crossover between public and private spheres that is offered by Facebook does not meet serious competition. Some alternatives, such as Diaspora (which is a distributed social network), Ello, or Vero could be mentioned, but none of these services should be considered to be mainstream.

---

[93] Article 20 (1) of the GDPR.

[94] Article 20 (2) of the GDPR.

[95] Recital 68 of the GDPR.

[96] De Hert et al. (2018). pp. 193–203.

Meta considers that its platform is fully compliant with the right to portability. The vice-president and chief privacy officer have published a paper on this issue, where they explain that

> In connection with the GDPR coming into force, we made DYI [the "Download Your Information" service provided by Facebook] better suited for portability by enabling people to receive their information in the commonly used structured JSON format.[97]

It remains to be seen whether this opening really facilitates an effective use of the right of portability in this context. Empiric analysis of the retrieved data through the DYI process tends to prove that no real portability to competitors is offered in practice. Specifically, it has been stated that "[p]orted data is simultaneously insufficient to replicate Facebook and too tailored to Facebook to be useful for much else."[98]

2.2.5 The Sharing of Data Between WhatsApp and the Main Platform: The Dangerous Relationships

2.2.5.1 The Merger and the Anticompetition Fine

WhatsApp is a company founded in 2009 by two former Yahoo employees that offers an instant messaging application through the Internet and operating on smartphones, using the phone number to login. The simplicity and effectiveness of the service quickly attracted a new public and the company's popularity soared. Meanwhile, Meta had already determined that the future of social networking will be focused on smartphone devices. In 2014, Facebook decided to buy WhatsApp for the astronomical amount of USD 19 billion. This is by far the most expensive investment the company has ever made and one of the biggest in the field in general.[99] The presumed intent was to merge the Facebook Messenger, Instagram, and WhatsApp messaging platforms into one cross-platform service. This merger was strongly debated. Facebook already had a messaging service—"Messenger"—and it was more than plausible that the company's true motivations for this acquisition were not the application itself but rather the opportunity to neutralize an emerging competitor. Furthermore, this acquisition adds more control over the personal data of many users who may not have created a Facebook account.

Because the transaction qualified as a concentration under the merger regulation, it fell within the scope of the European Commission's competence to control its legality. The European Commission first approved this move in 2014, considering at the time that the two companies were not competitors per se. However, in 2016, Facebook submitted a note to the Commission where it set out its plan for a better

---

[97] Egan (2019).

[98] Nicholas and Weinberg (2019).

[99] Deutsch (2020).

integration of the two services, through an updating of WhatsApp's privacy notice. The Commission then reconsidered its position, suspecting that it did not have possess all the necessary information at the time of its first assessment of the merger's legality. In 2017, the Commission decided to levy a EUR 110 million fine against Facebook for furnishing the European body with misleading information concerning its acquisition of WhatsApp.[100] The Commission mainly considered that Facebook was aware, at the time of the first investigation, of anticompetitive practices that technically would allow it to automatically match users' profiles from different apps. This finding means that the purpose of the acquisition, from the beginning, was maybe not to extend Facebook's services into new sectors but to integrate a rival messaging service into Facebook's ecosystem.

Meanwhile, allegations that the company has unlawfully maintained a monopoly by freezing out and buying up potential competitors are also rising outside the EU. In December 2019, the US Federal Trade Commission and 46 states sued the company over antitrust practices.[101] US judges, however, rejected this claim.[102] The Court considered that "[t]he FTC's Complaint says almost nothing concrete on the key question of how much power Facebook actually had, and still has, in a properly defined antitrust product market",[103] highlighting the difficulty in applying classic theories of dominance in the market to the specific situation of the social network (see Sect. 9.1.1).

2.2.5.2 The Privacy Threats Related to the Merger

In the context of the merger between WhatsApp and Facebook, one may wonder

> whether the Facebook-WhatsApp merger qualifies as a competition law case, in which the data wealth is tangentially relevant as one aspect of a classical merger assessment, or whether the fusion of the two companies is in fact a clear-cut case of a data protection legal issue.[104]

Indeed, the censure from the European Commission does not explicitly concern data protection issues, but this is the "elephant in the room" as regards the merger. The ultimate goal of fully merging the two communication services (Messenger and WhatsApp) remains plausible. This emerges from some new modifications to WhatsApp's privacy policy in 2019. Not only do users share some metadata with Facebook, such as user phone numbers and device information, but, under the new privacy policy (if accepted), payment and transaction data too. In parallel, Meta

---

[100] EU Commission, case No. M.8228 –FACEBOOK / WHATSAPP C (2017) 3192 final.

[101] Kendall (2021).

[102] US District Court of Columbia, Federal Trade Commisssion v. Facebook inc, 28/06/2021, Civil Action No. 20-3590 (JEB).

[103] p.31 of the decision.

[104] Gábor P. (2020) The Value of Personal Data from a Competition Law Perspective. Elte Law Journal. https://eltelawjournal.hu/the-value-of-personal-data-from-a-competition-law-perspective/.

continues its efforts to unify the underlying infrastructure of Messenger, WhatsApp, and Instagram, for instance through integrating a common encryption system.

In a statement, the Irish Data Protection Commission reacted to these new developments and announced that

> [t]he Irish DPC will be very closely scrutinising Facebook's plans as they develop, particularly insofar as they involve the sharing and merging of personal data between different Facebook companies. Previous proposals to share data between Facebook companies have given rise to significant data protection concerns and the Irish DPC will be seeking early assurances that all such concerns will be fully taken into account by Facebook in further developing this proposal. It must be emphasised that ultimately the proposed integration can only occur in the EU if it is capable of meeting all of the requirements of the GDPR.[105]

Indeed, the consequences of a fusion of the messaging services would be devastating in terms of data protection. Already in 2018, the Higher Administrative Court of Hamburg endorsed the Data Protection Authority's order[106] banning Facebook from using WhatsApp users' data extensively for its own purposes. The judge found that there was no valid consent from the users for the planned mass data exchange.[107]

In 2021, the Hamburg Commissioner for Data Protection and Freedom of Information (HmbBfDI), activating again Article 66 of GDPR on urgent provisional measures, issued an order prohibiting Facebook Ireland Ltd from processing personal data from WhatsApp for its own purposes.[108] However, the EDPB intervened in this matter (see Sect. 2.5.1). The EDPB remarks that "there was not enough information to establish with certainty whether Facebook IE already started to process WhatsApp IE user data as a (joint) controller for its own purposes of marketing communications and direct marketing."[109] Consequently, the EDPB asked the Irish Data Commission to conduct further investigation.

Furthermore, ICO handed down a ruling after 2 years of investigation into this issue. The authority found that, firstly, WhatsApp had not identified a lawful processing basis for any such sharing of personal data. Secondly, WhatsApp had failed to provide adequate fair processing information to users in relation to any such

---

[105] Irish Data Protection Commission (2019) Data Protection Commission statement on proposed integration of Facebook, WhatsApp and Instagram. Press release of the Data Protection Commission, https://dataprotection.ie/en/news-media/press-releases/data-protection-commission-statement-proposed-integration-facebook.

[106] From the Hamburg Commissionner for data protection and freedom of information.

[107] The Hamburg Commissioner for Data Protection and Freedom of Information (2018) Higher Administrative Court confirms the prohibition of data sharing between WhatsApp and Facebook. Press Release, The Hamburg Commissioner for Data Protection and Freedom of Information, https://datenschutz-hamburg.de/assets/pdf/Press_Release_2018-03-02_Higher_Administrative_Court_Facebook.pdf.

[108] The Hamburg Commissioner for Data Protection and Freedom of Information (2021) Order of the HmbBfDI: Ban of further processing of WhatsApp user data by Facebook. Press release. https://datenschutz-hamburg.de/assets/pdf/2021-05-11-press-release-facebook.pdf.

[109] EDPB (2021b) EDPB adopts urgent binding decision: Irish SA not to take final measures but to carry out statutory investigation. Press release. https://edpb.europa.eu/news/news/2021/edpb-adopts-urgent-binding-decision-irish-sa-not-take-final-measures-carry-out_en.

sharing of personal data. Thirdly, in relation to existing users, such sharing would involve the processing of personal data for a purpose that is incompatible with the purpose for which such data was obtained. And finally, it found that if they had shared the data, they would have been in contravention of the first and second data protection principles of the GDPR (principles of transparency and of purpose limitation).[110]

Moreover, in another case in Germany, the Bundeskartellamt (Federal Cartel Office) had ordered Facebook to stop collecting data on its users across its suite of products (Facebook, Instagram, WhatsApp, and Oculus). However, the order was blocked on appeal by the Higher Regional Court Düsseldorf in 2019.[111] Eventually, the German court asked the ECJ for guidance on this matter and the issue is still pending.[112]

The issue of the sharing of data between various Meta services is still pending a definitive result. However, the DMA proposal (see Sect. 9.2.2) aims to definitively close the question by stating as a principle that Facebook (as "gatekeeper") should

> refrain from combining personal data sourced from these core platform services with personal data from any other services offered by the gatekeeper or with personal data from third-party services, and from signing in end users to other services of the gatekeeper in order to combine personal data, unless the end user has been presented with the specific choice and provided consent in the sense of Regulation (EU) 2016/679.[113]

In other words, the merging of the dataset would be permissible only if the end-users opt in to this.

2.3   The Legal Bases for Data Processing of Facebook's Users

2.3.1   General Principles on the Lawfulness of Data Processing

Since the Data Protection Directive and pursuant to Article 8 of the Charter of Fundamental Rights of the European Union, no data processing should occur without a specific justification. This justification takes the shape of a two-step test: first, as explained above, the controller needs to indicate the purpose of the data processing. Then, all data processing must opt for one of only six possible lawful bases in order to justify its legitimacy. These lawful bases are listed in Article 6 (1) of the GDPR. They are consent, contract (the processing is necessary for the execution

---

[110] Denham (2018).

[111] Bundeskartellamt (2019).

[112] ECJ, C-252/21, Facebook v. Bundeskartellamt, logged in 24 March 2021.

[113] Article 5 (a) of the Proposal.

of a contract), legal obligation, vital interests, public task, and legitimate interests (unless the data subject's interest prevails). This part of the previous legal framework does not fundamentally change under the GDPR, even if the lawful basis of consent has received special attention from the EU legislator in order to close some potential loopholes as regards the definition and the exercising of consent.

The decision to choose one or more specific lawful bases for the data processing is essential. The matter affects both the legality of the activity and the extent of the data subject's rights. However, this obligation can be misleading: the fact that the lawfulness of the processing is guaranteed by the legal basis does not mean that the data processing is automatically legal—only that it is legitimate. It is in any case mandatory to apply the six fundamental principles of data processing specified above (see Sect. 2.2.3).

Normally, these lawful bases of the lawfulness of the data processing are mutually exclusive. However, it is possible to distinguish between kinds of processing that differ because of the nature of the data or of the circumstances of the collection, and to establish a specific lawful basis for each individual processing instance of processing. This is the approach that Facebook has adopted. It has opted for the second legal basis (execution of the contract) as the main basis for the most basic functions of the platform, but in conjunction with almost all the other lawful bases. It is clear that the lawful basis of the execution of the contract cannot cover the entire range of data processing operated by the platform. The EDPB remarks that

> [i]t is possible that another lawful basis than Article 6(1)(b) may better match the objective of the processing or be more appropriate because it better balances the interests of the parties. The identification of the appropriate lawful basis is tied to principles of fairness and purpose limitation.[114]

2.3.2   Facebook's Lawful Bases Under the GDPR: The Contract

To use this lawful basis, the controller basically needs to prove two elements: there is a valid contract, and the processing is necessary for the contract. As regards the first requirement, it has to be noted that the GDPR does not influence the core principles of contract law, as enshrined in each country's national legislation. Therefore, the controller must be aware that the validity of the consent to enter into a contractual relationship is subject to judicial control.

As regards the second requirement, in 2019 the EDPB published new guidelines on using the execution of a contract as a legal basis, in the context of the provision of online services.[115] The authority notes that the notion of necessary data for the execution of the contract has to be interpreted in the light of the general principles of

---

[114] EDPB (2019a).
[115] EDPB (2019a).

the GDPR, and mainly that "[b]oth purpose limitation and data minimisation principles are particularly relevant in contracts for online services, which typically are not negotiated on an individual basis".[116] However, the concept of necessity transcends the already strict principles of purpose and data minimization, as this legal basis "does not cover situations where the processing is not genuinely necessary for the performance of a contract, but rather unilaterally imposed on the data subject by the controller".[117]

Let's refer to exactly how Facebook justifies its activity under this lawful basis and for which kind of data processing. In the privacy policy, it is specified that

> [f]or all people who have the legal capacity to enter into an enforceable contract, we process data as necessary to perform our contracts with you (the Facebook Terms and Instagram Terms, together, "the Terms"). We describe the contractual services for which this data processing is necessary in the "Our Services" section of the Terms, and in the additional informational resources accessible from the Terms. The uses of core data, which are necessary for the provision of our contractual services, are: To provide, personalise and improve our Facebook Products; To promote safety, integrity and security; To transfer, transmit, store or process your data outside the EEA, including to within the United States and other countries; To communicate with you, for example, on product-related issues; and To provide a consistent and seamless experiences across the Facebook Company Products.

The policy clarifies, in accordance with the GDPR, why the data processing is necessary for the performance of the contract, listing five activities. However, some of these explanations can be rejected as inconsistent with the basis. For instance, the EDPB considers that "processing for service improvement" is not valid, as in most cases, a user enters into a contract to avail him- or herself of an existing service, which casts doubt on the legitimacy of the first and fifth points.[118] Likewise, as regards the second point, the EDPB considers that the processing for 'fraud prevention' exceeds the range of what is strictly necessary for the execution of the contract.[119]

Most importantly, Meta considers that the contract is the basis for all the platform's services, as a rule, and covers all the practical functions of the platform. This view endorses a philosophy of online services where personal data is perceived as a form of monetary payment. The EDPB, with a rare intensity, states that this view is not compatible with the EU's legal framework. As per the afore-mentioned guidelines, and commenting on the behavioral advertising as justification for data processing under the legal basis of performance of contract, it held that

> [c]onsidering that data protection is a fundamental right guaranteed by Article 8 of the Charter of Fundamental Rights, and taking into account that one of the main purposes of the GDPR is to provide data subjects with control over information relating to them, personal

---

[116] Par.16 of the precited Guidelines.

[117] Article29 Working Party (2014).

[118] Par.46 of the precited Guidelines.

[119] Par.47 of the precited Guidelines.

data cannot be considered as a tradeable commodity. Data subjects can agree to processing of their personal data, but cannot trade away their fundamental rights.[120]

In conclusion, this decision to place most data processing under the legal basis of contract is problematic from a legal point of view. On the one hand, it is justified as the platform is indeed merely an online service paid for with personal data. On the other hand, most users legitimately expect the platform to base the lawfulness of processing their activities on consent, not on the contract. Also, the EDPB points out that if certain processing activities are not necessary for the individual services requested by the data subject, but rather necessary for the controller's wider business model, the contract is not the appropriate lawful basis for those activities.[121] This position explains why, even if Facebook declares the contract as the main basis for its data processing, other legal bases are referred to as well.

2.3.3   Facebook's Lawful Bases Under the GDPR: Consent

2.3.3.1   Consent in General

The basis of consent plays a complementary role to that of contract in Facebook's contractual mechanism. First of all, it should be highlighted that the notion of consent here is to be understood as consent to the data processing, and not consent to enter into the contractual relationship. Once Facebook opts for the lawful basis of consent, it is not possible to switch to another lawful basis. Specifically, "it is not allowed to retrospectively utilise the legitimate interest basis in order to justify processing, where problems have been encountered with the validity of consent."[122]

As mentioned above, the GDPR has further restricted the conditions of validity of the data subject's consent. Under this basis, Facebook has a duty to obtain free, unequivocal, specific, and informed consent from its users. Consent must consist of a statement or clear affirmative action, be demonstrable, clearly distinguishable, intelligible and easily accessible, use clear language and be capable of being withdrawn.[123]

Facebook uses consent as a lawful basis only in specific contexts, where it is in fact legally bound to do so. Its privacy policy specifies that consent serves as lawful basis for the processing of only certain activities:

> For processing data with special protections (such as your religious views, political views, who you are "interested in" or your health, if you share this information in your Facebook profile fields or life events), so we can share with those you choose and personalise your content. For using facial recognition technology. For using data that advertisers and other

---

[120]Par.51 of the precited Guidelines.

[121]Par.36 of the precited Guidelines.

[122]Article 29 Working Party (2018), p. 23.

[123]See Article 29 Working Party (2011).

partners provide us with about your activity off Facebook Company Products, so we can personalise ads that we show you on Facebook Company Products, and on websites, apps and devices that use our advertising services. For sharing data that personally identifies you (information such as your name or email address, that by itself can be used to contact you or identifies who you are) with advertisers, such as when you direct us to share your contact information with an advertiser so they can contact you, for example, with additional information about a promoted product or service. For collecting information that you allow us to receive through the device-based settings you enable (such as access to your GPS location, camera or photos), so we can provide the features and services described when you enable the settings.

This first category of data collected under the basis of consent is what Facebook calls "data with special protections". It refers to the "specific categories of data"[124] under the GDPR, or, under the previous legislation, to "sensitive data". Indeed, sensitive data benefit from a special protection. As they concern information closely related to the core elements of an individual's personality, such as his philosophical, sexual, or political preferences, the GDPR prohibits their processing as a rule,[125] unless explicit consent has been obtained from the data subject. The platform, as a free forum of discussions on an infinite range of topics, collects "sensitive personal data" all the time. It is debatable whether Facebook complies with all the legal character-istics of consent as regards sensitive data, and specifically, the requirement that consent must be explicit.

Actually, in 2017, the Spanish data protection authority considered whether consent was a lawful basis for Facebook and decided to fine the company EUR 1,200,000.[126] The authority found that Facebook had collected details such as the gender, religious beliefs, personal preferences and browsing history of millions of Spanish users without informing them how such information would be used. Fur-thermore, the Spanish data authority ruled that

the consent cannot be specific where the information is given by means of imprecise wording which does not allow to understand the data processed and the purpose of the processing. The data collected is not proportional in connection with the purpose of the processing, much less where the user is giving a misinformed consent. The word "finished", instead of "I accept", is used when completing user registration. Furthermore, users are not required to have consulted the data privacy policy prior to consenting. Considering that the information shown by Facebook can confuse the average new technologies user, the consent can never be unequivocal or specific.[127]

---

[124] Article 9 of the GDPR.

[125] Article 9 (1) states that

Processing of personal data revealing racial or ethnic origin, political opinions, religious or philosophical beliefs, or trade union membership, and the processing of genetic data, biometric data for the purpose of uniquely identifying a natural person, data concerning health or data concerning a natural person's sex life or sexual orientation shall be prohibited.

[126] Lema (2017).

[127] Lema (2017) op.cit.

The Spanish data authority also held in the same decision that Facebook misguides users when obtaining consent, by not disclosing that personal data other than that directly provided by the user will also be collected and processed. It additionally reproached the company for not making the "data policy" clearly accessible and not making it mandatory to read it prior to registration.

2.3.3.2 Consent and Cookies

Cookies technology represents a strategic asset for Facebook, which uses it heavily. Through accessing information stored in users' devices, the platform is in a position to enrich its dataset on users. Cookies are also used by Facebook to track the behavior of non-registered visitors.

Facebook's data privacy notice mentions "collecting information that you allow us to receive through the device-based settings you enable". The Article 29 Working Party had in the past the opportunity to explain that

> advertising network providers are bound by Article 5(3) of the ePrivacy Directive pursuant to which placing cookies or similar devices on users' terminal equipment or obtaining information through such devices is only allowed with the informed consent of the users.[128]

In other words, for cookies technology and other device-based tracking mechanisms, data subject consent is the only available lawful basis. This consent is ruled by similar principles regulating consent under the GDPR. Specifically, the 2002 ePrivacy Directive, as amended in 2009, imposes the obligation to obtain informed consent before information is stored or accessed in the user's (or subscriber's) terminal device, which is exactly what a cookie does. It means that the traditional opt-out system, where consent is presumed, should be replaced with an opt-in system, as a positive action from the data subject is required.

Consequently, the question of cookies and data processing is only partially regulated by the GDPR, as the ePrivacy Directive intends to apply as lex specialis. Initially, the ePrivacy Directive was meant to be amended at the same time the GDPR was being enacted, but delays and lack of consensus on the content of the new ePrivacy Directive blocked its adoption. In 2021, the EU institutions finally reached an agreement on a new ePrivacy regulation.

Because of this dichotomy between the two legislative acts, Facebook adopted a special policy, distinct from its data policy, focusing on cookies.[129] Indeed, the legal regimes are similar but not identical. The ePrivacy Directive adds two exceptions to the requirement of informed consent, where the cookie is used "for the sole purpose of carrying out the transmission of a communication over an electronic communications network" or the cookie is "strictly necessary in order for the provider of an

---

[128] Article 29 Working Party (2010), p. 3.

[129] https://www.facebook.com/policies/cookies.

information society service explicitly requested by the subscriber or user to provide the service".

The Article 29 Working Party explained that these two exceptions must be strictly interpreted and, especially, that cookies installed under these exceptions "will likely be cookies that are set to expire when the browser session ends or even earlier."[130] Facebook uses both first-party cookies (cookies intended for the platform, such as authentication cookies or cookies identifying what advertisement was watched) and third-party cookies (cookies from other companies). However, the Working Party did not consider all cookies equal as regards the informed consent exception in the ePrivacy Directive. Specifically, it considers that "third party" cookies are usually not 'strictly necessary' to the user visiting a website since these cookies are usually related to a service that is distinct from the one that has been 'explicitly requested' by the user."[131]

The proposed ePrivacy Regulation aims to modify this regime.[132] While the logic of consent/exemptions is maintained, the list of exemptions is has grown quite a bit. In the proposal an exemption from the consent requirement for the processing of electronic communications data is possible if it is necessary for the purposes of network management or network optimization, if it is necessary for the performance of an electronic communications service contract to which the end-user is party, if it is necessary in order to protect the vital interest of a natural person, and, if (with conditions) it is necessary for scientific or historical research purposes or statistical purposes.[133]

Furthermore, in another article entitled "Protection of end-users' terminal equipment information". a general prohibition of the use without consent of "processing and storage capabilities of terminal equipment and the collection of information from end-users' terminal equipment" has been enshrined.[134] This article, therefore, directly concerns cookies and similar technologies. However, here again, a long list of exceptions follows. Cookies are authorized if they are necessary for the sole purpose of providing an electronic communication service, if they are strictly necessary for providing a service specifically requested by the end user, if they are necessary for the sole purpose of audience measuring, if they are necessary to maintain or restore the security of information society services or terminal equipment of the end-user, to prevent fraud or prevent or detect technical faults for the duration necessary for that purpose, or if they are necessary for a software update.

---

[130] Article 29 Working Party (2012). p. 5. Available at: https://ec.europa.eu/justice/article-29/documentation/opinion-recommendation/files/2012/wp194_en.pdf.

[131] Ibid, p. 5.

[132] Council of EU (2021) Proposal for a Regulation of the European Parliament and of the Council concerning the respect for private life and the protection of personal data in electronic communications and repealing Directive 2002/58/EC (Regulation on Privacy and Electronic Communications). Brussels, 10 February 2021, 6087/21.

[133] Article 6b of the Proposal.

[134] Article 8 of the Proposal.

Currently, a major concern, notably from the EDPB, is that the final text of the new ePrivacy Regulation marks a diminished level of protection. To avoid this, the EDPB insists on an adoption and interpretation of the ePrivacy Regulation's principles in the light of the GDPR. Specifically, it declares that

> provisions on consent under the GPDR apply in the context of the ePrivacy rules. Therefore, the EDPB considers that the necessity to obtain a genuine freely-given consent should prevent service providers from using unfair practices such as "take it or leave it" solutions, which make access to services and functionalities conditional on the consent of a user to the storing of information, or gaining of access to information already stored in the terminal equipment of a user (the so-called "cookie walls").[135]

In its cookies policy, Facebook lists a number of uses of cookies on the platform: authentication, security, site and product integrity, advertising, recommendations, insights and measurement, site features and services, performance, analytics and research, third-party websites and apps. Finally, it is possible for the user to completely block the installation of cookies through its browser settings or to opt-out from some tracking on the website of the European Interactive Digital Advertising Alliance, which is a "self-regulatory initiative aimed to foster transparency in the online advertising environment".[136]

Consequently, Facebook's heavy reliance on cookies and similar technologies poses serious legal issues. In addition, Facebook was condemned in Germany in 2018, as a location data tracker was activated by default in the Facebook app for mobile phones.[137] In addition, CNIL—the French data protection authority—imposed a 60 million euro fine on Facebook Ireland in 2022. The ratio of the decision makes a direct reference to the cookies policy.[138] The French authority reproaches the company for its "dark pattern" strategy (see Sect. 2.4.4). Specifically, the data authority highlights that the

> company did not make available to users located in France, on the website 'facebook.com', a means of refusing operations to read and/or write information in their terminals with the same degree of simplicity as the means provided to accept their use.[139]

Nevertheless, Meta may be forced to modify its policy, not through litigation, but because of technological changes. Indeed, two other GAFAM members have taken measures on this topic in the last version of its exploitation system for mobiles, Apple has decided to activate by default an opt-in mechanism for applications to access the "identifier for advertisers", which is a unique device identifier on every iPhone and iPad. Facebook reacted by announcing that it is working on new alternative tracking tools that could be available on Apple products.[140] Nevertheless

---

[135] EDPB (2021e).

[136] See http://www.youronlinechoices.eu/.

[137] LB Berlin 16 O 341/15, 16/01/2018, ECLI:DE:BVerwG:2018:160118B1VR12.17.0.

[138] CNIL, Deliberation of the restricted committee No. SAN-2021-024 of 31 December 2021 concerning FACEBOOK IRELAND LIMITED.

[139] Par.10 of the Decision.

[140] Facebook (2021).

the company estimated that this move cost it 10 billion dollars, only in 2022.[141] Second, Google has announced plans to stop using tracking cookies on its Chrome browser (which is estimated to dominate the market, with nearly 65% of the market share)[142] by 2022. The browser will instead use users' recent browsing history to generate a "cohort identity".

The ePrivacy Regulation proposal also includes some remarkable new means of protection. For instance, users shall be reminded of the possibility to withdraw their consent at periodic intervals,[143] and it is explained that consent directly expressed by an end-user shall prevail over software settings.[144]

2.3.4   Facebook's Lawful Bases Under the GDPR: The Legitimate Interest

The data privacy policy provides a third lawful basis for the processing: legitimate interest. This lawful basis differs profoundly from the others allowed by the GDPR. Whereas the other bases offer an absolute ground of lawfulness for the processing, this one is conditional. The purpose of legitimate interests in the processing pursued by the controller or by a third party should not be "overridden by the interests or fundamental rights and freedoms of the data subject".[145] In other words, this lawful basis is conditional upon a test of proportionality that adds a certain degree of uncertainty.

According to the GDPR itself, this basis could be totally relevant for Facebook. Indeed, the Recitals provide that "the processing of personal data for direct marketing purposes may be regarded as carried out for a legitimate interest".[146] However, as may be expected, the real degree of attraction of this lawful basis for Facebook is negligible. Even so, the company still makes extensive use of this basis, complementing the lawful basis of contract. First, it works as an umbrella in cases when the data subject is a minor, where the contract and/or the consent cannot serve as lawful use (see below, Sect. 2.4.3). Second, it adds two more grounds for data processing: the need to efficiently measure the effectiveness of its profiling tools and advertising campaigns, and, last but not least, the direct marketing's business model.

Specifically, the data privacy policy states that a legitimate interest is understood to be

> [o]ur legitimate interests or the legitimate interests of a third party, where not outweighed by your interests or fundamental rights and freedoms: (..) For all people, including those under

---

[141] Condon (2022).

[142] Source: https://gs.statcounter.com/browser-market-share.

[143] Article 4a (3) of the proposal.

[144] Article 4a (2aa) of the proposal.

[145] Article 6 (1) (f) of the GDPR.

[146] Recital 47 of the GDPR.

the age of majority: For providing measurement, analytics and other business services where we are processing data as a controller. The legitimate interests we rely on for this processing are: To provide accurate and reliable reporting to our advertisers, developers and other partners, to ensure accurate pricing and statistics on performance and to demonstrate the value that our partners realise using Facebook Company Products; and In the interests of advertisers, developers and other partners to help them understand their customers and improve their businesses, validate our pricing models and evaluate the effectiveness of their online content and advertising on and off the Facebook Company Products. For providing marketing communications to you. The legitimate interests we rely on for this processing are: To promote Facebook Company Products and issue our direct marketing. To research and innovate for social good. The legitimate interest we rely on for this processing is: To further the state-of-the-art or academic understanding on important social issues to affect our society and world in a positive way.

This lawful basis is presumably less attractive for Facebook because of the uncertainty surrounding the balancing test between the legitimate interests of the data subject and those of the data controller. The Article 29 Working Party interprets this test strictly, considering that it has to be read as a necessity test.[147] More precisely, the test, confirmed by the ECJ in the Fashion ID case,[148] is composed of three parts: the data controller must justify its legitimate interest, the data processing must be necessary for this legitimate interest, and the fundamental rights of the data subject should not be disproportionately threatened.

The EDPB, in its Guidance on the targeting of users on social media,[149] distinguishes between data provided by the user to the social media provider, data provided by the user of the social media platform to the targeter, targeting on the basis of observed data, and targeting on the basis of inferred data. Each of these instances of processing needs a specific and relevant legal basis. As regards the first category of data, the EDPB considered that "there are two legal bases which could justify the processing that supports the targeting of social media users: data subject's consent (Article 6(1)(a) GDPR) or legitimate interests (Article 6(1)(f) GDPR)".[150] Nevertheless, in the same Guidance the Board reminds us that the Article 29 Working Party had previously explained

> that it would be difficult for controllers to justify using legitimate interests as a legal basis for intrusive profiling and tracking practices for marketing or advertising purposes, for example those that involve tracking individuals across multiple websites, locations, devices, services or data-brokering.[151]

The legal basis of legitimate interest is, in conclusion, fundamental for Facebook. It is in most cases the only available basis to justify its data processing. However, the

---

[147] Article 29 Working Party (2014).

[148] ECJ, C-40/17, Fashion ID GmbH & Co.KG v. Verbraucherzentrale NRW eV, 29/07/2019, ECLI:EU:C:2019:629.

[149] EDPB (2021d).

[150] Par.49 of the Guidelines.

[151] Op.cit. par.56. See also Article 29 Working Party (2017b), p. 15.

exercise of this legal basis requires some precautions and abuses could be severely punished.

2.3.5   Facebook's Lawful Bases Under the GDPR: The Legal Requirement and Compliance with a Legal Obligation

As stipulated by the privacy data notice, Facebook processes personal data

> [t]o share information with others including law enforcement and to respond to legal requests. (..) The legitimate interests we rely on for this processing are: To prevent and address fraud, unauthorised use of the Facebook Company Products, breaches of our terms and policies, or other harmful or illegal activity; to protect ourselves (including our rights, property or Products), our users or others, including as part of investigations or regulatory enquiries; or to prevent death or imminent bodily harm

It further adds the compliance with a legal obligation as a lawful basis "[f]or processing data when the law requires it, including, for example, if there is a valid legal request for certain data".

Even without Facebook's collaboration, it has become apparent that the social network constitutes a very precious source of information for law enforcement agencies. It appears that 81% of law enforcement professionals consult the platform as an investigation tool.[152] Specifically,

> information posted through social media accounts can be utilized by law enforcement to identify criminal behavior, assist in identifying witnesses, verify alibis, provide evidence in ongoing criminal investigations, and be used during a trial to verify or contradict testimony.[153]

2.3.6   Facebook's Lawful Bases Under the GDPR: The Protection of Vital Interests

Facebook's policy also refers to the lawful basis of the protection of vital interests. Normally, this basis applies in circumstances where life is immediately threatened. For instance, the GDPR would not restrain life-saving acts which would include data processing (for instance, a blood test on a person in a coma) or the publication of an Amber Alert in order to find a missing child.

In this context, Facebook's reference to this basis could seem strange at first sight. Nevertheless, the policy explains that

> [p]rotection of your vital interests or those of another person: The vital interests that we rely on for this processing include protection of your life or physical integrity or that of others,

---

[152] Rice and Parkin (2016).

[153] Rice and Parkin (2016) op.cit. p. 3.

and we rely on it to combat harmful conduct and promote safety and security, for example, when we are investigating reports of harmful conduct or when someone needs help.

Moderation on Facebook may start by a notification or self-investigation through AI analysis of the content. In both cases, while a system of internal complaint is ongoing, data processing occurs. While not exactly in violation of the letter of the GDPR, the fact that the lawful basis of protection of vital interests is called upon to justify a specific case of the moderation process arguably leads to a fragmentation of the legal bases—something which is contrary to the spirit of the Regulation.

2.3.7 Facebook's Lawful Bases Under the GDPR: The Public Interest

Finally, Facebook even invokes the public interest to justify some data processing. The data privacy policy specifies that

[f]or undertaking research for social good and to promote safety, integrity and security, as described in our Data Policy under "How we do use this information?", where this is necessary in the public interest as laid down by Union law or Member State law to which we are subject.

Normally, the lawful basis of "public interest" of the data processing can only be invoked by persons when exercising official authority. In any case, the focus here is on the nature of the function, not the nature of the organization, which means that notwithstanding the private nature of the company, it is theoretically possible to use this lawful basis, assuming that Facebook carries out utility services in the public interest and that the data processing is necessary to accomplish them. As provocative as this assertion may seem, it is nevertheless arguable that the platform has acquired a de facto troubled status of a "digital public place" (see Sect. 8.2.2).

2.4 Specific Legal Issues of the GDPR's Enforcement Related to the Online Platform

2.4.1 Facial Recognition

Facial recognition is a feature introduced on the platform in 2010, allowing Facebook to automatically recognize and "name tag" the persons in pictures uploaded by users. The name "Facebook", itself a reference to the common practice in the US of publishing school yearbooks, implies at its core a list of portraits and names. AI first scans the picture, finds faces, and tries to guess the face's identity. This deep learning's AI, called "Deepface", scores a 97.25% success rate in recognizing a person.[154] Technically, the software only uses facial verification (it recognizes that two images show the same face) and not facial recognition, but given that a name is already attached to the first image of the comparison, the practical result is the same. The high level of the AI's efficiency and the huge practical impact on privacy has led to some speculation and even some conspiracy theories. When a new trend known as the "10 Years Challenge" appeared, asking users to post old and new photos, Facebook was accused of using it as a pretext to train its AI[155] and was ultimately obliged to officially deny having any such implication.[156]

From a legal perspective, however, this technique has been less successful. In the US, a class action suit that started in 2015 and concerned privacy issues over the facial recognition feature, was settled in 2021 for USD 650 million.[157] Under the GDPR, the face is sensitive biometric data. In other words, like fingerprints or voices, the face belongs to a special category of personal data that receives a specific protection. The GDPR defines biometric data as

> personal data resulting from specific technical processing relating to the physical, physio-logical or behavioural characteristics of a natural person, which allow or confirm the unique identification of that natural person, such as facial images or dactyloscopic data;[158]

Put otherwise, a picture representing a person or a group of persons will be deemed to be personal data; however, analyzing this picture to extract the face and link this face with a specific name transforms the nature of this data from (simply) personal into biometric. It has been written that "the eyes are the mirror of the soul and reflect everything that seems to be hidden; and like a mirror, they also reflect the person looking into them",[159] but in the digital era, the eyes (as well as all the other facial features), are also a key and can, for instance, unlock a mobile phone or a secure app.

Biometric data fall within the category of "special category of data" or sensitive data, which means, as mentioned above, that no processing should occur on princi-ple, unless one of the exceptions set out in Article 9 applies. It explains why Facebook does not use the contract or the legitimate interest as a lawful basis for facial recognition; rather, it relies on consent. The data privacy policy could not avoid specifically mentioning facial recognition. As explained by the Convention 108 Committee,

> using digital images that were uploaded on the Internet, including social media or online photo management websites or were captured passing through the lens of video surveillance

---

[154] Simonite (2014).

[155] O'Neill (2019).

[156] Read (2019).

[157] Lyons (2021).

[158] Article 4 (14) of the GDPR.

[159] Coelho (2013).

cameras cannot be considered lawful on the sole basis that the personal data were made manifestly available by data subjects.[160]

Facebook had stopped activating its face recognition tool in Europe in 2012 after concerns from regulators and privacy advocates. The Irish Data Protection Commissioner even asked Facebook to delete any data that it had garnered at the time through the facial recognition feature.[161] Ironically, the company brought back the feature in 2018 as an answer to the GDPR, justifying it through its interest in combating false accounts. However, some legal uncertainties continue to subsist. For instance, the requirement of express consent for the collection of the biometric data should also apply to further processing, specific uses of these data by other persons and/or for other purposes. However, although it is still possible for the users to control who has the right to name tag them in a photo, the mechanism of name tagging is often toggled on by default.

In this context, the Irish privacy data commission notes in its annual report for 2018 that

> While explicit consent of the data subject is required as a lawful basis for all users who choose to "opt-in" to the use of such technology, compliance with the GDPR extends beyond mere compliance with Article 9 of the GDPR. The broader compliance standard extends to account default settings, transparency obligations, the rights of users — and non-users or users who have not opted-in — and the scope and nature of the technical elements of the processing of biometric data.[162]

This constant pressure from lawmakers, courts, and data authorities is not without effect. Indeed, in 2021 Meta announced in 2021 that it plans to definitively stop using its facial recognition system, deleting the "facial recognition templates" of more than one billion people.[163]

2.4.2 The Rogue App Problem

2.4.2.1 A Story of Data Breaches

As analyzed above (see Sect. 2.3.4), the huge scandal related to Cambridge Analytica's collection and use of users' personal data for political purposes has heavily marred Facebook's public image. The incident concerned profile details from 87 million users. Much pressure was exerted on the company by official sources in the US and Europe in order to avoid further mass data breaches. At the

---

[160] Consultative committee of the Convention for the protection of individuals with regards to automatic processing of personal data - Convention 108 (2021), p. 6.

[161] Kharpal (2018).

[162] Data Protection Commissioner (2018).

[163] Dang and Culliford (2021).

time, Facebook faced a GBP 500,000 fine in the UK.[164] Facebook is nowadays bound by the GDPR to ensure the "confidentiality, integrity, availability and resilience of processing systems".[165]

However, in 2018, another hacking took place that exposed 29 million accounts.[166] Approximately three million Europeans were affected, according to the Irish Data Protection Commissioner.[167] The access token vulnerability used by the hacker permitted the unauthorized entry into 300,000 accounts. This led to litigation in the US for Facebook's negligence. The judge accepted the admissibility of the negligence action because of the substantial risk of identity theft but, as regards the nationwide and worldwide class actions, it considered that neither credit monitoring costs (the time the users spent in order to verify that their account had not been misused after the breach), nor the reduced value of stolen personal information could justify sufficient damages.[168] The judge partially accepted a class action as regards the injunction to improve security of the platform. Therefore, an injunctive relief-only settlement has been negotiated (the parties are still arguing over the amount of the remuneration of the plaintiff's lawyer, calculated by the plaintiff to be USD 10,7 million).[169]

In Europe, on the contrary, the GDPR clearly states that the right to compensation in case of a violation of the GDPR also encompasses "non-material damage".[170] Moreover, the GDPR also leaves open the possibility of a specific kind of class action, as Member States may provide that a not-for-profit body, organization or association has a right to lodge a complaint to claim compensation on a data subject's behalf even without a mandate from the affected data subjects.[171] Nevertheless, the Irish data authority considered that in this case Meta infringed articles 5(2) and 24(1) of the GDPR and imposed a fine of €17m. Specifically, it found "that Meta Platforms failed to have in place appropriate technical and organizational measures which would enable it to readily demonstrate the security measures that it implemented in practice to protect EU users' data".[172]

Once again, in 2021, a new giant leak of personal data was announced, concerning 500 million Facebook users.[173] The leak included users' phone numbers, Facebook IDs, full names, locations, birthdates, bios, and, in some cases, e-mail

---

[164] Osborne (2018).

[165] Article 32 (1) (b) of the GDPR.

[166] Munsif et al. (2018).

[167] Rodriguez (2018).

[168] District Court, N.D. California (2019) Adkins v. Facebook, Inc., 3:18-cv-05982.

[169] Merken (2021).

[170] Article 82 of the GDPR.

[171] Article 80 of the GDPR.

[172] Data Protection Commission (2022) Data Protection Commission announces decision in Meta (Facebook) inquiry. Press Release. https://www.dataprotection.ie/en/news-media/press-releases/data-protection-commission-announces-decision-meta-facebook-inquiry.

[173] Satter (2021).

addresses. Details of the database were sold on the dark web. Facebook issued a statement explaining that the data derived from a breach that had been fixed in 2019 (but evidently existed before then).[174] However, this means that the vulnerability had existed until 2019, that is, after the Regulation entered into force. Under the GDPR, Facebook has no more than 72 h after becoming aware of a personal data breach to notify the supervisory authority.[175] Therefore the date of the breach is immaterial.

It seems, however, that Facebook did send formal notifications at the time,[176] while Facebook's interpretation of the notification mechanism as regards the information to be provided to the supervisory authority is contestable.[177] Indeed, the company considers there was no breach in the first place, as the data were acquired not through hacking but through "scraping" (automatic collection of data in public access). However, if the data were publicly accessible, this was because of a vulnerability of the system in the first place. It was possible, through the import contact function and through trial and error, to determine the registered phone number of any user of the platform. In the light of the GDPR's overall philosophy and specifically of the privacy by default principle, both the method used and the result achieved should amount to a "breach", which triggers the company's duties. The Irish Data Commission declared that it had started investigations into this matter.[178]

2.4.2.2   Facebook's Rogue Apps

At the core of the Cambridge Analytica scandal is the thorny issue of the function and control of Facebook's apps. A Facebook app could be defined as

> [a]n interactive software application developed to utilize the core technologies of the Facebook platform to create an extensive social media framework for the app. Facebook Apps integrate Facebook's News Feed, Notifications, various social channels and other features to generate awareness and interest in the app by Facebook users.[179]

Some apps, such as Band Profile, which allows musicians to share the own music, are for entertainment. Other apps are just games, exploiting the various possibilities of interactions with the user's friends (multiplayer games, challenges, tournaments, etc.).

In this ocean of apps, some of them could be characterized as "rogue". These apps have been designed with a malicious intent, which could be to access profile information, to carry out fraudulent activity such as phishing, or even to facilitate

---

[174] Clark (2021).

[175] Article 33 (1) of the GDPR.

[176] Brandom (2018).

[177] Koch (2019).

[178] Manancourt (2021).

[179] See definition on Webodopia : https://www.webopedia.com/definitions/facebook-app/.

cybercriminal behavior (hacking, viruses injected through links sent to friends as a message, etc.). Facebook's responsibilities in this respect are under scrutiny as the platform is accused of not making enough effort to combat rogue apps. The Irish Data Protection Commission specifically declared that "we are focusing on Facebook's ability to govern and oversee in a comprehensive and effective manner the activities of app developers, especially their capacity to swiftly identify and respond to "bad actors" and misuse of personal data".[180]

Indeed, the safe harbor that protects hosting activities from liability (see Sect. 6.2.1) does not apply here, at least for privacy issues, as the platform shares data with the apps. Furthermore, controlling the app marketplace is not impossible. Technical solutions are feasible. In 2012, a team of researchers created a tool that gave the user transparency as regards the transfer of his or her private data to the app.[181] In 2015, another team showed that by analyzing the behavior pattern of malicious apps, AI could detect almost all malicious apps on Facebook.[182] In this context, it has to be remembered that the implementation of state of the art technical measures of protection is a GDPR imperative under the "privacy by design principle".[183]

2.4.3 Minors on Facebook

2.4.3.1 The Need for a Specific Protection of Children's Personal Data

The sooner and the younger a user enters the social network, the deeper the psychological dependency and the network effect produced (see Sect. 1.4). More data are produced, and the privacy risks increase. But the presence of minors on a social network also presents other dangers that are specific to them. Children may not be fully aware of the far-reaching consequences of the data processing.[184] Exploiting a minor's inexperience and ingenuousness, malevolent persons or sexual predators can force someone to send or steal "sexts" (messages with erotic content) to feed the child pornography market.

At the same time, the vital importance of protecting children should not lead to blind accusations against the social network. Some phenomena and risks that have been associated with social networks, such as the "blue whale" game (where the child is supposedly given some challenges that ultimately lead him/her to commit suicide), are often blown out of proportion.[185] It has been proved that the blue whale

---

[180] Data Protection Commissioner (2018), p. 21. https://www.dataprotection.ie/sites/default/files/uploads/2018-11/DPC%20annual%20Report%202018_0.pdf.

[181] Egele et al. (2012), pp. 1507–1515.

[182] Rahman et al. (2015), pp. 773–787.

[183] Rubinstein and Good (2013), p. 1333.

[184] See Recital 38 of the GDPR.

[185] Algavi et al. (2017), pp. 660–668.

challenge was largely fictional: although some Russian teenagers did commit suicide because they frequented the same forum that discussed this topic, it was not related to a conscious and malicious attempt to take their life, disguised as a game.[186]

Consequently, the news surrounding this topic should not give the false impression that the social network does not present increased risks for the children. Not just sexual predators, but all potential sources of harm on a social network, such as harassment, radicalization, online grooming, self-harm, have multiplied effects when the victim is a child.

It should firstly be noted that, despite a lack of intervention by the EU in this area, all Member States agree that the age of majority is 18 years, following the recommendations of the United Nations Convention of the Rights of the Child,[187] that defines children as all "human beings below the age of eighteen years". However, this apparent uniformity hides great divergences in Europe as regards minors' legal capacity to enter into contractual agreements. Although it is generally acknowledged that the minor has a reduced legal capacity, the content and scope of the exceptions differ from Member State to Member State.

Therefore, instead of addressing the issue of minors' protection as such, the GDPR prefers to use the more generic term "child". It specifies that

> children merit specific protection with regard to their personal data, as they may be less aware of the risks, consequences and safeguards concerned and their rights in relation to the processing of personal data. Such specific protection should, in particular, apply to the use of personal data of children for the purposes of marketing or creating personality or user profiles and the collection of personal data with regard to children when using services offered directly to a child. The consent of the holder of parental responsibility should not be necessary in the context of preventive or counselling services offered directly to a child.[188]

Children affect numerous mechanisms of the GDPR. The information provided must be adapted,[189] the right to be forgotten facilitated,[190] and the use of automated decisions prohibited.[191] One of the most fundamental aims is that the now-adult should not be burdened by the digital traces of his childhood. In the context of a risk assessment, if some personal data concern children, this is an aggravating factor when calculating the potential risks to the rights and freedoms of the involved natural persons.[192] Finally, the supervisory authority has a specific duty to inform children of their personal data protection.[193] In the UK, ICO has produced an Age Appropriate Design Code for online services processing children's data, that mainly

---

[186] Adeane A. (2019) Blue Whale: What is the truth behind an online 'suicide challenge'? BBC news. https://www.bbc.com/news/blogs-trending-46505722.

[187] Convention on the Rights of the Child (1989).

[188] Recital 38 of the GDPR.

[189] See recital 58 and article 12 of the GDPR.

[190] See recital 65 of the GDPR.

[191] See recital 71 of the GDPR.

[192] See recital 75 and article 6 (1) (f) of the GDPR.

[193] Article 57 (1) (b) of the GDPR.

focuses on the need to further strengthen the principle of privacy by design when addressing children.[194]

Additionally, the Irish Data Protection Commission has published a list of "fundamentals"[195] that sets out 14 basic principles that any online service should follow to enhance protections for children in the processing of their personal data. These principles apply to Facebook. Specifically, it is worth mentioning the third principle ("zero interference"),[196] the fourth ("know your audience"),[197] and the twelfth ("prohibition on profiling"), which specifies that

> [o]nline service providers should not profile children and/ or carry out automated decision making in relation to children, or otherwise use their personal data, for marketing/advertising purposes due to their particular vulnerability and susceptibility to behavioural advertising, unless they can clearly demonstrate how and why it is in the best interests of the child to do so.

2.4.3.2   Article 8 of the GDPR

Article 8 of the GDPR deals with the specific legal framework that applies to children's activity on Facebook. The article states that

> 1. Where point (a) of Article 6(1) applies, in relation to the offer of information society services directly to a child, the processing of the personal data of a child shall be lawful where the child is at least 16 years old. Where the child is below the age of 16 years, such processing shall be lawful only if and to the extent that consent is given or authorised by the holder of parental responsibility over the child. Member States may provide by law for a lower age for those purposes provided that such lower age is not below 13 years. 2. The controller shall make reasonable efforts to verify in such cases that consent is given or authorised by the holder of parental responsibility over the child, taking into consideration available technology. 3. Paragraph 1 shall not affect the general contract law of Member States such as the rules on the validity, formation or effect of a contract in relation to a child.

As has already been pointed out, the Regulation was the result of heavy negotiations and compromises, because of its horizontal approach, sensitive matter, and its extreme practical importance for e-commerce. Article 8 of the GDPR is the perfect illustration of this, as the EU legislator was not able to set a standard age of protection. The GDPR only proposes the age of 16 years as a guideline, offering Member States the possibility of lowering the threshold to 13 years. Nevertheless, the article aims to protect children when active in the "information society services".

---

[194] Information Commissioner's Office (2020).

[195] Data Protection Commission (2020).

[196] "Online service providers processing children's data should ensure that the pursuit of legitimate interests do not interfere with, conflict with or negatively impact, at any level, the best interests of the child".

[197] "Online service providers should take steps to identify their users and ensure that services directed at/intended for or likely to be accessed by children have child-specific data protection measures in place".

The GDPR does not provide an autonomous definition of these services,[198] but instead refers to the definition of the Directive (EU) 2015/1535.[199] In this directive, they are defined as "any Information Society service, that is to say, any service normally provided for remuneration, at a distance, by electronic means and at the individual request of a recipient of services".[200]

Does Facebook fall within the scope of the definition of an "information society service"? The question could seem odd initially, as the EU legislator certainly intended to include social networks in Article 8. However, at the same time, the definition mentions "service normally provided for remuneration", while the platform's access is free. This reference to remuneration was mandatory, as the notion of information society service belongs to the larger notion of a service, as defined in Article 50 of the EC Treaty.[201] However, the ECJ has provided a wide interpretation of this criterion, estimating that any consideration for an economic activity can constitute "remuneration". Specifically, it has been ruled that the notion of a service, as stated in the European Treaty, encompasses indirectly paid activities through advertisements.[202] In the light of this jurisprudence, no doubts remain that Facebook constitutes an information society service.

Furthermore, Article 8 only applies when the lawful basis of the processing is consent. As analyzed above (see Sect. 2.3.3), however, Facebook utilizes consent only as a basis complementary to that of lawful processing. Nevertheless, for Member States that leave the issue of minors' contractual capacity up to the discretion of the court, the age limit set as regards consent should, by extension, be a determinative criterion for judging the minor's capacity. The GDPR protects the freedom of the minor, stating that the minor himself can express his consent after the age of 16. Below the age limit, consent from the holder of parental responsibility is acquired.

Specific technical guarantees must be provided in order to verify this consent. In other words, a simple pop-up window asking for an individual to confirm that he or she is the holder of parental responsibility of the user before the child signs up does not correspond to "reasonable efforts". The efficiency of Facebook's various protection mechanisms has been the topic of much discussion, and the Italian data protection authority, for example, launched in 2021 a series of inquiries against Facebook, requesting detailed information on the mechanisms in place and the age

[198] Article 4 (25) of the GDPR.

[199] Directive (EU) 2015/1535 of the European Parliament and of the Council of 9 September 2015 laying down a procedure for the provision of information in the field of technical regulations and of rules on Information Society services, OJ L 241, 17.9.2015, p. 1–15, ELI: http://data.europa.eu/eli/dir/2015/1535/oj.

[200] Article 1 (b) of the Directive 2015/1535.

[201] Treaty establishing the European Community OJ C 325, 24.12.2002, p. 33–184, ELI: http://data.europa.eu/eli/treaty/tec_2002/oj.

[202] ECJ, C-352/85, Bond van Adverteerders v. the Netherlands 26/04/1988, ECLI:EU:C:1988:196.

verification methods applied to check compliance with the age threshold for registration.[203]

2.4.3.3 Facebook's Practice and Concern for Minors

Facebook's concern for children's personal data is obvious and clearly expressed. For instance, a specific version of Facebook Messenger, entitled "Messenger Kids", was launched in 2017. Facebook also recently unveiled plans to launch an Instagram app for under 13-year-olds. The cold logic behind this strategy is undeniable: the sooner the users sign up to the network, the stronger their emotional connection will be to it. However, it certainly underestimates the wide concern from parents and educators concerning the risk of preteen addictions to social networking. Furthermore, the privacy by default principle becomes even more necessary and simultaneously more complicated to apply, in the case of children's data. For instance, a technical error on the Messenger Kids app allowed communications between users without parental approval.[204]

The most immediate answer from Facebook to the legal obligations posed by Article 8 is to prohibit children from opening an account before the age of 13. Nevertheless, in violation of the platform's terms of service, a lot of children are still opening accounts, lying about their age. Research tends to demonstrate that, by creating a framework in which companies choose to restrict access to children, the law inadvertently undermines parents' ability to make choices and protect their children's data.[205] Furthermore, the obligation of parental consent does not seem to constitute a real obstacle. In the US, 55% of parents declared in 2011 that they knew that their underage children had signed up for the service.[206]

A fundamental difference between the general legal framework and the protection of minors' privacy data in the GDPR is that the lawful basis for the data processing differs. The data privacy policy states that:

> For people under the age of majority (under 18, in most EU countries) who have a limited ability to enter into an enforceable contract only, we may be unable to process personal data on the grounds of contractual necessity. Nevertheless, when such a person uses our Services, it is in our legitimate interests to:
> Provide, personalise and improve the Facebook Products. For people under their Member State's age of consent, we modify our Facebook Products to ensure special protections, and with some restricted features regarding the data used to select advertising. This includes processing information that people under the age of consent allow us to receive through device-based settings that they enable, to provide the features and services covered by those settings.

---

[203] EPDB (2021a).

[204] Lomas (2019).

[205] Boyd et al. (2011).

[206] Kang (2011).

Promote safety, integrity and security, including through tools focused specifically on threats to people under the age of majority; and

Provide non-marketing communications for product or customer service-related issues. The legitimate interests we rely on for this processing are:

To create, provide, support and maintain innovative products and features that enable people under the age of majority to express themselves, communicate, discover and engage with information and communities relevant to their interests, build community and utilise tools and features that promote their well-being.

To secure our platform and network, to verify accounts and activity, combat harmful conduct, detect and prevent spam and other bad experiences, keep the Facebook Company Products free of harmful or inappropriate content and investigate suspicious activity or breaches of our terms or policies; and to protect the safety of people under the age of majority, including to prevent exploitation or other harms to which such individuals may be particularly vulnerable.

In conclusion, although Facebook does collect children's personal data, in accordance with the principles set out by the Irish Data Protection Commission (see above), the policy does not refer to marketing communications.

2.4.4 Facebook's Dark Patterns

As analyzed above (see Sect. 2.3.3), the legal framework surrounding consent is arguably in opposition to the social network's practice in numerous respects. Not only is the consent, in some circumstances, not informed or specific, but it is also up for discussion whether the consent is really free. Indeed, recent years have seen the development on the Internet of a series of design techniques known as "dark patterns" (see Sect. 2.4.4 above).[207]

"Dark patterns" comprise all techniques used in order to influence the website's visitor by modifying visual, graphic or textual elements. For instance, the "I accept" button could be bigger, more colorful, and better placed than the "I refuse" button. In other words, through malicious design, it is possible to substantially affect the result of an apparent choice, and this technique is specifically used in the context of choices concerning privacy.[208] It has therefore been suggested that consent mechanisms based on dark patterns used by the GAFAM violate the principles of fairness, accountability and transparency and invalidate the lawfulness of the consent acquired.[209]

Dark patterns on Facebook do not concern only consent. As explained above, to arrive at a point where true deletion—and not only simple deactivation—of the account is offered, the user has to equip himself with patience and perspicacity, following pages and pages of information that, without being overtly misleading, hinder the final decision-making process.

---

[207] Gray et al. (2018), pp. 1–14.

[208] Bösch et al. (2016), pp. 237–254.

[209] Human and Cech (2021).

A lot of privacy settings have been added to the platform, sometimes voluntarily, sometimes after litigation or legislative reform. For instance, it is possible for the user to block who has access to older posts, to limit who can send him/her friend requests, to control if Google Search will display him/her, to block location, etc. Facebook has gradually introduced a lot of privacy tools allowing users to customize their experience. However, one may doubt the company's sincerity and the compatibility of the mechanisms with the GDPR's privacy by design principle. To clarify, the question is: since the settings are there, why are they not deactivated by default?

Dark patterns constitute a new legal challenge, which has not yet been sufficiently explored. Although it could be regarded as an unfair commercial practice (see Sect. 9.1.1), its effect is insidious and the burden of proving its existence could be crippling. Additionally, it should be noted that the EU institutions, through the Digital Services Act package, have multiplied the initiatives to impose a duty of fairness on social networks (see Sect. 9.2).

2.5 Responsibilities and Liability

2.5.1 Controller Versus Processor and the Principle of Accountability

2.5.1.1 General Principles

All of Chap. 4 of the GDPR is dedicated to the roles and interactions of the controller and the processor. In a nutshell, the philosophy is to consider the controller as being primarily accountable for compliance with the GDPR, as he or she "determines the purposes and means of the processing of personal data".[210] On the other hand, the processor is merely the person that "processes personal data on behalf of the controller".[211] The ECJ considers that a natural or legal person who exerts influence over the processing of personal data, for his own purposes, and who participates, as a result, in the determination of the purposes and means of that processing, may be regarded as a controller.[212]

The controller is responsible for the implementation of appropriate technical and organizational measures to ensure and to be able to demonstrate that processing is performed in accordance with this Regulation. He or she is also responsible for the data privacy policy.[213] The technical and organizational measures referred to here must be taken in accordance with the famous GDPR principle known as "privacy by design" and specified in Article 25 of the GDPR. This notion should not be

---

[210] Article 2 (7) of the GDPR.

[211] Article 2 (8) of the GDPR.

[212] ECJ, C-25/17, Jehovan todistajat, 10/07/2018, ECLI:EU:C:2018:551, par.68.

[213] Article 24 of the GDPR.

considered independent from the six basic principles that are the foundation of any processing. It aims to offer further explanations on the degree of the controller's liability in complying with these principles. Where a general duty of care with respect to, for instance, the principle of data minimization would open too large a range of interpretations, the notion of privacy by design intervenes to impose both legal and technical measures in this respect. In other words, the system must be designed in a way that offers by default the maximum possible privacy, taking into consideration the relevant state of the art technology. The notion embraces a paradox, as it is asked of the machine (and of the engineers) to "go beyond functional requirements and be responsive to human values in our increasingly technological society".[214] At the same time, the regulation wants to be technologically neutral, and in this sense, it does not give any examples of the required technologies.

2.5.1.2   Facebook and Page Administrators As Co-controllers

There is absolutely no doubt that Facebook is a controller as regards the processing of the user's personal data on the platform. The publication of news, posts, comments and profile information—basically all the interaction between the user and the platform—are analyzed for profiling purposes and are used primarily as resources for the company's business model. However, the situation is more complex when a parallel second level of processing occurs. When Facebook is used by some users to collect data on other users, or when the company obtains data from without the digital platform, a complex interaction occurs that cannot be fully rendered by the simple distinction between controller and processor.

As explained above (see Sect. 2.2.2), the Fashion ID case reveals that the installation of a "like" button on a third-party website makes Facebook a co-controller of the process. Even if Facebook does not initiate the data collection or decide on what information is being collected, the fact that the data are sent to the online platform to be processed for profiling purposes is enough to make them a co-controller. Nonetheless, the Fashion ID case built on the finding of another landmark decision that has direct consequences on Facebook's legal framework: the Wirtschaftsakademie case.[215]

In this case, the ECJ had to rule on the case of data processing occurring in the context of a Facebook Page. The Page tool is complex and efficient enough to be used as a front page not only for fans, groups, but more generally for a large panel of e-commerce services. An entity entitled "Wirtschaftsakademie" (hereinafter, the "academy") offers educational services through a fan page hosted on Facebook. The German supervisory authority ordered the academy to deactivate its page, on the ground that neither the academy nor Facebook informed visitors to the fan page that Facebook, through cookies, collected their personal data and then processed them. In

---

[214] Bednar et al. (2019), pp. 122–142.

[215] ECJ, C-210/16, Wirtschaftsakademie Schleswig-Holstein, 05/06/2018, ECLI:EU:C:2018:388.

the ensuing litigation, the Federal Court decided to refer some questions to the ECJ. Essentially, the German judges asked whether the EU data privacy legislation must be interpreted as allowing an entity to be held liable in its capacity as the administrator of a fan page on a social network where the rules on the protection of personal data are infringed, because it has chosen to make use of that social network to distribute the information it offers.

First, the ECJ stated that

> Facebook Inc. and, for the European Union, Facebook Ireland must be regarded as primarily determining the purposes and means of processing the personal data of users of Facebook and persons visiting the fan pages hosted on Facebook, and therefore fall within the concept of 'controller'.[216]

Facebook is the sole controller in the case of a user account. Then, the court explains why a personal page differs from the case of a fan page. Three reasons are advanced[217] to differentiate the fan page from individual users: first, the administrator of a fan page gives Facebook the opportunity to place cookies on the computer or other device of a person visiting its fan page; second, the creation of a fan page on Facebook involves the definition of parameters by the administrator, depending inter alia on the target audience and the objectives of managing and promoting its activities, which has an influence on the processing of personal data; third, contrary to a user's Facebook "timeline", a fan page is accessible even to non-Facebook users and in this case the page itself initiates a personal data process through cookies that would not otherwise occur.

It could certainly be countered that the administrator of the page only receives an anonymized version of the visitors' data, solely for statistical purposes only. However, the court considers that the data privacy law "does not, where several operators are jointly responsible for the same processing, require each of them to have access to the personal data concerned".[218] In other words, the designation of co-controller is not necessarily related to having access to the personal data concerned, a principle that the ECJ has reaffirmed in another decision (the Jehovah's Witnesses decision).[219]

Indeed, the fan page administrator, even if he does not process the data, substantially contributes to their collection, by creating and promoting the page, setting the parameters, and managing the activities. Consequently, the ECJ applies the designation of joint controller to the page administrator. At the same time, the court clarifies that the existence of joint controllership does not entail equal responsibility of the operators involved in the processing of personal data, introducing the principle that the responsibility of a controller should be dependent on the stages of the processing in which it is involved and on the degree of this involvement.[220] This

---

[216] Par.30 of the decision.

[217] Par.35, 36, and 41 of the decision.

[218] Par.38 of the decision.

[219] ECJ, C-25/17—Jehovan todistajat, 10/07/2018, ECLI:EU:C:2018:551.

[220] Cimina (2021), pp. 639–654.

position reflects an equilibrium in the assessment of the joint controllers' regime: the ECJ's extensive interpretation of the concept of joint controller has been accompanied by a dilution of the corresponding responsibility of the joint controller that has no substantive role in the data process. However, this approach is not without criticism, as the "lack of specificity and predictability might prove to be a source of major uncertainties in practice".[221]

Although the Fashion ID and Wirtschaftsakademie cases had been decided under the previous data privacy legislation, the principles are still relevant under the GDPR. Nonetheless, the GDPR innovates in consecrating this jurisprudential approach. Indeed, in Article 26 of the GDPR, the notion of joint controller is specifically regulated. Article 26 (1) of the GDPR states that

> [w]here two or more controllers jointly determine the purposes and means of processing, they shall be joint controllers. They shall in a transparent manner determine their respective responsibilities for compliance with the obligations under this Regulation, in particular as regards the exercising of the rights of the data subject and their respective duties to provide the information referred to in Articles 13 and 14, by means of an arrangement between them unless, and in so far as, the respective responsibilities of the controllers are determined by Union or Member State law to which the controllers are subject. The arrangement may designate a contact point for data subjects.

Therefore, the GDPR proposes a "soft law" resolution of the potential uncertainties related to the concept of joint controller. It is a matter of arrangement between the joint controllers to determine their respective responsibilities. As the EDPB remarked, an important criterion for the concept of joint controller is that the processing would not be possible without both parties' participation in the sense that the processing by each party is inseparable, i.e. inextricably linked.[222] It can be concluded that in most data processing situations where Facebook is involved, the company should be regarded as a joint controller.

2.5.1.3   The (Too Secret) Identity of Facebook's DPO

As mentioned in Sect. 2.1.2, the DPO is a novelty of the GDPR, introduced in order to create more flexibility in the previous legal framework. According to the principle of accountability, Facebook must be able to demonstrate that it fully complies with the multiple duties under the GDPR. This is the role of the DPO, who is responsible for supervising and monitoring the platform's compliance with the GDPR. The DPO also serves as a contact point, both for the public and the supervisory authority. Therefore, it could be said that the DPO has a hybrid role: internally, through his involvement in decision-making processes related to personal data[223] and

---

[221] Globocnik (2019), pp. 1033–1044.

[222] EDPB (2021c).

[223] Article 38 (1) of the GDPR states that "The controller and the processor shall ensure that the data protection officer is involved, properly and in a timely manner, in all issues which relate to the protection of personal data."

specifically in the drawing up of the company's data protection impact assessment,[224] he ensures the efficiency of the privacy by design principle and the adherence to the data breach notification obligation; externally, he is accessible to the public, in case of a complaint as regards the exercise of the data subject's rights,[225] and to the supervisory authority, offering full cooperation.[226]

The DPO is mandatory under the legislation in only three cases:

> the processing is carried out by a public authority or body, except for courts acting in their judicial capacity; the core activities of the controller or the processor consist of processing operations which, by virtue of their nature, their scope and/or their purposes, require regular and systematic monitoring of data subjects on a large scale; or the core activities of the controller or the processor consist of processing on a large scale of special categories of data pursuant to Article 9 or personal data relating to criminal convictions and offences referred to in Article 10.[227]

In the context of Facebook, it is clear that a DPO is mandatory as the activities fall within the scope of regular and systematic monitoring of data subjects on a large scale.

A set of is skills required for a DPO, which is not absolute but is to be commensurate with the sensitivity, complexity and amount of data organization processes.[228] Therefore, for Facebook, the nomination of a DPO was under high scrutiny. The company's Global Deputy Chief Privacy Officer Stephen Deadman took up the position in 2018.[229] However, it should be noted that no mention of the DPO's name or address is made on the platform. Facebook provides a simple communication interface entitled "Contact the Data Protection Officer (DPO)" which offers a closed list of available questions that the user is allowed to ask, while, actually, the only question that leads to the second phase of the communication form is "How can I get support for a privacy issue from the Data Protection Officer?".[230]

This communication mechanism poses two major legal issues. First, the lack of transparency concerning the identity and background of the DPO raises some concerns. The GDPR states that "[t]he controller or the processor shall publish the contact details of the data protection officer and communicate them to the supervisory authority."[231] The Article 29 Working Party had adopted Guidelines on the DPO in 2017,[232] which stated that this article did not impose a the publication of the name; nevertheless, Facebook's communication does not reflect the GDPR's

---

[224] Article 35 (2) of the GDPR.

[225] Article 38 (4) of the GDPR.

[226] Article 39 (1) (d) of the GDPR.

[227] Article 37 of the GDPR.

[228] Emili (2019).

[229] Pfeifle (2018).

[230] See: https://www.facebook.com/help/contact/540977946302970.

[231] Article 37 (7) of the GDPR.

[232] Article 29 data protection working party (2017a).

philosophy of proposing an efficient and informed interface of communication. Second, the communication interface that comprises an online form on the Facebook platform has a certain degree of needless complexity (the mandatory closed list and the mandatory format of communication is surprising and could be considered a "dark pattern" practice (see Sect. 2.4.4)).

An overall impression of underestimation of the DPO's role begins to emerge from the Facebook architecture. Characteristically, Facebook Germany, which is a Facebook branch that does not directly interfere with the platform, was fined EUR 51,000 by the German supervisory authority in 2019 for not having appointed a data protection officer.[233]

2.5.1.4   Violations of the GDPR by Users

Facebook is far from being the only source of GDPR violations on the platform. To Meta's great inconvenience, the platform has evolved from just a list of faces and names and has de facto become a public forum of expression. While some users still share their personal experiences, stories, and selfies with their friends and/or the rest of the world, others use it sometimes exclusively as a means of communication on a variety of topics, which, obviously, encompasses personal data processing.

It should be reminded in this context that normally online service providers are protected against litigation as regards the content they host, thanks to the safe harbor mechanism (see Chap. 6). However, data privacy legislation is expressly exempted from this mechanism. As stated by the e-Commerce Directive,

> [t]he protection of individuals with regard to the processing of personal data is solely governed by (. . .) [privacy data legislation] which are fully applicable to information society services; these Directives already establish a Community legal framework in the field of personal data and therefore it is not necessary to cover this issue in this Directive in order to ensure the smooth functioning of the internal market, in particular the free movement of personal data between Member States; the implementation and application of this Directive should be made in full compliance with the principles relating to the protection of personal data, in particular as regards unsolicited commercial communication and the liability of intermediaries; this Directive cannot prevent the anonymous use of open networks such as the Internet.[234]

Consequently, the issue of Facebook's liability in case of illegal data processing (for instance, posts in violation of the principle of transparency or of data minimization) cannot be resolved by using the safe harbor, but by reference to the inherent principles of the GDPR, and specifically, the notions of controller and/or joint controller.

Is, first of all, the average user a controller in the sense of the GDPR? Some elements of the answer are provided by the ECJ's Buivids decision.[235] Mr. Buivids

---

[233] EDPB (2019b).

[234] Recital 14 of the e-Commerce Directive.

[235] ECJ, C-345/17, Sergejs Buivids v. Datu valsts inspekcija, 14/02/2019, ECLI:EU:C:2019:122.

recorded a video at a police station of activity that he considered unlawful and posted it on YouTube to raise awareness of this public office's behavior. There is a process (the uploading of the video onto the social network platform), there are personal data (the faces and behavior of the police officers), and the household exception would not allow the video to be exempted from the GDPR, since the video was freely accessible on the Internet (see Sect. 2.2.1). Therefore, the data privacy legislation is applicable, albeit on a smaller scale, as the video's uploading and sharing

> may constitute a processing of personal data solely for journalistic purposes, within the meaning of that provision, in so far as it is apparent from that video that the sole object of that recording and publication thereof is the disclosure of information, opinions or ideas to the public, this being a matter which it is for the referring court to determine.[236]

Furthermore, the broad interpretation of the concept of joint controllership poses serious issues. Is the average user expected to prepare a privacy notice, to answer individual requests, and to indicate the lawful basis of his posts and stories? According to Buivids, the user of a social media platform is bound by the data privacy legislation. However, in the Wirtschaftsakademie case analyzed above, the ECJ peremptorily holds that "the mere fact of making use of a social network such as Facebook does not make a Facebook user a controller jointly responsible for the processing of personal data by that network".[237] This apparent contradiction is linked to the dynamic notion of data processing, defined by the purpose of the controller: each purpose is deemed to be a different data processing. Therefore, the users are accountable for the data processing related to the communication to the public of the data of other data subjects, and their publication should be protected by the specific regime related to data processing for a journalistic purpose. Indeed, it will on principle be covered by the journalistic purpose if the national legislator has thought about this, while Facebook is accountable for the profiling activity conducted on this user-generated content.

However, the issue remains whether Facebook could be considered a joint controller as regards the communication itself. The Irish Court in the case CG v. Facebook adopted an original point of view. Despite the fact that data protection is excluded from the scope of the e-Commerce Directive, the national judges found that user-generated content on Facebook fell within the scope of "matter covered by the e-Commerce Directive" which provides a "tailored solution" for the liability of intermediaries. It is worth mentioning that some GDPR principles are, in practice, similar to the e-Commerce Directive's notification mechanism. For instance, as regards the right to be forgotten, either as established by the landmark Google Spain[238] case or as enshrined in the GDPR, it could be argued that there is a convergence between European data protection and intermediary liability law.[239]

---

[236] Decision's conclusion.

[237] Par.35 of the Decision.

[238] ECJ, C-131/12, Google Spain SL and Google Inc. v. Agencia Española de Protección de Datos (AEPD) and Mario Costeja González, 13/05/2014, ECLI:EU:C:2014:317.

[239] Keller (2018), p. 287.

2.5.2 The Consequences of Facebook's Responsibility

2.5.2.1 The Potential Sanctions of the GDPR

The enforcement of the GDPR constitutes a challenge in the context of the GAFAM. How to establish a system of sanctions that can be fair and possesses a deterrent effect against companies that have billions in revenue? Administrative fines are considered in the GDPR to be the natural form of sanction.[240] The GDPR itself states about administrative fines that "[s]uch penalties shall be effective, proportionate and dissuasive."[241] As mentioned above (see Sect. 2.1.2) the GDPR establishes a new sanctions system that is directly based on the percentage of worldwide revenue of the responsible data controller.

Nevertheless, as impressive as a fine calculated on 2% of Facebook's revenues may sound, it must be remembered that it is only a potential maximum. First, it has been noted that there is a certain lack of interest and, of course, resources of data subjects and data protection authorities in initiating procedures.[242] Secondly, some scholars and data experts have recently criticized the Irish Data Protection Commission's (which is competent to impose the fine to Facebook—see below) efficiency, considering that "[t]he Irish regulator doesn't really have a track record of robust enforcement".[243]

Concerns have been expressed even by the European Parliament, which issued a report on the enforcement of the GDPR, saying that it

[u]nderlines the importance of the one-stop-shop mechanism in providing legal certainty and reducing the administrative burden for companies and citizens alike; expresses, however, great concern over the functioning of the mechanism, particularly regarding the role of the Irish and Luxembourg DPAs; notes that these DPAs are responsible for handling a large number of cases, since many tech companies have registered their EU headquarters in Ireland or Luxembourg; is particularly concerned that the Irish data protection authority generally closes most cases with a settlement instead of a sanction and that cases referred to Ireland in 2018 have not even reached the stage of a draft decision pursuant to Article 60(3) of the GDPR; calls on these DPAs to speed up their ongoing investigations into major cases in order to show EU citizens that data protection is an enforceable right in the EU; points out that the success of the 'one-stop shop-mechanism' is contingent on the time and effort that DPAs can dedicate to the handling of and cooperation on individual cross-border cases in the EDPB, and that the lack of political will and resources has immediate consequences on the extent to which this mechanism can function properly.[244]

---

[240] See Recital 148.

[241] Article 84 of the GDPR.

[242] Golla (2017), p. 70.

[243] Solon (2018).

[244] Commission evaluation report on the implementation of the General Data Protection Regulation two years after its application (2021).

Characteristically, the EDPB has delivered its first Binding Decision on this very specific topic.[245] The case concerned a violation of the GDPR by Twitter (lack of data breach notification) and the Irish Data Protection Commission imposed a fine of EUR 250,000. Multiple other national authorities objected to this decision, but the Irish Data Protection Commission rejected their arguments. Germany, for instance, considered that the fine was not dissuasive enough. Consequently, the EDPB was called upon to resolve the issue. It has been said that the number of objections itself and their subsequent rejection by the Irish Data Protection Commission indicate a deep lack of consistency in approach by different data protection authorities.[246]

The German Data Authority, specifically, had considered that

> the dissuasive effect of high fines can only be achieved if the amounts imposed cannot be easily paid because of large assets or high income, highlighting that the fine must have a dissuasive effect, particularly in relation to specific data processing. As a consequence, the threatened fine must be high enough to make data processing uneconomic and objectively inefficient.[247]

Although the EDPB accepted this objection, and those of Spanish and French data authorities as especially relevant, it also considered that the severity of penalties must be commensurate with the seriousness of the infringements and the fines cannot be disproportionate to the infringement viewed as a whole.[248] Consequently, the EDPB decided that the fine proposed in the Draft Decision (the initial decision taken by the Irish Data Protection Commission) was too low and returned the case to the authority, which went on to issue a higher fine of EUR 450,000.

2.5.2.2 The Potential Intervention from Multiple Supervisory Authorities

As supervisory authorities have the task of monitoring the application of the GDPR, their role is central to data protection legal framework. Under the previous data privacy legislation, the ECJ considered that multiple supervisory authorities could be involved. In the Wirtschaftsakademie case (see Sect. 2.5.1),[249] the ECJ held that the German supervisory authority was competent in respect of a case of data processing where the controller of the data concerned was established in Ireland, and the subsidiary that was established in Germany (namely Facebook Germany GmbH) was solely responsible for the sale of advertising spots and other marketing activities in Germany.

Nevertheless, the GDPR found a new compromise on this issue between the data subjects' interest, which is to have contact with the supervisory authority of their

---

[245] EDPB (2020a).

[246] Hodges (2021).

[247] Par. 169 of the Decision.

[248] Par. 196 of the Decision.

[249] ECJ, C-210/16, Wirtschaftsakademie Schleswig-Holstein, 05/06/2018, ECLI:EU:C:2018:388.

country, and the data controller's interest, which is to be in contact with the supervisory authority of the country of its establishment. Through the "one-stop shop" regime, the Regulation imposes a delicate system of cooperation between the relevant supervisory authorities. While the supervisory authority of the data controller's country of establishment becomes the "lead supervisory authority",[250] other supervisory authorities may be involved in the decision-making process.[251] Specifically, with respect to cross-border processing, the various national supervisory authorities concerned must cooperate in order to reach a consensus and a single decision, which is binding on all those authorities. Indeed, the lead supervisory authority's decision on the litigation is a draft decision only until the other involved supervisory authorities have intervened with comments and objections. The lead supervisory authority cannot just ignore its colleagues from other Member States, as involved supervisory authorities have the competence to block the draft decision of the lead supervisory authority, through reasonable objections transmitted within a period of 4 weeks after having been consulted.

The downside of the one-stop shop model is the centralization of all interests in a specific supervisory authority, in our case the Irish Data Protection Commission, thus facilitating Facebook's lobbying operations, as by definition, they have only one unique interlocutor to discuss with (see Sect. 2.1.2). Moreover, the social and political pressure on national supervisory authorities to intervene should not be underestimated. Put otherwise, the perceived responsibility incumbent on each of the Member States' national authorities to contribute to a high level of protection of their national may force them to take initiatives, while not being the lead supervisory authority.

In 2021, the ECJ had the opportunity to clarify the rules applying to this question, in a case concerning Facebook before the Belgian supervisory authority.[252] In 2015, the Belgian supervisory authority had initiated a court action, seeking an injunction against Facebook Ireland, Facebook Inc. (as it was then named) and Facebook Belgium, aiming to put an end to alleged infringements of data protection laws by Facebook. Those infringements consisted, inter alia, of the collection and use of information on the browsing behavior of Belgian internet users, whether or not they were Facebook account holders, by means of various technologies, such as cookies, social plugins or pixels. The first instance civil court held that the action was admissible. However, the Court of Appeal hesitated as regards the Belgian supervisory authority's competence: should not the Irish supervisory authority be competent in this case for injunctions under the GDPR?

Therefore, the Court's mission in this case was to specify the conditions under which a national supervisory authority, which does not have the status of lead supervisory authority in relation to an instance of cross-border processing, must

---

[250] Article 56 of the GDPR.

[251] Article 60 of the GDPR.

[252] ECJ, C-645/19, Facebook Ireland and Others v. Gegevensbeschermingsautoriteit, 15/06/2021, ECLI:EU:C:2021:483.

exercise its power to bring any alleged infringement of the GDPR before a court of a Member State and, where necessary, to initiate or engage in legal proceedings in order to ensure the application of that regulation.

The Court, first, confirms that the competence of the Irish Data Protection Commission in case of issues related to Facebook is the rule, while the competence of other supervisory authorities, the exception.[253] Moreover, the Court notes that

> the use of the 'one-stop shop' mechanism cannot under any circumstances have the consequence that a national supervisory authority, in particular the lead supervisory authority, does not assume the responsibility incumbent on it under Regulation 2016/679 to contribute to providing effective protection of natural persons from infringements of their fundamental rights as recalled in the preceding paragraph of the present judgment, as otherwise that consequence might encourage the practice of forum shopping, particularly by data controllers, designed to circumvent those fundamental rights and the practical application of the provisions of that regulation that give effect to those rights.[254]

In other words, in a "normal" procedure, the non-leading supervisory authority exercises its responsibility of monitoring the application of the GDPR through the process of sincere cooperation and consensus with the Irish data protection authority. This cooperation also works as a prerequisite for the exclusive competence of the Irish data protection authority. The ECJ provides some safeguards and explains that

> the exercise of the power of a Member State's supervisory authority to bring actions before the courts of that State cannot be ruled out where, after the mutual assistance of the lead supervisory authority has been sought, under Article 61 of Regulation 2016/679, the latter does not provide the former with the requested information.[255]

In conclusion, the Irish data protection authority does not possess an absolute exclusivity over litigation related to Facebook. First, an indirect influence of the other supervisory authorities is perceptible, as they are entitled to intervene, in a spirit of cooperation. Second, other supervisory authorities may also directly exercise their power against Facebook, counteracting the exclusivity of the lead authority, but only in some specific circumstances. The ECJ states that

> that power is exercised in one of the situations where that regulation confers on that supervisory authority a competence to adopt a decision finding that such processing is in breach of the rules contained in that regulation, and that the cooperation and consistency procedures laid down by that regulation are respected.[256]

The Court explicitly refers to the situation where the lead authority does not comply with its duty of information. In this case the supervisory authority is entitled to take provisionary measures if it considers that they are urgently needed. For definitive measures, however, the supervisory authority has to request an urgent binding decision from the EDPB.

---

[253] Par.63 of the decision.

[254] Par.68 of the decision.

[255] Par.71 of the decision.

[256] Par. 75 of the decision.

In parallel, the GDPR provides an additional means of action for the national data authorities through Article 66 of the GDPR. The article states that in exceptional circumstances, when a supervisory authority considers that there is an urgent need to act in order to protect the rights and freedoms of data subjects within its territory, it can adopt provisional measures that have a legal effect in their own territory for a maximum of 3 months.

Characteristically, Meta's constant efforts to increase its profiling power in the context of the merger with WhatsApp (see Sect. 2.2.5) has provoked growing tensions between the data authorities on this topic. Thus, the German data authority ordered Facebook to stop any further attempt at blending the databases, using Article 66 of the GDPR as a legal basis. Besides, the WhatsApp terms of service updates that provide a basis to this merger arguably violate consumer law protection (see Sect. 9. 1.1). However, the EDPB intervened and considered that there was not enough information available in order to make such an order and returned the case to the Irish data protection authority for further investigation.[257]

Furthermore, it has to be highlighted that the one stop shop mechanism does not extend to issues related to the eprivacy Directive. Indeed, the EDPB[258] expressly excluded the application of the "one-stop shop" mechanism to facts that are materially covered by the ePrivacy Directive. Therefore, national data authorities continue to intervene in topics such as the use of cookies on the platform and the French data authority, for instance, fined Facebook in 2022 for its cookies policy (see Sect. 2.3.3).

2.5.3   The War Over the Cross-Border Transfer

2.5.3.1   The EU's Data Imperialism

It would have been naïve of the EU to enact one of the most complete instruments for the protection of individuals as regards their data without also establishing some measures against unfair data processing by third parties. Without such a mechanism all the protection would fail to achieve its purpose, as the data processing would occur far from the eyes of the data subject, the supervisory authority, and the courts. Therefore, the GDPR continues to reinforce the previous mechanism of control over the transfer of data outside the EU, something which automatically introduces an extra-territorial impact to the GDPR. However, it has been said that this behavior

---

[257] EDPB (2021b).

[258] EDPB (2019) Opinion 5/2019 of 12 March 2019 on the interplay between the ePrivacy Directive and the GDPR, in particular regarding the competence, tasks and powers of data protection authorities.

amounts to a certain kind of EU imperialism, obvious from the binding effects on US companies,[259] or the adverse effect on African countries' e-commerce.[260]

This "data imperialism" has to be borne by the EU because of the particularities of the data marketplace. Let's not forget that not only Meta but all five GAFAM are established in the US. Nevertheless, this image of imperialism and unilateral action has to be more nuanced. Indeed, if in some way, the EU has become the "world's privacy cop", the strict application of the rule regarding the cross-border transfer of data requires a discussion—even a collaboration—between the EU and third countries as regards their data privacy legislation.[261]

Certainly, it has to be remembered first that the GDPR applies not only to processing that occurs in the EU but also to the processing of personal data of data subjects who are in the EU, independently of the nationality or of the place of the controller,

> where the processing activities are related to: a) the offering of goods or services, irrespective of whether a payment of the data subject is required, to such data subjects in the Union; or b) the monitoring of their behaviour as far as their behaviour takes place within the Union.[262]

Recital 23[263] explains that to determine whether an activity involving data processing targets EU citizens, it should be established that the controller's manifest intent is to monitor personal data from the EU. This intent is deduced from convergent objective factors such as the language, the currency, or the existence of an advertising campaign within the EU. Furthermore, it has to be highlighted that having personal data transferred from a Member State to a third country constitutes, in itself, processing of personal data.

---

[259] Klar (2020), p. 101.

[260] Mannion (2020), p. 685.

[261] Schwartz (2019), p. 771.

[262] Article 3 (2) of the GDPR.

[263] Recital 23:

> In order to ensure that natural persons are not deprived of the protection to which they are entitled under this Regulation, the processing of personal data of data subjects who are in the Union by a controller or a processor not established in the Union should be subject to this Regulation where the processing activities are related to offering goods or services to such data subjects irrespective of whether connected to a payment. In order to determine whether such a controller or processor is offering goods or services to data subjects who are in the Union, it should be ascertained whether it is apparent that the controller or processor envisages offering services to data subjects in one or more Member States in the Union. Whereas the mere accessibility of the controller's, processor's or an intermediary's website in the Union, of an email address or of other contact details, or the use of a language generally used in the third country where the controller is established, is insufficient to ascertain such intention, factors such as the use of a language or a currency generally used in one or more Member States with the possibility of ordering goods and services in that other language, or the mentioning of customers or users who are in the Union, may make it apparent that the controller envisages offering goods or services to data subjects in the Union.

2.5.3.2 The GDPR's Legal Framework on Cross-Border Transfers of Data

Assuming, then, that the GDPR applies to processing, any data transfer outside EU is subject to a strict legal framework, detailed in Chap. 5 of the GDPR. The core principle of this legal framework is to ensure that the data will travel to a place where the fundamental notions of the GDPR are respected. In other words, no transfer will be allowed, unless it is ensured "that the level of protection of natural persons guaranteed by this Regulation is not undermined."[264]

If Meta cannot guarantee that data subjects residing in the EU are sufficiently protected, the practical consequences would be enormous: either it would have to completely cease activities in Europe (the company, whether or not it may have been bluffing, has already expressed some threats that it will have to terminate its activity in Europe)[265] or to restructure its network in such a way to separate worldwide and EU servers into two independent platforms.

To allow cross-border transfers of data, the GDPR asks for some guarantees, which can be offered through three alternative means: an adequacy decision by the EU Commission, the establishment of appropriate safeguards, or individual agreements (for instance, express consent to the transfer). At first sight, Facebook would have an easy way out, basing its transfer on the express consent of the user. However, the GDPR intends this third way to be used as an exception only, for specific situations. It is therefore stated that this cannot justify a transfer where the transfer is of a repetitive nature.[266]

The second way to prove the existence of adequate guarantees is to establish appropriate safeguards. This can be done mainly through three options: standard contractual clauses (SCCs) (subject to the approval of the EU Commission), binding corporate rules set by the supervisory authorities, and contractual clauses (but subject to approval by the competent supervisory authority).[267]

To avoid long and costly negotiations and for more legal certainty, Meta—like all other giants of the tech industry—refers to the last means of establishing appropriate safeguards: the direct intervention of the Commission. The EU Commission can issue a decision concerning the level of data protection in the US, thereby protecting Facebook's activities. However, such a decision is not without legal uncertainties. Certainly, the US and the EU are major economic partners. However, not only do the EU and the US differ in their respective approaches to data privacy,[268] but the NSA scandal, following the revelations made by Edward Snowden and described as "the greatest mass surveillance project in human history",[269] has perceptibly affected

---

[264] Article 44 of the GDPR.

[265] Hern (2020).

[266] See Article 49 of the GDPR.

[267] Article 46 of the GDPR.

[268] Gady (2014), pp. 12–23.

[269] Salter (2015), pp. 183–201.

Europeans' confidence in the US authorities as regards the protection of privacy. The scandal had direct effects on an official level as the Commission issued a subsequent report expressing its growing concern over the protection of EU citizens' personal data in the US.[270]

2.5.3.3   Schrems I and II Decisions

The NSA scandal has impacted the confidence in the ability of US authorities to effectively protect the data of EU citizens. This issue is reflected in some major legal conflicts between the Commission and the ECJ in this regard, with Facebook at the epicenter of the discussion: the Schrems I and II decisions. However, before analyzing these decisions, it is important to highlight that the ECJ has, in general, adopted a strict approach as regards cross-border transfers. Indeed, in 2006 the ECJ annulled the 2004 Passenger Name Record (PNR) Agreement between the EU and the US,[271] and objected to the entry into force of the EU-Canada PNR Agreement in 2017.[272]

In the Schrems I decision,[273] Mr. Schrems commenced litigation against the Irish supervisory authority regarding Facebook Ireland's practice of transferring its users' personal data to the US and keeping it on servers located in that country. However, the EU Commission, through Decision 2000/520[274] known also as the "Safe Harbour arrangement",[275] had used its competence to issue "an adequacy decision" and protect the transfers of data to the US from the legal framework of cross-border transfers, shielding from litigation some companies that subscribed to the arrangement. Facebook, like many other Internet service providers located in the US, had subscribed to the Safe Harbour arrangement.

Therefore, the case poses two interrelated issues: one related to the legality of the Safe Harbour regime, in the light of Articles 7, 8 and 47 of the Charter of Fundamental Rights, and the other as regards the relationship between the adequacy decision and the supervisory authority. The ECJ, first, recalls the hierarchy of

---

[270] EU Commission (2013).

[271] ECJ, C-317/04 and C-318/04, European Parliament v. Council of the European Union and European Parliament v. Commission of the European Communities, 30/05/2006, ECLI:EU:C:2006: 346.

[272] ECJ, Opinion 1/15, ECLI:EU:C:2017:592, 26/07/2017.

[273] ECJ, C-362/14, Maximillian Schrems v. Data Protection Commissioner, 06/10/2015, ECLI:EU: C:2015:650.

[274] Commission Decision 2000/520/EC of 26 July 2000 pursuant to Directive 95/46/EC of the European Parliament and of the Council on the adequacy of the protection provided by the safe harbour privacy principles and related frequently asked questions issued by the US Department of Commerce (notified under document number C(2000) 2441), OJ L 215, 25.8.2000, p. 7–47, ELI: http://data.europa.eu/eli/dec/2000/520/oj.

[275] Which is not to be confused with the principle of non liability of intermediaries, known as "safe harbor" (see Sect. 6.2.1).

norms and states that "until such time as the Commission decision is declared invalid by the Court, the Member States and their organs, which include their independent supervisory authorities, admittedly cannot adopt measures contrary to that decision".[276] However, the fact that the adequacy decision is binding on the supervisory authority does not "prevent persons whose personal data has been or could be transferred to a third country from lodging with the national supervisory authorities a claim".[277] To resolve this apparent contradiction, the ECJ concludes that the supervisory authority is bound by the adequacy decision of the Commission, unless the decision itself is deemed to be violating the Charter.[278] Of course, the ECJ alone has jurisdiction on the matter of the validity of the adequacy decision and that means that where a supervisory authority believes that the adequacy decision violates fundamental rights, it has to make a reference to the European Court for a preliminary ruling.

This finding is itself fundamental as it greatly minimizes the practical protection offered by mechanisms such as the Safe Harbour. However, the decision goes on to address the question of the validity of this specific adequacy decision. Analyzing in detail the principles set out in Decision 2000/520, the ECJ found that it entails restrictions on the protection of the data subjects. These restrictions are interpreted as interferences with the data subject's fundamental freedoms, founded on national security and public interest requirements or on US domestic legislation.[279] Consequently, the Safe Harbour adequacy decision was declared invalid.

The ECJ's judgment does not automatically mean that all transfers to the US are illegal, but it certainly creates a great amount of legal uncertainty. In response to the ensuing panic from the technological sector, the EU Commission quickly proceeded in 2016 to enact a replacement for the Safe Harbour: the "privacy shield" agreement. The new system is more complex and differs from the previous mechanism, as it comprises on the one part a European Commission's Decision on SCCs[280] and on the other part a Privacy Shield adequacy decision.[281] As regards the decision on SCCs, the legal basis differs, as does the logic: the decision does not take into consideration the overall legal framework of the concerned territory. However, it was apparent as soon as they were enacted that these two legal instruments only

---

[276] Par.52 of the Decision.

[277] Par.53 of the Decision.

[278] Par.60 of the Decision.

[279] Par.87 of the Decision.

[280] Commission Implementing Decision (EU) 2016/2297 of 16 December 2016 amending Decisions 2001/497/EC and 2010/87/EU on standard contractual clauses for the transfer of personal data to third countries and to processors established in such countries, under Directive 95/46/EC of the European Parliament and of the Council; OJ L 344, 17.12.2016, p. 100–101, ELI: http://data.europa.eu/eli/dec_impl/2016/2297/oj.

[281] Commission Implementing Decision (EU) 2016/1250 of 12 July 2016 pursuant to Directive 95/46/EC of the European Parliament and of the Council on the adequacy of the protection provided by the EU-U.S. Privacy Shield (notified under document C(2016) 4176), C/2016/4176, ELI: http://data.europa.eu/eli/dec_impl/2016/1250/oj.

partially addressed the prerequisites imposed by the ECJ in the Schrems I case.[282] Like its predecessor, the privacy shield is based in practice on a system of certification, and, although it aims to offer better protection, it relies on letters of intention from US public authorities, rather than actual legal commitments.

In this context, a "round 2" was unavoidable. The landmark decision "Schrems II"[283] is the direct continuation of the previous litigation, as, after the Schrems I decision, the Irish High Court had asked Mr. Schrems to reformulate his complaint in the light of the new regulation, the invalidity of the Safe Harbour, and the new privacy shield system.

First, the High Court sought clarification from the ECJ on the level of protection required to accept a third country as having adequate safeguards, under the mechanism of standard data protection clauses. The ECJ answered that

> although not requiring a third country to ensure a level of protection identical to that guaranteed in the EU legal order, the term 'adequate level of protection' must, as confirmed by recital 104 of that regulation, be understood as requiring the third country in fact to ensure, by reason of its domestic law or its international commitments, a level of protection of fundamental rights and freedoms that is essentially equivalent to that guaranteed within the European Union by virtue of the regulation, read in the light of the Charter.[284]

In other words, it is not asked of the processor located in the third country to implement a literal copy of the GDPR, but to ensure that the fundamental principles woven into the data privacy legislation are respected. This analysis requires a holistic approach, that includes not only the quality and obligations of the processor, and its relationship with the controller, but also the overall influence of the legal framework of the third country on the effective protection of the data subject.

Second, the ECJ reiterates the Schrems I finding that a Commission adequacy decision is binding in its entirety on all Member States, which means that if the supervisory authority has some doubts concerning the validity of the adequacy decision after an individual has lodged a complaint, it has the duty to bring an action before the national court, asking for a suspension of all cross-border transfers to a country that does not ensure an adequate level of protection, and assumes that the national court will in its turn ask for a preliminary ruling from the ECJ.[285] Consequently, the ECJ finds that the mechanism of SCCs as implemented by the EU Commission, does not violate any fundamental principles of the data privacy legislation.

Third, the question of the validity of the privacy shield is discussed. Much progress had been made following the annulment of the Safe Harbour decision, so as to correct the defects of the previous legal framework:[286] under the privacy shield mechanism, the recipient of personal data established in a third country is

---

[282] Tracol (2016), pp. 775–777; Terpan (2019), pp. 1045–1059.

[283] ECJ, C-311/18, Facebook Ireland and Schrems, 16/07/2020, ECLI:EU:C:2020:559.

[284] Par.94 of the decision.

[285] Par.120 of the decision.

[286] Monteleone and Puccio (2017).

contractually bound to comply with the European data privacy legislation and to inform the controller of any inability to comply with those clauses. An ombudsperson's mechanism is also inserted. However, one major concession from the EU Commission to the US remains: the continuation of the US surveillance program for reasons of national security and its enforcement against EU citizens. Ironically, it must be recalled that the GDPR does not provide a substantial protection in this case, as matters of national security are exempted from the application of the Regulation.[287] However, the GDPR is not the only relevant legal instrument in EU and the legality of surveillance programs is still under scrutiny.

In this case, the Court refers to Article 47 of the Charter, relating to the right to an effective judicial remedy. The Court remarks that

> [a]ccording to settled case-law, the very existence of effective judicial review designed to ensure compliance with provisions of EU law is inherent in the existence of the rule of law. Thus, legislation not providing for any possibility for an individual to pursue legal remedies in order to have access to personal data relating to him or her, or to obtain the rectification or erasure of such data, does not respect the essence of the fundamental right to effective judicial protection, as enshrined in Article 47 of the Charter.[288]

The mass processing of personal data in the name of national security does not fall within the control of the US judiciary. In conclusion, it cannot be said that the US ensures a level of protection essentially equivalent to that guaranteed in Europe. As a consequence, for the ECJ, the statement made by the EU Commission in Article 1 of the Privacy Shield Decision, namely that the US provides an adequate level of protection, is wrong. This error affects the validity of the decision in its entirety, which is declared invalid.

The consequence of the decision is clear and immediately concerns Facebook: transfers on the basis of the privacy shield's legal framework are illegal. However, the practical impact of the Schrems II decision, while tremendous, has to be put into perspective. Meta has not yet split its infrastructure into two. Facebook was using Standard Contract Clauses in the Safe Harbour era and, as the privacy shield falls, the company is returning to the Standard Contract Clauses Decision as a last resort to justify the cross-border transfers.

However, the Standard Contract Clauses as a legal basis are more fragile. Even if the Schrems II decision confirms the validity of the corresponding EU Commission mechanism, the subsequent finding as regards the level of protection offered by the US has indirect implications on its validity. As noted by the EDPB,

---

[287] See Article 2 (2) (a) of the GDPR and Recital 16, which states that

> This Regulation does not apply to issues of protection of fundamental rights and freedoms or the free flow of personal data related to activities which fall outside the scope of Union law, such as activities concerning national security. This Regulation does not apply to the processing of personal data by the Member States when carrying out activities in relation to the common foreign and security policy of the Union.

[288] Par.187 of the decision.

[w]hether or not you can transfer personal data on the basis of SCCs will depend on the result of your assessment, taking into account the circumstances of the transfers, and supplementary measures you could put in place. The supplementary measures along with SCCs, following a case by-case analysis of the circumstances surrounding the transfer, would have to ensure that U.S. law does not impinge on the adequate level of protection they guarantee.[289]

Furthermore, the legality of this basis depends on the strict enforcement by the data exporter of its contractual duties. One of these duties, stated by the Decision, is to stop any transfer to the US if data confidentiality would be in peril. In this context, if it could be proved that Facebook had complied with any request from the US authorities arising under the US surveillance law, this would be deemed to violate the Decision. A simple solution from a legal perspective but quite a bit more complex from a geopolitical point of view would be for the US to simply reform its surveillance laws, as proposed by the EPDB.[290]

As a result, Facebook's practices and business had pushed the digital world towards a point of non-return, with only two possible paths ahead. One path includes the danger of a digital world being fractured into data spheres of influence. The other option is that it is possible, while very uncertain, to achieve the declared goal of potential convergence of data protection standards on an international level.[291]

After the Schrems II ruling, the Irish supervisory authority proceeded with additional inquiries into Facebook's compliance with the GDPR with respect to cross-border data transfers. In 2020, it issued a Preliminary Draft Decision where it characteristically stated that "I am therefore bound to conclude that US law does not provide a level of protection that is essentially equivalent to that provided by the EU law". Moreover, the decision notes that "standard contractual clauses cannot compensate for the inadequate protection provided by US law; and Facebook Ireland does not appear to have in place any supplemental measures which would compensate for the inadequate protection provided by US law". The company sought a judicial review of the legality of this inquiry, citing various procedural issues. This review was rejected by the High Court.[292]

Compliance with Schrems II, therefore, means that transfers of personal data to third countries such as the US are not permitted without implementing supplementary measures. Facebook must be in a position to prove that it carried out periodic assessments of the situation in order to verify that it had taken all necessary technical measures (for instance, encryption) to protect the data. This situation obviously puts the company in a very difficult position, and it should not be a surprise that Meta has issued threats against the EU institutions, stating that it would have to leave the EU market if no solution is found to the cross-border transfer of data.[293]

---

[289] EPDB (2020c), p. 3.

[290] EPDB (2020b).

[291] European Parliament (2020).

[292] High Court (Ireland), Facebook Ireland ltd v. Data Protection Commission and Maximilian Schrems, 14/05/2021, 2020No.617 JR., 2020 No. 126 COM.

[293] Deutsch and Bodoni (2022).

In parallel, the EU Commission has issued the final version of the updated SCCs for international data transfers to third countries.[294] Learning from previous failed attempts, the EU Commission has introduced here new obligations for data transfers to third countries—mainly safeguards against public authority access. It also adopted a modular approach, regulating different situations separately (transfer from controller to processor, from controller to controller, etc.). At the same time, the EU Commission and US Department of Commerce jointly declared that they are working together intensively on a new and enhanced EU-US Privacy Shield framework.[295]

References

Adeane A (2019) Blue Whale: What is the truth behind an online 'suicide challenge'? BBC news. https://www.bbc.com/news/blogs-trending-46505722

Algavi LO, Kadyrova SN, Rastorgueva NE (2017) The blue whale game: the five dimensions of news storytelling. J Stud Literature Journalism 22(4):660–668

Article 29 data protection working party (2017a) Guidelines on Data Protection Officers ('DPOs'), WP 243rev.01

Article 29 Data Protection Working Party (2017b) Opinion 2/2017 on data processing at work, WP 249, p 11

Article 29 Working Party (2010) Opinion 2/2010 on online behavioural advertising (WP171), p 3

Article 29 Working Party (2011) Opinion 15/2011 on the definition of consent, WP 187

Article 29 Working Party (2012) Opinion 04/2012 on Cookie Consent Exemption (WP 194), p 5. Available at: https://ec.europa.eu/justice/article-29/documentation/opinion-recommendation/files/2012/wp194_en.pdf

Article 29 Working Party (2013) Opinion 03/2013 on purpose limitation (WP203), p 15

Article 29 Working Party (2014) Opinion 06/2014 on the notion of legitimate interests of the data controller under Article 7 of Directive 95/46/EC (WP217)

Article 29 Working Party (2017a) Guidelines on the right to data portability, 16/EN, WP 2042

Article 29 Working Party (2017b) Opinion on profiling and automated decision making, WP 251, rev. 01, p 15

Article 29 Working Party (2018) Guidelines on consent under Regulation 2016/679, WP259, p 23

Bboyd D, Hargittai E, Schultz J, Palfrey J (2011) Why parents help their children lie to Facebook about age: Unintended consequences of the 'Children's Online Privacy Protection Act'. First Monday, 16(11). https://doi.org/10.5210/fm.v16i11.3850

Bednar K, Spiekermann S, Langheinrich M (2019) Engineering privacy by design: are engineers ready to live up to the challenge? Information Soc 35(3):122–142

Bösch C, Erb B, Kargl F, Kopp H, Pfattheicher S (2016) Tales from the dark side: privacy dark strategies and privacy dark patterns. Proc Privacy Enhancing Technol 2016(4):237–254

---

[294] Commission Implementing Decision (EU) 2021/914 of 4 June 2021 on standard contractual clauses for the transfer of personal data to third countries pursuant to Regulation (EU) 2016/679 of the European Parliament and of the Council, C/2021/3972, OJ L 199, 7.6.2021, p. 31–61, ELI: http://data.europa.eu/eli/dec_impl/2021/914/oj.

[295] Raimondo (2021).

Brandom R (2018) The Facebook hack could be Europe's first big online privacy battle. The Verge. https://www.theverge.com/2018/10/1/17922946/facebook-breach-gdpr-lawsuit-privacy-com missioner-europe

Bundeskartellamt (2019) Bundeskartellamt prohibits Facebook from combining user data from different sources. Background information on the Bundeskartellamt's Facebook proceeding. Press Release, Source: https://www.bundeskartellamt.de/SharedDocs/Publikation/EN/ Pressemitteilungen/2019/07_02_2019_Facebook_FAQs.pdf?__blob=publicationFile&v=6

Cadwalladr C, Graham-Harrison E (2018) Revealed: 50 million Facebook profiles harvested for Cambridge Analytica in major data breach. The Guardian 17:22

Cimina V (2021) The data protection concepts of 'controller', 'processor' and 'joint controllership' under Regulation (EU) 2018/1725. ERA Forum 21:639–654. https://doi.org/10.1007/s12027-020-00632-8

Clark M (2021) The facts on news reports about Facebook data. About Facebook. https://about.fb. com/news/2021/04/facts-on-news-reports-about-facebook-data/

CNIL (16 May 2017) Facebook sanctioned for several breaches of the French Data Protection Act, https://www.cnil.fr/en/facebook-sanctioned-several-breaches-french-data-protection-act

Coelho P (2013) Manuscript found in Accra. Knopf Publishing Group, New York

Commission evaluation report on the implementation of the General Data Protection Regulation two years after its application (2021) European Parliament resolution of 25 March 2021 on the Commission evaluation report on the implementation of the General Data Protection Regulation two years after its application (2020/2717(RSP))

Condon S (2022) Meta estimates Apple's iOS changes will cost it $10B in 2022. ZDnet. https:// www.zdnet.com/article/meta-estimates-apples-ios-changes-will-cost-it-10b-in-2022

Consultative committee of the Convention for the protection of individuals with regards to automatic processing of personal data - Convention 108 (2021) Guidelines on Facial Recognition. Publications of the Conseil Council of Europe. T-PD(2020)03, p 6

Council of Europe (1981) Explanatory Report to the Convention for the Protection of Individuals with regard to Automatic Processing of Personal Data, par.28, available at

Dang S, Culliford E (2021) Facebook will shut down facial recognition system. Reuters. https:// www.reuters.com/technology/facebook-will-shut-down-facial-recognition-system-2021-11-02/

Das S, Kramer A (June 2013) Self-censorship on Facebook. In Proceedings of the International AAAI Conference on Web and Social Media (Vol. 7, No. 1)

Data Protection Commission (2020) Fundamentals for a child-oriented approach to data processing_draft version for consultation. https://www.dataprotection.ie/sites/default/files/ uploads/2020-12/Fundamentals%20for%20a%20Child-Oriented%20Approach%20to%20Data %20Processing_Draft%20Version%20for%20Consultation_EN.pdf

Data Protection Commissioner (2018) Final Report 2018. Data Protection Commission, p 21. https://www.dataprotection.ie/sites/default/files/uploads/2018-11/DPC%20annual%20Report% 202018_0.pdf

De Hert P, Papakonstantinou V, Malgieri G, Beslay L, Sanchez I (2018) The right to data portability in the GDPR: Towards user-centric interoperability of digital services. Comp Law Secur Rev 34(2):193–203

Denham E (2018) Blog: A win for the data protection of UK consumers. ICO blog. https://ico.org. uk/about-the-ico/news-and-events/news-and-blogs/2018/03/blog-a-win-for-the-data-protec tion-of-uk-consumers/

Deutsch A (2020) WhatsApp: the best Facebook purchase ever? Investopedia, https://www. investopedia.com/articles/investing/032515/whatsapp-best-facebook-purchase-ever.asp

Deutsch J, Bodoni S (2022) Meta renews warning to EU it will be forced to pull Facebook. Bloomberg

Devergranne T (2018) GDPR : why Facebook will have to delete 80% of their European user's' data. "Données personnelles" blog. https://www.donneespersonnelles.fr/gdpr-why-facebook-will-have-to-delete-80-of-their-european-users-data

EDPB (2019a) Guidelines 2/2019 on the processing of personal data under Article 6(1)(b) GDPR in the context of the provision of online services to data subjects. https://edpb.europa.eu/sites/edpb/files/consultation/edpb_draft_guidelines-art_6-1-b-final_public_consultation_version_en.pdf, par.18

EDPB (2019b) Hamburg Data Protection Commissioner's €51,000 fine against Facebook Germany GmbH, edpb. https://edpb.europa.eu/news/national-news/2019/hamburg-data-protection-com missioners-eu51000-fine-against-facebook-germany_en

EDPB (2020a) Decision 01/2020 on the dispute arisen on the draft decision of the Irish Supervisory Authority regarding Twitter International Company under Article 65(1)(a) GDPR, 09 November 2020

EDPB (2020b) EDPS Statement following the Court of Justice ruling in Case C-311/18 Data Protection Commissioner v. Facebook Ireland Ltd and Maximilian Schrems ("Schrems II"). https://edps.europa.eu/press-publications/press-news/press-releases/2020/edps-statement-fol lowing-court-justice-ruling_en

EDPB (2020c) Frequently asked questions on the judgment of the Court of Justice of the European Union in Case C-311/18 - Data Protection Commissioner v. Facebook Ireland Ltd and Maximillian Schrems. EDPB, https://edpb.europa.eu/sites/edpb/files/files/file1/20200724_edpb_faqoncjeuc31118_en.pdf, p 3

EDPB (2021a) Children and social networks: Italian DPA requests information on processing from Facebook and Instagram. EDPB. https://edpb.europa.eu/news/national-news/2021/children-and-social-networks-italian-dpa-requests-information-processing_en

EDPB (2021b) EDPB adopts urgent binding decision: Irish SA not to take final measures but to carry out statutory investigation. Press release. https://edpb.europa.eu/news/news/2021/edpb-adopts-urgent-binding-decision-irish-sa-not-take-final-measures-carry-out_en

EDPB (2021c) Guidelines 07/2020 on the concepts of controller and processor in the GDPR. V.2

EDPB (2021d) Guidelines 8/2020 on the targeting of social media users. V2.0

EDPB (2021e) Statement 03/2021 on the ePrivacy Regulation Adopted on 9 March 2021. https://edpb.europa.eu/system/files/2021-03/edpb_statement_032021_eprivacy_regulation_en_0.pdf

Egan E (2019) Data portability and privacy. Facebook. p 6. https://about.fb.com/wp-content/uploads/2020/02/data-portability-privacy-white-paper.pdf

Egele M, Moser A, Kruegel C, Kirda E (2012) PoX: protecting users from malicious Facebook applications. Comp Commun 35(12):1507–1515

Emili AM (2019) Data Protection Officer. In: Bartolini A, Cippitani R, Colcelli V (eds) Dictionary of statuses within EU Law. Springer, Cham. https://doi.org/10.1007/978-3-030-00554-2_16

EU (2019) Special Eurobarometer 487a – March 2019 "The General Data Protection Regulation" Report, https://doi.org/10.2838/43726

EU Commission (2013) Communication to the European Parliament and the Council 'Rebuilding Trust in EU-US Data Flows' (COM(2013) 846 final

European Parliament (2012) Interparliamentary Committee Meeting European Parliament - National Parliaments, The reform of the EU Data Protection framework - Building trust in a digital and global world, LIBE_OJ(2012)1009_1

European Parliament (2020) The CJEU judgment in the Schrems II case. European Parliament, p 3. https://www.europarl.europa.eu/RegData/etudes/ATAG/2020/652073/EPRS_ATA(2020)652073_EN.pdf

Facebook (2021) Apple's iOS 14 changes are almost here: how to finish preparing and what's changing. announcements, April 21, available at https://www.facebook.com/business/news/how-to-prepare-for-changes-to-facebook-ads-from-ios-14-update

Finck M, Pallas F (2020) They who must not be identified—distinguishing personal from non-personal data under the GDPR. Int Data Privacy Law 10(1):11–36. https://doi.org/10.1093/idpl/ipz026

Fowler M (2019) Revealed: Facebook's global lobbying against data privacy laws, The Guardian, https://www.theguardian.com/technology/2019/mar/02/facebook-global-lobbying-campaign-against-data-privacy-laws-investment

Gady FS (2014) EU/US approaches to data privacy and the "Brussels Effect": a comparative analysis. Georgetown J Int Aff:12–23

Gábor P (2020) The value of personal data from a competition law perspective. Elte Law Journal. https://eltelawjournal.hu/the-value-of-personal-data-from-a-competition-law-perspective/

Globocnik J (2019) On joint controllership for social plugins and other third-party content – a case note on the CJEU Decision in Fashion ID. IIC 50:1033–1044. https://doi.org/10.1007/s40319-019-00871-4

Golberk J (2013) On Second Thought … , Slate.com, https://slate.com/technology/2013/12/facebook-self-censorship-what-happens-to-the-posts-you-dont-publish.html

Golla SJ (2017) Is data protection law growing teeth: The current lack of sanctions in data protection law and administrative fines under the GDPR. J Intell Prop Info Tech Elec Com Law 8:70

Graef I (2013) Mandating portability and interoperability in online social networks: regulatory and competition law issues in the European Union (22 July). Telecommunications Policy2015 39(6):502–514

Graef I, Gellert R, Husovec M (2018) Towards a holistic regulatory approach for the European Data Economy: why the illusive notion of non-personal data is counterproductive to data innovation. TILEC Discussion Paper No. 2018-029, Available at SSRN: https://ssrn.com/abstract=3256189 or https://doi.org/10.2139/ssrn.3256189

Gragl P (2017) An Olive Branch from Strasbourg: interpreting the European Court of Human Rights' Resurrection of Bosphorus and Reaction to Opinion 2/13 in the Avotins Case: ECtHR 23 May 2016, Case No. 17502/07, Avotins v. Latvia. EuConst, 13, 551

Gray C, Kou Y, Battles B, Hoggatt J, Toombs A (2018) The dark (patterns) side of UX design. In: Proceedings of the 2018 CHI Conference on Human Factors in Computing Systems (CHI '18). Association for Computing Machinery, New York, NY, USA, Paper 534, pp 1–14. https://doi.org/10.1145/3173574.3174108

Greenleaf G (2012) The influence of European data privacy standards outside Europe: implications for globalization of Convention 108. Int Data Privacy Law 2(2):68–92

Hazelhorst M (2017) Free movement of judgments and the European Convention on Human Rights. In: Free movement of civil judgments in the European Union and the right to a fair trial. T.M.C. Asser Press, The Hague. https://doi.org/10.1007/978-94-6265-162-3_5

Hern A (2020) Facebook says it may quit Europe over ban on sharing data with US. The Guardian. https://www.theguardian.com/technology/2020/sep/22/facebook-says-it-may-quit-europe-over-ban-on-sharing-data-with-us

Hill K (2012) Max Schrems: The Austrian Thorn In Facebook's Side. Forbes. https://www.forbes.com/sites/kashmirhill/2012/02/07/the-austrian-thorn-in-facebooks-side/?sh=31f311d7b0b7

Hodges C (2021) Comments on GDPR Enforcement EDPB Decision 01/020 (January 10, 2021). Available at SSRN: https://ssrn.com/abstract=3765602 or https://doi.org/10.2139/ssrn.3765602

Holpuch A (2015) Facebook still suspending Native Americans over 'real name' policy, The Guardian, https://www.theguardian.com/technology/2015/feb/16/facebook-real-name-policy-suspends-native-americans

Human S, Cech F (2021) A human-centric perspective on digital consenting: the case of GAFAM. In: Zimmermann A, Howlett R, Jain L (eds) Human centred intelligent systems. Smart innovation, systems and technologies, vol 189. Springer, Singapore. https://doi.org/10.1007/978-981-15-5784-2_12

Information Commissioner's Office (2020) Age appropriate design: a code of practice for online services. https://ico.org.uk/for-organisations/guide-to-data-protection/key-data-protection-themes/age-appropriate-design-a-code-of-practice-for-online-services/

Irish Data Protection Commission (2019) Data Protection Commission statement on proposed integration of Facebook, WhatsApp and Instagram. Press release of the Data Protection Commission, https://dataprotection.ie/en/news-media/press-releases/data-protection-commission-statement-proposed-integration-facebook

Kang C (2011) Parents help underage children lie to get on Facebook, survey fi nds. [Online] The Washington Post. http://www.washingtonpost.com/blogs/post-tech/post/parents-help-under age-children-lie-to-get-on-facebook-survey-finds/2011/11/01/gIQA-F6D1cM_blog.html

Keller D (2018) The Right tools: Europe's intermediary liability laws and the EU 2016 General Data Protection Regulation. Berkeley Tech Law J 33:287

Kendall B (2021) Facebook seeks to dismiss antitrust suits, saying it hasn't harmed consumers. The Wall Street Journal. https://www.wsj.com/articles/facebook-seeks-to-dismiss-antitrust-suits-saying-it-hasnt-harmed-consumers-1161540004

Kharpal A (2018) Facebook brings back its controversial facial recognition feature to Europe after closing it in 2012, CNBC, https://www.cnbc.com/2018/04/18/facebook-brings-back-facial-recognition-to-europe-after-closing-it-in-2012.html

Klar M (2020) Binding effects of the European General Data Protection Regulation (GDPR) on US companies. Hastings Sci Technol Law J 11:101

Koch R (2019) The GDPR meets its first challenge: Facebook. Gdpr.eu. https://gdpr.eu/the-gdpr-meets-its-first-challenge-facebook/

Lema J (2017) Spanish Data Protection Authority fines Facebook €1.2 million for data protection infringements. ECIJA, available at https://ecija.com/en/sala-de-prensa/spanish-data-protection-authority-fines-facebook-e1-2-million-data-protection-infringements/

Libert T, Graves L, Nielsen RK (2018) Changes in third-party content on European News Websites after GDPR. In: The World Wide Web Conference (WWW '19). Association for Computing Machinery, New York, NY, USA, pp 1590–1600. https://doi.org/10.1145/3308558.3313524

Lomas N (2019) Facebook fails to keep messenger kids' safety promise. Techcrunch. https://techcrunch.com/2019/07/23/facebook-fails-to-keep-messenger-kids-safety-promise

Lyons K (2021) Judge approves $650 million Facebook privacy settlement over facial recognition feature. The Verge. https://www.theverge.com/2021/2/27/22304618/judge-approves-facebook-privacy-settlement-illinois-facial-recognition

Mahieu R, van Hoboken J (2019) Fashion-ID: introducing a phase-oriented approach to data protection?. European Law Blog. Available at SSRN: https://ssrn.com/abstract=3548487

Manancourt V (2021) Ireland to probe Facebook following massive data leak. Politico. https://www.politico.eu/article/ireland-to-probe-facebook-following-massive-data-leak/

Mannion C (2020) Data imperialism: the GDPR's disastrous impact on Africa's E-Commerce markets. Vand J Transnational Law 53:685

Merken S (2021) Facebook's lawyers blast attorney fees bid in deal over 2018 data breach. Reuters. https://www.reuters.com/article/us-dataprivacy-facebook-idUSKBN2B12JD

Monteleone S, Puccio L (2017) From safe harbour to privacy shield: advances and shortcomings of the new EU-US data transfer rules. European Parliamentary Research Service, European Parliament. https://doi.org/10.2861/09488

Munsif V, Arjun P, Paresh D (2018) Facebook says big breach exposed 50 million accounts to full takeover. Reuters. https://www.reuters.com/article/us-facebook-cyber-idUSKCN1M82BK

Nicas J (2019) Does Facebook really know how many fake accounts it has? The New York Times, https://www.nytimes.com/2019/01/30/technology/facebook-fake-accounts.html

Nicholas G, Weinberg M (2019) Data portability and platform competition is user data exported from Facebook actually useful to competitors? Endelberg Center on innovation Law and policy, p 2. https://www.law.nyu.edu/sites/default/files/Data%20Portability%20and%20Platform%20 Competition%20-%20Is%20User%20Data%20Exported%20From%20Facebook%20Actually %20Useful%20to%20Competitors.pdf

O'Neill K (2019) Facebook's '10 Year Challenge' Is Just a Harmless Meme—Right? Wired. https://www.wired.com/story/facebook-10-year-meme-challenge/

OECD (2013) Privacy guidelines. OECD Publishing, Paris, available at https://www.oecd.org/sti/ieconomy/oecd_privacy_framework.pdf

Osborne C (2018) Facebook faces £500,000 fine in UK over Cambridge Analytica scandal. Zdnet. https://www.zdnet.com/article/uk-watchdog-to-give-facebook-500000-fine-over-data-scandal/

Øverby H (2018) Network effects in Facebook. ICEEG '18: Proceedings of the 2nd International Conference on E-commerce, E-Business and E-Government. Association for Computing Machinery, New York, pp 37–40

Ozanne M, Cueva Navas A, Mattila AS, Van Hoof HB (2017) An investigation into Facebook "Liking" behavior an exploratory study. Social Media + Society. https://doi.org/10.1177/2056305117706785

Pfeifle S (2018) Facebook names Deadman first DPO. IAPP. https://iapp.org/news/a/facebook-names-deadman-first-dpo/

Purtova N (2018) The law of everything. Broad concept of personal data and future of EU data protection law. Law Innov Technol 10(1):40–81

Rahman S, Huang TK, Madhyastha HV, Faloutsos M (2015) Detecting malicious Facebook applications. IEEE/ACM Trans Networking 24(2):773–787

Raimondo G (2021) Intensifying negotiations on trans-atlantic data privacy flows: a joint press statement by U.S. Secretary of Commerce Gina Raimondo and European Commissioner for Justice Didier Reynders. Press Release, U.S. Secretary of Commerce. https://www.commerce.gov/news/press-releases/2021/03/intensifying-negotiations-trans-atlantic-data-privacy-flows-joint-press

Read M (2019) Facebook doesn't need to fool you. New York Magazine. https://nymag.com/intelligencer/2019/01/facebook-doesnt-need-to-fool-you.html

Rice SK, Parkin WS (2016) Social media and law enforcement investigations. Oxford Handbooks Online. https://doi.org/10.1093/oxfordhb/9780199935383.013.9

Ridley K (2021) Facebook faces 2nd UK class action lawsuit over data harvesting scandal, Insurance Journal, https://www.insurancejournal.com/news/international/2021/02/10/600758.htm

Rodriguez S (2018) Facebook hack affected 3 million in Europe, creating the first big test for privacy regulation there. CNBC. https://www.cnbc.com/2018/10/16/facebook-hack-affected-3-million-in-europe-first-big-test-for-gdpr.html

Rodriguez S (2021) Facebook revenue rises 48%, driven by higher-priced ads. CNBC. https://www.cnbc.com/2021/04/28/facebook-fb-earnings-q1-2021.html

Rodriguez MM, Abellan-Matamoros C (2018) Deleting a Facebook account is almost impossible, says expert, Euronews, https://www.euronews.com/2018/04/06/deleting-a-facebook-account-is-almost-impossible-says-expert

Rubinstein IS, Good N (2013) Privacy by design: A counterfactual analysis of Google and Facebook privacy incidents. Berkeley Technol Law J 28:1333

Salter L (2015) Framing Glenn Greenwald: Hegemony and the NSA/GCHQ surveillance scandal in a news interview. Int J Media Cultural Politics 11(2):183–201

Satter R (2021) Leaker says they are offering private details of 500 million Facebook users. Reuters. https://www.reuters.com/article/us-facebook-cyber-leak/leaker-says-they-are-offering-private-details-of-500-million-facebook-users-idUSKBN2BQ0J8

Schwartz PM (2019) Global data privacy: the EU way. NYUL Rev 94:771

Schwartz PM, Janger EJ (2007) Notification of data security breaches. Mich Law Rev 105(5):913–984

Scott M, Cerulus L, Overly S (2019) How Silicon Valley gamed Europe's privacy rules, Politico, https://www.politico.eu/article/europe-data-protection-gdpr-general-data-protection-regulation-facebook-google/

Simonite T (2014) Facebook Creates Software That Matches Faces Almost as Well as You Do. MIT Technology Review, https://www.technologyreview.com/2014/03/17/13822/facebook-creates-software-that-matches-faces-almost-as-well-as-you-do/

Solon O (2018) Facebook faces $1.6bn fine and formal investigation over massive data breach. The Guardian. https://www.theguardian.com/technology/2018/oct/03/facebook-data-breach-latest-fine-investigation

Specht-Riemenschneider L, Schneider R (2020) Stuck Half Way: the limitation of joint control after fashion ID (C-40/17). GRUR Int 69(2):159–163

Tang Q, Whinston AB (2020) Do reputational sanctions deter negligence in information security management? A field quasi-experiment. Production Operations Manag 29(2):410–427

Terpan F (2019) EU-US data transfer from safe harbour to privacy shield: back to square one? EurPapers A J Law Integr 2018(3):1045–1059

The Hamburg Commissioner for Data Protection and Freedom of Information (2018) Higher Administrative Court confirms the prohibition of data sharing between WhatsApp and Facebook. Press Release, The Hamburg Commissioner for Data Protection and Freedom of Information, https://datenschutz-hamburg.de/assets/pdf/Press_Release_2018-03-02_Higher_Administrative_Court_Facebook.pdf

The Hamburg Commissioner for Data Protection and Freedom of Information (2021) Order of the HmbBfDI: Ban of further processing of WhatsApp user data by Facebook. Press release. https://datenschutz-hamburg.de/assets/pdf/2021-05-11-press-release-facebook.pdf

Tracol X (2016) EU-US privacy shield: the Saga continues. Comp Law Secur Rev:775–777

Wachter S, Mittelstadt B (2019) A right to reasonable inferences: Re-thinking data protection law in the age of big data and AI. Colum Bus Law Rev:494

Wagner K (2018) This is how Facebook collects data on you even if you don't have an account, Vox, https://www.vox.com/2018/4/20/17254312/facebook-shadow-profiles-data-collection-non-users-mark-zuckerberg

Wong Q, Brown S (2019) Facebook takes down more than 3 billion fake accounts, Cnet, https://www.cnet.com/news/facebook-took-down-more-than-3-billion-fake-accounts/

York J, Kayyali D (2014) Facebook's 'Real Name' Policy Can Cause Real-World Harm for the LGBTQ Community, Electronic Frontier Foundation, https://www.eff.org/deeplinks/2014/09/facebooks-real-name-policy-can-cause-real-world-harm-lgbtq-community

Zuckerberg M (2018) Facebook post, https://www.facebook.com/zuck/posts/10104712037900071

Chapter 3
User-Generated Content on Facebook and Intellectual Property Rights

Facebook's business model indirectly feeds off user-generated content. The more original and captivating the content is, the more time users will spend on the platform and watch advertisements. Surprisingly, only a few major cases concerning intellectual property and Facebook have arisen. This does not mean, however, that the topic should be neglected. Intellectual property law, a relatively specific field of law, has emerged over the past few years as one of the major legal challenges to the main actors of the digital era.

Intellectual property is a vast area that notably encompasses copyright law, trade mark law, patent law, design law and domain name protection. However, copyright law retains most of our attention here, as the platform mainly consists of protected works. Indeed, in its most basic form, Facebook can be considered an exploitation of information goods. Information goods of various kinds are uploaded, shared and broadcasted and although Facebook does not directly exploit them, it indirectly earns revenues from analyzing their circulation.

Therefore, this chapter will first explain why copyright law—mainly—plays a substantial role in the service's legal framework (Sect. 3.1). It will then focus more specifically on the issue of linking and sharing (Sect. 3.2), analyzing the legality of the users' activity on Facebook. In parallel, the legality of Facebook's activity has to be determined as regards the new, ambiguous and controversial filter duty imposed by the European legislator after many discussions (Sect. 3.3). Finally, the related questions of industrial property law will be discussed (Sect. 3.4).

3.1   Facebook User-Generated Content As a Protected Intellectual Creation

3.1.1   Facebook Data As an Intellectual Creation

3.1.1.1   The Notion of a Protected Work in the EU

One of the most surprising discoveries for the legal scholar who is not accustomed to the specific legal field of intellectual property lies in the significant legal uncertainty governing copyright law, especially as regards the subject matter of the protection. In common law tradition, a—very loosely defined—closed list of protected works applies (traditionally the protection concerns literary, dramatic, musical and artistic works), while continental law, on the other hand, considers any kind of intellectual work as being potentially protectable, regardless of its specific form of expression.

In this respect, EU law has inherited principles from the Berne Convention—the result of lengthy efforts to internationalize the field.[1] As a consequence, no definition of the protected work is imposed on the member states, and, in accordance with a core principle of the Berne Convention, copyright protection subsists from the moment of the creation of the work, without any formalities such as requiring registration.[2] Therefore, any message posted on Facebook, whether photography or video, with or without music, or even a simple text message, is theoretically and, provided certain conditions are met, eligible for protection.

In 2011, a lawsuit was filed in the US that addressed this issue.[3] Apparently, Facebook used various posts, information, and pictures in a promotion campaign called "sponsored stories". In short, sponsored stories turned personal posts into ads. The complaint, which took the form of a class action, argued that this technique violated the users' copyright in their posts. The lawsuit was settled for USD 20 million, which proves that the company took the lawsuit's arguments very seriously.

As copyright law is strictly related to most of the EU's objectives (free movement of services, digital single market, etc.), the EU legislator has heavily intervened for a deep harmonization of EU copyright law. However, the definition of the protected work has never been dealt with by the EU legislator. In an audacious act of judicial activism,[4] the ECJ has rectified this omission, justifying this intervention by recognizing that the EU legislator's goal of harmonization could not be achieved without a common understanding of the notion of a protected work. The ECJ has distinguished

---

[1] Berne Convention for the Protection of Literary and Artistic Works (adopted in 1886, last amended in 1979).

[2] Article 5 (2) of the Berne Convention: "The enjoyment and the exercise of these rights shall not be subject to any formality".

[3] Angel Fraley, et al. v. Facebook, Inc. and Does 1-100, no. 11-CV-01726, N.D. Cal., filed Apr. 4, 2011.

[4] Bently and Sherman (2014).

three cumulative criteria for the notion of a protected work: originality, a concrete form distinct from a mere idea, and an objective form of expression.

It is certainly accepted that the vast majority of texts and pictures uploaded on Facebook's platform are of somewhat low artistic value. Nevertheless, as a general principle of EU copyright law, no criteria than those stated above are relevant. This prohibition of other criteria specifically refers to the use of aesthetic or qualitative criteria in establishing the potential protection of an intellectual creation. In other words, it does not matter if the users only post pictures of their pets or of their food; they should still obtain copyright law protection for their creations. Judicial reluctance to address aesthetic considerations is not, however, absolute. It has been demonstrated that these implicitly appear in the determination of a subject matter's originality.[5]

The ECJ's decision in the Cofemel case[6] confirms the irrelevance of aesthetic criteria in copyright law. The Court examined the situation from the perspective of design law. A design may benefit in some cases from the simultaneous protection of design law and copyright law. However, some national legislations have traditionally limited the use of copyright law for protecting merely functional designs, requiring that a design generate a specific, aesthetically significant visual effect for copyright protection to subsist. The Court states in this decision that this practice violates EU law, explicitly confirming the "no other criteria" rule as a general principle of EU copyright law.

In parallel, Facebook's terms of service assume that part of the content may be protected by copyright law. It states that

> [y]ou own the intellectual property rights (things such as copyright or trademarks) in any such content that you create and share on Facebook and the other Facebook Company Products you use. Nothing in these Terms takes away the rights you have to your own content.

3.1.1.2 The Concept of Originality

The lack of a common definition of originality in the EU was seen as very unfortunate, as there are two conflicting approaches: one, more often applied in common law countries, refers to an objective approach and defines originality by reference to the individuality of the protected work (that is, mainly, that is in not a copy of previous works), while the other, mainly developed in continental countries, attaches to the concept of originality a subjective approach and discusses originality by reference to the personality of the author.

---

[5] van Gompel and Lavik (2013), pp. 100–295.
[6] ECJ, C-683/17, Cofemel – Sociedade de Vestuário SA v. G-Star Raw CV, 12/09/2019, ECLI:EU: C:2019:721.

The EU legislator had originally imposed a definition of the concept of originality in the specific cases of software,[7] databases,[8] and photography.[9] In these situations, originality is defined as "the author own's intellectual creation". In the seminal Infopaq case,[10] which discussed the protection of press article abstracts, the ECJ extended a definition of the concept of originality established by the legislator for specific works to all categories of intellectual creations. This position has been subsequently confirmed, first of all, by the Painer case,[11] relating to the protection of a portrait. Subsequently, the BSA[12] case applied the unified definition of originality to computer program interfaces, the Flos[13] case to industrial designs, and the Football Association Premier League[14] to video broadcasts.

The European definition of originality is a fragile compromise between the two opposite theories of originality. Indeed, the reference to "own" and to "creation" suggests the individuality criterion of the objective approach, while the reference to "author" and to "intellectual" implies that the personality of the author should also be taken into consideration in the definition of the concept. In practice, this means that the threshold of protection should not be so low as to encompass any kind of intellectual activity, but it also should not be so high so as to reject subject matter from protection if the work denotes some creative choices. In conclusion, it is safe to assume that most content accessible on the platform, whether audiovisual content or text (in posts, stories or even in comments) are sufficiently original to be eligible for copyright law protection.

3.1.1.3   The Objective Expression of the Work

Originality alone does not suffice. The intellectual creation should also have an objective expression. This principle has been highlighted by the landmark Levola

---

[7] Article 1 (3) of the Directive 91/250/EEC now Directive 2009/24/EC of the European Parliament and of the Council of 23 April 2009 on the legal protection of computer programs, ELI: http://data. europa.eu/eli/dir/2009/24/oj.

[8] Article 3(1) Directive 96/9/EC of the European Parliament and of the Council of 11 March 1996 on the legal protection of databases, ELI: http://data.europa.eu/eli/dir/1996/9/oj.

[9] Article 6 of Directive 2006/116/EC of the European Parliament and of the Council of 12 December 2006 on the term of protection of copyright and certain related rights, ELI: http://data.europa.eu/eli/dir/2006/116/2011-10-31.

[10] ECJ, C-5/08 Infopaq International A/S v. Danske Dagblades Forening, 16/07/2009, ECLI:EU:C:2009:465.

[11] ECJ, C-145/10 Eva-Maria Painer v. Standard Verlags GmbH, Axel Springer AG, Süddeutsche Zeitung GmbH, Spiegel-Verlag Rudolf Augstein GmbH & Co KG, Verlag M. DuMont Schauberg Expedition der Kölnischen Zeitung GmbH & Co KG, 1/12/2011, ECLI:EU:C:2011:798.

[12] ECJ, C-393/09, Bezpečnostní softwarová asociace – Svaz softwarové ochrany v. Ministerstvo kultury22/12/2010, ECLI:EU:C:2010:816.

[13] ECJ, C-168/09, Flos SpA v. Semeraro Casa e Famiglia SpA, 27/01/2011, ECLI:EU:C:2011:29.

[14] ECJ, C-403/08, Football Association Premier League Ltd and Others v. QC Leisure and Others, 04/10/2011, ECLI:EU:C:2011:631.

case of the ECJ.[15] The case discussed the copyright protection of the characteristic taste of a cheese. Although the facts of the case seem, at first sight, very far from the current legal issues related to social networks, the consequences of the decision extend well beyond the culinary field. Indeed, the Court sets out a general principle that copyright protection presupposes the possibility of an objective access to the subject matter. In other words, purely subjective experiences—such as taste, but also smell—cannot be objectively analyzed and the Court cannot justify classifying them as original.

Text, pictures, video, and music automatically pass this test. It would not be so evident for other potential uses of the platform, such as the personal feelings linked to specific juxtapositions or an arrangement of the various stories of a timeline, or a specific subjective experience linked to a virtual environment.

3.1.1.4   The Precise Expression of the Work and the Issue of Raw Data Protection

Furthermore, the expression of the work must be precise enough. This prerequisite is known as the principle of non-protection of the mere idea and has been established as a cornerstone of copyright law from the start. The principle is divided into a list of non-protected intellectual creations: style, news, history, historical incidents, facts, scientific principles, descriptions of an artwork, mere principles or schemes, methods of operation, and general ideas for entertainment are out of the scope of copyright law.[16] For instance, the use of a specific Instagram filter on a picture, a specific marketing method of a group, the style of a message or of a story, the news (but not the article itself, which is protected) are outside the scope of copyright law.

This principle also means that author of the creation is the person that brings a substantial intellectual contribution to the expression of the work. This consequence has recently become problematic with the rise of AI technology. The various engineers programming the AI are only giving "ideas" to the machine, which is alone responsible for the specific expression of the work. For instance, a specific AI technology is used to automatically produce some basic messages ("bot messages") and which are effective in the framework of individual conversations ("chats") on Messenger. From a legal point of view, the issue of protecting such bot-produced messages through copyright law is therefore complicated. If the bot only reproduces predetermined answers, the programmer is deemed to be the creator of the message. If, on the other hand, the bot is associated by a "real" deep learning AI, endowed with a capacity of auto-learning, bot messages are not protected under the current framework of copyright law.

The non-protection of ideas also means that "raw data" are not protected by copyright law, although some discussions about non-personal data protection have

---

[15] ECJ, C-310/17, Levola Hengelo BV v. Smilde Foods BV, 11/13/18, ECLI:EU:C:2018:899.
[16] Vaver (2002), pp. 15–20.

emerged in the EU (see Sect. 4.1.2). As an exception, organized collections of data that demonstrate a substantive qualitative or quantitative investment are protected by the sui generis right available to the producer of a database.[17] The producer's right protects him against systematic appropriation of the content of the database. As groups and pages on Facebook place much importance on the stories they post, it is a matter of debate whether their activities belong to the legal definition of a database. For sure, it constitutes a collection of individual works and the contents are independently accessible. Following this logic, the systematic publication of the same contents, in the same chronology, by a third-party fan page could constitute a violation of copyright law (a reutilization of a quantitively substantial part of the database).

However, in 2004, sensitive to the censure from multiple critics as regards the danger that creating an exclusive right to data would have for the freedom of expression, the ECJ has considerably reduced the impact of EU legislation, by applying a strict interpretation of the criterion of substantial investment. Specifically, in the British Horseracing case,[18] the court adopted a very narrow approach of the criteria of protection by estimating that the notion of investment in obtaining the content does not include the resources used for the creation of materials which make up the contents of a database. In other words, the analysis of the investment criterion should exclusively refer to the database, not to the data. It is now extremely improbable that a court would accept that the creation of a page or a group on the platform constitutes, on its own, a substantial investment.

3.1.2   The Right Holder's Exclusive Protection and Its Limits

3.1.2.1   The Scope of Copyright Law's Prerogatives in the Online Environment

The European Union has harmonized the economic rights associated with copyright law by imposing a common definition and duration[19] (on principle, 70 years after the author's death). The distinction between the two main economic rights constitutes a fundamental division of copyright law; if someone copies and multiplies the number of existing intellectual creations, his or her act belongs to the right of reproduction, while if he or she displays this work, without copying it, to a number of persons that exceeds his or her strict social and familial environment, this act belongs to the right

---

[17] Directive 96/9/EC of the European Parliament and of the Council of 11 March 1996 on the legal protection of databases, OJ L 77, 27.3.1996, p. 20–28, ELI: http://data.europa.eu/eli/dir/1996/9/oj.

[18] ECJ, C-203/02, British Horseracing Board Ltd v. William Hill Organisation Ltd, 09/11/2004, ECLI:EU:C:2004:695.

[19] Directive 2006/116/EC of the European Parliament and of the Council of 12 December 2006 on the term of protection of copyright and certain related rights (codified version), ELI: http://data.europa.eu/eli/dir/2006/116/oj.

of communication to the public. Certainly, all content uploaded on the platform is protected against copying under the right of reproduction, while the issues of sharing and linking to user-generated content are governed by the principles on the right of communication to the public (see below next section).

Other economic rights are recognized, such as the right of distribution, the droit de suite (resale right), and the rights of lending and renting. However, their practical influence on the functioning of the platform is very limited and therefore their analysis exceeds the scope of this study.

The "Infosoc Directive"[20] defines the right of reproduction in Article 2 as the "right to authorise or prohibit direct or indirect, temporary or permanent reproduction by any means and in any form, in whole or in part". The concept of reproduction is not to be reduced to the mere act of copying the physical support of a protected work. Reproduction also occurs if the form or the expression changes and even when reproduction is partial. For instance, although fictional characters from a book or a movie are only part of an intellectual creation, their copying will be regulated by the reproduction right.

In this context, it should be highlighted that infringement of the economic rights is not conditional upon an economic benefit. It does not matter if the publisher of the infringing content does not receive any remuneration for his or her act. Therefore, the mere act of "copy-pasting" a message, or photographing and then uploading it (instead of sharing it), amounts to a violation of the right of reproduction, independently of the motivation of the second publication's author (unless one of the exceptions applies, see below). However, the lack of an economic benefit plays a role when determining the appropriate sanction. Indeed, as stated by the TRIPS Agreement[21] from the World Trade Organization, criminal sanctions should be available only in cases of infringement on a commercial scale.[22] For a non-economic activity such as use of the platform by a basic user, the only consequences in terms of liability would therefore be civil and not criminal.

In conclusion, although economic rights are protected on social networks, the absence of criminal sanctions strongly diminishes the effective enforcement of the legal framework, as it is highly improbable for a collective management organization to sue an individual for his activity on the platform: not only would the cost of the litigation exceed the compensation awarded, but it would also be ruinous for the right-holders' public image. Criminal sanctions of course would have even more adverse effects on the public opinion and their enforcement would raise serious legal issues in terms of human rights protection (freedom of speech). Nevertheless, intellectual property infringing content will trigger a moderation mechanism.

---

[20] Directive 2001/29/EC of the European Parliament and of the Council of 22 May 2001 on the harmonisation of certain aspects of copyright and related rights in the information society, ELI: http://data.europa.eu/eli/dir/2001/29/oj.

[21] Agreement on Trade-related Aspects of Intellectual Property.

[22] See Article 61 of the TRIPS agreements.

In the same way, the fact that the protected work is already freely circulating on the Internet is irrelevant for the appreciation of the infringement of economic rights. The landmark Renckhoff decision[23] discusses the case of a student using a photograph of the town of Cordova for her presentation in a language workshop. The picture was taken from an online travel portal, which had licensed it from its author. The teacher uploaded the presentation onto the school's website, and the photographer sued the state (it was a public school) for copyright law infringement. It should be noted that in the decision the submissions almost entirely focus on the right of communication to the public, and not the right of reproduction. It could be said that the ECJ adopts a holistic approach to economic rights in the online environment, perceiving them as a general right to control the access to the work.[24] Characteristically, the Court remarks that, in this case, the uploading of the photograph onto the school's website resulted in the photographer's loss of control over his work. The Court indicates that

> even if the holder of the copyright holder decides no longer to communicate his work on the website on which it was initially communicated with his consent, that work would remain available on the website on which it had been newly posted.[25]

Consequently,

> to allow such a posting without the copyright holder being able to rely on the rights laid down in Article 3(1) of Directive 2001/29 would fail to have regard to the fair balance, referred to in recitals 3 and 31 of that directive, which must be maintained in the digital environment between, on one hand, the interest of the holders of copyright and related rights in the protection of their intellectual property, guaranteed by Article 17(2) of the Charter of Fundamental Rights of the European Union and, on the other hand, the protection of the interests and fundamental rights of users of protected subject matter, in particular their freedom of expression and information guaranteed by Article 11 of the Charter of Fundamental Rights, as well as the public interest.[26]

The ECJ concludes that uploading a protected work onto the Internet without authorization infringes copyright law, even if the work is already freely accessible on Internet.

Economic rights can be licensed or transferred (assigned). Any publication can take place on the platform without fear of litigation, assuming the prior consent of the right-holder has been obtained. On the contrary, "moral rights", that are the prerogative of the author related to the protection of his or her personality, are non-transferable. Two moral rights have been recognized by the Berne Convention: the right of paternity (i.e. of attribution) and the right to protect the integrity of the work. The right of paternity creates a duty for a third party to mention the name of the author in each exploitation of the work and to the extent of the technical feasibility of the mention. The right to protect the integrity of the work forbids any

---

[23] ECJ, C-161/17, Land Nordrhein-Westfalen v. Dirk Renckhoff, 7/08/2018, ECLI:EU:C:2018:634.

[24] Synodinou (2019), pp. 21–33.

[25] Renckhoff, par.31.

[26] Par.41 of the Decision.

intervention on the work that alters the user's experience in such a way that the author's reputation could be hurt.

3.1.2.2 Exceptions to Copyright Law Relevant to the Main Facebook Activities

EU copyright law works on the basis of an exhaustive list of recognized exceptions (defenses), codified in the Infosoc Directive.[27] These exceptions have a defensive nature, as they cannot be used as the basis of a complaint (i.e. they are a shield and not a sword). Nevertheless, they function de facto as user's rights, in the sense that the user is authorized to freely access the protected work even without the consent of the right-holder. Subsequently, if an act is covered by an exception, the relevant economic right is overridden. It means the content does not infringe copyright law and should not be moderated.

The closed nature of the list of exceptions in Europe corresponds to a long legal tradition and can be linked to the principles of the three-step test. The three-step test, present in the Berne Convention[28] but also in the TRIPS Agreement[29] and EU law, explains that exceptions should cover specific purposes, should not conflict with the normal exploitation of the work, and should not disproportionately prejudice the legitimate interests of the right-holder. The opposite approach is taken in the US; although the country is a member of the Berne Convention, users' freedom to interact with the work fall within the scope of a general clause called the fair use exception.[30]

The ECJ has recently adopted a very strict approach to the balancing of interests in the Spiegel Online case.[31] The Court considered that the list of exceptions constitutes an balance between the opposing interests of the right-holders and the users. Users' human rights, and specifically the freedom of expression, are already incorporated in the exceptions list. This means that it is not permitted to refer to human rights in copyright law as a way to limit the exclusive prerogatives of the right-holder. The Court indeed states without ambiguity in this case that

> [f]reedom of information and freedom of the press, enshrined in Article 11 of the Charter of Fundamental Rights of the European Union, are not capable of justifying, beyond the exceptions or limitations provided for in Article 5(2) and (3) of Directive 2001/29, a derogation from the author's exclusive rights of reproduction and of communication to the public.

Instead, human rights indirectly influence the regime, as criteria to interpret the existing exceptions, in order to protect the full effectiveness of the exception.

---

[27] Article 5 of the Directive 29/2001.

[28] Article 9 (2) of the Convention.

[29] Article 13 of the TRIPS Agreement of the Word Trade Organization.

[30] Stewart (2012), p. 93.

[31] ECJ, C-516/17, Spiegel Online v. Volker Beck, 29/07/2019, ECLI:EU:C:2019:625.

This inflexibility of the legal framework in Europe in comparison to the US is especially highlighted by a lack of a specific exception related to "user-generated content". User-generated content covers two meanings: firstly, in a general sense, user-generated content means any content created by users of an online service. This broad definition does not allow for any specific, and more favorable for the users, legal regime. Secondly and more specifically, user-generated content may refer to the use of a pre-existing protected work as raw material for a derivative work created without commercial intent. For instance, a fan work that creates a new story in the universe of his or her favorite fiction, a protected music playing in the background while creating a homemade video, or a "meme" (use of a known picture with the addition of custom text incorporated in the picture) are user-generated content in the second sense of the term. In Canada, a specific exception has been created to cover this activity.[32]

As regards the most common uses of Facebook, a few exceptions stand out from the list, namely the use for information purposes by the press, caricature, quotation exceptions, and incidental use. But first, it should be noted that under EU copyright law, all of these exceptions are optional and some Member States can decide to not implement one or even all of them (however, some of them are mandatory under the Berne Convention, and it is arguable that exceptions cited by Article 17 of the Digital Single Market Directive—see Sect. 3.3.1—are de facto mandatory). This uncertainty as regards the legal nature of these exceptions is subject to criticism, as it does not only create significant variations between the different national frameworks but it also, in the light of the Spiegel Online decision, appears clear that these exceptions serve a fundamental purpose (applying the human rights approach to copyright law and ensuring that EU copyright law remains compatible with the Fundamental Charter of Human Rights).

The use for information purposes by the press is governed by Article 5 (3) (c) of the Infosoc Directive, that states that

> reproduction by the press, communication to the public or making available of published articles on current economic, political or religious topics or of broadcast works or other subject-matter of the same character, in cases where such use is not expressly reserved, and as long as the source, including the author's name, is indicated, or use of works or other subject-matter in connection with the reporting of current events, to the extent justified by the informatory purpose and as long as the source, including the author's name, is indicated, unless this turns out to be impossible.

The exception is limited to use by the press, but it could be argued that the definition of the press should cover any activity that focuses on the dissemination of information on current events. Therefore, some Facebook groups and pages activities could fall within the scope of this exception.

However, the exception is restricted to specific information and a specific purpose. For instance, a UK decision relating to a website where short visual abstracts of cricket were shared, held that the videos did not serve an informative purpose but a

---

[32] Section 29.21 of Canada's Copyright Act.

recreational one.[33] In the Spiegel Online case already discussed above, the ECJ added that main criterion for the application of this exception is the contribution of this particular information to democratic society.

Nevertheless, most of these activities may be covered by a second exception, which has a broader scope: the exception of quotation. This exception is defined as

> quotations for purposes such as criticism or review, provided that they relate to a work or other subject-matter which has already been lawfully made available to the public, that, unless this turns out to be impossible, the source, including the author's name, is indicated, and that their use is in accordance with fair practice, and to the extent required by the specific purpose.[34]

The quotation exception has probably been designed as an exception for the use of literary works only, and for using only a small part of it. However, no explicit reference to this appears in the law and it has to be assumed that nowadays quotation can apply to various works, such as pictures, video, and music. In addition, no reference exists to partial use of the work. Indeed, the only fundamental criterion of application of this exception does not lie in a specific category of work(s) but in the purpose of the use, which has to be criticism or review. The ECJ's case "Metall auf Metall",[35] related to the legality of the sampling technique, confirms that quotation exception could extend its reach to protected musical works and also to complete use of works.

Moreover, and even more importantly, the Court proposes a definition of the exception in this decision. It notes that

> the essential characteristics of a quotation are the use, by a user other than the copyright holder, of a work or, more generally, of an extract from a work for the purposes of illustrating an assertion, of defending an opinion or of allowing an intellectual comparison between that work and the assertions of that user, since the user of a protected work wishing to rely on the quotation exception must therefore have the intention of entering into 'dialogue' with that work.[36]

It is clear that review or criticism is incompatible with an economic exploitation of the quoted work. For example, it means that the user of an extract of a phonogram is only required to ask for authorization if the sample is unmodified and can be recognized in the new work.[37]

The prerequisite of a dialogue implies the existence of a communication. Applied to Facebook, it can be concluded that the quotation exception could potentially protect any uploaded protected work such as pictures, photography, video or text, depending on the context. However, the mere fact that the publication is open to

---

[33] High Court of England and Wales, Chancery Division, England And Wales Cricket Board Ltd & Anor v. Tixdaq Ltd & Anor, HC-2015-002993, 18 /03/2016.

[34] Article 5 (3) (d) of the Infosoc directive.

[35] ECJ, C-476/17, Pelham GmbH, Moses Pelham, Martin Haas v. Ralf Hütter, Florian Schneider-Esleben, 29/07/2019, ECLI:EU:C:2019:624.

[36] Par.71 of the decision.

[37] Jütte (2019), pp. 827–829.

comments is not sufficient to prove the existence of dialogue. Indeed, the dialogue should be perceptible in the original publication, independently of the comments. Furthermore, the Court states that the dialogue should be a dialogue "with that work" and not "on that work". This "indicates that the quoting work must have its own intellectual structure and integrity, into which the quotation can be placed".[38] A lot of the platform's groups focus on publishing artistic or funny content and specialize in showing protected works. The fact that they use the works as a resource to feed their flow of content could be an indicator that no real dialogue exists.

In conclusion, the quotation exception would most certainly protect a lot of personal publications on the platform that insert protected works, as long as the publication is accompanied by some personal remarks proving a dialogue. Conversely, this exception cannot be extended to massive reproduction of protected works without any real purpose of opening a dialogue with the work.

Furthermore, the InfoSoc Directive implements the exception of caricature through Article 5 (3) (k). The article succinctly states the "use for the purpose of caricature, parody or pastiche" is authorized. Once again, the ECJ offers substantial guidelines towards an interpretation of this exception, through the Deckmyn case.[39] The court reviewed the parody exception with respect to a flyer, from an extreme right political party, that used the main elements of a famous cover page from a comic. One of the issues was that the comic was not the topic of the parody, but only the means (the parody targeted the town's mayor). This kind of use of protected works as pure material for parodying someone or something has become extremely popular on the Internet, in the light of the so-called "meme" culture. Therefore, the definition adopted by the ECJ is clearly fundamental for the operation of social network. It states that

> the essential characteristics of parody, are, first, to evoke an existing work, while being noticeably different from it, and secondly, to constitute an expression of humour or mockery. The concept of 'parody', within the meaning of that provision, is not subject to the conditions that the parody should display an original character of its own, other than that of displaying noticeable differences with respect to the original parodied work; that it could reasonably be attributed to a person other than the author of the original work itself; that it should relate to the original work itself or mention the source of the parodied work.

In other words, the ECJ opts for a broad interpretation of the concept of parody. That the protected work is only a means to the parody and not its purpose is irrelevant for the application of the exception. Similarly, the parody does not need to be so original that it constitutes a derivative work. A parody to be protected only needs to display "noticeable differences" and to constitute an attempt at humor. Nevertheless, the ECJ in this decision places a limit on what can be seen as a "freedom to parody". The court considered that the parody cannot be used in a way that would disproportionately hurt the reputation of the author of the original work. In other words, the parody

---

[38] Adeney (2013), p. 142.
[39] ECJ, C-201/13, Johan Deckmyn and Vrijheidsfonds VZW v. Helena Vandersteen and Others, 3/09/2014, ECLI:EU:C:2014:2132.

exception obviously supersedes the moral right to protest against the alteration of the work, but with a limit: if it can be proved that the author is known to be against the specific message carried by the caricature, the parody is not legal.

Furthermore, the Infosoc Directive protects against litigation for the "incidental inclusion of a work or other subject-matter in other material".[40] Since copyright law extends to a quasi-infinite range of works, it is common for a picture or a short video to incorporate the image of a protected work of architecture, music from a neighbor, an image of a poster, or even clothes or objects of a certain and original design. The exception in these situations will protect the user against litigation. The incidental character of the inclusion means, first, that the inclusion should be accidental, that is without intent of inclusion from the user, and, secondly, that it should not be a central part of the final realization.

It should be noted, as explained in the landmark Adam case,[41] that all these exceptions require a lawful use to be applied. Users cannot receive protection from an exception to the right-holders' prerogative if did not have legitimate access to the protected work in the first place.

Finally, specific mention should be made of the new data mining exception. It is doubtless that the platform contains a huge variety of freely accessible data that have an enormous potential research interest. The Digital Single Market Directive[42] added this exception to the database producer prerogatives, with the purpose of providing access to this data, mainly for researchers. Moreover, access to huge amounts of data is required for the deep learning of AI. Consequently, the Directive creates two separate legal frameworks. In Article 3, an exception is created in favor of researchers, while Article 4 proposes a regime of data mining even for commercial purposes (however, the company that owns the data is free to opt out from it). A lot of research in various fields, such as hate speech, build data crawlers that retrieve the comments of public posts[43] and the Digital Single Market Directive provides the adequate legal framework for this field to flourish.

3.1.2.3 The License to Facebook Included in the Terms of Service

Copyright law is highly dependent on contractual arrangements. The field of contractual copyright law has not been unified at EU level, and some Member States even accept the general transfer of the exclusive rights on a protected work, while in other Member States the question is regulated through the principle of specialty of the transfer. Meta, conscious of the various potential legal issues related to the

---

[40] Article 5 (3) (i) of the Infosoc Directive.

[41] ECJ, C-435/12, ACI Adam BV and Others 10/04/2014, ECLI:EU:C:2014:254.

[42] Directive (EU) 2019/790 of the European Parliament and of the Council of 17 April 2019 on copyright and related rights in the Digital Single Market and amending Directives 96/9/EC and 2001/29/EC. ELI: http://data.europa.eu/eli/dir/2019/790/oj.

[43] For instance, see Del Vigna et al. (2017), pp. 86–95.

practical management of the platform, inserted a clause on copyright law in its general terms of service. Specifically, it is stipulated that

> when you share, post or upload content that is covered by intellectual property rights on or in connection with our Products, you grant us a non-exclusive, transferable, sub-licensable, royalty-free and worldwide licence to host, use, distribute, modify, run, copy, publicly perform or display, translate and create derivative works of your content.

As a simple, non-exclusive license to host, use and display the protected content, this contract does not present insuperable legal difficulty. As no transfer of rights takes place, the mechanism avoids the various national legal frameworks which limit the duration or the extent of the transfer and/or impose some formalities. Nevertheless, the clause possesses a certain ambiguity, as the act of creating derivative works, for instance, mentioned in the clause, could have easily been interpreted as a form of exploitation of the protected work.

Still, Facebook's use of user-generated content in order to feed the platform with original content poses issues such as non-remunerated exploitation of a work. The EU Digital Single Market Directive introduces a new principle of appropriate and proportionate remuneration. Specifically, it states that "where authors and performers license or transfer their exclusive rights for the exploitation of their works or other subject matter, they are entitled to receive appropriate and proportionate remuneration."[44]

Furthermore, the Directive mentions that

> [i]n the implementation in national law of the principle set out in paragraph 1, Member States shall be free to use different mechanisms and take into account the principle of contractual freedom and a fair balance of rights and interests.[45]

The principle of contractual freedom implies that a contractual regulation of the remuneration (or the lack of it) would prevail based on the principle of proportionate remuneration of the author. In other words, the duty to remunerate the author should be interpreted as being restricted to commercial utilization of the work, while on the other hand, the validity of free licenses should not be challenged on the basis of the principle of fair remuneration.[46]

In conclusion, Facebook's choice to include a free license in its terms of service, which is explained by its litigation history in the US, does not fit comfortably with EU law. First, the license could be considered abusive in the light of the consumer protection framework (see Sect. 9.1.1). Second, the free license arguably conflicts with the new principle of remuneration introduced by Article 18 of the Digital Single Market Directive, where Facebook would alternatively have been entitled to justify its use of the works under various exceptions (such as the quoting exception).

---

[44] Article 18 (1) of the Directive 2019/790.

[45] Article 18 (2) of the Digital Single Market Directive.

[46] Paramythiotis (2021), pp. 77–97.

3.1.3 The Question of Facebook Apps

The platform itself is protected by copyright as a software and as a database. However, the platform authorizes third-party developers to interact with its code for their own creations. These "Facebook apps" constitute derivative works, contractually linked to the platform. The specific terms and conditions of the contract between the company and the developer regulate the topic. Facebook offers

> a limited, non-exclusive, non-sublicensable (except to Service Providers as described below), non-transferable, non-assignable license to use, access, and integrate with Platform, but only to the extent permitted in these Terms and all other applicable terms and policies.

With the license, the developers become a legal user in the sense of the EU Software Directive. However, they do not automatically receive all users' rights. Facebook's policy specifies that

> [y]ou will not sell, transfer, or sublicense Platform to anyone. Except as expressly licensed herein, you will not use, access, integrate with, modify, translate, create derivative works of, reverse engineer, or otherwise exploit Platform or any aspect thereof. The Facebook Companies reserve all rights, title, and interest (including the right to enforce any such rights) not expressly granted in these Terms.[47]

3.2 About Linking and Sharing of Protected Content

3.2.1 Hyperlinking and Sharing As Acts of Communication to the Public

3.2.1.1 General Jurisprudential Framework on the Right of Communication to the Public

The last decade has seen tremendous case-law development related to the right of communication to the public and, more specifically, as regards its enforcement in the online environment. In hindsight, this should not have been a surprise. A major trend of digitalization has been taking place over the past three decades. The rise of cloud, streaming and Web 2.0 technologies are driving users even further from "old" storage techniques. Therefore, from a copyright law perspective, we see a decline of the importance of the right of reproduction in favor of the right of communication to the public. This right-holder's prerogative appeared in international copyright law with the amendment of the Berne Convention in 1928. It has been transposed into EU copyright law through Article 3 of the Infosoc Directive, which states that

> the exclusive right to authorise or prohibit any communication to the public of their works, by wire or wireless means, including the making available to the public of their works in

---

[47] https://developers.facebook.com/terms/.

such a way that members of the public may access them from a place and at a time individually chosen by them.

The notion of "communication to the public" has been examined by the landmark Rafael Hoteles decision,[48] relating to broadcasts of television programs in hotel rooms. The ECJ concluded that this activity does belong to the right of communication to the public. It emerges from this decision that communication to the public requires two cumulative analyses: communication and the public. "Communication" is broadly interpreted as any kind of intervention in the process of the dissemination of the protected work. For instance, in this case, the connection of TV devices to a central antenna was deemed to be a sufficient interference.

The "public" is defined by reference to a series of criteria: the existence or not of an economic benefit in the communication, a new public, and an audience that is larger than one user's own private or family circle. The concept of an economic benefit has provoked reactions from the academic community, since it is absent from the international legal framework. However, its usefulness has been demonstrated in subsequent cases, such as the Del Corso decision.[49] In this case, the ECJ rejected the application of the right of communication to the public to the installation of a radio device in the waiting room of a dentist's office, considering that the radio broadcast cannot be part of the economic services provided by the office, as it does not give the service a "competitive advantage".

Furthermore, the notion of the "new public" acquires a critical importance. The concept is used in the frame of a retransmission, in order to ensure that the second communication is ontologically independent from the first. Therefore, a comparison is made between the public at whom the original right-holder's communication was aimed and the public that is concerned by the litigious second communication. For instance, in the TV Catch up case, a company took the initiative of casting a TV channel's analog television signal on the Internet. The company profited from the advertisement(s) shown on the edge of the screen. Users were contractually bound to declare that they were from the country (implicitly, that they already had the opportunity to receive the analog signal). Nevertheless, the Court decided that the change in the nature of the transmission (from analog to digital) had, as an automatic consequence, the creation of a new public. In other words, the original target of the transmission was the owner of a television in the country while the new transmission concerned any Internet user in the country.

---

[48] ECJ, C-306/05, Sociedad General de Autores y Editores de España (SGAE) v. Rafael Hoteles SA, 7/12/2006, ECLI:EU:C:2006:764.

[49] ECJ, C-135/10, Società Consortile Fonografici (SCF) v. Marco Del Corso, 15/03/2012, ECLI:EU:C:2012:140.

3.2.1.2 Legal Issues Relating to Hyperlinks

Through the Rafael Hoteles and Reha Training[50] decisions, as well a series of subsequent decisions applying this test to various situations (another hotel,[51] café-bar,[52] and spa[53]) the ECJ has provided a rich jurisprudence and a very broad definition of communication to the public. However, this extensive definition potentially conflicts with the classic degree of freedom that governs the Internet. Most content on Facebook is not "original content" in the sense that it does not belong to the user who uploads or shares it. On the other hand, the platform has become a digital place to share articles, videos, pictures, text, and music, with or without comments. No reproduction is involved in the process of sharing. The user posts on the platform a hyperlink that leads to the source content and by default Facebook adds a "preview snippet" to the link, which transforms the link into a visual thumbnail of the source content. By extension, the same logic applies to the "share" button on the platform, which could be seen as an internal hyperlinking mechanism. The "like" button indirectly serves the same purpose, as content is promoted to friends' news feeds through this action.

Promoting access to protected content through a hyperlink constitutes, in the light of the above jurisprudence, an intervention that facilitates access to the work. However, to accept that Facebook's users, and even the platform itself to some extent, would be making an act of communication to the public in such situations would have potentially disastrous consequences for the Internet.[54] The seminal decision Svensson[55] solves this dilemma and provides the basis of a specific legal framework for hyperlinking. This decision builds upon previous decisions relating to communication to the public and separates its reasoning into two main aspects of the discussion: the notion of communication and the notion of the public.

As regards communication, although some scholars (amongst which is the prestigious European Copyright Society) considered it abusive to regard a hyperlink as an act of communication,[56] the ECJ was bound by its previous jurisprudence to recognize that hyperlinks belong to the notion of intervention facilitating access to the work.

---

[50] ECJ, C-117/15, Reha Training, 31/06/2016, ECLI:EU:C:2016:379.

[51] ECJ, C-136/09, Organismos Sillogikis Diacheirisis Dimiourgon Theatrikon kai Optikoakoustikon Ergon v. Divani Akropolis Anonimi Xenodocheiaki kai Touristiki Etaireai, 18/03/2010, ECLI:EU:C:2010:151.

[52] ECJ, C-403/08, Football Association Premier League Ltd v. QC Leisure, 4/10/2011, ECLI:EU:C:2011:631.

[53] ECJ, C-351/12, Ochranný svaz autorský pro práva k dílům hudebním o.s. (OSA) / Léčebné lázně Mariánské Lázně as, 27/02/2014, ECLI:EU:C:2014:110.

[54] Arezzo (2014), p. IIC 524.

[55] ECJ, C-466/12, Nils Svensson, Sten Sjögren, Madelaine Sahlman, Pia Gadd v. Retriever Sverige AB, 13/02/2014, ECLI:EU:C:2014:76.

[56] European Copyright Society (2013).

Nevertheless, without a public, an act of communication alone does not trigger copyright protection. The ECJ specifically focuses on the criterion of the new public, which is normally as explained above, dependent on the right holder's intent with regard to the first act of communication. However, here the right-holder's intent is to be decided objectively: as soon as the content is freely accessible on the Internet, it is presumed that the right-holder had wanted to reach all Internet users as a public. The second act of communication (the hyperlink) in this context does not create a new public. Therefore, hyperlinking activities do not fall under the right-holder's exclusive right.

Despite the fact that this decision has been much criticized, it provides an elegant solution to the tense opposition between two approaches, one of copyright law and the other of the Internet. By default, hyperlinks are legitimate, without denying the existence of exclusive rights on the source content. However, the legality of hyperlinks has not been completely settled with the Svensson decision. Indeed, three basic issues remain: what acts and behaviors are covered by this specific rule? What if the first communication occurred without the consent of the right-holder? What if the right-holder's intent is clearly expressed in the first communication and does not cover all Internet users?

To answer these questions, it should be noted, first, that this specific application of the concept of communication to the public has been perceived as technologically neutral. In the Svensson case, the ECJ refused to differentiate between various kind of hyperlinks (in addition to a simple hyperlink on a webpage, it is possible to distinguish a frame link, a deep link to specific content, and an embedded link that actually presents the content). This approach has been confirmed in other cases. For instance, torrent keys, which are small files that provide access to a specific peer-to-peer network, have been assimilated into the definition of hyperlinks in the Pirate Bay case.[57] Also, in the Kodi box case,[58] the ECJ considered that the settings of a TV Android box that provide the user with access to private servers also fell within the scope of the Svensson jurisprudence. Therefore, a broad interpretation of the Svensson jurisprudence may be adopted, which encompasses any kind of technology that works in practice as a vessel towards access to the online content. In this context, Facebook's sharing and liking are deemed to facilitate access and should be assimilated into the definition of hyperlinks.

Secondly, as mentioned above, the Svensson case does not specify whether its scope extends to content that has been illegally communicated in the first place. For instance, if a video was illegally uploaded onto any social media platform and a user decides to share it with his or her friends on Facebook, a dilemma arises: if it is accepted that this situation falls within the scope of the Svensson jurisprudence, then the illegal sharing of content becomes legal, and copyright law provisions are de facto obsolete. If, on the other hand, we conclude that the illegality of the first

---

[57] ECJ, C-610/15, Stichting Brein v. Ziggo BV, XS4ALL Internet BV, 14/06/2017, ECLI:EU: C:2017:456.

[58] ECJ, C-527/15, Stichting Brein v. Jack Frederik Wullems, 26/04/2017, ECLI:EU:C:2017:300.

communication cannot be cured by the sharing, the end user ends up bearing a burden to acknowledge, at each moment, the status of the content as regards copyright law, and this burden is considered disproportionate in the light of Article 11 of the Charter, which protects freedom of expression.

The GS Media case[59] resolves this issue and completes the legal framework of hyperlinks introduced by the Svensson case. In this case, a newspaper published an article about a "playmate", a nude model affiliated with Playboy. It added some links to pictures of the model. The pictures were stored on an anonymous storage server without the consent of the right-holder. The ECJ states that, as a principle, there cannot be infringement of the right to communication to the public without intent, which implies full knowledge of the legal consequences of its action.[60]

Therefore, as a rule, the mere user who shares ordinary protected content does not infringe the right of communication to the public. On the other hand, "where it is established that such a person knew or ought to have known that the hyperlink he posted provides access to a work illegally placed on the internet",[61] the sharing is illegal. It is a matter of an in concreto assessment whether the content is of such a nature, or the circumstances are so clear, that it is possible to prove the real or constructed knowledge of the illegality of the content.

If we conclude that the basic user remains relatively protected by this ruling, the same cannot be said about the professional user. Indeed, the ECJ continues its reasoning and states that

> when the posting of hyperlinks is carried out for profit, it can be expected that the person who posted such a link carries out the necessary checks to ensure that the work concerned is not illegally published on the website to which those hyperlinks lead, so that it must be presumed that that posting has occurred with the full knowledge of the protected nature of that work and the possible lack of consent to publication on the internet by the copyright holder.[62]

In other words, the presumption of ignorance becomes a presumption of knowledge in the case of profit-making activities. This constitutes a simple presumption: whether a reasonable and diligent professional would have been in a position to detect the illegality of the first communication to the public.

As mentioned above, the Svensson/GS Media jurisprudence lacked clarity on one last point: what happens if the right-holder's intent to give free access to all Internet users in the first publication is not clearly expressed? Svensson's ratio decidendi is built on a technical presumption that uploading something on the Internet automatically means that all Internet users are the public for this communication, but in practice the right-holder may reserve his or her rights. In the situation where, through a disclaimer for instance, the right-holder indicates that he does not wish any kind of hyperlinks to his work to be posted, does the objective presumption that the upload

---

[59] ECJ, C-160/15, GS Media BV v. Sanoma Media Netherlands BV and Others, 08/09/2016, ECLI: EU:C:2016:644.

[60] Par.35 of the decision.

[61] Par.49 of the decision.

[62] Par.51 of the decision.

reaches the entire Internet landscape still stand or does it collapse and allow room for the declared intent that the concerned public targeted by the communication consists only of the website's visitors?

The Stephanie Sinclair case[63] from the US is characteristic of this problem. The photographer denied a newspaper the use of one of her photographs and the newspaper solved this issue by just embedding her Instagram photo in its article. The court at first dismissed the photographer's action, arguing that, pursuant to the terms and conditions of the service, Instagram may sublicense the content. However, the case reopened after evidence that Instagram never explicitly consented to the embedding of the photograph on the online newspaper, so the newspaper could not use Instagram's Platform Policy as a legal defense against Sinclair's copyright infringement claim.

From an EU law point of view, the newspaper apparently does not violate the photographer's exclusive right: the first publication was legitimate and was freely accessible; therefore the linking does not reach a new public. However, in 2020, Advocate General Maciej Szpunar delivered his Opinion in the case of VG Bild-Kunst,[64] a further case concerning the legality of linking. The Advocate General proposes a new interpretation of the Svensson / GS Media jurisprudence, which distinguishes between simple hyperlinks and inline hyperlinks that automatically execute.[65]

In the end, the Court did not follow this proposal in its decision,[66] opting for a simpler and more pragmatic one. Considering the overall need for the certainty of a legal framework, the ECJ reasoned that it is not practical to restrict the public of a specific website, if no technical measures of protection exist. Characteristically, it states that

> [i]t must be made clear that, in order to ensure legal certainty and the smooth functioning of the internet, the copyright holder cannot be allowed to limit his or her consent by means other than effective technological measures, (. . .). In the absence of such measures, it might prove difficult, particularly for individual users, to ascertain whether that right holder intended to oppose the framing of his or her works. To do so might prove even more difficult when that work is subject to sub-licences.[67]

Therefore, the fact that the protected work is in open access is enough to decide that no new public is involved in the new act of communication through the hyperlink, regardless of any disclaimer or other declaration of intent—provided, however, that

---

[63] Court Reopens Photographer's Lawsuit Against Mashable Over Instagram Embedding, https://petapixel.com/2020/06/24/court-reopens-photographers-lawsuit-against-mashable-over-instagram-embedding/.

[64] Szpunar (2020).

[65] Synodinou (2020).

[66] ECJ, C-392/19, VG Bild-Kunst v. Stiftung Preußischer Kulturbesitz, 09/03/2021, ECLI:EU:C:2021:181.

[67] Par. 46 of the decision.

the specific rules of the GS Media case as regards the illegality of the first act of communication are taken into account.

In conclusion, any intervention that facilitates access to a protected work is an act of communication. This applies to hyperlinks but also to the use of the "share" button on the platform. Even the "like" button is relevant, as the platform presents to the user's friends the content that he or she has liked. However, for a simple user, these activities do not touch a new public, as the content is already freely accessible on the Internet. This extends even to illegal content, unless the user knows or ought to know the illegality. The situation is more complex for professionals. This concerns, for instance, companies that use pages or groups in order to promote their business. In this case, and following the Svensson/GS Media jurisprudence, the publication of hyperlinks by the administrator or moderator would be heavily scrutinized and, if it transpires that the content was originally illegal, the person responsible for the illegal sharing will be liable for copyright law infringement.

3.2.1.3 Facebook's Liability for Hyperlinks

The above considerations mainly concern the user's liability for providing access to protected content through the platform. What of Facebook's liability in this context? In a sense, the platform also provides access to the content. However, some specificities apply here. First, as an Internet service provider, Facebook is protected from liability by the safe harbor mechanism (see Chap. 6).

Second, the ECJ has explained that the notion of facilitating access inherent to the concept of an act of communication has to be interpreted as operating in conjunction with an intent. In the YouTube decision, the Court underlined that it

> has, first, emphasised the indispensable role played by the platform operator and the deliberate nature of its intervention. That platform operator makes an 'act of communication' when it intervenes, in full knowledge of the consequences of its action, to give its customers access to a protected work, particularly where, in the absence of that intervention, those customers would not, in principle, be able to enjoy the broadcast work.[68]

In other words, Facebook does not even need the safe harbor mechanism as it is not liable in the first place: no act of communication occurs without intent to communicate the specific content.

For clarity, the Court also adds that

> the mere fact that the operator knows, in a general sense, that protected content is made available illegally on its platform is not sufficient ground to conclude that it intervenes with the purpose of giving internet users access to that content. The situation is, however, different where that operator, despite having been warned by the rightholder that protected

---

[68] ECJ, C-682/18 and C-683/18, Frank Peterson v. Google LLC, YouTube Inc., YouTube LLC, Google Germany GmbH (C-682/18), and Elsevier Inc. v. Cyando AG (C-683/18), 22/06/2021, ECLI:EU:C:2021:503, par.68.

content is being communicated illegally to the public via its platform, refrains from expeditiously taking the measures necessary to make that content inaccessible.[69]

However, the EU legislator has intervened in this debate and imposed a different approach, through Article 17 of the Digital Single Market Directive. This article is of extreme importance as it imposes some specific duties on Facebook to prevent copyright law infringement under some circumstances. These duties are justified by a principle, posed as an irrebuttable presumption, and in opposition with the ECJ's findings: Facebook does perform an act of communication to the public. Specifically, Article 17 (1) states that

> Member States shall provide that an online content-sharing service provider performs an act of communication to the public or an act of making available to the public for the purposes of this Directive when it gives the public access to copyright-protected works or other protected subject matter uploaded by its users. An online content-sharing service provider shall therefore obtain an authorisation from the rightholders referred to in Article 3(1) and (2) of Directive 2001/29/EC, for instance by concluding a licensing agreement, in order to communicate to the public or make available to the public works or other subject matter.

This lex specialis counteracts both the general principles of copyright law and the safe harbor mechanism. However, it does not mean that Facebook would be automatically liable for any illegal content shared on the platform. Article 17 (4) establishes specific duties (see Sect. 3.3.1) and, in case of compliance, allows for a rebuttal of the presumption created by Article 17 (1).

3.2.2   Hyperlinks to Press Articles, the Value Gap, and the Press Publisher's Exclusive Right

Facebook and press publishers have a complicated relationship. On the one hand, social networks contribute the most to the advertisement of content, as it is estimated that 30% of an online newspaper's traffic comes from social networks.[70] On the other hand, 6 out of 10 users are satisfied with just reading the title and won't continue with reading the article,[71] which is catastrophic for press publishers as their website is not visited. Therefore, we arrive at a paradoxical situation where Facebook becomes a primary news source, while not actually spending any money on news creation. At the other end of the scale, although online newspapers are remunerated by exploiting the traffic on their own websites, they do not receive any remuneration while being the creator of the content.

This situation is characteristic of a phenomenon described as the "value gap": online platforms economically exploit creations that constitute the huge majority of the content they host, and the creator does not receive the benefits. In the case of

---

[69] Par.85 of the decision.

[70] Gabielkov et al. (2016).

[71] Gabielkov et al. (2016) op.cit.

Facebook specifically, the platform automatically "reads" the hyperlink and produces a snippet with the picture and the headline of the article, which further aggravates the situation.

In order to combat the value gap, the EU legislator has introduced a new neighboring right into copyright law through the Digital Single Market Directive:[72] the press publisher's exclusive right on online uses of their articles. According to Article 15 of the Directive, press publishers receive protection for 2 years against the online use of their articles by information society service providers. This right was conceived as a bargaining tool in the discussions between press publishers and online service providers.

This directive at first was not meant to apply only to news aggregators, such as Google News. On the contrary, as mentioned above, a value gap also exists on social media. However, the application of Article 15 to social networks was the subject of extensive debate and much lobbying. In its final version, Article 15 explicitly excludes Facebook from its scope, stating that

> [t]he rights provided for in the first subparagraph shall not apply to private or non-commercial uses of press publications by individual users. The protection granted under the first subparagraph shall not apply to acts of hyperlinking.

Consequently, the status quo remains. On the one hand, the absence of an exclusive right to online use of articles on social networks corresponds to a traditional vision of copyright law and is in line with the defense of fundamental freedoms. Indeed, the news itself is only information and cannot be protected by copyright law, while the quoting of an article is protected as an exception to economic rights. On the other hand, the real problem of the value gap is left unresolved as regards social networks. It could be argued that article 15 only created a "private use" exception in favor of the users, but that it does not exempt Facebook from requiring licenses. Characteristically, a German collective management society adopted this interpretation and has submitted to Facebook a licence agreement for the amount of 190 million euros and concerning the use of press publishers' rights for 2022.[73] In other parts of the world, the debate is still going on, with Australia for instance, pushing for its own press publishers' right that would mainly apply to Google and Facebook.[74]

---

[72] Directive (EU) 2019/790 of the European Parliament and of the Council of 17 April 2019 on copyright and related rights in the Digital Single Market and amending Directives 96/9/EC and 2001/29/EC, ELI: http://data.europa.eu/eli/dir/2019/790/oj.

[73] Corint Media (2022).

[74] Furgal (2020).

3.3   Facebook's Duty to Filter Content Infringing Copyright Law

3.3.1   Article 17 of the Digital Single Market Directive

The potential liability of the platform's users in case of copyright law infringement must be viewed in context. In practice, litigation against mere users is rare and often counterproductive. Another, more efficient, strategy would be to directly involve the platform in the process of combating infringement. After much controversy, this was achieved with the enactment of a new legal framework that creates some duties for social media: the much-discussed Article 17 of the Digital Single Market Directive. This article constitutes a derogation from the general legal framework, which is normally a lot more protective of the online intermediary.[75]

The article concerns online content-sharing service providers, as defined in Article 2 of the Directive. The notion of content-sharing service providers (OCSSP) is strictly defined, as a means to protect the freedom of commerce and the freedom of expression of small platforms with an altruistic purpose. The directive defines the 'online content-sharing service provider' as

> a provider of an information society service of which the main or one of the main purposes is to store and give the public access to a large amount of copyright-protected works or other protected subject matter uploaded by its users, which it organises and promotes for profit-making purposes.[76]

However, this definition has to be completed, as the most innovative part of Article 17 (the ambiguous and controversial duty to filter) does not concern businesses "which have been available to the public in the Union for less than three years and which have an annual turnover below EUR 10 million".[77] In any case, Facebook doubtlessly meets the conditions of the definition of an OCSSP.

The principal purpose of Article 17 is to compel OCSSPs to obtain blanket licenses for each Member State from collective management organizations.[78] The blanket licenses do not concern sharing and hyperlink activities but the uploading of protected content by the users. The Directive stipulates that an OCSSP performs an act of communication to the public or an act of making available to the public when it gives the public access to copyright-protected works or other protected subject matter uploaded by its users.[79]

The main mechanism of Article 17 lies in the fourth paragraph:

---

[75] See article 17 (3) of the Directive, that explicitly states the regime as a derogation to the system of limitation of liability.

[76] Article 2 (6) of the Digital Single Market Directive.

[77] Article 17 (6) of the Digital Single Market Directive.

[78] Castro (2021), pp. 49–76.

[79] Article 17 (1) of the Digital Single Market Directive.

If no authorisation is granted, online content-sharing service providers shall be liable for unauthorised acts of communication to the public, including making available to the public, of copyright-protected works and other subject matter, unless the service providers demonstrate that they have:

(a) made best efforts to obtain an authorisation, and
(b) made, in accordance with high industry standards of professional diligence, best efforts to ensure the unavailability of specific works and other subject matter for which the rightholders have provided the service providers with the relevant and necessary information; and in any event
(c) acted expeditiously, upon receiving a sufficiently substantiated notice from the rightholders, to disable access to, or to remove from their websites, the notified works or other subject matter, and made best efforts to prevent their future uploads in accordance with point (b).

Point (a) of the article establishes the principle of negotiations with right-holders and point (c) reiterates the importance of the reporting system and the duty to quickly react to the report that had already been implemented in the e-Commerce Directive. Article 17 (4) (b) innovates as it creates a new kind of duty: the "best efforts to ensure the unavailability of specific works". Therefore, no explicit reference is made to a filtering duty. This point was indeed one of the most controversial of the Directive due to its adverse effect on the freedom of expression[80] and references to a filter disappeared from the final version of the text. However, it is difficult to imagine how it will be possible to ensure the unavailability of the potentially infringing content without some automatization, since on principle the rule refers to hosting services of massive content.[81]

3.3.2   The Ambiguous Interpretations of Article 17

Article 17 (4) presents a legal challenge for the scholar: on the one hand, it lacks the clarity and the explicit mandate to generalize ex ante control of the content; on the other hand, it imposes the obligation to ensure the unavailability of the content. Furthermore, an ex ante control would constitute a serious limitation to the freedom of expression. Besides, Poland had even asked the ECJ to judge the compatibility of Article 17 with the Charter of Fundamental Rights. However, the Advocate General considered in its opinion that Article 17 is compatible with the Charter and should not be annulled.[82] Very lucidly, the Advocate General admits that Article 17 (4) de facto imposes the use of content recognition tools.[83] Consequently, Article 17's enforcement entails an 'interference' with the freedom of expression of the users of sharing

---

[80] Guzel (2021), pp. 205–229.

[81] Metzger et al. (2020).

[82] Øe (2021).

[83] Par. 62 of the Opinion.

services. Nevertheless, the Advocate General does not see this interference as disproportionate.

The EU Commission, in its guidance on Article 17, proposes a compromise to solve this uncertainty.[84] It recommends limiting automated ex ante blocking of content identified by right-holders to 'manifestly infringing uploads' only. It implies both the existence of an efficient AI analysis and a risk-based approach that filters only content manifestly flagged as infringing copyright law. The ECJ confirmed this position and dismissed the Poland's action, considering that the mitigation measures and safeguards against the potential negative effects of the filtering system implied in article 17 were sufficient to justify, under the principle of proportionality, a restriction to freedom of expression. Notably, the existence of complaint and redress mechanisms or the mandatory protection of copyright law's exception such as parody have to play a substantial role in the practical function of the article 17.[85]

The concept of preventive action against illegal content had already been implemented on a voluntary basis by Google for its YouTube service in 2007. The system, called "content ID", works as a digital fingerprinting system. When a work is uploaded, its "digital fingerprint" is compared to those of the existing works in the database and a (quite efficient, but not perfect)[86] conclusion can be drawn as to whether the work infringes a previous existing work. In 2016, Facebook introduced a similar tool, called the "Rights Manager".[87] It offers the opportunity to "creators and publishers who have a large or growing catalog of content that people love to share" to register their content in order to track where it has been uploaded by another user on the platform. The service, originally conceived for videos, was extended to photos in 2020.

Are the existing measures in line with the provisions of Article 17 (4) (b)? The reference to "high industry standards" seems to refer to various levels of digital fingerprinting. Indeed, a very basic transposition would be to just compare the "hash" of the files in order to determine if the files are identical. In this case, the system would be very easy to manipulate: changing a video length for one second or the photography size would suffice to obtain a different digital fingerprint. Therefore, to pass the "high industry standards" test, the digital fingerprinting needs to be more sophisticated, so as to analyze the content itself.

Nevertheless, it is not expected that automatic analysis will be perfect, especially in a field of law where the fragile equilibrium between exclusive rights and exceptions requires the expert eyes of a specialist. The system of notice and review is

---

[84] EU Commission (2021).

[85] ECJ, C-401/19, Republic of Poland v. European Parliament, 26 April 2022, ECLI:EU:C:2022:297.

[86] von Lohmann (2009).

[87] https://rightsmanager.fb.com/.

basically kept. The difference is that under the previous regime, the notice and take down approach created a massive burden on right-holders. In other words, the previous system would necessitate a continuous monitoring of the social network by the right-holders, as the users would have been free to re-upload the same infringing content for an indefinite number of times. Now, the mechanism is reversed: as the system automatically recognizes the potentially litigious character of the content, the burden falls on the user to report a false result. Nevertheless, the use of automatic decision-making should also trigger the user's right to explanation (see Sect. 8.3.2).

Furthermore, it should be noted that the mechanism does not necessarily result in a loss of content and interaction from the users. Indeed, Article 17 places an emphasis on licensing, and in practice both YouTube and Facebook's filtering mechanisms offer alternative solutions. The right-holder on YouTube often chooses not to block the infringing content but to "monetize" it, that is to claim revenues from its profits. Similarly, in addition to blocking measures, Facebook's mechanism includes the options to monitor the content or attribute credit via an ownership link.

3.4 Facebook and the Industrial Property Laws

3.4.1 Trade Mark Law, Hashtags, and Domain Name Protection

3.4.1.1 Facebook As a Trade Mark

Trade mark law provides virtually perpetual protection for a sign, provided that it is periodically (every 10 years) renewed. Parallel to the harmonized legal framework of national trade marks in the EU, the EU legislator has also instituted an EU trade mark regime with unitary effect.[88] However, as a fundamental principle of trade mark law, the protection is not absolute. Only the specific link established in the mind of the average consumer between a company and a product or service deserves trade mark protection, which means that the registration of the trade mark must declare what product or service is concerned. Practically, the EU trade mark system uses the international Nice Classification[89] for this purpose.[90]

---

[88] Regulation (EU) 2017/1001 of the European Parliament and of the Council of 14 June 2017 on the European Union trade mark, OJ L 154, 16.6.2017, p. 1–99, ELI: http://data.europa.eu/eli/reg/2017/1001/oj.

[89] Nice Agreement Concerning the International Classification of Goods and Services for the Purposes of the Registration of Marks, 1957.

[90] Article 33 of the Regulation.

Facebook registered the word Facebook as a European trade mark in 2001 in classes 16,[91] 35,[92] 38,[93] and 41.[94] In 2010, the company filed a figurative trade mark, comprising the word Facebook, written in a specific font and in white characters on a blue rectangular background. Over the years, through additional registrations, both the word and the figurative representations have been protected in additional classes (for instance, for alcoholic beverages), the practical result being that the word is protected in virtually all industry sectors. This evolution was completed in 2018 with a general registration in classes 1 to 45. In addition to the "Facebook" sign, the company also registered various other trade marks, amongst which the stylized "f" in both black and white or with the iconic blue background, the stylized "like with a thumbs up icon" sign, the figurative sign showing a hand forming a thumbs up, and the messenger app icon (a horizontal white bolt of lightning on a pink and blue background).

The validity of this registration depends, notably, on the distinctive character of the sign. However, this specific sign is composed of two banal words: "face", and "book", which are descriptive. Nevertheless, the "BABY-DRY" jurisprudence could apply by analogy. In this case, the ECJ considered that the "descriptiveness must be determined not only in relation to each word taken separately but also in relation to the whole which they form."[95] Consequently, a word combination may provide a distinctive character to a sign. Nevertheless, the sign "Facebook" does not refer to a book of faces stricto sensu. The use of this sign for a social media platform denotes a distinctive character.

However, although the concern that the word should not be appropriated by third parties for merchandising purposes is understandable, it could be argued that the company's strategy of overreaching protection of its trade mark(s) is potentially dangerous. Indeed, the ECJ has explained, in the landmark IP Translator case,[96] that a core component of EU trade mark law is the principle of specialty. The court considers that the application of the EU trade mark law regime depends, to a great

---

[91] "Printed matter, newspapers, books, periodicals, journals, printed publications, magazines, photographs".

[92] "Advertising; business management; business administration; office functions; advertising and information distribution services, namely, providing classified advertising space via the global computer network; promoting the goods and services of others over the Internet; compilation and management of on-line computer databases and on-line searchable database".

[93] "Telecommunications; telecommunications via Internet networks, communications by computer terminals."

[94] "Education; providing of training; entertainment; sporting and cultural activities; providing an online directory information service featuring information regarding, and in the nature of, collegiate life, general interest, classifieds, virtual community, social networking, photo sharing, and transmission of photographic images."

[95] ECJ, C-383/99 P, Procter & Gamble v. OHIM, 20/09/2001, ECLI:EU:C:2001:461.

[96] ECJ, C-307/10, Chartered Institute of Patent Attorneys v. Registrar of Trade Marks, 19/06/2012, ECLI:EU:C:2012:361.

extent, on whether the goods or services covered by a registered trade mark are indicated with sufficient clarity and precision.[97]

Nevertheless, it is fair to assume that the trade mark has acquired the status of a well-known mark and its protection exceeds the range of the services it is registered in. Indeed, in this case, the Regulation recognizes additional prerogatives to the right-holder. Overall, Article 9 of the EU Trade Mark Regulation institutes three rights for the trade mark owner: the right to oppose the use of his trade mark in the same specialty, the right to oppose to the use of a similar but not identical sign in the same specialty, but on the condition that "exists a likelihood of confusion on the part of the public", and, finally—only in the case of well-known trademark—the right to oppose the use of an identical or similar sign irrespective of the specialty, where the "use of that sign without due cause takes unfair advantage of, or is detrimental to, the distinctive character or the repute of the EU trade mark".

Meta has had to defend its trade mark in the past in various disputes against owners of various signs, arguably similar to Facebook. For instance, Bearbook, PlaceBook, Shagbook, FacebookOfPorn, Faceporn, Lamebook, and Teachbook signs have been served a lawsuit from the company.[98] In some cases, the lawsuit is just a first move towards settlement. In the Lamebook case, Facebook settled with the parody site, when the latter agreed that it would not apply for trade mark protection of its sign.[99] This strategy is not without risk. In the Shagbook case, which concerned an adult dating network, the other company counter-attacked, challenging the validity of Facebook's trade mark before the US courts.[100]

3.4.1.2   Facebook and the Hashtag Function

One of the most interesting issues concerning Facebook and EU trade mark law consists in the uses and misuses of the so-called "hashtag" function.[101] A hashtag is a metadata tag that is prefaced by the hash symbol, #. It has been popularized mainly through Twitter, which generalizes its use as a user-generated tagging and indexing function. Through the hashtag, a user may find other content that incorporates the same keyword. The popularity of this function has slowly grown to its current form as an indispensable tool for some popular movements, such as "#JeSuisCharlie" or "#MeToo". Facebook introduced it on the platform in 2015.

While in principle, Facebook, as an online intermediary, is protected against liability for the use of hashtags that infringe trade marks (see Chap. 6), the situation differs as regards the author of the hashtag. Unless the trade mark includes the hash symbol, which is possible but not common, the use of a protected word as a hashtag

---

[97] Par.42 of the decision.

[98] Sganga (2013), p. 301.

[99] Bruce (2011).

[100] Online personals Watch (2013).

[101] Butwin (2015), p. 110.

would be prohibited as it may result in a likelihood of confusion with regard to similar signs in the mind of the average user. As hashtags nowadays play an integral role in companies' overall marketing strategies, the temptation for a competitor to use an "illegal" hashtag to attract new clients is real. In the US, some cases have already condemned the use of a trademarked word in a hashtag without the permission of the trade mark owner.[102]

The same conclusion could be reached under EU law. However, it does not mean that every use of a trade mark in a hashtag is illegal. In addition to the need to prove the likelihood of confusion, the ECJ has often insisted on interpreting the trade mark owner's rights in the light of the essential function of the trademark.

The ECJ's Interflora case[103] is, in this matter, of specific interest. Using the "AdWords" referencing service, Marks & Spencer's selected the keyword "Interflora", which is protected as a trade mark. Consequently, when internet users entered the word "Interflora" or one of its variants as a search term into Google's search engine, a Marks & Spencer's advertisement appeared under the heading "sponsored links", offering an online flower-delivery online service.

First of all, the ECJ states as a principle that "the proprietor of the trade mark cannot prevent the use of a sign identical to its trade mark as a keyword", unless all the conditions provided for this in the trade mark legislation are met.[104] In other words, the third party using the trade mark is liable only if the use has an adverse effect on one of the functions of the mark. The ECJ has listed three essential functions of the mark: the protection of the origin of the activity (which implies the protection of the quality of the good or service), the protection of the advertising, and the protection of the communication investment function (the protection of the client's loyalty related to the general reputation of the mark's owner).

With regard to the function of protection of the origin of the activity, the use of a protected keyword (and the same reasoning works for a hashtag too) does not automatically entail liability. It actually depends on the knowledge of a reasonably well-informed and reasonably observant internet user: is he or she aware that the keyword or hashtag is being used by someone who is not the trade mark owner, or, on the contrary, does this use confuse him or her as regards the origin of the product or service?

With regard to the advertising function of the mark, the ECJ considers that the third party using the mark is not liable. The court notes that

> Internet advertising on the basis of keywords corresponding to trade marks constitutes such a practice in that its aim, as a general rule, is merely to offer internet users alternatives to the goods or services of the proprietors of those trade marks.[105]

---

[102] US District Court for the Eastern District of Louisiana, TWTB, Inc. v. Rampick, No. CV 15-3399, 2016 WL 236313; US District Court, Massachusetts, Pub. Impact, LLC v. Boston Consulting Grp., Inc., No. 15-13361-FDS, 2016 WL 1048884.

[103] ECJ, C-323/09, Interflora Inc., Interflora British Unit v. Marks & Spencer plc, Flowers Direct Online Ltd, 22/09/2011, ECLI:EU:C:2011:604.

[104] Par.32 of the decision.

[105] Par.58 of the decision.

Finally, with regards to the investment function of the mark, the ECJ estimates that the use has an adverse effect on the function only "if it substantially interferes with the proprietor's use of its trade mark to acquire or preserve a reputation capable of attracting consumers and retaining their loyalty".[106]

Finally, the situation is significantly different if the trade mark has a reputation ("well-known trade mark"), but, once again, the third party is not automatically liable for its use. It depends on the context of the situation. The Court demands proof that

> the competitor thereby takes unfair advantage of the distinctive character or repute of the trade mark (free-riding) or where the advertising is detrimental to that distinctive character (dilution) or to that repute (tarnishment). Advertising on the basis of such a keyword is detrimental to the distinctive character of a trade mark with a reputation (dilution) if, for example, it contributes to turning that trade mark into a generic term.[107]

In conclusion, a company that wishes to use hashtags on Facebook for a promotion campaign has to be aware of the potential legal consequences. While principles of freedom of expression and freedom of competition influence the answer, the Interflora case shows that it is a matter of carrying out an in concreto analysis of each specific situation as to whether the hashtag infringes the rights of the trade mark owner.

Furthermore, Facebook's liability in case of trade mark infringement cannot not be completely excluded, as one may consider that the company plays an active role in certain cases (see Sect. 6.1.2). On one hand, the ECJ has held, as regards the operation of an e-commerce platform, that the use of signs that are identical or similar to trade marks in offers for sale displayed in an online marketplace is made by the sellers who are customers of the that marketplace's operator and not by that operator itself.[108] Moreover, the ECJ also ruled that an e-commerce platform is not liable for any counterfeit products it stores on behalf of the seller.[109] However, new developments concerning the intermediary's safe harbor requires a stricter approach to the platform's liability. The pending Louboutin case[110] will certainly provide much guidance in resolving the remaining issues. In this case, the question directly concerns the liability of a platform in case of an advertisement that is infringing a trade mark. While the court at first instance accepted that the platform was liable, the Court of Appeal partly reversed the decision.[111]

---

[106] Par.66 of the decision.

[107] Par.83 of the decision.

[108] ECJ, C-324/09, L'Oréal and Others, 12/07/2011, EU:C:2011:474, par.103.

[109] ECJ, C-567/18, Coty Germany GmbH v. Amazon Services Europe Sàrl, Amazon Europe Core Sàrl, Amazon FC Graben GmbH, Amazon EU Sàrl, 02/04/2020, ECLI:EU:C:2020:267.

[110] ECJ, C-148/21, Louboutin, pending.

[111] Court of Appeal of Brussels (9th Chamber), Amazon Europe Core sàrl, Amazon EU sàrl and Amazon Services Europe sàrl v. Mr. C. Louboutin, 25 June 2020, published in Ing. Cons. 2020/2, p. 509.

3.4.2   Patent Law

Facebook's success is arguably based on various mathematical or commercial methods of interaction with its users and most of these methods could qualify as an algorithm. However, patent law does not protect algorithms per se, as mathematical methods do not fall within the scope of the definition of an invention.[112] The same principle also applies to computer programs, as they are normally protected through copyright law.[113] However, in practice, the European Patent Office (EPO), created by the European Patent Convention (EPC),[114] shows more flexibility, as it is possible to patent an algorithm-based invention if the contribution made by the mathematical method to the technical character of an invention serves a technical purpose.[115]

Facebook certainly uses this flexibility, following a general trend of Internet giants relying on patent law for the protection of innovative products and methods. In 2013, Meta owned (only) 127 patents in the US, in comparison to 1317 patents registered in 2019.[116] For instance, Meta has been granted various patents protecting the graphic interface of its platform.[117] More recently, the company proceeded to file a new wave of patents to accompany its investment strategy on multiverse. The patents contain inventions such as a system for tracking a user's facial expressions through a headset that will then adapt media content based on those responses.[118]

This strategy of exponentially expanding its patent portfolio could be seen as a preventive measure, as Meta itself has confessed that it does not really mean to use all of its patents in future products.[119] Put otherwise, fear of patent trolls (companies that maliciously register fallacious and abusive patent applications without any intent of really applying them in an industrial context, but only for purpose of blackmailing industries that use the methods covered by the patent), has tended to transform the GAFAM into patent trolls themselves.

Some of these patents propose new methods of profiling based on identification of pattern algorithms that are very intrusive for the user.[120] For instance, the US Patent "US20160316341A1"[121] protects the social networking implications of a "[d] eviation from the estimated routine of the user may be calculated based on the

---

[112] Article 52 (2) (a) of the European Patent Convention.

[113] Article 52 (2) (c) of the European Patent Convention.

[114] European Patent Convention, 17th edition, 2020.

[115] See OEB, T 1358/09, Classification/BDGB ENTERPRISE SOFTWARE, 21.11.2014.

[116] Tankovska (2021).

[117] See Patent USD912075S1, Display device or portion thereof with graphical user interface, https://patents.google.com/patent/USD912075S1/en ; patent USD910032S1, Display device or portion thereof with graphical user interface, https://patents.google.com/patent/USD910032S1/en.

[118] Murphy (2022).

[119] Chan (2019).

[120] Chinoy (2018).

[121] Routine deviation notification (2013) https://patents.google.com/patent/US20160316341A1/en.

distance between the current ambient-location reading and the routine location expected for the particular time of day and day of the week". In other words, the platform would identify the user's life habits and notify for instance nearby friends in case of a deviation from the registered habits.

However, these US patents do not necessarily reflect the EPO's position on this issue. Meta, like most tech giants, files its patent applications via the Patent Cooperation Treaty (PCT)[122] route. A PCT application is an application before a national office (for Facebook, the US Patent and Trademark Office (USPTO) is usually preferred), which establishes a filing date for all contracting states. A PCT patent is not a unitary international patent, but only a unified procedure. As regards the validity of a PCT patent from a substantive law perspective, the EPO is certainly not bound by the administrative or judicial decisions in the US. On the contrary, under the European Patent regime delivered by the EPO, harmonization of substantive patent law is achieved; however, the protection of the patent is ensured at national level by the contracting parties of the EPC. Simultaneously, the EU is still in the process of implementing an EU unitary patent, which would also be managed by the EPO, and which would provide one patent with unitary effect on the entire EU.[123]

In this context, it should be noted that the EPO is known to be stricter than the US office in assessing the substantive conditions for the grant of a patent. The patent should be an invention, novel, showing an inventive step, and susceptible of industrial application. As explained above, there is some flexibility as regards the notion of invention, that could indirectly cover algorithms in certain cases. However, the algorithm must pass the "inventive step" test, which is more demanding. The invention is considered to involve an inventive step if, having regards to the state of the art, it is not obvious to a person skilled in the art. [124] In this context, the so-called "problem-solution approach" is applied by the EPO, which consists of three stages: (1) determining the "closest prior art", (2) establishing the "objective technical problem" to be solved, and (3) considering whether or not the claimed invention, starting from the closest prior art and the objective technical problem, would have been obvious to the skilled person.

Applying this problem-solution approach to most of Facebook's patents would potentially lead to the invalidation of some of them in Europe. The most characteristic and famous example of the differences in approach between the US and Europe in this field is the case of Amazon's 1-click button. In 2009, a patent was granted by the USPTO for the commercial method consisting of linking cookies technology and e-commerce in order to offer a button leading to a shopping cart. A similar application, however, was rejected by the EPO.[125] Of course, it is important to avoid using

---

[122] Patent Cooperation Treaty, Washington, 1970.

[123] The two EU regulations establishing the Unitary Patent system (No 1257/2012 and No 1260/2012) entered into force in 2013, but they will only apply as from the date of entry into force of the Unitary Patent Convention Agreement, which encountered legal difficulties (litigation in Germany about its constitutionality).

[124] See EPO (2021), p. 803.

[125] EPO, T 1244/07, 1-Click/AMAZON, 27.1.2011.

hindsight when judging the inventive step and the validity of a 1999 application should not be doubted just because the technology became trivial afterwards. However, the Board noted that the 1-click button was more an immediate application of a new programming feature as soon as it had become available in that field,[126] obvious for the skilled computer scientist.

The EPO Board of Appeals has taken a position on some of Facebook's patents. In the first case, a patent application that related to social graphs and performing searches for objects within a social-networking environment was refused by the Examining Division. The invention involved a search process which maps natural language text input to elements of a social-graph database in the context of a social network. In other words, when the system encounters a vague search, the ambiguous word or expression is interpreted with respect to its relevance in the social-graph analysis[127] and the invention consists in the addition of keywords selected from a user's long-term interest to disambiguate the query. On appeal, the EPO considered that this application lacked inventive step, as the distinguishing features of the invention do not contribute to the solution of a technical problem.[128]

In the second case,[129] the ground for refusing Facebook's application was lack of novelty. The invention concerned a method of sharing locations of members participating in an online social networking service. The technical effect provided by the distinguishing features is that, since both location information and status information are updated, the location-based matching can consider which members of the group are actually in proximity to each other, instead of being based on registrations for an event at a particular location. The Board considered that this solution did not differ from the prior state of the art in this field.

In conclusion, the European legal framework on patents, through the double test of novelty and inventive step, has successfully prevented (until now) the abuse of patent law and it is cited as an example in a US plagued by patent trolls.[130] For Meta, however, this means that its relatively new strategy of large-scale patent applications (notably on the model of Apple) will encounter legal difficulties in Europe. These difficulties have to be put into context, as, in the digital era, the partial validity of a patent in the US is enough to successfully prevent competitors from copying the invention. Indeed, the alternative would be for competitors to offer the online service that incorporates the invention to non-US users only.

---

[126] Par.20 of the decision.

[127] The Social-graph analysis views social relationships in terms of network theory consisting of nodes and edges (Nodes represent the individual actors within the networks, and edges represent the relationships between the actors).

[128] EPO, T 1089/17, Ambiguous queries on online social networks/FACEBOOK, 7.2.2020.

[129] EPO, T 0572/15, Locating web-based social network members/FACEBOOK, 11.12.2019.

[130] Mayergoyz (2009), p. 241.

References

Adeney E (2013) Appropriation in the name of art: is a quotation exception the answer? Aust Intellect Prop J 23:142, Available at SSRN: https://ssrn.com/abstract=2853788 or. https://doi.org/10.2139/ssrn.2853788

Arezzo E (2014) Hyperlinks and making available right in the European Union — what future for the internet after Svensson? Int Rev Intellect Prop Compet Law 45(5):IIC 524

Bently L, Sherman B (2014) Brad intellectual property law, 4th edn. Oxford University Press, Oxford

Bruce K (2011) Facebook and Lamebook settle trademark dispute. AdLaw By Request. https://www.adlawbyrequest.com/2011/09/articles/in-the-courts/facebook-and-lamebook-settle-trademark-dispute

Butwin BA (2015) # Trademarklaw: protecting and maximizing the value of trademarks in an evolving social media marketplace. Cybaris Intellect Prop Law Rev 7:110

Castro RV (2021) How Article 17 of the digital single market directive should be implemented: a personal view. In: Synodinou J, Markou P-M (eds) EU internet law in the digital single market. Springer, Cham, pp 49–76

Chan J (2019) How patents drive innovation at Facebook. Facebook Newsroom. https://about.fb.com/news/2019/08/how-patents-drive-innovation/

Chinoy S (2018) What 7 creepy patents reveal about Facebook. The New York Times. https://www.nytimes.com/interactive/2018/06/21/opinion/sunday/facebook-patents-privacy.html

Corint Media (2022) Corint Media submits to Facebook a licence agreement for the use of press publishers' right. Press Release, https://www.corint-media.com/wp-content/uploads/2021/12/211202_PR-Corint-Media_GmbH_Corint-Media-submits-licence-agreement-to-Facebook.pdf

Del Vigna F, Cimino A, Dell'Orletta F, Petrocchi M, Tesconi M (2017) Hate me, hate me not: hate speech detection on facebook. In: Proceedings of the First Italian Conference on Cybersecurity (ITASEC17). pp. 86–95

EPO (2021) Guidelines for examination in the European Patent Office, Part G – Chapter VII-1, p. 803

EU Commission (2021) Guidance on the application of Article 17 of the new Copyright Directive. COM/2021/288 final

European Copyright Society (2013) Opinion on the reference to the CJEU in Case C-466/12 Svensson. https://europeancopyrightsociety.org/opinion-on-the-reference-to-the-cjeu-in-case-c-46612-svensson/

Furgal U (2020) Making google and facebook pay? Comparing the EU press publishers' right and Australian Draft Media Bargaining Code. CREATe. https://www.create.ac.uk/blog/2020/09/15/making-google-and-facebook-pay-comparing-the-eu-press-publishers-right-and-australian-draft-media-bargaining-code/

Gabielkov M, Ramachandran A, Chaintreau A, Legout A (2016) Social clicks: what and who gets read on Twitter?. ACM SIGMETRICS/IFIP Performance 2016, Antibes Juan-les-Pins, France. hal-01281190

Guzel SG (2021) Directive on Copyright in the Digital Single Market and Freedom of Expression: The EU's Online Dilemma. In: Synodinou TE, Jougleux P, Markou C, Prastitou-Merdi T (eds) EU Internet Law in the Digital Single Market. Springer, Cham, pp 205–229

Jütte B (2019) CJEU permits sampling of phonograms under a de minimis rule and the quotation exception. J Intellect Prop Law Practice 14(11):827–829. https://doi.org/10.1093/jiplp/jpz120

Mayergoyz A (2009) Lessons from Europe on how to tame US Patent Trolls. Cornell Int Law J 42: 241

Metzger A, Senftleben M, Derclaye E et al (2020) Selected aspects of implementing Article 17 of the Directive on copyright in the digital single market into National Law – Comment of the European Copyright Society. SSRN Electronic J. https://doi.org/10.2139/ssrn.3589323

Murphy H (2022) Facebook patents reveal how it intends to cash in on metaverse. Financial Times. https://www.ft.com/content/76d40aac-034e-4e0b-95eb-c5d34146f647

Øe S (2021) Opinion on Case C-401/19 Republic of Poland v. European Parliament, Council of the European Union, 15/07/2021, ECLI:EU:C:2021:613

Online Personals Watch (2013) Facebook Vs Shagbook: Facebook trademark at risk? https://www.onlinepersonalswatch.com/news/2013/11/facebook-vs-shagbook-facebook-trademark-at-risk.html

Paramythiotis Y (2021) Fairness in copyright contract law - remuneration for authors and performers under the copyright in the digital single market directive. In: Synodinou T, Jougleux P, Markou C, Prastitou-Merdi T (eds) EU Internet law in the Digital Single Market. Springer International Publishing, Cham, pp 77–97

Sganga J (2013) Trademark owner's strategy: litigation versus the UDRP. Pepp Disp Resol Law J 13:301

Stewart DR (2012) Can I use this photo I found on Facebook-applying copyright law and fair use analysis to photographs on social networking sites republished for news reporting purposes. J Telecomm High Technol Law 10:93

Synodinou ET (2019) The Renckhoff case: 6 degrees of separation from the lawful user. ERA Forum 20:21–33. https://doi.org/10.1007/s12027-019-00558-w

Synodinou ET (2020) Copyright law trapped in the web of hyperlinking: the AG's Opinion in the VG Bild-Kunst case (Part I). Kluwer Copyright Blog, http://copyrightblog.kluweriplaw.com/2020/10/22/copyright-law-trapped-in-the-web-of-hyperlinking-the-ags-opinion-in-the-vg-bild-kunst-case-part-i/

Szpunar M (2020) Opinion on VG Bild-Kunst v. Stiftung Preußischer Kulturbesitz, case C-392/19, ECLI identifier: ECLI:EU:C:2020:696

Tankovska H (2021) Number of patents in the United States granted to Facebook from 2013 to

van Gompel S, Lavik E (2013) Quality, merit, aesthetics and purpose: An inquiry into EU copyright law's eschewal of other criteria than originality. RIDA (236):100–295

Vaver D (2002) Principles of copyright, cases and material. World International Property Organization, Geneva. Publication No. 844(A/E/F), pp 15–20

von Lohmann F (2009) Testing YouTube's Audio content ID system, Electronic Frontier Foundation, https://www.eff.org/deeplinks/2009/04/testing-youtubes-aud

Chapter 4
Data Ownership (and Succession Law)

The protection of personal data is enshrined in the fundamental right to personality. Nevertheless, this paradigm obscures another reality: data, both personal and non-personal, have become a commodity. However, while intellectual property rights accept ownership over intangible goods, mere information is considered, as a general principle, to be free of protection from intellectual property regimes. Simultaneously, academic challenges, theoretical obstacles and legal uncertainty have not prevented the market from treating data in practice as a commodity. For example, Google buys data on a daily basis for the "Google Maps" service. Facebook's raison d'être is to economically exploit its users' data, presented as the flip side of the free access to the service.

Interestingly, scholars, some case-law, and even sometimes the EU legislator, concur in discerning or creating some embryonic forms of data protection (see Sect. 4.1). For Facebook, this theory has a direct practical impact. The main issue appears after the death of a user. Should the Facebook account, in accordance with the rules of succession law, be transferred to the heirs (see Sect. 4.2)?

4.1 Ownership of Accounts

4.1.1 The Contract Law Perspective

4.1.1.1 The User As a Sole Party

In the context of account ownership, before even discussing its practical and theoretical aspects, it should be recalled that some content is eligible for protection under copyright law (see Sect. 3.1.1). Therefore, both ownership and inheritance of these data are ensured by the legal framework, although the result of a court action would remain uncertain due to the flexibility of the concept of originality.

Furthermore, the burden of proving that specific content hosted on the platform is the property of an author will fall on his heirs.

The issue of account ownership should be dealt with first of all by applying principles of contract law. While in the previous Statement of Rights and Responsibilities, Facebook made a reference to the topic, explaining that "[y]ou own all of the content and information you post on Facebook, and you can control how it is shared through your privacy and application settings.", this phrase has now disappeared from the new Terms of Service.[1]

There is no established EU contract law principle as regards personal contracts. However, the notion of an "intuitu personae" contract, established in countries influenced by the French Civil Code, or the principle of "actio personalis moritur cum persona" ("a personal right of action dies with the person") in common law countries, seem to show that a consensus exists on the point that the contract automatically terminates at the moment of the death of one party when the parties have intended to regard this contract as a personal one. It is arguable that a contract with Facebook is personal in nature.[2] For instance, the user's account is, per the terms, non-transferable.

The question concerning ownership of fan pages and groups is more delicate. A page may sometimes be the result of a lot of time and energy expended by the owner. Through the number of persons following the page, it may have acquired real economic value (although in practice, at least 100,000 followers are needed in order to enter the market).[3] An underground market concerning pages has consequently developed: popular pages are sold by their owners to businesses interested by quickly reaching a massive number of persons (advertisement, political messages, etc.). However, from a legal point of view, these actions are questionable. Facebook's policy is quite confusing. On the one hand, the policy states that any transfer of a page is legal only with Facebook's written permission. On the other hand, the platform allows the page's owner to add other administrators and even to leave the administration, in practice opening the door to transfer. In other words, while transfers are legally heavily regulated, technically no limitations exist at all.

Nevertheless, the legal issue of the data produced during the execution of the contract remains. The EU legislator implicitly took a position on this topic when it modernized the rules applying to digital contracts in 2019. Indeed, instead of formulating one general legal framework applicable to digital contracts, it distinguished between two regimes: the sale of goods,[4] and the contracts for the supply of

---

[1] See https://www.facebook.com/legal/terms/plain_text_terms.

[2] Harbinja (2017), p. 177.

[3] See for instance the site "viralaccount.com" that specialises in acquiring fanpages.

[4] Directive (EU) 2019/771 of the European Parliament and of the Council of 20 May 2019 on certain aspects concerning contracts for the sale of goods, amending Regulation (EU) 2017/2394 and Directive 2009/22/EC, and repealing Directive 1999/44/EC (Text with EEA relevance.), PE/27/2019/REV/1, OJ L 136, 22.5.2019, p. 28–50, ELI: http://data.europa.eu/eli/dir/2019/771/oj.

digital content and digital services.[5] The supply of digital content, where no physical medium is involved, is exclusively governed by the Directive on digital content, not by the Directive on sale of goods. It could be concluded that the legislator does not regard digital content as goods in the first place. However, this element was not widely discussed. As the legislator states,

> [t]his Directive should also not determine the legal nature of contracts for the supply of digital content or a digital service, and the question of whether such contracts constitute, for instance, a sales, service, rental or sui generis contract, should be left to national law.[6]

4.1.2 Data As Intangible Goods

4.1.2.1 The Civil Law Doctrines on the Notion of Res

It is both quite audacious and surprisingly easy to categorize data as goods, for scholars of both civil law and common law countries have not traditionally bothered to explicitly reject the idea. Countries that follow the Roman tradition generally appear to agree on the basic elements of the concept of ownership. It is described as the most absolute right in rem. For instance, ownership is characterized in France as a combination of three prerogatives: *usus* (the right to use the thing), *fructus* (the right to receive the fruits of the thing), *abusus* (the right to dispose of the thing). However, in some legislations, the notion of res is defined, often in a restrictive manner and/or without ontological coherence. For example, in the Greek Civil Code, under Article 947 (which is similar to the German equivalent),[7] it is stated that

> [t]hings, within the meaning of the law, are only tangible objects. Natural forces or energies are also considered, in particular electricity and heat, if they are subject to power, when confined to a certain space.[8]

In Roman law, the concept of "*res*" occupied an essential place. Indeed, Gaius and Justinian accepted a triple division of the law: "Omne autem ius quo utimur vel ad personas pertinet vel ad res vel ad actiones", which is to say, "The whole of the law observed by us relates either to persons or to things or to actions".[9] Applying the notion of res to data would even make sense for personal data, as in this context it could be possible to refer to the notion of "res extra commercium" to explain the

---

[5] Directive (EU) 2019/770 of the European Parliament and of the Council of 20 May 2019 on certain aspects concerning contracts for the supply of digital content and digital services (Text with EEA relevance.), PE/26/2019/REV/1, OJ L 136, 22.5.2019, p. 1–27, ELI: http://data.europa.eu/eli/dir/2019/770/oj.

[6] Recital 12, Directive 2019/770.

[7] See. Article 90 of the German Civil Code.

[8] Laskaridis (2013), p. 7.

[9] Domingo (2011).

specific rule of "dynamically limited alienability"[10] governing the field (the fact that transactions with data are allowed but at the same time heavily regulated).

Therefore, based on the general ambiguity of modern civil law and the deep roots of the concept of res in antiquity, some commentators have begun, over the last few decades, to develop a revised theory of ownership according to which information, subject to conditions, belongs to the definition of a good. In France, this phenomenon has been expressed by Pierre Catala.[11] The scholar considered that information protection is quite similar to property rules concerning tangible things, since the monopoly of exploitation resulting from protection has the essential function of ownership: enforcing it against everyone (an erga omnes characteristic). In Germany, a similar doctrine has emerged, the Dateneigentum (data ownership),[12] which argues that the doctrine of privacy, which is the prevailing approach to personal data,[13] does not adequately cover the scope of data exploitation possibilities in the digital age.[14]

The debate on the protection of information is not only academic; in specific cases, the courts have been persuaded to apply an ownership regime to data. For example, in France, information theft is recognized by the criminal courts.[15] In Germany, some decisions have left open the question of data ownership being independent from the ownership of the storage medium,[16] while in other cases the courts remain attached to the letter of the German Civil Code and reject the characterization of data as a thing.[17] Also worth mentioning is an attempt to circumvent this difficulty by referring to the general theory that things that are considered neither rights nor goods can, however, be the subject of a sales contract. Based on this idea, the Nuremberg Court of Appeal developed a theory known as "Skripturakt",[18] which recognizes a right to the data creator. However, this theory falls within the framework of criminal law and has not been applied in civil cases.[19]

More generally, some national courts have various traditional mechanisms at their disposal for protecting trade secrets at national level. In Germany, a former employee was accused of taking with him some technical documents to produce his own products which he offered to the company's customers at a lower price. The issue was that some of this information belonged to the public sector and some of it could be covered by trade secret protection. The Supreme Court considered that in

---

[10] Janeček and Malgieri (2020), pp. 924–943.

[11] Catala (1983), pp. 245–262.

[12] Amstutz (2018), pp. 438–551 (114).

[13] Zech (2016), pp. 51–79.

[14] Hoeren (2014), p. 751.

[15] Cass crim, 28, 2017, No. 16-81113.

[16] LG Karlsruhe, Urt. v. 3 U 15/95, liability for Destruction of computer data, 07 November 1995. BGH, 10/07/2015 – 154/14.

[17] LG Konstanz, Urt. v., 1 S 292/95 = NJW 1996,266, 10 x 1996.

[18] OLG Nuremberg, 1st Senate, 1 Ws 445/12, 23 – 2013.

[19] LAG Sachsen, 2 Sa 808/05, MMR 2008, 4, 17 – 2007.

the present case the distinction between the nature of the various files did not matter. The fact that the documents contained, even in part, trade secrets, made them all trade secrets.[20]

A similar evolution is to be discerned in common law countries. In England, information is not expressly considered to be an object of ownership that may be stolen, subject to a lien[21] (that is a right of retention), or over which ownership can be claimed.[22] In the case Fairstar Heavy Industries v. Adkin,[23] the employer was entitled to access e-mails stored on a former employee's personal computer. However, the judges reached this conclusion through the law of agency, explicitly avoiding taking a position on the ownership of the e-mail messages. In particular, they considered that

> [i]t would be unwise, for example, for this court to endorse the proposition that there can never be property in information without knowing more about the nature of the information in dispute and the circumstances in which a property right was being asserted.[24]

Furthermore, information in common law is protected through a traditional tort known as "breach of confidence". The main features of the tort were set out in a 1968 case:[25] it presupposes information which possesses an element of secrecy, which has been given under circumstances which give rise to an obligation of confidentiality, and which has been used without authorization to the detriment of the person in charge of the information. By taking a modern approach to these three criteria, the UK Court of Appeal gradually outlined a regime for the protection of confidential information, through the landmark Douglas v. Hello![26] decision. It should be highlighted that while the tort is often used as a way of protecting privacy, it actually protects information per se because of its value.

In this context, the reference case is Fraser v. Thames Television Ltd in 1984.[27] An actor and singer put together a partly autobiographical story of a rock band to submit to a TV producer. However, the producer proceeded to implement the idea without the actor's contribution. In other words, an idea was usurped—except that in intellectual property ideas are not protected. Since intellectual property does not offer a means of protection, other methods of protection can be explored. In this case, the court reached some useful conclusions: the information is protected, whatever its form (even oral); the information must be clearly expressed; and a non-specific idea cannot be protected. In conclusion, here, the plaintiff was entitled to damages for breach of confidence.

---

[20] BGH, NoI ZR 71/05, Schweißmodulargenerato, 13/12/2007.

[21] Oxford v. Moss [1979] 68 Cr App Rep 18.

[22] Your Response v. Datateam Business Media [2014] EWCA Civ 281.

[23] Fairstar Heavy Industries v. Adkin, [2013] EWCA Civ 886.

[24] Par.48 of the decision.

[25] Coco v. AN Clark (Engineers) Ltd [1968] F.S.R. 415, 01/07/1968.

[26] Douglas v. Hello! [2005] EWCA Civ 595, [2006] QB 125.

[27] Fraser v. Thames Television Ltd [1984] 1 Q.B. 44 (High Court).

Therefore, not all information under this regime is protected—only specific information goods that combine two characteristics: a form of originality (it is understood here that the concept is interpreted more leniently than it is in intellectual property law; otherwise, the intangible good would be protected as an intellectual creation) and an element of secrecy, in the sense that it has not already been spread throughout the world. In this context, it has to be recalled that not all data communicated to Facebook are communicated to the public or to friends. The user may have various interactions with the platform that are known only to him/her and to Facebook: all posts published under the "Only Me" privacy setting, or the "save for later" option on some publications. In other words, it is arguable that Facebook is in some cases in a position of trust with respect to the confidentiality of the information.

The courts have had the opportunity to apply and interpret the principles of breach of confidence in a series of judgments. In the case De Maudsley v. Palumbo[28] it was considered that the idea of a nightclub with general descriptions of the decoration or the type of music did not fall within the protection offered by this tort, as no specific context of secrecy had arisen. In the case Mars v. Teknowledge[29] it was considered that the internal mechanism of a vending machine is not protected: once the appliance is on the market, the holder may open it and have access to the information. Similarly, in the case BBC v. Harper Collins[30] the protagonist of a TV show who always wears a helmet that hides his true identity decided to write his autobiography. The disclosure of his true identity, however, did not constitute a breach of confidence as several press publications had already shared evidence of it. In other words, the information had already lost its confidentiality. The same conclusion was reached by the court in the case AG v. Observer Ltd,[31] about the autobiography of a secret agent. It was no longer confidential as it had already entered the "public domain", i.e. the information was generally accessible. Indeed, in this case, the agent's memoirs had already been published abroad.

In conclusion, it is quite impressive that the courts borrow several concepts from intellectual property law. As with intellectual property law, there are exceptions on public policy and morality grounds. In the case Stephens v. Avery,[32] it was held that information which is "immoral" is not entitled to protection (in this case, the applicant's homosexuality was not regarded as immoral information). Nevertheless, in any case a special relationship must be established between two persons in order to establish an obligation of confidentiality. It could be said that, in general, in both common law and civil law countries in Europe the concept of confidentiality plays a similar role to the notion of possession in the ownership regime. However, there is

---

[28] De Maudsley v. Palumbo [1996] FSR 447.

[29] Mars v. Teknowledge [1999] EWHC 226 (Pat).

[30] BBC v. Harper Collins (2010) EWHC 2424.

[31] AG v. Observer Ltd [1990] 1 AC 109.

[32] Stephens v. Avery [1988] 2 WLR 1280, [1988] I Ch 449, [1988] 2 All ER 477.

no national legislation in the EU that explicitly refers to the problem of ownership of information.[33]

4.1.2.2   The Protection of Data Under Contemporary Legal Regimes and the Protection of Facebook's User Account

Data are defined as "reinterpretable representation of information in a formalized manner suitable for communication, interpretation, or processing".[34] Through the introduction of the special EU database protection regime in 1996,[35] a form of exclusivity has been established in the systematic presentation of data with individual access, resulting from the essential investment of the database creator. The sui generis database right could be seen as the legal regime that best aligns with the idea of data ownership. However, this is an incomplete protection. The isolated data escape the reach of the sui generis right of the database creator, which only concerns substantial or systematic extraction and reuse of the database. Meanwhile, EU intellectual property law continues to flirt with the concept of data ownership. For instance, a new right is available to the online press publisher, while it is not even certain that it concerns only protected works (see Sect. 3.2.2).

It is also possible to find some indirect protection of information outside the field of intellectual property law. The concept of ownership entails absolute protection, both civil and criminal. In the area of criminal law, specifically, the EU legislator initiatives have multiplied. Based on the principles expressed in the Council of Europe's Convention on Cybercrime,[36] known as the Budapest Convention, the EU legislator, first by a 2005 Framework Decision, then by the 2013 Directive on cyberattacks,[37] lays the foundations of criminal computer law.

Articles 3, 4, and 5 of the Directive establish the offenses of illegal access to information system, illegal system interference and illegal data interference. The first offense is defined as the access without right, to the whole or to any part of an information system, where committed by infringing a security measure. The condition of infringing a security measure adds some legal uncertainty to the offense. Indeed, when someone, through brute force technique or social phishing, discovers a Facebook user's password, should it be regarded as an infringement of a security measure? The platform falls within the category of an information system, and a user account is a part of this. Furthermore, as the platform security measures consist in a

---

[33] Van Asbroeck et al. (2017), p. 23.

[34] International Organization for Standardization (2015) ISO/IEC 2382:2015.

[35] Directive 96/9/EC of the European Parliament and of the Council of 11 March 1996 on the legal protection of databases, OJ L 77, 27.3.1996, p. 20–28 ELI: http://data.europa.eu/eli/dir/1996/9/oj.

[36] The Convention on Cybercrime of the Council of Europe (CETS No.185), 23/11/2001.

[37] Directive 2013/40/EU of the European Parliament and of the Council of 12 August 2013 on attacks against information systems and replacing Council Framework Decision 2005/222/JHA, OJ L 218, 14.8.2013, p. 8–14, ELI: http://data.europa.eu/eli/dir/2013/40/oj.

verification of identity, it is reasonable that any misuse of personal identification data, and any identity theft for the purpose of accessing the Facebook account without right, falls within the definition of a security measure infringement. Therefore, the access to a user account by a third party, without the right to do so, is criminalized.

In this context, it is important to also refer to Article 7 of the Cyberattacks Directive, which adds that

> the intentional production, sale, procurement for use, import, distribution or otherwise making available of (...) a computer password, access code, or similar data by which the whole or any part of an information system is capable of being accessed

is also a criminal offense. Revealing a user's Facebook password, even without direct economic gain, would be dealt with by this Article.

In general, the EU legislator began adopting a new approach on the issue of non-personal data ownership some years ago.[38] In a new 2017 report,[39] the EU Commission discusses the possibility of introducing a new exclusive right, the data producer right. It states that this right would be a

> right to use and authorise the use of non-personal data could be granted to the "data producer", i.e. the owner or long-term user (i.e. the lessee) of the device. This approach would aim at clarifying the legal situation and giving more choice to the data producer, by opening up the possibility for users to utilise their data and thereby contribute to unlocking machine-generated data. However, the relevant exceptions would need to be clearly specified, in particular the provision of non-exclusive access to the data by the manufacturer or by public authorities, for example for traffic management or environmental reasons. Where personal data are concerned, the individual will retain his right to withdraw his consent at any time after authorising the use. Personal data would need to be rendered anonymous in such a manner that the individual is not or no longer identifiable, before its further use may be authorised by the other party. Indeed, the GDPR continues to apply to any personal data (whether machine generated or otherwise) until that data has been anonymised.[40]

In conclusion, multiple studies and efforts on the recognition of ownership in non-personal data have emerged in the past decade at the EU level.[41] However, the European Commission has not yet come up with a concrete proposal. One major issue with the recognition of such a right is that creating new monopolies capable of restricting open access to data may, in fact, result in a threat to the development of an EU data market.[42]

---

[38] EU Commission (2014) Towards a Thriving Data-Driven Economy, Communication, COM (2014) 442 final. EU Commission (2015) A Digital Single Market Strategy for Europe, Communication, COM(2015) 192 final.

[39] EU Commission (2017() Building a European data economy. Communication. COM/2017/09.

[40] Section 3.5 of the Communication.

[41] Barbero et al. (2018).

[42] Banterle (2020).

4.1.2.3 The Trade Secrets Directive and the Golden Algorithm

In the context of a discussion on data ownership, Directive 2016/943 on the protection of trade secrets[43] merits a closer analysis. Indeed, while its title ("trade secrets") suggests a narrow field of application, the legislation actually covers a wide range of information. The Directive follows a global trend in this area,[44] compatible with the provisions of the TRIPS Agreement.[45]

The protection of the trade secret holder is quite impressive and arguably goes beyond a mere fault-based regime of responsibility. It could be said that the EU legislator's intent here is to create a regime of protection of quasi-intellectual property law.[46] The core element of the regime lies in the definition of the trade secret. A trade secret

> means information which meets all of the following requirements: (a) it is secret in the sense that it is not, as a body or in the precise configuration and assembly of its components, generally known among or readily accessible to persons within the circles that normally deal with the kind of information in question; (b) it has commercial value because it is secret; (c) it has been subject to reasonable steps under the circumstances, by the person lawfully in control of the information, to keep it secret.[47]

This sets out the three conditions governing the whole regime (the confidential character of the information, its commercial value, the expressed intent to protect it), which are quite similar to the common law tort of breach of confidence.

Three prerogatives are available to the trade secret holder. Such a holder shall be granted protection against unlawful acquisition, use and disclosure.[48] At the heart of the protection lies the concept of illegal acquisition. In order to be found to be unlawful, the acquisition of the information must correspond to two characteristics: the absence of the consent of the holder and one of the following two situations:

> (a) unauthorised access to, appropriation of, or copying of any documents, objects, materials, substances or electronic files, lawfully under the control of the trade secret holder, containing the trade secret or from which the trade secret can be deduced; (b) any other conduct which, under the circumstances, is considered contrary to honest commercial practices.[49]

The truly revolutionary element of the Directive appears in Article 4 (4). So far, the trade secret holder's prerogatives could be summarized as a quasi-contractual duty of confidence. However, in some cases, the obligation extends to a third party, de

---

[43] Directive (EU) 2016/943 of the European Parliament and of the Council of 8 June 2016 on the protection of undisclosed know-how and business information (trade secrets) against their unlawful acquisition, use and disclosure (Text with EEA relevance) OJ L 157, 15.6.2016, p. 1–18, ELI:http://data.europa.eu/eli/dir/2016/943/oj.

[44] Patel et al. (2016).

[45] See article 39 of the TRIPS agreement.

[46] See recitals 1 and 2 of the Directive.

[47] Article 2 of the Directive.

[48] Article 4 (1) of the Directive.

[49] Article 4 (2) of the Directive.

facto transforming the nature of the obligation into an in rem right. Article 4 (4) states that

> [t]he acquisition, use or disclosure of a trade secret shall also be considered unlawful whenever a person, at the time of the acquisition, use or disclosure, knew or ought, under the circumstances, to have known that the trade secret had been obtained directly or indirectly from another person who was using or disclosing the trade secret unlawfully within the meaning of paragraph 3.

A prerequisite is that the third party must have acquired the information in bad faith. As with movable property, a bona fide third party that acquires possession of the information good is protected against liability as a general principle.[50] The article, then, explains the notion of unlawful acquisition of the secret, which must be in breach of either a contractual duty of confidentiality or a similar contractual duty to limit the use of the secret, or a non-contractual duty to not disclose or limit the use of the secret.

Finally, the Directive introduces some exceptions to the regime, placing an overall emphasis on freedom of expression, repeating in various articles the principle that trade secret protection should not be interpreted in an absolute manner. On the contrary, a compromise with freedom of expression is required, in the light of the principle of proportionality. Specific legislation has been introduced on this point in order to ensure that potential whistle-blowers would not be affected by the trade secret holder's rights.[51] It is necessary to proceed with an in concreto analysis of the concept of "contribution to a debate involving the whole society". For example, in a recent French case,[52] a website specializing in financial information revealed a lot of sensitive information about a company that was bankrupt. The French court considered, however, that this information was not generally aimed at the general public so as to take precedence over the trade secret protection, but only at a specific audience of registered users, and so the disclosure of the sensitive information was regarded as not contributing to a general debate involving the whole society. From time to time, some internal documents from Facebook are leaked that reveal some vital information on moderation techniques and strategies. It is clear that these publications are protected under this regime against litigation for trade secret infringement.

In the context of the social network, the general applications of the Trade Secrets Directive are still uncertain. A lot of data are acquired by the platform in confidential or semi-confidential contexts. From the user's point of view, the biggest legal challenge consists in determining what data correspond to the "commercial value" criterion. Taking a broad approach, it could be said that all personal data pass the test, as by definition they serve as an economic consideration for the service. From Facebook's point of view, the Directive also has some critical uses. From the

---

[50]Zimmermann et al. (2000).

[51]Directive (EU) 2019/1937 of the European Parliament and of the Council of 23 October 2019 on the protection of persons who report breaches of Union law, PE/78/2019/REV/1, OJ L 305, 26.11.2019, p. 17–56, ELI: http://data.europa.eu/eli/dir/2019/1937/oj.

[52]Cass.civ., 13/02/2019, 17-18.049. ECLI:FR:CCASS:2019:CO00198.

accumulated data of trained AI to algorithm functions, the platform not only feeds on data but also produces them. The trade secret protection would in this case serve as the closest legal regime to ownership that is available in the EU.

Facebook's main algorithm would certainly be entitled to receive trade secret protection. First, it has to be noted that an algorithm, as a mathematical notion, cannot be protected either by copyright law (see Sect. 3.1.1) or by patent law, but for some substantial exceptions (see Sect. 3.4). By Facebook's algorithm, we mean here the main function of the platform, that is to control the ordering and presentation of the user's friends' posts, suggestions, and, of course advertisements. The general idea of the algorithm is known: present content in the news feed that is the most relevant for the user, using four main ranking signals: recentness, popularity, content type, and relationship.[53] However, even if the GDPR requests more transparency in this field (see Sects. 8.3.1 and 8.3.2), the algorithm is seen as a black box and its secrecy has fed some famous myths, such as the "26 friends limit".[54]

In conclusion, a lot of pressure exists on Facebook to give more details about its algorithm. However, from an intellectual property perspective, Facebook's interest is to keep the actual algorithm secret, as it is entitled this way to protection as a trade secret.

4.2 Facebook Versus Succession Law: The Digital Graveyard's Perspective

4.2.1 The Memorial State and the Digital Inheritance

The problematic issue of transferring a deceased user's account dataset to his or her heirs is known in the literature as "digital inheritance". This question touches upon various fields of law: copyright law, personal data protection, succession law, property law, and contract law.[55] As presented above (see Sect. 4.1), the nature of data as goods in certain situations is still highly debated. Most scholars adopt a conservative approach to this question and consider that, as data is not corporeal, it cannot be a thing, and therefore succession law does not apply.[56]

The GDPR's perspective represents a major aspect of the digital inheritance regime. It is established as a general principle of data privacy law, that only living persons may be data subjects in the sense of the GDPR. However, contrary to the

---

[53] However, overall thousands of signals are used in order to build the machine learning (ML) ranking system that powers the News Feed. See the explanations from Facebook: Akos L, Meihong W, Tak Y (2021) How does News Feed predict what you want to see? Tech@facebook. https://tech.fb.com/news-feed-ranking/.

[54] Facebook (2019).

[55] Nemeth and Carvalho (2017), p. 253.

[56] Mackenrodt (2018).

previous legislation, the GDPR does not explicitly exclude the protection of personal data of the deceased. On the contrary, Recital 27 leaves the decision to extend the protection to deceased persons up to the discretion of the Member States. Some Member States, such as Denmark, have indeed inserted special provisions in this sense. The Danish legal regime extends the protection to 10 years after the death of the data subject.[57] However, the ECtHR has explained that the right to privacy could also, in some cases, cover the reputation of the deceased, in the sense that the reputation of a deceased member of a person's family might affect that person's private life and identity, and thus fall within the scope of Article 8 of the Convention.[58]

Unless specified otherwise, therefore, in national legislation, the GDPR does not constitute an obstacle to digital inheritance, but for one major exception. Indeed, ironically, Facebook could find a sound argument in the GDPR for refusing the digital inheritance. One of the six fundamental principles (see Sect. 2.2.3), the principle of storage limitation, imposes a time limit on the duration of the data processing. This time limit is linked to the purpose of the processing. By definition, no advertiser can be interested in the profile of a deceased person and no new profiling can occur. The processing's purpose has been fulfilled, which means that all personal data should be automatically deleted. In other words, the user's account data cease, in principle, to be personal data after his or her death, but if, by exception, the data privacy law continues to apply, the issue of data inheritance would be immediately resolved, as a complete deletion of the account would be required. To support this theory that data privacy law continues to apply, it would be possible to argue that the GDPR does not apply to data processing that occurs after the death of the data subject, but still applies at the moment of his or her death, necessitating the immediate deletion of data.

Nevertheless, from a psychological point of view, the automatic deletion of a deceased person's account would have dramatic repercussions on the platform. Arguably, Facebook has a role to play in the mourning process.[59] The company has found a compromise, the legality of which is debatable: the "memorial state". After a report from a user, the account is locked. It does not appear anymore in the timelines of the deceased's friends (for instance, it does not show birthday reminders); nor does it appear in third persons' "People You May Know" suggestions, or in Facebook ads.

It should be noted that memorialization is only one of the three available options in this context. Facebook also recognizes that the heirs are entitled to request the deletion of the account. Furthermore, the terms and conditions introduce the concept of a legacy contact. The users are allowed either to signal that they wish their account to be deleted after their death, or to

---

[57] Article 2(5) of the Data Protection Act.

[58] ECtHR, Putistin v. Ukraine, no16882/03, 21 November 2013.

[59] See Brubaker et al. (2013), pp. 152–163; Church (2013), pp. 184–189.

designate a person (called a legacy contact) to manage your account if it is memorialised. Only your legacy contact or a person who you have identified in a valid will or similar document expressing clear consent to disclose your content upon death or incapacity will be able to seek disclosure from your account after it is memorialized.[60]

4.2.2 The Jurisprudential Positions on Digital Inheritance

4.2.2.1 The German Law Decisions

A 15-year-old girl died under circumstances that looked like suicide. The conductor of the metro that was involved in the death sued the family. Under these circumstances, the mother, who claimed that her deceased daughter had given her Facebook password, tried to log in to it in order to understand more about this sad situation, but the account had already been already blocked. Facebook, after a notification from an unknown source, had given the account "memorial status".

These are the facts of three very interesting German decisions that have had to take a position on the thorny issue of the application of succession law to a Facebook account.[61] The court at first instance considered that if the girl had left a personal diary, the question of its transfer of ownership would not even be posed. At the same time (and in a contradictory fashion), it is thought that the account falls within the scope of the definition of a service, which can be transferred to the heirs upon the death of the contracting party. Furthermore, it noted that, as a rule, data privacy legislation does not apply to personal data of deceased persons. It concluded that the mother should have access to her daughter's account.[62]

However, on appeal by Facebook, the Court of Appeal reversed the first instance judgment and dismissed the action.[63] On the one hand, the Court agreed with the first decision as regards the availability of the transfer of a social media account through succession law, as a principle, but remarked that the principle of secrecy of telecommunications in practice interferes with such a transfer and prohibits it.

The Supreme Court, therefore, intervened.[64] It noted that

> [t]he Court underlined that the contract of use between the plaintiff's daughter and Facebook was transferred to the heirs by way of universal succession. Its inheritability was not excluded by contractual provisions. Nor did the nature of the contract imply that the contractual relationship was not inheritable.[65]

---

[60] https://www.facebook.com/legal/terms/plain_text_terms.

[61] Fuchs (2021), pp. 1–7, https://doi.org/10.1007/s12027-021-00652-y.

[62] LG Berlin, 20 O 172/15, ECLI:DE:LGBE:2015:1217.20O172.15.0A.

[63] Kammergericht, Judgment of 31 May 2017 – 21 U 9/16, ECLI:DE:KG:2017:0531.21U9.16.0A.

[64] BGH, Judgment of 12 July 2018 – III ZR 183/17, ECLI:DE:BGH:2018:120718UIIIZR183.17.0.

[65] Fuchs (2021) op.cit.

Moreover, the Court rejected the objection raised by the Court of Appeal as regards the secrecy of telecommunications, considering that an individual should expect a considerable decrease in his personal rights post-mortem.

The parents gained access to the account. However, the decision's enforcement gave rise to another litigation. Facebook sent the parents a USB key with one large PDF file of 14,000 pages. The parents considered that this file did not allow them real access to the account, because of its lack of structure. Facebook answered that it could not give them access to the account, as it would be in fact a kind of identity theft if the parents would be in a position to post or comment on their daughter's page. However, the Court remarked that a technical colossus such as Facebook should have the savoir faire in order to give "read only" access to an account. In conclusion, the German court condemned Facebook for a second time, judging that the USB key had not provided what the court injunction had ordered.[66]

This decision was appealed, and then reviewed by the Supreme Court. The Court of Appeal, first, disagreed with the first instance court.[67] However, the Supreme Court[68] agreed with the first instance court, explaining that, through universal enforcement of succession law, the heirs should have access to the account, not only to a simple copy of it. The double litigation ended with a victory for the family over Facebook. At the same time, even if a precedent has been created that opens the door to future litigation as regards the ownership of data, the question is far from settled. Multiple issues remain, such as the ownership of a page.

References

Amstutz M (2018) Data ownership, function and form, heading: treatises and discussion reports. Archive for Civilist Practice (AcP) (2-4):438–551. (114)

Banterle F (2020) Data ownership in the Data Economy: a European dilemma. In: Synodinou T-E et al (eds) EU Internet Law in the Digital Era. Springer International Publishing, Cham

Barbero M, Cocoru D, Graux H, Hillebrand A, Linz F, Osimo D, Siede A, Wauters P (2018) Study on emerging issues of data ownership, interoperability, (re-)usability and access to data, and liability, SMART number2016/0030 https://doi.org/10.2759/781960

Brubaker JR, Hayes GR, Dourish P (2013) Beyond the grave: Facebook as a site for the expansion of death and mourning. Information Soc 29(3):152–163

Catala P (1983) Ebauche d'une théorie juridique de l'information, Revue de droit prospectif, Université d'Aix-Marseille III, n1, Dalloz 1984, chron. p 97

Catala P (1998) La propriété de l'information, in Le droit à l'épreuve du numérique. Jus ex Machina, coll. "Droit, Éthique, Société". PUF, Paris, pp 245–262

Church SH (2013) Digital gravescapes: digital memorializing on Facebook. Information Soc 29(3): 184–189

Domingo R (2011) Gaius, Vattel, and the new global law paradigm. Eur J Int Law 22(3):627–647

---

[66] LG Berlin, Order of 13 February 2019 – 20 O 172/15, ECLI:DE:LGBE:2019:0213..20O172.15.00.

[67] Kammergericht, Order of 9 December 2019 – 21 W 11/19.

[68] BGH, Order of 27 August 2020 – III ZB 30/20, ECLI:DE:BGH:2020:270820BIIIZB30.20.0.

Facebook (2019) No, your news feed is not limited to posts from 26 friends. Facebook Newsroom. https://about.fb.com/news/2019/02/inside-feed-facebook-26-friends-algorithm-myth/

Fuchs A (2021) What happens to your social media account when you die? The first German judgments on digital legacy. ERA Forum 22:1–7. https://doi.org/10.1007/s12027-021-00652-y

Harbinja E (2017) Post-mortem social media:law and Facebook after death. In: Mangan D, Gillies LE (eds) The legal challenges of social media. Edgar Law, Technology and Society, New York, p 177

Hoeren T (2014) Big Data and the ownership in data: recent developments in Europe. EIPR 36(12): 751

Janeček V, Malgieri G (2020) Commerce in data and the dynamically limited alienability rule. German Law J 21(5):924–943. https://doi.org/10.1017/glj.2020.47

Laskaridis E (2013) Interpretation of Article 947. In: Georgiadis A (ed) Short interpretation of the Civil Code, vol II. P N Sakkulas, Athen, p 7

Mackenrodt M (2018) Personal data after the death of the data subject—exploring possible features of a holistic approach. In: Bakhoum M, Conde Gallego B, Mackenrodt MO, Surblyt-è-Namavičienė G (eds) Personal data in competition, consumer protection and intellectual property law. MPI studies on intellectual property and competition law, vol 28. Springer, Berlin. https://doi.org/10.1007/978-3-662-57646-5_11

Nemeth K, Carvalho JM (2017) Digital Inheritance in the European Union. EuCML 2017:253

Patel AB, Pade JA, Cundiff V, Newman B (2016) The global harmonization of trade secret law: the convergence of protections for trade secret information in the United States and European Union. Def Counsel J 83:472

Van Asbroeck B, Debussche J, César J (2017) Building the European data economy data ownership, white book, bird&bird, p 23

Zech H (2016) Data as a tradable commodity. In: Franceschi D (ed) European Contract Law and the digital single market. Intersentia, Cambridge, pp 51–79

Zimmermann R, Whittaker S, Bussani M (2000) Good faith in European Contract Law. Cambridge University Press, Cambridge

Chapter 5
Defamation and Personal Attacks

The Internet, and social media specifically, has given a voice to the crowd, thereby revolutionizing society. Nevertheless, this evolution from a centralized to a decentralized form of expression is not an exclusively positive development. As Umberto Eco noted,

> [s]ocial media gives legions of idiots the right to speak when they once only spoke at a bar after a glass of wine, without harming the community. Then they were quickly silenced, but now they have the same right to speak as a Nobel Prize winner. It's the invasion of the idiots.[1]

It could also be said that the intrinsic ambiguity and fluidity of the self—or, indeed, of other boundaries—on the Internet leads to online disinhibition.[2]

In any case, the observation remains that social media enables a constant flow of personal attacks. Facebook's attempt to fight hate speech or fake news is discussed later (see Chap. 7), as it is worth analyzing independently from the issue of defamation, for three reasons. First, the ECtHR itself makes a distinction between the topics and has deeply influenced EU defamation law (see Sect. 5.1). Second, defamation law has traditionally taken a broad approach to the notion of communication, which leads to new issues. Should someone be liable merely for interacting with the platform through the "like" button? (See Sect. 5.2.) Third, defamation involves a personal attack, usually (but not always) against one Facebook user and it therefore has to be analyzed under the scope of contract law too (see Sect. 5.3).

---

[1] Martini (2017).

[2] Ballam and Fullwood (2010), pp. 391–399.

P. Jougleux, *Facebook and the (EU) Law*, Law, Governance and Technology Series 48, https://doi.org/10.1007/978-3-031-06596-5_5

5.1   The Labyrinth of Defamation Laws and the Breadcrumb Trail of ECtHR Case-Law

5.1.1   The Alignment of Laws and Practices Concerning Online Defamation

EU law is silent on the question of defamation. It is clear that defamation places a kind of limit to freedom of expression (see Chap. 8). However, in some Member States defamation is an offense, while in others it is simply a civil wrong. Defamation law tends to be handled more and more as a civil law issue. Indeed,

> [w]hile we cannot talk of decriminalisation on a mass scale (only 10 of the 47 member states have fully decriminalised defamation to date), there is a clear trend towards abolition of sentences restricting freedom of expression and a lightening of sentences in general.[3]

Besides, the Council of Europe has adopted a resolution that nudges its member states towards decriminalization of defamation.[4]

It could be argued that there are no substantive law arguments to justify maintaining defamation as a criminal offense. Furthermore, the fear of criminal sanctions automatically gives rise to a chilling effect on the freedom of expression (see Sect. 8.1.2). However, from a procedural perspective, the designation of defamation as an offense does provide certain advantages for the victim. Assuming the offense is categorized as a "serious" one, the victim could be entitled to ask for the secrecy of correspondence that protects the identity of the perpetrator to be lifted. It should be recalled here that confidentiality of electronic communications is protected at an EU level by the ePrivacy Directive, Article 5.[5]

The ECtHR has diligently exercised its powers to assess the compatibility of defamation law with the freedom of expression. As it is a restriction to Article 10, much case-law emphasizes the need for defamation to pass the famous three-part test (the restriction must be prescribed by law, adopted in pursuit of a legitimate aim—namely for the protection of the reputation of another—and be necessary in a democratic society—see Sect. 8.1.2).[6] Specifically, the national court, in an action for defamation, should carefully weigh the competing interests at stake and efficiently explain the grounds it has relied on to justify the interference with the author of the statement's right to freedom of expression.[7]

---

[3] Directorate General of Human Rights and Legal Affairs, Media Division (2012), p. 7.

[4] Parliamentary Assembly of the Council of Europe (2007). See Parliamentary Assembly Resolution 1577 & Recommendation 1814.

[5] Directive 2002/58/EC of the European Parliament and of the Council of 12 July 2002 concerning the processing of personal data and the protection of privacy in the electronic communications sector (Directive on privacy and electronic communications), OJ L 201, 31.7.2002, p. 37–47, ELI: http://data.europa.eu/eli/dir/2002/58/oj.

[6] European Court of Human Rights Press Unit (2021).

[7] See for instance, ECtHR, Cicad v. Switzerland, 7 June 2016.

Defamation, and by extension online defamation, is not defined by the ECHR. However, it is established that protection of one's reputation falls within the scope of Article 8 of the Convention concerning protection of the personality.[8]

Some essential points of the civil wrong of defamation are clearly discernable. As a result, a general definition emerges that could be summarized as follows: "the act of defamation consists of making a false or untrue statement about another person that tends to damage his/her reputation in the eyes of reasonable members of society."[9] In other words, defamation has four characteristics: a communication, a lie, a specific person or specific persons targeted by the message, and reputational damage. The court adds one more criterion: an attack on a person's reputation must involve a certain level of seriousness and in a manner causing prejudice to the personal enjoyment of the right to respect for private life.[10]

The lie requirement does not mean that the statement must absolutely be true. It is enough for the statement to have been without factual foundation. Furthermore, it is not mandatory for the defendant to absolutely prove veracity. In Braun v. Poland,[11] an author accused a well-known professor on radio of being an informant of the secret political police during the communist era. The national courts considered that if the author had been a journalist, the criterion for liability would have been a standard of due diligence and good faith. Otherwise, the defendant would have had to prove the veracity of his allegations and thus meet a higher standard. This higher level of responsibility for non-journalists was found to be incompatible with the ECHR. The court considered that the ECHR offers protection to all participants in debates on matters of legitimate public concern. Furthermore, there cannot be condemnation for defamation where an obligation on the defendant to demonstrate the truth of his statements would amount to an unreasonable, if not impossible, task.[12] In another case, it was clearly highlighted that behind the lie criterion, it is in fact required to prove that the applicant had acted in bad faith or without due diligence.[13]

Furthermore, in the case of defamation, the fact that the statement concerns matters of public interest constitutes an absolute defense.[14] Specifically, public— mostly, but not only, political—figures should expect scrutiny and harsh criticism. The classic legal notion of a public figure finds a new definition on the Internet. In a world of "influencers", should the notion be defined by the number of likes, or followers? Pinning down a definition depends on the circumstances of each case and is better left to the discretion of the courts. Nevertheless, the court should avoid

---

[8] ECtHR, Bédat v. Switzerland [GC], no. 56925/08, 29 March 2016.

[9] McGonagle (2016), p. 14.

[10] ECtHR, Axel Springer AG v. Germany [GC], no. 39954/08, 7 February 2012.

[11] ECtHR, Braun v. Poland, 4 November 2014.

[12] ECtHR, Smolorz v. Poland, 16 October 2012.

[13] ECtHR, Erla Hlynsdottir v. Iceland (no. 2), 21 October 2014.

[14] ECtHR, Axel Springer AG v. Germany (no.2), 18 July 2014.

applying this regime, which is less protective of the victim, just because the victim possesses an account on the platform.[15]

5.1.2   Specificities of Online Defamation

Online defamation does not essentially differ from the general regime of defamation, as regards the civil wrong's substantive criteria. The ECtHR case Olafsson v. Iceland[16] gives some insight into the fundamental issue on the Internet of the hosting service's secondary liability. It discusses the instance of a publication on a web-based media site of articles insinuating that a political candidate had sexually abused children. The Supreme Court of Iceland held the applicant liable for defamation. However, the ECtHR found that the Supreme Court of Iceland had failed to strike a reasonable balance between the measures restricting the applicant's freedom of expression, and the legitimate aim of protecting the reputation of others.

First, the court considered that the subject of the allegations had been standing for political office and should have anticipated public scrutiny. Furthermore, the articles about him had been published in good faith, in compliance with ordinary journalistic standards, and had contributed to a debate of public interest. In addition, whilst the allegations had been defamatory, they were being made not by the journalist himself, but by others (the sisters of the politician). And last, the court found it significant that the political candidate had chosen not to sue the persons making the claims (the sisters) and had thus potentially prevented the applicant from establishing that he had ascertained the truth of the allegations.

On Facebook, it is difficult to predetermine when a message will become "viral", that is, shared and commented on numerous times. In this case, through the snowball effect, the original message is often over-amplified and distorted. In the Kanellopoulou v. Greece[17] case (which was not, however, about online defamation), the ECtHR held that it was important not to confuse the intentions of the applicant with those of the sensationalist press, which had taken an interest in the case because the doctor implicated in the case was well-known. It could be deduced that the author is not liable for the harmful consequences of multiple shares, or even for the comments.

In general, online defamation is treated in the same way as defamation through the press. For instance, in the ECtHR case Egill Einarsson v. Iceland,[18] a well-known blogger considered he had been defamed by the words "Fuck you rapist bastard" used in an Instagram post about him, posted a week after prosecutors had dismissed rape and sexual offence accusations against him. The Supreme Court of Iceland,

---

[15]Lafferman (2012), p. 199.

[16]ECtHR, Olafsson v. Iceland, 16 March 2017.

[17]ECtHR, Kanellopoulou v. Greece, 11 October 2007.

[18]ECtHR, Egill Einarsson v. Iceland, no. 24703/15, 07 November 2017.

however, gave precedence to freedom of expression and rejected the complaint. The applicant objected that the Supreme Court judgment meant that he could be called a rapist without being charged or convicted of such a crime and without being able to defend himself.

The court held that there had been a violation of Article 8 (the right to respect for private life) of the Convention finding that, overall, the domestic courts had not struck a fair balance between the applicant's right to respect for his private life and the right to freedom of expression of the person who had posted the remark. Indeed, in the specific context of the case (the discontinued criminal procedure), the word "rapist" was not to be interpreted as a judgment value but as a statement of fact, and even public persons who had begun a heated debate did not have to tolerate being accused of violent criminal acts without such statements being supported by facts.

Furthermore, simple vulgarity does not automatically lead to online defamation. In the case Høiness v. Norway,[19] the Norwegian courts refused to impose civil liability on an Internet forum host after vulgar comments about the applicant, a well-known lawyer, had been posted on the forum. The ECtHR did not find any manifest error of appreciation from the Norwegian court (see also Sect. 6.2.2 for this case).

It should be noted that in cases of online defamation the plaintiff has to be careful with the requested remedies. In the case Wegrzynowski and Smolczewski v. Poland,[20] two lawyers had been defamed by a newspaper's article and, after litigation, received compensation. However, the online version of the article remained available. The court considered that the first set of proceedings before the Polish courts did not create a "legitimate expectation" that the article would be removed from the newspaper's website, as the lawyers had not made claims during the proceedings regarding the presence of the article on the Internet. Indeed, in refusing to proceed with the removal of the defamatory content, the Polish courts had struck a fair balance between the public's right to access to information, on the one hand, and the applicant's right to have his reputation protected, on the other hand. On the contrary, it means that completely removing the contested article from the newspaper's archive would have been disproportionate.

5.1.3   Online Defamation and Forum Shopping

Which court is competent to hear a case of defamation on Facebook? Confronted with the multitude of national points of contact, the plaintiff is naturally attracted to choose the best—that is, the strictest—court for his defamation case. The court itself is tempted to accept defamation cases, as there is "a growing tendency by courts in content-related disputes to exercise personal jurisdiction over internet companies

---

[19] ECtHR, Høiness v. Norway, no. 43624/14, 19 March 2019.

[20] ECtHR, Węgrzynowski and Smolczewski v. Poland, 33846/07, 16 July 2013.

that are located abroad"[21] has been noted. The jurisdiction election phenomenon, or forum shopping, is known in all fields of law, but in the case of online defamation, various arguments tend to amplify it, to the point that it has acquired a specific label: "libel tourism".[22]

Assuming that the defamation case is dealt with as a tort, the general principle relevant here is the lex loci delicti rule—the rule of the competence of the jurisdiction of the domicile of the defendant—which is imposed by Article 4(1) of the Brussels I (recast) Regulation.[23] The same rule pertains to the applicable law, by virtue of Article 4(1) of the Rome II Regulation. In the Facebook context, in Europe, it means that any case that involves Facebook's liability should only be heard by the courts of Ireland.

However, this general principle is not absolute in the case of complex tort situations. In complex tort situations, such as online defamation, the plaintiff can still elect the jurisdiction, in accordance with some criteria. The ECJ first developed a "mosaic approach" in the landmark "Shevill" case,[24] giving the plaintiff the choice to sue either before the courts of the place of publication, either before each jurisdiction where harm has been suffered, including the place of habitual residence of the plaintiff, but only for a limited amount of damages that corresponds to the damage suffered in this jurisdiction. This solution has been adopted in the digital era. In the eDate/Martinez case,[25] the ECJ added the courts of the EU Member State in which the plaintiff's center of interests is based as an additional available choice of jurisdiction for the plaintiff. As the place of center of interests may not always coincide with the place of habitual residence, "the ECJ has in fact reinforced its "mosaic approach" by allowing claimants an even wider choice of forums."[26]

In this context, the Bolagsupplysningen case in 2017[27] plays a substantial role in clarifying the situation and adapting the mosaic approach to the digital era. A Swedish company published on its website information on an Estonian company, stating that the company was carrying out acts of fraud and deceit. The Estonian company sued for defamation before the Estonian courts. The Estonian court, however, declined competence, remarking that the comments were written in

---

[21] Expert Committee on human rights dimensions of automated data processing and different forms of artificial intelligence (2019), p. 7. https://rm.coe.int/liability-and-jurisdictional-issues-in-online-defamation-cases-en/168097d9c3.

[22] Hartley (2010), pp. 25–38.

[23] Regulation (EU) No 1215/2012 of the European Parliament and of the Council of 12 December 2012 on jurisdiction and the recognition and enforcement of judgments in civil and commercial matters, OJ L 351, 20.12.2012, p. 1–32, ELI: http://data.europa.eu/eli/reg/2012/1215/oj.

[24] ECJ, C-68/93, Shevill and Others v. Presse Alliance, 07/03/1995, ECLI:EU:C:1995:61.

[25] ECJ, C-509/09 and C-161/10, eDate Advertising GmbH and Others v. X and Société MGN Limited, 25/10/2011, ECLI:EU:C:2011:685.

[26] Expert Committee on human rights dimensions of automated data processing and different forms of artificial intelligence (2019). Op.cit. p.14.

[27] ECJ, C-194/16, Bolagsupplysningen OÜ and another v. Svensk Handel AB, 17/10/2017 ECLI:EU:C:2017:766.

Swedish, and without a translation, they were incomprehensible to persons residing in Estonia. The Supreme Court decided to stay the proceedings and ask for guidance from the ECJ on the question of jurisdiction.

The ECJ considers, on principle, that in matters relating to tort, the courts for the place where the harmful event occurred or may occur are usually the most appropriate for deciding the case. Recalling the Shevill/edate rule, the Court then recalls that, on the one hand, the victim can bring an action for reparation before the courts of each Member State in which the publication was distributed and where the victim claims to have suffered injury to his reputation (Shevill), but, on the other hand, in the specific context of the internet, the victim must also have the option of bringing an action for damages before the courts of the Member State in which the center of his interests is based (edate). Therefore, it confirmed the mosaic approach that gives a partial competence (limited to the damage that occurs in the particular place) in cases of online defamation.

Nonetheless, this approach is confined to situations where the victim claims compensation for the damage suffered. The victim of a tortious internet publication can only seek an order for rectification and removal of the incorrect information in the courts that have jurisdiction over the entirety of the harm sustained and not before the courts that only enjoy jurisdiction regarding the damage suffered in their territory. Indeed, the court considers that

> in the light of the ubiquitous nature of the information and content placed online on a website and the fact that the scope of their distribution is, in principle, universal (. . .), an application for the rectification of the former and the removal of the latter is a single and indivisible application and can, consequently, only be made before a court with jurisdiction to rule on the entirety of an application for compensation for damage (. . .), and not before a court that does not have jurisdiction to do so.[28]

This distinction based on the nature of the remedies certainly has the merit of restricting the mosaic approach. It is, at the same time, arguably regrettable that a court of a Member State, which has jurisdiction to hear an extra-contractual action for damages, is not also entitled to rule on the issue of all the remedies that are available under national law.[29]

Consequently, in a case of alleged defamation against Facebook, the plaintiff may sue not only in Ireland (which is both the place of domicile of Facebook in Europe and its center of interest for the EU), but also in the place of his habitual residence. Furthermore, if the victim wishes not only to seek compensation but also to block, rectify, or delete the defamatory content on Facebook, the only competent court will be in Ireland. It should be noted, additionally, that the mosaic approach should also be examined from the perspective of human rights. Indeed, in relation to the right to effective access to justice, the ECtHR considers that in online defamation cases, a

---

[28] Par.48 of the decision.

[29] Vanleenhove (2018), pp. 640–646.

court should not refuse its competence where a "strong connection" exists between the country and the case.[30]

It is worth mentioning that this case law has recently been confirmed by the Grand Chamber of the European Court in the Gtflix Tv v DR case.[31] The court found that

> person who, considering that his or her rights have been infringed by the dissemination of disparaging comments concerning him or her on the internet, seeks not only the rectification of the information and the removal of the content placed online concerning him or her but also compensation for the damage resulting from that placement may claim, before the courts of each Member State in which those comments are or were accessible, compensation for the damage suffered in the Member State of the court seised, even though those courts do not have jurisdiction to rule on the application for rectification and removal.[32]

5.2   Defamation Through Reactions or the Dilemma of the "Like" Button

5.2.1   The Hyperlink's Analogy

Online defamation poses various issues of secondary liability. First, we should recall that Facebook is protected from litigation under the safe harbor mechanism, unless it does not fulfil the conditions of the immunity (see Chap. 6). Nevertheless, the platform offers multiple ways of interactions between the users, some of them new to the digital era. For instance, the iconic "like" button currently provides six non-verbal modes of expression to the user who wishes to react to a post: thumbs up, love, care, laugh, surprised, sad, and angry.

While extremely basic (and sometimes ambiguous), these reactions can convey a lot of information in some contexts. For instance, a lot of media articles covering the coronavirus pandemic presented news about hospitalizations or deaths. A laugh icon in this context does not necessarily mean that the user finds it funny, but it implies a judgment on the news, accusing the news report of being fake or overdramatic. This conveys a message that will be distributed to other users, depending on the context. While some may ignore this message, others may be influenced, and others may be hurt.[33] It should be noted that reactions cannot be moderated. By default, only the three most popular reactions to the specific post are shown underneath.

Another consequence of the reaction button is the automatic rebroadcasting of the content. While Facebook's algorithm alone is in a position to decide what will be published in which news feed (see Sect. 8.3), in some cases a reaction from a user A on some content will lead to an indirect kind of notification to the user B. User B, a

---

[30] ECtHR, Arlewin v. Sweden, no. 22302/10, 1 March 2016.

[31] ECJ, C-251/20, Gtflix Tv v DR, 21 December 2021, ECLI:EU:C:2021:1036.

[32] Par.43 of the decision.

[33] Bin (2021). https://www.thedailystar.net/shout/news/my-problem-facebooks-haha-react-2031165.

friend of A, likes to follow what A is doing, and the algorithm shows him content that A interacted with, that otherwise would not have shown up in his news feed.

From a legal point of view, this means that the reaction button is not innocent. It is a form of expression, which has to answer to media law, and it is also a form of rebroadcasting of the message (for repercussions under copyright law, see Sect. 3. 2.1). Indeed, through the reaction, the defamatory content is directed to a new, different audience. While national defamation laws are not harmonized, it is accepted as a general principle that the fact that a message has been rebroadcasted by a defendant is not a valid defense in a defamation case.

Some cases are beginning to raise this specific issue. Specifically, in Switzerland, the Supreme Court[34] had to decide the case of a person who had commented on, liked and shared several posts from third parties on Facebook in which an animal protection association was accused of having an antisemitic, national socialist and racist background and of using racist expressions. The court considered that a liked or shared post can amount to defamation if such action facilitates the distribution of defamatory statements to third parties and imposed a fine on the individual. However, the decision does not clearly take a position on the legal consequences of liking and sharing, as in this case three other facts had a substantial effect on the decision: the defendant had also sent an e-mail to the plaintiff, commented on the third parties' publications, and showed a multiplicity of reactions targeting the plaintiff.

Although liability may be found in the case of liking and sharing, this cannot be automatic. Indeed, in the case Magyar Jeti Zrt v. Hungary[35] the ECtHR provided substantial clarifications on this matter. While the case does not discuss the specific liking and sharing reactions, its rationale could arguably be extended to them. In this case, a news portal published an article about an incident at a Roma school, where a group of drunk passers-by had thrown beer bottles and shouted insults and threats to the children. A local Roma leader accused a political party of having been involved in this attack, and the article referred to this, adding a hyperlink to the YouTube video that contained the accusations. Does, therefore, the insertion of a hyperlink constitute rebroadcasting of the defamatory content?

The ECtHR considered that hyperlink technology has four characteristics: it has a navigational function, it is a referencing tool, its author does not control the content, and its author does not create new content. Therefore, there is no automatic liability for the insertion of a hyperlink that leads to a defamatory content. However, in this context, liability for defamation was to be asserted in the light of five main elements: did the journalist endorse the impugned content, did the journalist repeat the impugned content (without endorsing it), did the journalist merely insert a hyperlink to the impugned content (without endorsing or repeating it), did the journalist know or could reasonably have known that the impugned content was defamatory or otherwise unlawful, and, finally, did the journalist act in good faith, respecting the

---

[34] Supreme Court of Switzerland, Decision 6B_1114/2018 of 29/01/2020.
[35] ECtHR, Magyar Jeti Zrt v. Hungary, no 11257/16, 04/12/2018.

ethics of journalism and performing the due diligence expected in responsible journalism?

In conclusion, many uncertainties remain as regards the legal consequences of liking and sharing. Following the Magyar case, it could be said that the main element of consideration should be the good faith (or lack thereof) of the interacting user. In some contexts, where it is manifest for the average reader that the user has acted in bad faith, that is with the malicious intent of propagating the defamatory content (such as in the situation of the Swiss case, where the multiplication of the interventions showed the obsession of the defendant), even the simple act of using Facebook's reaction buttons could have legal repercussions.

It should be added that the use of hashtags on Facebook falls within the same problematic. In some circumstances, a hashtag serves as a means to spread a message, which can be found to be defamatory. The case Biancardi v Italy[36] illustrates this situation. In this case, the chief editor of an online journal was held liable not for not removing a defamatory article, but for not having de-indexed it. The indexation—or tags—added to the article indeed helped potential search engines to refer to it, and consequently greatly contributed to its dissemination. The Court found that this injunction to de-index the defamatory article was, on the facts of the case, compatible with the protection of freedom of expression.

5.2.2   The Melike Case

The ECtHR Melike v. Turkey[37] case provides some useful insight into the impact of "likes" on freedom of expression and its limits. In this case, an individual working under contract with the Ministry of Education was dismissed because she had "liked" certain Facebook content published by third parties that accused teachers of rape and contained violent political accusations against officials and political parties. The authorities considered that "liking" such provocative content was likely to disturb the peace and quiet of her workplace.

The Court observed that "the use of likes on social media, which could be seen as a way of showing interest or approval for content, is, as such, a common and popular form. exercise of freedom of expression online".[38] This way, reactions such as like, laugh and angry are recognized as a distinct form of communication, and it is implied that media law can apply to them.

However, the Melike case also highlights another consequence of accepting the "like" button as a form of communication: it is protected by freedom of expression. The three-part test for the legitimacy of a restriction to freedom of expression (see

---

[36] ECtHR, Biancardi v. Italy, no 77419/16, 25 November 2021.

[37] ECtHR, Melike v. Turkey, no 35786/19, 15 June 2021.

[38] Par.44 of the decision (translation from French by the author).

Sect. 8.1.2) imposes, amongst other requirements, a strict analysis of proportionality between the impact of the communication and the sanction.

This analysis requires a concrete estimation of the practical consequences of the action. Had the action of "liking" had a real impact? The Court sets out two lines of reasoning, one in abstracto and one in concreto. First, as a principle, it notes that

> the act of adding a "like" to a content cannot be considered as carrying the same weight as sharing content on social networks, insofar as a "like" mention only expresses a sympathy for published content, not an active desire to distribute it.[39]

It then observed there was no proof that the content in question had reached a very wide audience. Some of this content had received only about ten "likes" and a few comments in total, and, in any case, because of the limited reputation and presence of the applicant in her workplace, her activities on Facebook could not have a significant impact on students, parents, teachers and other employees. It was not even proven that they had access to the applicant's Facebook account and had only seen the "likes" in the context of the litigation.

The ECtHR finally held that, without any clear indication that

> the "likes" expressed by the applicant for the content in question had been noticed or denounced by the pupils, parents of pupils, teachers or other employees of the same workplace and whether these mentions had caused incidents likely to endanger the peace and order of the workplace,[40]

the administrative sanction of terminating a contract without compensation is manifestly disproportionate and violates the freedom of expression.

In conclusion, the Melike case should not be interpreted as an authority that "liking" does not entail any legal consequences. However, the fact that the "like" button is protected by freedom of expression does limit these legal consequences, as it has to be proven that the "liking" behavior had a measurable negative effect on a legitimate interest such as the protection of personality.

5.3 Promising That the Platform Is Safe: An Unfair Commercial Practice?

As e-commerce continues to grow and became almost mandatory during the coronavirus pandemic, a bad review could mean the death of a small enterprise. It is accepted that the right to reputation also covers legal persons, and, in this context, there is no reason to exclude false reviews from the scope of online defamation.[41] This is not the only relationship between anti-defamation laws and competition law

---

[39] Par.51 of the decision (translation from French by the author).

[40] Par.52 of the decision (translation from French by the author).

[41] Vroman et al. (2020).

(see Sect. 9.1.2) and the EU Commission hopes to regulate this issue of false reviews (see Sect. 9.2).

In 2021, Reporters Without Borders (Reporters Sans Frontières—RSF), an independent non-governmental organization (NGO) that focuses on the protection of the freedom of expression and the defense of journalists, filed a criminal complaint against Facebook for 'deceptive commercial practices' in France. The complaint is based on the observation, first, that the platform's fight against fake news is manifestly inefficient, and second, that hateful content and threats against journalists proliferate.

According to Article 6 of the Unfair Commercial Practices Directive,[42]

> [a] commercial practice shall be regarded as misleading if it contains false information and is therefore untruthful or in any way, including overall presentation, deceives or is likely to deceive the average consumer, even if the information is factually correct, in relation to one or more of the following elements, and in either case causes or is likely to cause him to take a transactional decision that he would not have taken otherwise: (. . .) (c) the extent of the trader's commitments, the motives for the commercial practice and the nature of the sales process, any statement or symbol in relation to direct or indirect sponsorship or approval of the trader or the product.

Therefore, the existence of an unfair commercial practice is closely related to the contractual provisions. The terms and conditions of Facebook state, under the section "3. Limits on liability", that

> [n]othing in these Terms is intended to exclude or limit our liability for death, personal injury or fraudulent misrepresentation caused by our negligence, or to affect your statutory rights. We will exercise professional diligence in providing our Products and services to you and in keeping a safe, secure and error-free environment. Provided that we have acted with professional diligence, we do not accept responsibility for losses not caused by our breach of these Terms or otherwise by our acts; losses that are not reasonably foreseeable by you and us at the time of entering into these Terms; and events beyond our reasonable control.

The NGO bases its complaint on this specific term, interpreting it as a recognition by Facebook of a contractual duty to ensure a "safe" environment. The logic behind the complaint is that the lack of efficient measures against the incessant defamations against journalists on the platform violates this duty to provide a safe platform.

However, this legal basis of the complaint remains fragile. Even if the court accepts the argument, it would be possible for Facebook to unilaterally modify its terms of service (though updates of terms of service by online platforms will be closely scrutinized; see Chap. 9). Nevertheless, the interpretation of the contractual duty to provide a safe environment is subject to debate. The company indicates it provides a "safe, secure and error-free environment". It could be argued that in this

---

[42] Directive 2005/29/EC of the European Parliament and of the Council of 11 May 2005 concerning unfair business-to-consumer commercial practices in the internal market and amending Council Directive 84/450/EEC, Directives 97/7/EC, 98/27/EC and 2002/65/EC of the European Parliament and of the Council and Regulation (EC) No 2006/2004 of the European Parliament and of the Council (Unfair Commercial Practices Directive), ELI: http://data.europa.eu/eli/dir/2005/29/2022-0 5-28.

context the notion of "safety" does not include the content posted on the platform and the psychological safety of the users, but only the physical safety of the interacting device and of its user.

In conclusion, the interaction of contract law with issues related to freedom of expression as regards online platforms constitutes a relatively new field of law that needs to be further explored before the courts. This use of consumer protection law to solve fundamental issues concerning Facebook could arguably be seen as evidence of a new trend towards a stronger protection of the platform's user (see also Sect. 8.2.3).

References

Ballam D, Fullwood C (2010) Fluidity of personal boundaries in online social media: implications for netiquette. Contemp Ergonomics Hum Factors:391–399

Bin IF (2021) My problem with Facebook's Haha react. The Daily Star. https://www.thedailystar.net/shout/news/my-problem-facebooks-haha-react-2031165

Directorate General of Human Rights and Legal Affairs, Media Division (2012) Study on the alignment of laws and practices concerning defamation with the relevant case-law of the European Court of Human Rights on freedom of expression, particularly with regard to the principle of proportionality. CDMSI(2012) Misc11Rev2

European Court of Human Rights Press Unit (2021) Fact sheet – Protection of reputation. available at www.echr.coe.int/Documents/FS_Reputation_ENG.pdf

Expert Committee on human rights dimensions of automated data processing and different forms of artificial intelligence (2019) Liability and jurisdictional issues in online defamation cases. Council of Europe study. DGI(2019)04. https://rm.coe.int/liability-and-jurisdictional-issues-in-online-defamation-cases-en/168097d9c3

Hartley TC (2010) 'Libel Tourism' and conflict of laws. Int Comp Law Q:25–38

Lafferman M (2012) Do Facebook and Twitter make you a public figure: how to apply the Gertz Public figure doctrine to social media. Santa Clara Comp High Tech Law J 29:199

Martini KR (2017) Umberto eco and emotions in the time of internet. Int J Soc Educational Innov (IJSEIro) 4(7):51–58

McGonagle T (2016) Freedom of expression and defamation, A study of the case law of the European Court of Human Rights. Council of Europe Publishing, Strasbourg, p 14

Parliamentary Assembly of the Council of Europe (2007) Towards decriminalisation of defamation. Resolution 1577. The resolution was reaffirmed in 2015. See Parliamentary Assembly Resolution 1577 & Recommendation 1814

Vanleenhove C (2018) The European Court of Justice in Bolagsupplysningen: The Brussels I Recast Regulation's jurisdictional rules for online infringement of personality rights further clarified. Comp Law Secur Rev 34(3):640–646. https://doi.org/10.1016/j.clsr.2017.11.010

Vroman ME, Stulz K, Hart C, Mullins K (2020) The business cost of online defamation. Int J Trade Econ Finance 11(4)

Chapter 6
Intermediaries' Liability: Where Is My Chair?

"Chairs are like Facebook". Facebook is not about "friends" anymore. It can be many different things for many people: a forum of political expression, an online gallery, a dating service, a team management device, an e-commerce tool, a way to keep in touch with family, etc. But how does Facebook see itself? In 2012, to celebrate reaching one billion active users, the company launched an advertisement campaign in the form of a short video made by Academy Award-nominated director Alejandro González Iñárritu. The video aims to demonstrate the utility and versatility of the platform, by comparing it with. . . a chair.[1]

The metaphor is direct enough: we are not related to the user-generated content we host, just as we do not know who will sit down and what will be put down on our chair; we only provide a means, being just an infrastructure. This point of view, far from being innocent or isolated in a single advertisement, has been enshrined as a major principle of EU Internet law: the intermediaries are not to be held liable for the content they give access to, transfer, or even host.

This principle was developed during a time where the Internet had a totally different shape; As the Internet keeps evolving, the principle has changed too, under the pressure of civil society and the ECJ's scrutiny (see Sect. 6.1). Calls and initiatives are militating against maintaining a wild immunity for the intermediaries. As intermediaries such as Facebook are asked by the EU to be more involved in the co-regulation of the Internet, it is only reasonable to make them accountable for their participation (see Sect. 6.2).

---

[1] Berkowitz (2012).

6.1   Origin and Operation of the Legislative Umbrella

6.1.1   The e-Commerce Directive

While the Internet was still in its infancy, and Web 2.0 was a future concept, Americans—and, later, Europeans—adopted a clear position in favor of the online service providers, protecting them from liability. In other words, an immunity against monetary liability was created. The reasoning behind this is based on multiple logical observations: this (at the time) emerging sector needed more flexibility to develop, and the economic consequences of a legal duty would have been a disaster. It was mainly argued that no liability should be borne in case of illegal content, as no malicious intent existed from the side of the online service providers. Simply put, intent presupposes knowledge, and having knowledge is technically impossible in this case. To take Facebook as an example, and specifically its photos, it is estimated (statistics from 2018) that 350 million photos are uploaded every day (that is 4000 photo uploads per second!).[2]

While the US had created multiple sectorial safe harbors through specific legislative provisions and case-law which lacked standardization,[3] the EU opted from the beginning for a horizontal protection aiming at any potential civil litigation, through the e-Commerce Directive.[4] Therefore, the safe harbor concerns all civil legal proceedings as regards copyright law, privacy, defamation, breach of confidence, or right to publicity. The safe harbor not only protects the online provider from primary liability, which is the negligence in permitting or hosting the illegal content, but also "secondary liability" (mainly used in common law countries) that "cover[s] in general those liabilities which are dependent on the illegal behaviour of a third party, such as the vicarious liability of employers".[5]

The directive does not focus only on establishing a safe harbor, and also (for instance) lays down some principles as regards the validity of electronic contracts. The safe harbor itself is divided into three independent situations: the "mere conduit" (Article 12), the "caching" (Article 13), and the hosting service (Article 14). Facebook can be categorized as a hosting service with respect to almost all of its features. To state the obvious, without the user-generated content it hosts on its servers (posts, interactions, profiles, stories, groups, pages, etc.) the platform would only be an empty shell.

Specifically, Article 14 (1) of the e-Commerce Directive states that

---

[2] https://www.omnicoreagency.com/facebook-statistics/.

[3] Lemley (2007), p. 101.

[4] Directive 2000/31/EC of the European Parliament and of the Council of 8 June 2000 on certain legal aspects of information society services, in particular electronic commerce, in the Internal Market ('Directive on electronic commerce'), OJ L 178, 17.7.2000, p. 1–16, ELI: http://data.europa.eu/eli/dir/2000/31/oj.

[5] Sartor (2017), p. 9.

[w]here an information society service is provided that consists of the storage of information provided by a recipient of the service, Member States shall ensure that the service provider is not liable for the information stored at the request of a recipient of the service, on condition that: (a) the provider does not have actual knowledge of illegal activity or information and, as regards claims for damages, is not aware of facts or circumstances from which the illegal activity or information is apparent; or (b) the provider, upon obtaining such knowledge or awareness, acts expeditiously to remove or to disable access to the information.

As specified in the article, the concept of liability is intertwined with the concept of knowledge. In this context, not only is the intermediary authorized to ignore the content, but any legal provision that would oblige the intermediary to exercise a general surveillance on the content would, in accordance with Article 15 of the Directive, be incompatible with EU law. While a system of notification is not expressly stated to be mandatory or even mentioned in Article 14, the second requirement laid down in the article does not permit any other interpretation: the intermediary is eligible for immunity only if it provides a mechanism for the user to bring to its attention a specific instance of illegal content.

On Facebook, this notification system is embedded as the "find support or report" option, available for any post or advertisement in the advanced options (the "three dots"), or through the "Legal Removal Request" option. The ECJ's YouTube's decision also emphasizes that point. The Court explains that the condition of awareness of the illegal content

cannot be regarded as not being satisfied solely on the ground that that operator is aware, in a general sense, of the fact that its platform is also used to share content which may infringe intellectual property rights and that it therefore has an abstract knowledge that protected content is being made available illegally on its platform.[6]

Consequently, the safe harbor mechanism requires lack of awareness of the illegality of specific content, while such awareness may be brought about either through the Internet sharing platform's own investigations or through the notification system that must be installed in the platform.

6.1.2 The Theory of the Passive Role

As explained above, the intermediary's immunity is based on the double conditions enshrined in Article 14: no actual or constructive knowledge, and fast reactions to a report. However, much uncertainty surrounds the first condition, and the ECJ, in its efforts to clarify it, has elucidated an extremely important theory called the "passive role" theory. Central to this theory is Recital 42 of the e-Commerce Directive, that refers to services of a

---

[6]ECJ, C-682/18 and C-683/18, Frank Peterson v. Google LLC, YouTube Inc., YouTube LLC, Google Germany GmbH (C-682/18), and Elsevier Inc. v. Cyando AG (C-683/18), 22/06/2021, ECLI:EU:C:2021:503, par.111.

mere technical, automatic and passive nature, which implies that the information society service provider has neither knowledge of nor control over the information which is transmitted or stored.

The Google Adwords case[7] discusses the liability of an intermediary for trade mark infringement. Adwords, Google's paid referencing service, enables any economic operator, by reserving one or more keywords, to obtain an advertising link to its site, in the event that an Iinternet user types one of those reserved keywords into Google's search engine. Google does not check whether the operator has the right under intellectual property law to reserve the specific word, and in this case, a competitor of the Vuitton company could reserve the word "Vuitton" to advertise its own products. This use is certainly illegal from a trade mark law and competition law perspective. However, Google cannot be found liable if it has installed a notification system. Indeed, as stated by the Court,

> in order to establish whether the liability of a referencing service provider may be limited under Article 14 of Directive 2000/31, it is necessary to examine whether the role played by that service provider is neutral, in the sense that its conduct is merely technical, automatic and passive, pointing to a lack of knowledge or control of the data which it stores.[8]

The Grand Chamber in the subsequent L'Oreal decision[9] confirms the importance of neutrality within the context of the intermediary's passive role. Once again, the case concerned trade mark infringements—but on the eBay platform this time. The Court reaffirmed that the intermediary has to demonstrate its neutrality and adds that

> [t]hat is not the case where the service provider, instead of confining itself to providing that service neutrally by a merely technical and automatic processing of the data provided by its customers, plays an active role of such a kind as to give it knowledge of, or control over, those data.

In this case, it was demonstrated that eBay processed the data entered by its customer-sellers, set the conditions in accordance with the sales made, and even provided assistance to optimize or promote certain offers for sale. Therefore, the immunity here could not be invoked.

Furthermore, in the Papasavvas decision[10] the ECJ had to decide, in the context of a defamation case, whether the status of online service provider applies to a website that reproduces the content of printed newspapers. The Court, applying only the principles established above, concluded that the safe harbor did not apply to this case, as the newspaper publishing company which operates a website on which the

---

[7]ECJ, C-237/08 and C-238/08, Google France SARL and Google Inc. v. Louis Vuitton Malletier SA, Google France SARL v. Viaticum SA and Luteciel SARL and Google France SARL v. Centre national de recherche en relations humaines (CNRRH) SARL and Others, 23/03/2010, ECLI:EU:C:2010:159.

[8]Par.114 of the Decision.

[9]ECJ, C-324/09, L'Oréal SA and Others v. eBay International AG and Others, 12/07/2011, ECLI:EU:C:2011:474.

[10]ECJ, C-291/13, Sotiris Papasavvas v. O Fileleftheros Dimosia Etairia Ltd, Takis Kounnafi, Giorgos Sertis, 11/09/2014, ECLI:EU:C:2014:2209.

online version of a newspaper is posted has knowledge of the information posted and exercises control over that information, whether or not access to that website is free of charge.

In conclusion, contrary to the US courts and while the legislative frameworks are very similar on this point, European courts broadly construe the conditions of Article 14 and, typically, to the general disadvantage of intermediaries.[11] Through the theory of the passive role, the ECJ intends to limit the immunity offered to the intermediaries, probably with the intention of forcing them to undertake more responsible action in a coregulating approach to the Internet. This action is not an isolated one, but rather belongs to a certain judicial activism that is generally present in the area of Internet law.[12]

However, one major shortcoming of the passive role theory is the uncertainty surrounding the voluntary interventions by the hosting provider. When Facebook, for instance, takes the initiative to block and even delete some content that is detected as violating the Community Standards, without a report from users or third parties, is it still acting within the limits of the passive role? From a strict interpretation of the L'Oreal decision, it is arguable that Facebook is taking an active role, but this solution would lead, in practice, to the illogical result that a company would lose its safe harbor status if it contributes to the fight against illegal content.

This specific issue has been fixed. First, the ECJ had the opportunity in the YouTube decision, to observe that the fact that

> the operator of a video-sharing platform, such as YouTube, implements technological measures aimed at detecting, among the videos communicated to the public via its platform, content which may infringe copyright, does not mean that, by doing so, that operator plays an active role giving it knowledge of and control over the content of those videos.[13]

Second, the EU legislator also intervened and explained in its "Digital Services Act" proposal that the existence of a moderation policy does not, on its own, negate a passive role (see Sect. 6.2.4).

---

[11] Ericsson (2016).

[12] Callamard (2017), pp. 323–339.

[13] ECJ, C-682/18 and C-683/18, Frank Peterson v. Google LLC, YouTube Inc., YouTube LLC, Google Germany GmbH (C-682/18), and Elsevier Inc. v. Cyando AG (C-683/18), 22/06/2021, ECLI:EU:C:2021:503, par.109.

6.1.3   Uses and Abuses of the Notice and Take Down Procedure

6.1.3.1   The Lack of Formalities in the Notification Process: The CG v. Facebook Case

As analyzed above, the e-Commerce Directive does not regulate the practical function of the notice and take down procedure. This flexibility had some shortcomings. For instance, online service providers tended to consider that only the use of the online report tool compels them to act. On the contrary, the e-Commerce Directive only specifies the knowledge, actual or constructive, of the illegal content as a criterion. In 2012, the Commission recognized that the e-Commerce Directive needed improvement on this point, and that it was necessary to provide clarifications.[14]

The case CG v. Facebook in Ireland highlights this problematic.[15] A person set up a Facebook page entitled 'Keeping Our Kids Safe from Predators' in which he published details of individuals who had criminal convictions relating to sexual offences involving children. An injunction was applied for, on the basis of the extreme violence of the comments, that threatened the life of the persons concerned, requesting that Facebook be ordered to close the page. However, the same person immediately set up a second page on the same topic. On this new page, again, sensitive information was posted (photos of the convicted persons, disclosure of their home address) and shared 1622 times, accompanied by calls for violent actions against them, discussions about where they lived, and support for those who would act. One of these concerned persons, CG, commenced legal action against Facebook, claiming defamation, harassment, and violation of privacy. The company responded that the online report tool must be used to file a complaint, but the plaintiff's lawyers explained that CG did not want to have any interaction with the platform. Almost one month later, Facebook removed the page's contents, but the litigation process had already started.

One legal issue in the case was whether the previous injunction against the first version of the page was enough to bring Facebook's attention to potential future threats. Specifically, it is arguable that knowledge of the illegal content could be derived from the previous behavior of the page's creator. The court answered in the negative, considering that such a duty would indirectly violate the general prohibition of general monitoring in Article 15 of the e-Commerce directive. On the contrary, the letter from the solicitor was accepted by the court as an acceptable form of notification, which activated the duty to act expeditiously to remove the content. Facebook's delay in removing the content justifies its liability and CG was ultimately awarded GBP 2000 in damages.

---

[14]EU Commission (2012).

[15]Irish Court of Appeal, CG v. Facebook ([2016] NICA 54.

Nowadays, Facebook offers EU citizens a specific report option called the "Legal Removal Request".[16] A priori this option is similar to the report option available for any posts and comments on the platform, but with two major differences. First, an account is not needed to proceed with the notice. Second, the legal basis of the "Legal Removal Request" is the violation of the law directly, not the violation of the Community Standards (as it is for the report option). It is arguable that some content can be illegal on the basis of national law, while not infringing the user's contractual obligations. Furthermore, the modality and formalities of the notice system have been revised by the Digital Services Act (see Sect. 6.2.4).

6.1.3.2   The Facebook "Judgment" on Reporting and Its Strange Passivity

One other issue of the notification system is that is creates a burden on the Internet service provider to judge whether there are sufficient grounds to regard the content as illegal. This is problematic, first, because, due to the high number of notifications and the related costs, Facebook surely does not employ staff with sufficient qualifications in communications law to monitor the content. Second, there is an obvious conflict of interest in requiring that the company that profits from the existence of the content determine whether it should remove it or not.

Specifically, the corresponding lack of diligence of Facebook in assessing the seriousness of a report had already led to new court decisions. In J20 v. Facebook Ireland Ltd,[17] an individual initiated privacy and harassment proceedings against Facebook as his name and portrait were mentioned on several pages with rather unflattering comments ("Loyalist bigot", "woman beating snake", "tout"). The concerned person used the platform's online report system. At first, Facebook decided not to remove the material when the complaint was made because it concluded that the posts did not violate its Community Standards. It took almost one month for the platform to revise its opinion and delete the information, after a complaint was filed with the court.

The High Court considered a series of elements in deciding whether Facebook could benefit from the safe harbor. First, the report was very vague on the legal arguments supporting the view that the content was illegal. However, the Court considered the plaintiff merely used the report tool at his disposal and the burden of the classification of the publications as misuse of private information and/or defamation burdens Facebook, not the plaintiff. Second, the response time of the platform to delete the illegal content did not correspond to the definition of an expeditious reaction.

In conclusion, whilst this case is interesting it does not offer any substantial clarification concerning Facebook's liability. Nevertheless, this refusal to moderate

---

[16] See https://www.facebook.com/help/2214522878809427/.

[17] High Court. J20 v. Facebook Ireland Ltd ([2016] NIQB 98.

is characteristic of a general trend by the social network. It could be said that Facebook's notice and take down mechanism is surprisingly inefficient, and, in this, Facebook seems to have taken a different approach from other online service providers. Indeed, most online service providers apply a risk-based approach and weigh the risk of loss of revenue related to the deletion of specific, presumably illegal, content that has been reported against the risk associated with the non-deletion, which is a potentially costly court proceeding. In this context, the notice and take down procedure is bound to create some abuse, or a "broad censorial attitude",[18] with adverse effects on the freedom of expression. The danger of private censorship by online service providers is well-documented[19] and in 2015 the EU Commission recognized in a Communication that

> today the disabling of access to and the removal of illegal content by providers of hosting services can be slow and complicated, while content that is actually legal can be taken down erroneously.[20]

However, the exact opposite trend can be discerned on Facebook, whose visible reluctance to comply with notifications is slowly becoming more obvious to the public. For instance, Germany's Federal Office of Justice (BfJ) fined the company EUR 2 million for underreporting the number of complaints it had received about illegal content on its platform.[21] This general stance cannot be the result of statistical error. On the contrary, it must be admitted that this underestimation of the reports is the result of the company's deliberate policy.

A possible explanation of this strange conduct is that the company considers the removal of illegal content to be a kind of reputational damage: perhaps it fears that accusations of censorship would create a domino effect undermining the platform's credibility. Characteristically, when after months of various violations and following the riots in the Capitol, Facebook decided to suspend President Trump's account, the US far-right movement decided to boycott the platform en masse and to virtually gather in alternative social networks.[22] Moreover, past mergers show the company's great concerns about challenges posed by emerging competitors. In this context, lack of moderation was arguably internally perceived as a marketing advantage, notwithstanding the legal cost.

---

[18] Sartor (2017), p. 13.

[19] Kuczerawy (2015), pp. 46–56.

[20] European Commission (2015).

[21] Source: https://www.dw.com/en/germany-fines-facebook-for-underreporting-hate-speech-com plaints/a-49447820.

[22] Siladitya (2021).

6.1.4   The Recurrent "Take Down, Stay Down" Theory

6.1.4.1   Origin, Justification, and Dismissal of the Theory

The safe harbor has the practical consequence of putting the burden of policing the Internet on the victim, in the sense that it is the responsibility of the victim of an illegal post to report it to the intermediary. However, most social networks allow broad access to their service. Even on Facebook, where the policy asks the user to announce his real identity, the number of fake accounts is impossible to ignore. Within the first three months of 2018 alone, the company deleted 583 million fake accounts.[23] As a consequence, the reporting of illegal content, even when associated with a ban of the author for violating the Community Standards, can sometimes be only the beginning of a game between the victim and the author of the illegal content. This game has been described as a "whack-a-mole" problem: every time the content is taken down, it reappears elsewhere on the Internet.[24] The consequences are many: not only does each new recommunication increase the risk that the victim will lose heart and abandon his efforts, but the inefficiency of the enforcement method also enhances a general feeling of impunity on the Internet.

A simple solution to this problem would be to accept an addition to the "notice and take down" approach, which would be to consider the complaint as sufficient ground to alert the intermediary of a risk, and to create an enhanced duty of the intermediary to pre-emptively block any further attempt to communicate the illegal content. However, this "take down, stay down" theory has one fundamental weakness: its incompatibility with the provisions of Article 15 on the prohibition of general monitoring. Therefore, the theory has been rejected by national courts such as the Supreme Court in France in the Google France v. Bac Films decision.[25]

The ECJ, too, has expressed its position on this point. In the Scarlet Extended case[26] the Court had to discuss the compatibility with EU law of an injunction against an Internet service provider which required it to install a system for filtering access to some musical, cinematographic or audiovisual works available on the Internet in breach of copyright law. This injunction was ruled incompatible with the principle of prohibition of general monitoring. However, it is important to highlight the fact that the case does not refer to hosting services but to Internet providers.

---

[23] Rosen (2018).

[24] Besek (2020).

[25] France, Court of Cassation, First civil chamber, Google France v. Bac Films, 12/07/2012, ECLI: FR:CCASS:2012:C100831.

[26] ECJ, C-70/10 Scarlet Extended v. Société belge des auteurs, compositeurs et éditeurs SCRL (SABAM), 24/11/2011, ECLI:EU:C:2011:771.

A few months later, a second decision on this topic was published, that, this time, directly concerned a hosting service. In the Netlog NV case,[27] the same collective management organization requested an injunction to filter the content, but this time against a hosting platform, which

> runs an online social networking platform where every person who registers acquires a personal space known as a 'profile' which the user can complete himself and which becomes available globally.[28]

The court considered that the legitimate interest of enforcing copyright law must weighed against, first, the freedom to conduct business enjoyed by operators such as hosting service providers (as the Court remarks that

> such an injunction would result in a serious infringement of the freedom of the hosting service provider to conduct its business since it would require that hosting service provider to install a complicated, costly, permanent computer system at its own expense,[29]

and, second, the users' fundamental rights of privacy and freedom of information.[30] Therefore, such an injunction was illegal.

6.1.4.2   The Eva Glawischnig-Piesczek v. Facebook Case

The Eva Glawischnig-Piesczek[31] case provides a new perspective on the futility of the take down procedure, when not accompanied by the take down, stay down doctrine. In this case, a Facebook Service user shared on his personal page an article from an Austrian online news magazine, entitled 'Greens: Minimum income for refugees should stay', which had the effect of generating on that page a "thumbnail" of the original site, containing the title and a summary of the article, as well as a photograph of Ms. Glawischnig-Piesczek (the politician whose ideas were described in the article). Furthermore, the user added to the hyperlink a personal insulting and defamatory message about the politician.

The setting of the post was "public" and anyone could access it. The politician sent a letter requesting the deletion of the message in July and, in the absence of any action from the platform, decided to sue Facebook in December. It is not disputed here that Facebook had lost the privilege of the safe harbor, being considerably late in its reaction to the notification of the illegal content. The interesting part of the case lies in the demand of Ms. Glawischnig's solicitor, who not only requested the

---

[27] ECJ, C-360/10, Belgische Vereniging van Auteurs, Componisten en Uitgevers CVBA (SABAM) v. Netlog NV, 16/02/2012, ECLI:EU:C:2012:85.

[28] Par. 16 of the Decision.

[29] Par. 46 of the Decision.

[30] Par. 49 and 50 of the Decision.

[31] ECJ, C 18/18, Eva Glawischnig-Piesczek v. Facebook Ireland Limited, 03/10/2019, ECLI:EU: C:2019:821.

message to be deleted but also wished to prevent the publication of the same message or messages with equivalent meaning in the future.

In this context, the national court turned to the ECJ for some clarifications. First, if such an injunction is found to be compatible with the principles of the e-Commerce Directive, should it have a regional or a global range? Second and most importantly, is the prohibition on posting messages of equivalent meaning compatible with these principles?

As regards the issue of the global or regional reach of such an injunction, the ECJ considered that the e-Commerce Directive does not provide for any limitation, including a territorial limitation, on the scope of the measures which Member States are entitled to adopt in accordance with that directive,[32] and therefore there is no reason to limit the territorial impact of such an injunction.

As regards the issue of legality of such an injunction, although at first sight it could be seen as incompatible with the general prohibition of surveillance in Article 15, the ECJ did not consider that such injunction an injunction would be illegal on principle. The court remarks that

> [i]n those circumstances, in order to ensure that the host provider at issue prevents any further impairment of the interests involved, it is legitimate for the court having jurisdiction to be able to require that host provider to block access to the information stored, the content of which is identical to the content previously declared to be illegal, or to remove that information, irrespective of who requested the storage of that information. In particular, in view of the identical content of the information concerned, the injunction granted for that purpose cannot be regarded as imposing on the host provider an obligation to monitor generally the information which it stores, or a general obligation actively to seek facts or circumstances indicating illegal activity, as provided for in Article 15(1) of Directive 2000/31.[33]

However, this kind of injunction is not automatically valid. Its validity depends on two aspects: the details in the injunction (name, words, description of the content and of the meaning), and the interpretation that should apply to the concept of "equivalent message". Indeed, for the ECJ, such an injunction does not violate the principle of prohibition of general monitoring if it is very strictly interpreted as encompassing only messages that are substantially identical. Specifically, it considers that

> [i]n light of the foregoing, it is important that the equivalent information referred to in paragraph 41 above contains specific elements which are properly identified in the injunction, such as the name of the person concerned by the infringement determined previously, the circumstances in which that infringement was determined and equivalent content to that which was declared to be illegal. Differences in the wording of that equivalent content, compared with the content which was declared to be illegal, must not, in any event, be such as to require the host provider concerned to carry out an independent assessment of that content.[34]

---

[32] Par.49 of the Decision.

[33] Par.37 of the Decision.

[34] Par.45 of the Decision.

This interpretation offers a way for the injunction to be valid within the context of the prohibition of general monitoring. It could be said that the ECJ works under the assumption[35] that equivalent information in this context is information that can be identified as such through technological means, which implicitly means the use of AI, while it is unclear whether such a practice is feasible without incurring disproportionate costs.

6.2   Contemporary Doubts on the Safe Harbor Legitimacy

6.2.1   The Safe Harbor As Outdated Model

All arguments used in favor of the safe harbor have undergone fundamental alterations several decades later. As seen above, the reasoning behind the safe harbor is, first of all, based on the lack of knowledge of the Internet service provider. However, this lack of knowledge is nowadays debatable. The contemporary rise of AI has allowed for multiple new solutions to be found to the problem of illegal content. Furthermore, the immunity was also justified at the time for economic reasons, while nowadays the rise of the GAFAM rather shows monopolistic tends. Finally, as shown above (see Sect. 6.1.2), the immunity is closely dependent on proof of a passive role. This notion of a passive role is challenged today. Is Facebook's practical functioning neutral as regards user-generated content? Converging elements (see Chap. 8) indicate that the platform's operations are based on algorithms that do not treat all information in the same way. Facebook itself has publicly recognized in the context of defending a US lawsuit that it is not just a neutral platform anymore, but acts de facto as a publisher.[36]

Specifically, as regards Facebook, it has been remarked that

> services Facebook provide regarding information of interest to Facebook users (News Feed algorithm and content recommendation algorithm, as well as Ad Match services), may mean that the question of neutrality and passivity here is at least worthy of investigation, in that Facebook may promote certain content.[37]

These new facts, perspectives, and evolutions lead to a substantial paradigm shift.[38] As the platform grows in power, both economically and politically,[39] the intermediary's safe harbor is not seen as a positive outcome anymore. It is therefore considered that "the onus falls primarily upon social media platforms to update their organizational responsibilities in order to adhere to the law".[40]

---

[35] Woods (2019).

[36] Leven (2018).

[37] Woods (2017).

[38] Mac (2020), pp. 1–21.

[39] Busch et al. (2021).

[40] Rochefort (2020), pp. 225–260.

Exemptions to the safe harbor regime were already in place from the start and data privacy legislation is notably excluded from this field (see above Sect. 2.5.2). It is explicitly stated that the e-Commerce Directive shall not apply to "questions relating to information society services covered by Directives 95/46/EC and 97/66/EC".[41]

Nevertheless, legal developments questioning the safe harbor mechanism in specific fields of law have multiplied in recent years. Intellectual property law is particularly affected (see Sect. 6.2.3). Other sector-specific legislations have been passed that affect the intermediary's safe harbor.

First, the field of child pornography is relevant. Article 25 (1) of the Directive 2011/93/EU on combating the sexual abuse and sexual exploitation of children[42] states that

> Member States shall take the necessary measures to ensure the prompt removal of web pages containing or disseminating child pornography hosted in their territory and to endeavour to obtain the removal of such pages hosted outside of their territory,

while Article 25 (2) adds an option to block access to web pages containing or disseminating child pornography to Internet users within their territory. Even if the EU legislation refers to "web pages" and not to "content", it is arguable that Facebook is also affected. It is worth mentioning that providers are not directly exempted from the obligation to ensure the "prompt removal" of content, but the legislation gives a lot of latitude to Member States in transposing this obligation in their national framework.

Second, the intermediary's behavior in case of hate speech is scrutinized. In the revised Audiovisual Media Services Directive[43] (AVMSD) it is explained that "video-sharing platform providers" provide information society services within the meaning of the e-Commerce Directive.[44] However, the AVMSD contains numerous provisions related to video sharing services that aim to bind the social networks to some basic principles for the protection of minors and protection against hate speech (see Sect. 7.1.4 for a detailed analysis). Initiatives are also taken on national level to hinder the safe harbor on that point. Characteristically, in Germany, the regulation known as "Netzwerkdurchsetzungsgesetz" (Network Enforcement Act, or just NetzDG) imposes a strict duty to remove certain forms of illegal content in less than 24 h.

---

[41] Article 1 (5) (b) of the e-Commerce Directive.

[42] Directive 2011/93/EU of the European Parliament and of the Council of 13 December 2011 on combating the sexual abuse and sexual exploitation of children and child pornography, and replacing Council Framework Decision 2004/68/JHA, OJ L 335, 17.12.2011, p. 1–14, ELI: http://data.europa.eu/eli/dir/2011/93/oj.

[43] Directive (EU) 2018/1808 of the European Parliament and of the Council of 14 November 2018 amending Directive 2010/13/EU on the coordination of certain provisions laid down by law, regulation or administrative action in Member States concerning the provision of audiovisual media services (Audiovisual Media Services Directive) in view of changing market realities, PE/33/2018/REV/1, OJ L 303, 28.11.2018, p. 69–92 ELI: http://data.europa.eu/eli/dir/2018/1808/oj.

[44] Recital 44 of the Directive.

Third, a new regulation on preventing the dissemination of terrorist content online has been prepared by the EU Commission and adopted in 2021.[45] The regime provides for an extremely fast system of online terrorist content removal:[46] after receiving the removal order from the competent authority, the social network has one hour to comply and remove the content,[47] unless he can show objectively justifiable technical or operational reasons that justify a delay.[48] The hosting service provider has to comply. If it believes that the removal order was unlawful, it has the right to request—within 48 h—that the order be scrutinized by the competent authority of its country of establishment.[49] Furthermore, Facebook does not have to wait for the removal order. Not only is it compelled to add provisions against anti-terrorist content in its Community Standards, but it must also take some initiatives, "specific measures to protect its services against the dissemination to the public of terrorist content".[50] Lastly, in accordance with the general trend in this field (see Sect. 8.2.2), a general duty of transparency, diligence and non-discrimination is instituted.[51]

In conclusion, this fragmentation and erosion of the safe harbor regime could be seen as the end of the horizontal approach on this issue. It has been proposed that a vertical approach would anyway better fit the realities of the Internet today, in the sense that calibrating the system contributes to achieving a truer "fair balance" between the various interests at stake.[52]

---

[45] Regulation (EU) 2021/784 of the European Parliament and of the Council of 29 April 2021 on addressing the dissemination of terrorist content online, OJ L 172, 17.5.2021, p. 79–109, ELI: http://data.europa.eu/eli/reg/2021/784/oj.

[46] Online Terrorist content is defined at article 2 (7) of the Regulation as any material that

(a) incites the commission of one of the offences referred to in points (a) to (i) of Article 3(1) of Directive (EU) 2017/541, where such material, directly or indirectly, such as by the glorification of terrorist acts, advocates the commission of terrorist offences, thereby causing a danger that one or more such offences may be committed; (b) solicits a person or a group of persons to commit or contribute to the commission of one of the offences referred to in points (a) to (i) of Article 3(1) of Directive (EU) 2017/541; (c) solicits a person or a group of persons to participate in the activities of a terrorist group, within the meaning of point (b) of Article 4 of Directive (EU) 2017/541; (d) provides instruction on the making or use of explosives, firearms or other weapons or noxious or hazardous substances, or on other specific methods or techniques for the purpose of committing or contributing to the commission of one of the terrorist offences referred to in points (a) to (i) of Article 3(1) of Directive (EU) 2017/541; (e) constitutes a threat to commit one of the offences referred to in points (a) to (i) of Article 3(1) of Directive (EU) 2017/541;

[47] Article 3 (3) of the Regulation.

[48] Article 3 (7) of the Regulation.

[49] Article 4 (4) of the Regulation.

[50] Article 5 (2) of the Regulation.

[51] Article 7 of the Regulation.

[52] Angelopoulos and Smet (2016), pp. 266–301.

6.2.2   The Safe Harbor from a Human Rights Perspective

6.2.2.1   The Delfi Case

Any kind of legal immunity is by essence an anomaly in a rule of law system. In the past, the ECtHR has had some violent clashes with the UK courts as regards the "fair, just and reasonable" criterion in establishing a case of negligence under tort law. Originally, the ECtHR had decided in the famous Osman decision[53] that, as this criterion excludes some acts related to the general interest from civil liability, it works de facto as an immunity. The decision was later overturned as regards the law of negligence,[54] but the principle remains that immunity is incompatible (provided that this restriction does not pursue a legitimate interest and is disproportionate) with the general principle of free access to justice enshrined in Article 6 of the Convention. It is stated that "[i]mmunity is to be seen here not as qualifying a substantive right but as a procedural bar to the national courts' power to determine that right".[55]

The safe harbor is not an absolute immunity, but a conditional one. Furthermore, it could be argued that it serves a legitimate interest. Therefore, it could be argued that it is not a disproportionate restriction to Article 6. Nevertheless, it is established that EU law does not directly bind the ECtHR. Still, it is worth mentioning that as a principle the ECtHR agrees with the safe harbor philosophy. Liability is, on principle, personal in a democratic society, and liability of third parties should remain an exception.

Characteristically, in the Editorial Board of Pravoye Delo and Shtekel v. Ukraine case,[56] a newspaper published an anonymous letter posted on an Internet site that accused senior local officials of being involved in various criminal activities. The newspaper indicated the source of the information and specified that the content of the letter was not verified and might thus be false. The newspaper was held liable for defamation. The ECtHR considered that this decision violated journalists' freedom of expression. The newspaper was only reporting the content in good faith. However, this does not automatically mean that the ECtHR considers the safe harbor to be a manifestation of the freedom of expression. In this case, the court was more interested in the absence of a sufficient legal framework for the protection of journalists.

The landmark Delfi AS decisions[57] (of the Chamber in 2013 and of the Grand Chamber in 2015) have noticeably influenced the issue. Delfi was an online newspaper that had a notorious history of publishing defamatory and degrading comments. However, a notice and take down mechanism existed on the website to

---

[53] ECtHR, Osman v. the United Kingdom, no 23452/94, 28/10/1998.

[54] ECtHR, Z and Others v. the United Kingdom, no. 29392/95, 10/05/2001.

[55] ECtHR (2020) Guide on Article 6 of the European Convention on Human Rights, Council of Europe/European Court of Human Rights.

[56] ECtHR, Editorial Board of Pravoye Delo and Shtekel v. Ukraine, no. 33014/05, 05/05/2011.

[57] ECtHR, Delfi AS v. Estonia, no. 64569/09, (Chamber) 10/102013, (Grand Chamber) 6/06/2015.

prevent the dissemination of illegal content. In this context, the website published an article on a public company's gross negligence and its repercussions on the public. The article attracted a lot of passionate discussions and comments (twenty of them were personal threats against the director of the company). About 6 weeks after their publication, but on the same day the targeted director complained and sued the website, the offensive comments were removed. In other words, the website operated what could be described as "fairly standard measures: a disclaimer as to illegality, a filtering mechanism, the separation of the comments section from the article, and immediate removal upon notice.".[58] However, the filtering mechanism was manifestly ineffective. The national court held the newspaper liable for defamation.

It appears very important to highlight the fact that in this case the national court decided to reject the application of the safe harbor. The Supreme Court, a little too harshly, considered that the website indeed exercised strict control over the comments, contrary to the principles of a passive role. The ECtHR, both at first instance and in the Grand Chamber, held that it was not its role to intervene in the debate whether the online newspaper was a publisher or a provider of the comments. On the contrary, it found that the issue was not important here, as the true question was whether the newspaper's obligation to ensure that comments posted on its Internet portal did not infringe the personality rights of third persons was in accordance with the guarantees set out in Article 10 (freedom of expression).

Although most commentators expected the Chamber in 2013 to find against Estonia and to simultaneously enshrine the safe harbor into the protection of fundamental rights, the Court actually held that the decision against the newspaper did not violate Article 10 of the Convention, as it pursued a legitimate aim (the protection of reputation). This radical position justified the intervention of the Grand Chamber.

Therefore, the Court noted at the outset that

> user-generated expressive activity on the Internet provides an unprecedented platform for the exercise of freedom of expression. (...). However, alongside these benefits, certain dangers may also arise. Defamatory and other types of clearly unlawful speech, including hate speech and speech inciting violence, can be disseminated like never before, worldwide, in a matter of seconds, and sometimes remain persistently available online. These two conflicting realities lie at the heart of this case. Bearing in mind the need to protect the values underlying the Convention, and considering that the rights under Articles 10 and 8 of the Convention deserve equal respect, a balance must be struck that retains the essence of both rights.[59]

The court found that the defamatory comments were predictable, due to the sensitive content of the article and to the "tradition" of the newspaper. Consequently, the online newspaper "was in a position to assess the risks related to its activities and that it must have been able to foresee, to a reasonable degree, the consequences which

---

[58] Par. 36 of the joint dissident opinion of judges Sajo and Tsotsoria.
[59] Par.110 of the decision.

these could entail."[60] It was therefore confirmed by the Grand Chamber that the newspaper's liability for the illegal comments was compatible with the Convention. However, it must be highlighted that the Court explicitly exempts social media from this jurisprudence,[61] as the provider in such cases does not provide any content. Consequently, Facebook is not directly affected by this jurisprudence. The newspaper's liability in this case, despite apparently being triggered by anonymous comments from a third party, is actually strictly associated with its own publishing activity.

6.2.2.2 The Post-Delfi Era

Nevertheless, the Delfi case, by confirming the provider's liability, casts a shadow over the legitimacy of the safe harbor and the case indirectly affects Facebook's legal framework. In this context, new decisions in the "post-Delfi era" were expected to bring more clarifications on the status of intermediaries. Although two more cases of intermediaries' liability were indeed brought to the Court's attention, the decisions arguably blurred the situation even further.

In the case MTE v. Hungary[62] in 2016, a major Internet news portal once again allowed users to comment on the news. The system had a notice and take down mechanism. An article about the alleged unethical conduct of two real estate management websites provoked violent comments. The concerned company found that the comments were offensive, insulting and humiliating and sued the online newspaper. National courts considered that indeed the comments went beyond the acceptable limits of freedom of expression, but did not justify in detail why they did not apply the safe harbor in this case.

As already mentioned, restrictions on human rights must pass the famous three-part test: they must be prescribed by law, have one or more legitimate aims, and be necessary in a democratic society (see Sect. 8.1.2). It could be concluded that the facts of this case are very similar to the facts of Delfi, but, on the contrary, the court distinguished the two cases, finding that they differed on a substantial point. In this case, "[a]lthough offensive and vulgar (...), the incriminated comments did not constitute clearly unlawful speech".[63] Consequently, the Court found here that the decision against the intermediary constituted a violation of Article 10 of the Convention.

A second post-Delfi case, Pihl v. Sweden,[64] once again raised the issue of the hosting provider's civil liability for anonymous comments. In this case, a small

---

[60]Par.129 of the decision.

[61]Par.116 of the decision.

[62]ECtHR, Magyar Tartalomszolgáltatók Egyesülete and Index.hu Zrt v. Hungary, no. 22947/13, 02/02/2016.

[63]Par.64 of the decision.

[64]ECtHR, Pihl v. Sweden, no. 74742/14, 09/03/2017.

not-for-profit organization ran a personal blog where it posted an article accusing Mr. Pihl of being a member of the Nazi party. A comment under the post added "that guy pihl is also a real hash-junkie according to several people I have spoken to". However, the national courts refused to uphold the claim for defamation, taking into account the protection of the organization's freedom of expression. Mr. Pihl turned to the Court, alleging a violation of Article 8 of the Convention (right to personality).

Once again, the ECtHR made a distinction: the comments were "only" defamatory and had not amounted to hate speech or an incitement to violence. Continuing its previous jurisprudence, it concluded that Mr. Pihl's application was to be rejected.

In conclusion, the Delfi case on the one hand, and the MTE and Pihl on the other, have to be interpreted as contributing to a general picture of the safe harbor's compatibility with human rights. The Court reflects that the degree of "unlawfulness" of the content matters. With hate speech and calls for violence, considering the increased risk this entails for society and individuals, the provider has to intervene as soon as it obtains constructive knowledge of the content. However, for any other kind of unlawful content, the fundamental role exerted by the hosting service in guaranteeing the freedom of expression has the effect of annulling the intermediary's civil liability and no constructive knowledge should be used against it.

This conclusion has also been recently confirmed in the case Høiness v. Norway.[65] The ECtHR confirmed the decision of the national courts that the intermediary (a discussion forum under a news portal) was not liable for anonymous vulgar comments. The Court considered that the comments did not belong to the category of hate speech and calls for violence, that the forum had a warning system that was very efficient (the messages were deleted thirty minutes after notification), the comment section was clearly defined and designed to be separate from the news content, and the forum was regulated by moderators. Therefore, in dismissing the applicant's complaint, the courts had exercised their discretion to strike a balance between freedom of expression and protection of reputation.

Consequently, the ECtHR does confirm the validity and significance of the safe harbor in principle, but it also adds a substantial restriction to this principle, exempting one category of illegal content: serious cases of hate speech and call for violence.

---

[65] ECtHR, Høiness v. Norway, no. 43624/14, 19 March 2019.

6.2.3 Copyright Law As Lex Specialis and the Erosion of the Safe Harbor Mechanism Through Injunctions

6.2.3.1 Copyright Law As Lex Specialis

As explained above, the safe harbor has a horizontal effect. However, several mechanisms under copyright law can practically counteract the intermediary's immunity. This is quite ironic as copyright law has historically constituted the main field of application of the safe harbor, through the DMCA legislation in the US. Nevertheless, as it has become increasingly clear that copyright law enforcement through individual litigations or technical measures of protection will fail, the intermediaries' unique position to affect the enforcement of online copyright law has triggered some legislative and jurisprudential evolutions.

First, the court tends to accept the intermediary's constructive knowledge as a criterion when its reason d'être is closely associated with the copyright infringement. For instance, in the Pirate Bay case,[66] the ECJ discussed the liability of a famous website that offers its visitors the opportunity to share torrent keys which allow files to be downloaded on peer-to-peer networks. As soon as the website's owners create categories of protected works (movies, e-books, music, etc.), collect significant revenues from the website's activities as well as through advertisement, and present the website as way to access protected works, they obviously have knowledge that the content they are hosting in the peer-to-peer networks they offer access to, are illegal.

Second, Article 17 of the Digital Single Market Directive has substantially modified the impact of the safe harbor as regards copyright law (see Sect. 3.3.1). The hosting provider that makes available protected works is considered, on principle, to be making an act of communication to the public. Moreover, it is recognized that most major actors (such as Meta) have a duty to detect and prevent future acts of communication to the public. The general notice and take down system is reversed: the burden lies with the content's uploader to report an abuse of the filtering system. The Directive states that

> an online content-sharing service provider performs an act of communication to the public or an act of making available to the public for the purposes of this Directive when it gives the public access to copyright-protected works or other protected subject matter uploaded by its users.[67]

The Digital Single Market Directive declares, as a general principle, that it shall leave intact and shall in no way affect existing rules laid down by the e-Commerce Directive,[68] and it confirms the intermediary's new duty laid down in Article 17 that "[t]he application of this Article shall not lead to any general monitoring

---

[66] ECJ, C 610/15, Stichting Brein v. Ziggo BV, XS4ALL Internet BV, 14/06/2017, ECLI:EU:C:2017:456.

[67] Article 17 (1) of the Directive 2019/790 on the Digital Single Market.

[68] Article 1 (2) of the Directive.

obligation".[69] However, the distinction is subtle: although providers are still protected by the safe harbor even if the content infringes copyright law, the most important companies (typically the GAFAM) have the duty to exercise their best efforts to obtain authorization and a license for this content. Alternatively, they must demonstrate that they have made best efforts to ensure the unavailability of specific works and other subject matter for which the right-holders have provided the service providers with the relevant and necessary information in order to prevent their future uploads.[70] As explained above (see Sect. 3.3.2), even if the text of the Directive, after long discussions and negotiations, avoids using the term "filtering", this specific legal framework implies, in practice, an AI-based content recognition mechanism.

   In conclusion, Article 17 indirectly affects the safe harbor as the intermediary is liable in case it has not proceeded with extreme diligence (best effort) to ensure the unavailability of specific works for which the right-holders have provided a list.

6.2.3.2 Safe Harbor and Injunctions

In the Eva Glawischnig-Piesczek case discussed above (see Sect. 6.1.4), the ECJ explained that Article 14 of the Directive is not a general immunity from every legal obligation, meaning that national authorities remain competent to require a host to terminate access to or remove illegal information. This limitation of the safe harbor was already clear in the text of the e-Commerce Directive: the intermediary's immunity concerns liability as regards the illegal content, not liability for not complying with an administrative or judicial injunction.

   This distinction had a huge impact on copyright law, specifically. Not just any injunctions are permitted, since injunctions that are too general would violate the prohibition of general monitoring (see decisions Netlog and Scarlet, Sect. 6.1.4). Nevertheless, in the landmark decision UPC Telekabel Wien,[71] the court recognized the validity of a court injunction prohibiting an online service provider from allowing its customers access to a "pirate" website. In other words, online service providers may be requested to actively participate in the efforts against online copyright law infringement.

   Each time the safe harbor takes a step back, even indirectly, issues appear as regards the protection of freedom of expression. The Court explicitly handled this question, by adding two safeguards to the mechanism of injunctions against intermediaries. First, it must be ensured that the measures taken to comply with the injunction do not unnecessarily deprive Internet users of lawful access to the information available. In other words, the Telekabel mechanism will never apply against a legitimate website such as Facebook, even if illegal content is detected on

---

[69] Article 17 (8) of the Directive.

[70] Article 17 (4) (b) and (c) of the Directive.

[71] ECJ, C-314/12, UPC Telekabel Wien GmbH v. Constantin Film Verleih GmbH and Wega Filmproduktionsgesellschaft mbH, 27/03/2014.

their servers. Second, those measures must be effective. In a world of VPN servers and proxies, the effectiveness of a filtering measure is certainly relative, but the decision anticipated the criticism, adding that the effectiveness must be understood

> at least, of making it difficult to achieve and of seriously discouraging internet users who are using the services of the addressee of that injunction from accessing the subject-matter that has been made available to them in breach of the intellectual property right.

The purpose is not to completely block the access, but to make it more difficult in order to discourage users from attempting the access.

McFadden[72] illustrates the various injunctions that can be issued against intermediaries. The case concerned free Wi-Fi Internet access from a provider of access to a communication network. As the connection is anonymous, the right-holder could not determine who had downloaded its protected works. Therefore, it requested a court injunction to compel the provider to prevent third parties from making a particular copyright-protected work or parts thereof available to the general public from an online (peer-to-peer) exchange platform via an Internet connection. The provider remains free to choose which technical measures to take in order to comply with the injunction. It could be an identification system, a prevention of peer-to-peer exchanges on the network, or password protection. The court remarked that even a single measure consisting in password-protecting the Internet connection, provided that those users are required to reveal their identity in order to obtain the required password and may not therefore act anonymously, would be legitimate in this context.

6.2.4 The Proposed EU Digital Services Act

The most important manifestation of the contemporary doubts about the legitimacy of the safe harbor takes the shape of a Regulation proposal from the EU Commission. For a decade, the EU has been preparing the involved actors, through various evaluations and reports, for the need to modify the safe harbor regime.[73] Finally, in December 2020, the EU Commission officially proposed the Digital Services Act (DSA).[74] This proposal explicitly aims to correct the shortcomings of the e-Commerce directive as regards the safe harbor. However, the DSA on multiple points perpetuates the philosophy and mechanism of the e-Commerce Directive, adjusting its functioning only on some problematic points. Therefore, the immunity of the hosting service (Article 5), the prohibition of general monitoring (Article 7), and the possibility of injunctions against intermediaries (Article 8) are confirmed in the new regulation.

---

[72] ECJ, C-484/14, Tobias Mc Fadden v. Sony Music Entertainment Germany, 15/09/2016.

[73] Madiega (2020).

[74] Proposal for a Regulation of the European Parliament and of the Council on a Single Market For Digital Services (Digital Services Act) and amending Directive 2000/31/ECCOM(2020) 825 final.

The DSA uses a technique of scaled obligations. Intermediaries' duties are adjusted in accordance with their economic capacity. Three steps are distinguished. Very small providers are exempt from the obligations altogether and just receive the benefit of the safe harbor. For "normal" online providers, additional obligations are added, mainly as regards the procedure of notification. Finally, for very big providers (which, obviously, concerns Facebook), enhanced additional duties are specified.

The importance of the DSA is therefore not to be underestimated. First, in Article 6, the DSA implicitly refers to the passive role theory, explaining that acts of

> voluntary own-initiative investigations or other activities aimed at detecting, identifying and removing, or disabling of access to, illegal content, or take the necessary measures to comply with the requirements of Union law

do not mean the intermediary has lost its "passive role" stance.

Second, as expected, the DSA corrects one of the main issues of the e-Commerce Directive, which is the lack of precision and transparency on the notice and take down procedure. Article 14 of the DSA clarifies that the procedure is mandatory, and that the procedure should be "easy to access, user-friendly, and allow for the submission of notices exclusively by electronic means.". Furthermore, it specifies that the notice shall contain mandatory elements: an explanation of the reasons why the individual or entity considers the information in question to be illegal content; a clear indication of the electronic location of that information; the name and an electronic mail address of the individual or entity submitting the notice, except in the case of information considered to involve one of the offenses referred to in Articles 3 to 7 of Directive 2011/93/EU (crimes related to the exploitation of children and child pornography); and a statement confirming the good faith belief of the individual or entity submitting the notice that the information and allegations contained therein are accurate and complete.

Third, it could be argued that under the DSA the notice and take down procedure has evolved into a quasi-judicial procedure. The author of the alleged illegal content is informed in detail through a statement of the reasons of the moderation (Article 15). Furthermore, two systems of "appeal" are instituted, one internal (Article 17) and one external, through out-of-court dispute settlement with the involvement of a certified out-of-court dispute settlement body (Article 18). Both the complainant and the author of the message are entitled to use these mechanisms. Both the complainant and the author are subject to sanctions in case of abuse (for example, repeated unfounded notices or repeated posting of illegal content), which will first be a warning, then the suspension of the possibility to submit a notice or to post, respectively (Article 20).

This new system brings some changes to Facebook's moderation mechanism, which will have to implement the warning measure as a mandatory step before suspending any account. Another novelty can be found in Article 21, as regards a new obligation on hosting services to alert the authorities when the reported illegal content is a "serious criminal offence involving a threat to the life or safety of persons has taken place, is taking place or is likely to take place" (see Sect. 7.2.3).

Finally, the legal framework for very large online platforms adds enhanced duties, that are in essence very similar to the functioning of the GDPR. Facebook will have to appoint a compliance officer, responsible for monitoring its compliance with the DSA (Article 32), and establish and publish a risk assessment (Article 26), which has two uses: first, it serves as a tool of transparency as regards the moderation policy; second, it is a prerequisite for the fundamental new risk management obligation in Article 27. It is stated that

> [v]ery large online platforms shall put in place reasonable, proportionate and effective mitigation measures, tailored to the specific systemic risks identified pursuant to Article 26. Such measures may include, where applicable: (a)adapting content moderation or recommender systems, their decision-making processes, the features or functioning of their services, or their terms and conditions; (b)targeted measures aimed at limiting the display of advertisements in association with the service they provide; (c)reinforcing the internal processes or supervision of any of their activities in particular as regards detection of systemic risk; (d)initiating or adjusting cooperation with trusted flaggers in accordance with Article 19; (e)initiating or adjusting cooperation with other online platforms through the codes of conduct and the crisis protocols referred to in Article 35 and 37 respectively.

In other words, a "due diligence" obligation of risk mitigation is established, obliging Facebook to operate a moderation service independently of the notification system. This moderation works on the basis of the specific risks involved. This duty does not mean that Facebook is not automatically liable for any illegal content available on the platform. Put otherwise, the immunity as regards Facebook's secondary liability for the publication of the illegal content remains. What is added is a primary liability where it has been shown that Facebook does not demonstrate an acceptable level of diligence in managing the platform's conformity with the rule of law.

This "due diligence" obligation of risk mitigation could be subject to judicial control (Article 42). But before that, Facebook would be obliged to periodically conduct an independent audit of its compliance. Independently of the modifications, clarifications, and additions to the existing safe harbor mechanisms, the DSA follows a clear path, established by the GDPR, of imposing checks on the private sector as regards citizens' fundamental rights. The GDPR's supervisory authority becomes a "Digital Services Coordinator" (a European board for Digital Services is also constituted), the Data Protection Officer is a "Compliance Officer", and the Data Protection Impact assessment becomes a Risk Assessment". It should be mentioned that, in accordance with Article 42, the Digital Services Coordinator is given the power to impose fines for failure to comply with this Regulation.[75]

Consequently, if adopted, the DSA proposal would be the culmination of a long maturation of the liability regime of online intermediaries. For Facebook specifically, the legislation will have huge practical consequences: the institutionalization of the moderation procedure, the strict control over the platform's operations, and, mainly, the establishment of this new and enhanced duty of care, that pushes the boundaries of the safe harbor to its limit.

---

[75] Article 41 (2) (c) of the DSA.

References

Angelopoulos C, Smet S (2016) Notice-and-fair-balance: how to reach a compromise between fundamental rights in European intermediary liability. J Media Law 8(2):266–301. https://doi.org/10.1080/17577632.2016.1240957

Berkowitz J (2012) Facebook's first major marketing message? That It Is Like a Chair. FastCompany. https://www.fastcompany.com/1681706/facebooks-first-major-marketing-message-that-it-is-like-a-chair

Besek MJ (2020) Thorny copyright issues—development on the horizon? Landslide 13(1)., September/October. https://www.americanbar.org/groups/intellectual_property_law/publications/landslide/2020-21/september-october/thorny-copyright-issues-development-horizon/

Busch C, Graef I, Hofmann J, Gawer A (2021) Uncovering blindspots in the policy debate on platform power: Final report. European Commission. https://platformobservatory.eu/app/uploads/2021/03/05Platformpower.pdf

Callamard A (2017) Are courts re-inventing Internet regulation? Int Rev Law Comp Technol 31(3):323–339. https://doi.org/10.1080/13600869.2017.1304603

Ericsson S (2016) The commodification of internet intermediary safe harbors: avoiding premature harmonization around a suboptimal standard. In: Ullrich H, Hilty R, Lamping M, Drexl J (eds) TRIPS plus 20. MPI studies on intellectual property and competition law, vol 25. Springer, Berlin. https://doi.org/10.1007/978-3-662-48107-3_8

EU Commission (2012) A coherent framework for building trust in the Digital Single Market for e-commerce and online services. Communication to the EU parliament and the Council. COM/2011/0942 final

EU Commission (2015) A Digital Single Market Strategy for Europe. Communication to the EU Parliament and the Council. COM(2015) 192 final

Kuczerawy A (2015) Intermediary liability & freedom of expression: Recent developments in the EU notice & action initiative. Comp Law Secur Rev 31(1):46–56

Lemley MA (2007) Rationalizing internet safe harbors. J Telecomm High Technol Law 6:101

Leven S (2018) Is Facebook a publisher? In public it says no, but in court it says yes. The Guardian. https://www.theguardian.com/technology/2018/jul/02/facebook-mark-zuckerberg-platform-publisher-lawsuit.

Mac SD (2020) The road to responsibilities: new attitudes towards Internet intermediaries. Inf Communications Technol Law 29(1):1–21. https://doi.org/10.1080/13600834.2020.1677369

Madiega T (2020) Reform of the EU liability regime for online intermediaries, Background on the forthcoming digital services act. European Parliamentary Research Service. PE 649.404. https://www.europarl.europa.eu/RegData/etudes/IDAN/2020/649404/EPRS_IDA(2020)649404_EN.pdf

Rochefort A (2020) Regulating social media platforms: a comparative policy analysis. Commun Law Policy 25(2):225–260. https://doi.org/10.1080/10811680.2020.1735194

Rosen G (2018) Facebook publishes enforcement numbers for the first time. Facebook newsroom. https://about.fb.com/news/2018/05/enforcement-numbers/

Sartor G (2017) Providers liability: from the e Commerce Directive to the future. Directorate General for Internal Policy, European Parliament, IP/A/IMCO/2017-07

Siladitya R (2021) The far-right is flocking to these alternate social media apps — not all of them are thrilled. Forbes. https://www.forbes.com/sites/siladityaray/2021/01/14/the-far-right-is-flocking-to-these-alternate-social-media-apps%2D%2D-not-all-of-them-are-thrilled/

Woods L (2017) When is Facebook liable for illegal content under the E-commerce Directive? CG v. Facebook in the Northern Ireland courts. EU Law analysis. http://eulawanalysis.blogspot.com/2017/01/when-is-facebook-liable-for-illegal.html

Woods L (2019) Facebook's liability for defamatory posts: the CJEU interprets the e-commerce Directive. EU Law Analysis. http://eulawanalysis.blogspot.com/2019/10/facebooks-liability-for-defamatory.html

Chapter 7
Hate Speech, Fake News, and the Moderation Problem

While attacks against reputation (Chap. 5) are a huge practical issue on Facebook, they do not normally result in the platform's liability (Chap. 6). Nevertheless, the two legal issues of hate speech and misinformation differ on this point, as the influence of hate speech and fake news on democratic societies provokes much greater pressure from legislators and courts to regulate these issues. Unlike attacks against reputation, which are harmful to individuals, hate speech and fake news threaten society itself, in the sense that massive dissemination of such content on social networks induces in average users the false realization that their extreme political movements are strongly supported by the general population. This eventually leads to real life violence and/or to a modification of the political equilibrium in Member States. Even if this phenomenon mainly concerns hate speech, fake news is closely associated with it too, as it is in practice often produced in combination with hate speech.

Although it is not always straightforward to demonstrate due to the particularities of Member States' national electoral laws, it is widely accepted that the past decade has seen a surge both in jihadism and in right-wing extremism in Europe. As Interpol notes in its 2002 TeSAT report, "[b]oth jihadist and right-wing extremist propaganda incite individuals to perpetrate acts of violence autonomously and praise perpetrators as 'martyrs' or 'saints', respectively".[1] While Facebook announced a crackdown on 'white supremacy'[2] following the Christchurch attacks,[3] the social network remains a place where right-wing extremists still enjoy many freedoms.[4]

Online harmful content literally works as a virus on social media: content generated by hateful users tends to spread faster and farther, reaching a much

---

[1] Europol (2020) European Union Terrorism Situation and Trend report – TeSAT. Europol, p. 6.

[2] Conway et al. (2019).

[3] A mass shooting in a mosque that killed 51 persons in New Zeeland. The video of the attack was live-streamed, notably on Facebook.

[4] Europol (2020) European Union Terrorism Situation and Trend report, op.cit., p. 73.

P. Jougleux, *Facebook and the (EU) Law*, Law, Governance and Technology Series 48, https://doi.org/10.1007/978-3-031-06596-5_7

wider audience compared to the content generated by normal users.[5] In order to successfully combat this pandemic of online hate speech and fake news distribution, the two phenomena have been criminalized. However, significant issues remain as regards the definition of the notions (Sect. 7.1). Nevertheless, substantive laws criminalizing the behaviors are not tackling the trend sufficiently and Facebook has been asked to intervene in an innovative and still developing co-regulation mechanism (Sect. 7.2).

7.1   The Cybercrimes of Hate Speech and Fake News

7.1.1   To Hate Speech or Not to Hate Speech: General Elements of the Crime

7.1.1.1   The International Background

Identifying a comment as hate speech on Facebook is commonly considered to be highly subjective. Both the public and the platform seem to lack the appropriate landmarks in order to appreciate whether content is legal or not. Indeed, this uncertainty is not entirely their fault, as the definition of the crime of hate speech, from a legal perspective, poses serious issues.

Formulating hate speech as a criminal offense was the result of many influences at international and EU level. In 1948, the offence of incitement to genocide was introduced and adopted by the General Assembly of the United Nations.[6] In 1965, the International Convention on the Elimination of All Forms of Racial Discrimination proposed to criminalize

> all dissemination of ideas based on racial superiority or hatred, incitement to racial discrimination, as well as all acts of violence or incitement to such acts against any race or group of persons of another colour or ethnic origin, and also the provision of any assistance to racist activities, including the financing thereof.[7]

The International Covenant on Civil and Political Rights of 1966 further defines hate speech, specifying the fundamental elements of the offense:

> the list of protected characteristics is short and closed (national, racial or religious hatred), it requires 'advocacy', that is, an intentional and public promotion of hatred; the advocated 'hatred' is supposed to constitute incitement to discrimination, hostility or violence, i.e. illegal material actions.[8]

---

[5] Mathew et al. (2019), pp. 173–182.

[6] Convention on the Prevention and Punishment of the Crime of Genocide.

[7] Article 4 (a) of the International Convention on the Elimination of All Forms of Racial Discrimination.

[8] Bayer and Bard (2020), p. 27.

The most fundamental milestone at international level was an additional protocol to the Convention of Europe's so-called "Budapest Convention" on cybercrime.[9] The sensitive nature of the hate speech regime prevented it from being discussed in the general cybercrime framework, and the topic is later addressed in an additional protocol.[10] The contracting states are invited to introduce in their legislation a certain number of new offenses, amongst which three merit special attention here: the dissemination of racist and xenophobic material through computer systems (Article 3), the racist and xenophobia-motivated insult (Article 5), and denial, gross minimization, approval or justification of genocide or crimes against humanity (Article 6).

The offenses of Articles 3 and 5 are closely related. Both consist of an attack against a specific group of persons, defined by a closed list of criteria that are deemed to be racist: race, color, descent or national or ethnic origin, as well as religion. Furthermore, in both cases, the mens rea of the offense is clearly stated to be intention. Finally, a communication to the public is needed, as both articles refer to a public.

However, the various international interventions on this topic should not hide the fact that there are serious divergences in points of view between proponents of a near absolute freedom of speech on the one hand, who interpret the conditions of a hate speech offense extremely strictly, and those who would misuse the offense of hate speech, on the other hand, in order to establish as predominant a specific ideology. At the UN level, a tentative conciliation entitled the "Rabat Plan of Action"[11] has been adopted, which contains a six-part threshold test for forms of speech that are prohibited under criminal law. Specifically, the test takes into consideration the elements of incitement to hatred, the speaker, intent, content, extent of the speech, and likelihood of causing harm. The "Rabat Plan", therefore, is important guidance for the courts in evaluating the legality of the content.

7.1.1.2   The Hate Speech Crime and Its Consecutive Elements

The additional protocol of the Budapest Convention created a very specific binding framework for the EU legislator's intervention. Nevertheless, the institutions felt the need to establish the offense at EU level, probably estimating that combating hate speech belongs to the core values of the EU. Council Framework Decision 2008/913[12] states that

---

[9]Convention on Cybercrime, ETS No.185, Budapest, 23/11/2001.

[10]Additional Protocol to the Convention on Cybercrime, concerning the criminalisation of acts of a racist and xenophobic nature committed through computer systems, ETS No.189, Strasbourg, 28/01/2003.

[11]OHCHR (2011).

[12]Council Framework Decision 2008/913/JHA of 28 November 2008 on combating certain forms and expressions of racism and xenophobia by means of criminal law, OJ L 328, 6.12.2008, p. 55–58, ELI: http://data.europa.eu/eli/dec_framw/2008/913/oj.

[e]ach Member State shall take the measures necessary to ensure that the following intentional conduct is punishable: (a) publicly inciting to violence or hatred directed against a
group of persons or a member of such a group defined by reference to race, colour, religion,
descent or national or ethnic origin.[13]

Therefore, four elements define the offense of hate speech at EU level: a discrimination against a group of persons based on a closed list of criteria defining these
persons, an intention, an act of public communication, and a damage, which is the
potential consequence of inciting to violence or hatred against these persons. The
first element is to be interpreted differently depending on the kind of discrimination
(see below Sect. 7.1.2).

The second element—the intention—is sometimes and unfortunately restrictively
interpreted by the courts as not the intent to make the public statement, but the intent
to actually provoke the hatred. A racist motive is required. However, the courts
should adopt an objective analysis of the perpetrator's behavior and not base their
estimation purely on his or her psychology. Indeed, because self-awareness of
racism—or "explicit racism"—is much rarer nowadays,[14] limiting the offense to
individuals considering themselves racist would make the protection meaningless.
For instance, in Greece, an author wrote in a newspaper, misquoting Marco Polo:
"The militant Muslim is the person who beheads the infidel, while the moderate
Muslim holds the feet of the victim.". The Court considered that the author did not
intend to disseminate hate speech, as the topic of the article was a more general
discussion on multiculturalism and its boundaries.[15]

The third element—the communication to the public—is, in the context of
Facebook, a very sensitive topic. What, in the era of social networks, should be
considered public, semi-public, or private communication? The technical settings of
a Facebook pos do not provide a satisfactory answer, as, from a legal point of view,
the practical impact of the communication matters. This has been underlined by the
ECtHR in multiple cases.

For instance, in Stankov and the United Macedonian Organisation Ilinden v.
Bulgaria[16] the Court took into account the fact that the group making the statements
had no real influence, even locally, and that its rallies were not likely to become a
platform for the propagation of violence or intolerance. In other words, while it was a
public rally, the Court implicitly considered that it was of such limited impact that it
was equivalent to a private gathering.

Moreover, in Bon v. Croatia,[17] the ECtHR had to discuss the condemnation of an
activist for insult and defamation, for some rude remarks he made against an official

---

[13] Article 1 (1) of the Framework Decision.

[14] Levy (2017), pp. 534–551.

[15] Ekathimerini.com (2018).

[16] ECtHR, Stankov and the United Macedonian Organisation Ilinden v. Bulgaria, nos. 29221/95 and
29225/95, 2 October 2001, ECHR 2001-IX.

[17] ECtHR, Bon v. Croatia, Application no. 26933/15, 18 March 2021.

in a public speech, that were recorded and later posted on a local NGO's website. The Court considered that

> the impugned statement had been made only to a limited number of people with a particular interest. It does not appear from the facts, as submitted by the parties, that the applicant had intended to make his presentation available to the general public. However, without his knowledge or consent, the applicant's presentation had been privately recorded and posted on the website of a local NGO and had thus had only a limited impact.[18]

Consequently, the limited impact of the dissemination (40 attendees at the conference, plus the low number of visitors to the local blog) did not justify classifying it as a communication to the public.

It can be argued that the concept of communication to the public has evolved along with social networks. A "friends only" communication should not prevent a communication from being found to be public. However, the more limited impact of such a communication should also be taken into consideration when assessing the proportionality of a sentence.

The fourth element of the hate speech offense is damage to society. Hate speech is punishable because of the potential incitement to hate crime. It is a highly debated criterion, as it could be argued that the content of the hate speech communication suffices as proof of the incitement to violence. However, one of the most controversial findings of the ECtHR, in the context of its fruitful jurisprudence on hate speech, is that assessments on the content of hate speech should be context-based.[19]

In the case Perinçek v. Switzerland,[20] Perinçek, Chairman of the Turkish Workers' Party in Switzerland, made public statements denying the Armenian genocide. The Switzerland-Armenia Association filed a criminal complaint against him and the Swiss court found against him; he therefore applied to the ECtHR for violation of his freedom of expression. The Grand Chamber considered that there are three factors involved in determining whether restricting the applicant's freedom of expression was, in this case, necessary for a democratic society.

The first factor is whether the statements were made against a tense political or social background; the presence of such a background has generally led the Court to accept that some form of interference with such statements was justified. The second factor is whether the statements, fairly construed and seen in their immediate or wider context, could be seen as a direct or indirect call for violence or as a justification of violence, hatred or intolerance. Finally, the third factor analyzes the way the statements were made, and their capacity—whether direct or indirect—to lead to harmful consequences.

The ECtHR notes that it is the interplay between these various factors rather than any one of them taken in isolation that determines the outcome of the case,

---

[18] Par.35 of the decision.

[19] Bayer and Bard (2020). Op.cit., p. 38.

[20] ECtHR, Perinçek v. Switzerland, Application No. 27510/08, 17 December 2013, (grand chamber), 15 October 2015.

concluding that this approach is "highly context-specific".[21] In this case, the Court found that the declarations on the Armenian genocide apparently included an element of exaggeration as they sought to attract attention. In other words, in the opinion of the Court, the author of the publication only wished to discuss historical events and did not incite people to hatred or violence against today's Armenians.

However, it is important to distinguish incitement to hatred from incitement to violence. Indeed, the ECtHR has ruled that inciting hatred does not necessarily entail a call for an act of violence or other criminal acts. Attacks on persons by insulting, holding up to ridicule or slandering specific groups of the population can be sufficient for the authorities to favor combating racist speech where freedom of expression has clearly been exercised in an irresponsible manner.[22] While at international level only the incitement to violence is referred to, in the EU legislation both an incitement to hatred and an incitement to violence would trigger the state's intervention.

In conclusion, it must be highlighted that the interpretation of the hate speech offense and its practical enforcement cannot be separated from a human rights perspective. Indeed, the ECtHR has developed a rich jurisprudence on hate speech and how to achieve a fair balance between the legitimate interests protected by the offense and the freedom of expression (see Sect. 8.1.2).

7.1.1.3 Online Hate Speech Enforcement on Facebook

Many studies have focused on the specificity of online hate speech, with a focus on the involvement of AI detection and monitoring mechanisms.[23] Nevertheless, in the light of the ECtHR jurisprudence analyzed above, the four cumulative elements of the offense of hate speech are being interpreted in a subjective way that enormously complicates its enforcement in an online environment. The intent, the public character, and the damaging consequences must be interpreted in the light of the publication's specific context. Furthermore, the fight against online hate speech presents special requirements. The implementation report on the Framework Decision that created the offense on an EU level underlines the special demands on law enforcement and judicial authorities in terms of expertise, resources, and the need for cross-border cooperation.[24]

Facebook includes these categories of hate speech in its report system: "Race or ethnicity, National origin, Religious affiliation, Social caste, Sexual orientation, Sex or gender identity, Disability or disease, something else". Pages, groups, profiles,

---

[21] Par.208 of the decision.

[22] ECtHR, Vejdeland and Others v. Sweden, no. 1813/07, 9 February 2012, § 55.

[23] Dikaiakos et al. (2016), p. 49.

[24] Report from the Commission to the European Parliament and the Council on the implementation of Council Framework Decision 2008/913/JHA on combating certain forms and expressions of racism and xenophobia by means of criminal law, COM(2014)27 final.

individual content and comments can be reported for hate speech, but as already highlighted, the platform has, until now, been notoriously reluctant to validate a report (see Sect. 6.1.3). In the Community Standards, which work as a moderation guide for Facebook, the company refers to hate speech in Chapter 12, in the section for "objectionable content". It defines hate speech as

> a direct attack against people on the basis of what we call protected characteristics: race, ethnicity, national origin, disability, religious affiliation, caste, sexual orientation, sex, gender identity and serious disease. We define attacks as violent or dehumanising speech, harmful stereotypes, statements of inferiority, expressions of contempt, disgust or dismissal, cursing and calls for exclusion or segregation. We consider age a protected characteristic when referenced along with another protected characteristic. We also protect refugees, migrants, immigrants and asylum seekers from the most severe attacks, though we do allow commentary and criticism of immigration policies.[25]

Interestingly, the Community Standards also provide for the idea of sharing hate speech content without the intent of disseminating hatred and specifies that

> [w]e recognise that people sometimes share content that includes someone else's hate speech to condemn it or raise awareness. In other cases, speech that might otherwise violate our standards can be used self-referentially or in an empowering way. Our policies are designed to allow room for these types of speech, but we require people to clearly indicate their intent. If intention is unclear, we may remove content.

These principles set by the Community Standards seem to be in line with the four elements of the EU offense and the text is also compliant with the international framework and the Rabat Plan. It even goes beyond what is requested in terms of protected minorities, as the list also includes, for instance, protection of persons with disabilities. The issue here is the practical enforcement of these Community Standards by Facebook in its day-by-day moderation of the platform.

The company's lack of diligence has led to additional reactions from the EU (see Sect. 7.2.2 about the Code of Conduct) and from national legislators. For instance, Germany's response to hate speech has been remarked upon.[26] The adoption of the NetzDG in 2017[27] aimed to counter the epidemic of hate speech in social media. This law implements administrative measure that are binding for some big social networks (mainly Facebook). Its main provision is the obligation placed on Facebook to delete or block hate speech content upon notification within 48 h (within 24 h of receipt for content that is manifestly unlawful). The law also creates an administrative offense where a social network fails to "provide, to provide correctly or to provide completely" a procedure.

However, even in Germany the issue of the account status of the hate speech content's author is left unregulated. The EU offense obviously concerns the author's criminal liability, and the administrative mechanisms put in place in Germany further enhanced the notification and take down procedure implied by the

---

[25] Available at https://www.facebook.com/communitystandards/objectionable_content.

[26] Article 19 (2018) Germany: Responding to 'hate speech'. Article19.org.

[27] NetzDG, 30 June 2017. Federal Law Gazette 2017 I. Nr. 61, p. 3352.

e-Commerce Directive (amended by the Digital Services Act), but no provisions refer to the suspension or blocking of the account.

Facebook's terms of service explicitly mention the Community Standards, stating that "[y]ou may not use our Products to do or share anything: That breaches these Terms, our Community Standards and other terms and policies that apply to your use of Facebook". Therefore, the Community Standards are deemed to be part of the binding contract between the user and Facebook. It means that the company is theoretically entitled to proceed to terminate the service (account deletion) in case of a breach of contract related to Community Standards. This mechanism could be regarded as a double sanction and obviously has severe consequences on the freedom of expression. The Community Standards only specifies that

> [t]he consequences for violating our Community Standards vary depending on the severity of the violation and the person's history on the platform. For instance, we may warn someone for a first violation, but if they continue to violate our policies, we may restrict their ability to post on Facebook or disable their profile. We may also notify law enforcement when we believe that there is a genuine risk of physical harm or a direct threat to public safety.

The two criteria—severity of the violation and the person's history on the platform—are logical, but very imprecise.

It is arguable whether such a serious issue should be left entirely to the platform's discretion, as it creates a disproportionate risk of private censorship. Empirical evidence suggests that without relevant detailed knowledge of the subject, hate speech is hard to comment on.[28] The actual system is obviously subject to judicial control, in the sense that some members of a targeted protected group could lodge a complaint against Facebook in case it fails to moderate hate speech content that has been reported. Nevertheless, in practice, penalties for violation of Community Standards are becoming more and more codified, under the pressure for more transparency (see Sect. 8.1.3).

7.1.2   The Diversity of Hate Speech: Strengths and Weaknesses of the Closed List

7.1.2.1   Discrimination Based on Race, Origin, Nationality or Ethnicity

It is worth remembering that the entire EU structure and philosophy is founded on the principle of non-discrimination based on nationality among the Member States. In this context, the notion of race itself, which anyway lacks any scientific basis, is not recognized in EU law. Therefore, the reference to "race" in hate speech legislation is to be understood as alleged race, defined as set of physical characteristics (hair, skin color, morphology, etc.) that would distinguish one person from another. The two references to origin and ethnicity complete this protection against racist

---

[28] Waseem (2016), pp. 138–142.

content, as the concept of origin refers to alleged ancestry by implied reference to a (largely imaginary) common DNA legacy, while the concept of ethnicity is defined as a common national or cultural tradition characterizing a specific group.

The notion of discrimination based on nationality, on the contrary, presents more difficulty. In today's international context, where armed conflicts are still a reality, nationality remains a very strong marker of identity, but it also constitutes a necessary reference point for discussing international events. Furthermore, national clichés and stereotypes are part of more than one cultural tradition. The legal classification of such content as discrimination based on nationality depends in fact on the virulence of the speech. In the case Aksu v. Turkey, about book, which received funding from the public authorities, that contained stereotypes of the Roma (i.e. their involvement in illegal activities),[29] the ECtHR considered that the publication did not amount to hate speech (the book was written by an academic, emphasis was placed on the aim to shed light on the unknown world of the Turkish Roma community, which had been ostracized and vilified on account of prejudice). However, it accepted the idea that the negative stereotyping of an ethnic group is capable, when reaching a certain level, of having an impact on the group's sense of identity and on its members' feelings of self-worth and self-confidence.

The issue has also arisen of whether a call for boycotts against a specific country for political reasons should be incriminated by the offense. The call for a boycott is manifestly discriminatory and it is, by definition, based on nationality. However, the political motives of the call would normally indicate that there is no intent of dissemination of hatred against a population. For instance, in France, a group supporting Palestinians published a call to boycott goods imported from Israel, "until Israel complies with its obligations under international law, especially in relation to its illegal settlements and the right of Palestinian refugees to return to their homes". The French court had condemned the initiative as hate speech, but the ECtHR considered that France had, in this case, violated the support group's freedom of expression.[30] The Court's reasoning is based on the political nature of the debate. In other words, because of its political motive, this specific call for a boycott did not entail discrimination based on nationality. Nevertheless, it also means that other calls to boycott that are not justified by a political purpose could still be regarded as a form of hate speech.

7.1.2.2 Discrimination Based on Religion

The inclusion of religion as one of the illegal bases of hate speech has historically been amply justified, as past massacres related to religious hatred have flourished in history, from Biblical wars to the St. Bartholomew's Day massacre, from the medieval Jewish pogroms to the Holocaust. However, this issue of religious hate

---

[29] ECtHR, Aksu v. Turkey, nos. 4149/04 and 41029/04, 15 March 2012.

[30] ECtHR, Baldassi & Others v. France, no. 15271/16, 11 July 2020.

speech remains extremely sensitive because, in this context, religion is characterized by a hybrid nature: it is both a group of persons (whether or not a minority), sharing the same moral values and traditions, whose identity is not to be mocked—and a philosophical-mystical group of ideas. In other words, the offense of hate speech aims to protect the persons, not the ideas,[31] and religious hate speech is not to be confused with the crime of blasphemy. While the first offense is legitimate as a restraining tool to protect persecuted groups of persons, the second should be seen as an anachronistic tool of ideological oppression which should progressively disappear from the legal regimes of Member States.

However, even blasphemy has been considered by the ECtHR in the past to be a legitimate restriction of the freedom of expression. In 1996, in the Wingrove v. UK decision,[32] the Court upheld the British Board of Film Classification's refusal to certify a short movie for committing the criminal offense of blasphemy by depicting the wounded body of the crucified Christ as a participant in the erotic desire of St. Teresa. The Court was satisfied that the national law passed the three-part test for restrictions to the freedom of expression (see Sect. 8.1.2).

Nevertheless, this distinction between attacks against religion (blasphemy) and attacks against a religious community (hate speech) is a fine line in practice. In both cases, from the perspective of the believers, the content is seen as harmful and characteristic of an incitement to hatred. In both cases also, we have a communication to the public. The combined action of the last two criteria will allow this separation between lawful and lawful criticism of a religion: the intent and the act of discrimination against a group of persons. Criticism against the alleged absurdity or the immorality of a specific religious dogma or the parodic and humorous presentation of a religion would therefore avoid the restriction, as, first, they do not concern persons, only ideas, and second, they show an intent to engage in dialogue or entertainment, not to disseminate hate. The six-factor test in the Rabat Plan of Action (see Sect. 7.1.1) is particularly useful in this context.

Although prohibition of religious hate speech must be limited through a strict interpretation of the offense, numerous examples subsist in the ECtHR of situations where content directly targeting religious groups was treated as hate speech. For instance, in the Le Pen v. France case,[33] the leader of the extreme right wing political party in France declared in an interview that "the day there are no longer 5 million but 25 million Muslims in France, they will be in charge" and received a fine for hate speech. In the same way, in Norwood v. the United Kingdom,[34] a member of an extreme right-wing political party placed a poster on his apartment window that called for the removal of all Muslims from Britain and the condemnation for hate speech was found, by the ECtHR, to have been justified. The application of the offense obviously is not limited to attacks against Muslims. Various anti-Semitic

---

[31] Temperman (2008), pp. 517–545.

[32] ECtHR, Wingrove v. United Kingdom, No. 17419/90, 25 November 1996.

[33] ECtHR, Le Pen v. France, no.: 18788/09, 7 May 2010.

[34] ECtHR, Norwood v. the United Kingdom, no. 23131/03, 16 November 2004.

statements have also come before the ECtHR, which obviously considers that their suppression through the criminal law is legitimate.[35]

7.1.2.3   Discrimination Based on Sexual Preference

The notion of racism has gradually evolved from a traditional restrictive view which considered such only in terms of discrimination based on color. Nowadays, any kind of discriminatory behavior is considered by extension to be "racist", even if there is no relationship to racial discrimination. Nevertheless, the closed list of minorities protected by the hate speech offense as defined at EU level does not include discrimination based on sexual preference (see above, Sect. 7.1.1).

However, a legal basis exists for including the protection of sexual identity in the list. Article 10 of the Treaty on the Functioning of the European Union (TFEU) requires the Union, in defining and implementing its policies and activities, to aim at "combatting discrimination based on sex, racial or ethnical origin, religion or belief, disability, age or sexual orientation". Moreover, Article 19 of the TFEU provides a legal basis for the Union to take appropriate action to combat discrimination based (amongst other grounds) on sex or sexual orientation and Article 67(3) of the TFEU states that the EU must

> ensure a high level of security through measures to prevent and combat crime, racism and xenophobia, and through measures for coordination and cooperation between police and judicial authorities and other competent authorities, as well as through the mutual recognition of judgments in criminal matters.

Also, the Charter of Fundamental Rights of the European Union expressly protects human dignity (Article 1), and Article 21 provides that any discrimination based on a large list of topics that includes sex or sexual orientation shall be prohibited.

Therefore, the EU Commission has communicated its intent to proceed with better regulation on this topic.[36] Specifically, the EU Commission has focused on the protection of the "LBGTI+" community.[37]

At the same time, the ECtHR has also taken a position on this topic. First, in the Vejdeland and Others v. Sweden case,[38] which concerned allegations that homosexuals were attempting to play down pedophilia and were responsible for the spread of HIV (and, consequently, AIDS), the Court had stressed that "discrimination based on sexual orientation is as serious as discrimination based on 'race, origin or colour'".[39]

---

[35] ECtHR, Pavel Ivanov v. Russia, no. 35222/04, 20 February 2007; ECtHR, Kasymakhunov and Saybatalov v. Russia, nos. 26261/05 and 26377/06, 14 March 2013.

[36] European Commission (2020).

[37] Under the acronym "LGBTI+" is regrouped Lesbian, Gay, Bisexual, Transgender and Intersex persons.

[38] ECtHR, Vejdeland and Others v. Sweden, no. 1813/07, 9 February 2012.

[39] Par.55 of the decision.

Second, the Court reiterated its position on discrimination founded on sexual preference in the case Beizaras and Levickas v. Lithuania,[40] which is of particular interest as it concerns Facebook. On 8 December 2014, the first applicant posted a photograph on his Facebook page depicting a same-sex kiss between him and the second applicant, with the intention of announcing the beginning of the applicants' relationship. The picture was accessible not only to his Facebook "friends", but also to the public. Unfortunately, the post attracted a slew of comments aimed at inciting hatred and violence against LGBT people in general, such as "I'm going to throw up – they should be castrated or burnt; cure yourselves, jackasses – just saying".

The applicants attempted to open criminal investigations as regards the comments, but the prosecutor dismissed the case as not being of a criminal nature. On appeal, the Court confirmed the prosecutor's decision, adding that a person who posted a picture "of two men kissing" in a public space should and must have foreseen that such "eccentric behaviour really did not contribute to the cohesion of those within society who had different views or to the promotion of tolerance". For the national court, the owner of a social network profile on which such an image was posted, when exercising his freedom to express his convictions and freedom to promote tolerance, had to take into account the fact that that freedom was inseparable from the obligation to respect the views and traditions of others.

The ECtHR condemned Lithuania, considering that comments that amount to hate speech and incitement to violence, and are thus prima facie clearly unlawful, may in principle require the Member States to take certain positive measures. The ECtHR found violations of Article 14 (prohibition of discrimination), Article 8 (right to private life), and Article 13 (right to effective legal remedy).

It could be concluded that references to general principles and self-regulation principles on Facebook successfully cover the lack of protection against gender-based discrimination. However, data shows that the moderation system itself is a victim of biases. For instance, male nudity and female nudity are not treated the same way and it has been argued that "gender-based censorship" exists on Facebook.[41]

7.1.3   Fake News and Real Threats

7.1.3.1   The Multiple Faces of Fake News

The issue of fake news is, in practice, often closely related to hate speech. Their relationship could be characterized as a means to an end. Incitement to hatred is commonly carried out on social networks through fake news. Furthermore, fake news and hate speech have the same consequence: as fake news directly impacts the right to information, it also constitutes a danger to democratic society.

---

[40] ECtHR, Beizaras and Levickas v. Lithuania, no. 41288/15, 14 January 2020.
[41] Nurik (2019), p. 21.

Nevertheless, it would be a mistake to consider the phenomenon solely in the light of hate speech, as the offenses differ on several points. First, unlike hate speech, fake news does not necessarily entail incitement to violence. Second, fake news on specific topics may have disproportionate consequences on public health, as the Covid-19 pandemic has demonstrated. Finally, while hate speech is a known and quantifiable threat, fake news benefits from new technological developments that add further uncertainty on the future of the phenomenon.

Specifically, the recent popularization of deepfake technology,[42] that is the combination of video editing software and AI learning algorithms for the purpose of replacing one face for another, casts a shade of doubt not only on texts and photography but even on video. Through the deepfake technology, actors, politicians, and other celebrities seem to willingly participate in some video, while in reality their face is only retrospectively added to the video through AI analysis, by replacing the face of the true actor. Although this technology can be used for parodic or artistic purposes, its destructive potential in terms of a reputation's credibility is extreme. The Artificial Intelligence Act imposes a transparency duty for all uses of this technology (see Sect. 8.3.3).

Sometimes, and even more disturbingly, misinformation occurs not in the content itself but in the way it is presented, exploiting a gap in the legal protection. For instance, during the US presidential election campaign, some viral videos implied that a candidate encountered difficulty in expressing himself, while in fact the video was only played at 70% of its normal speed. Facebook did not moderate the content as fake news, as the video was real.[43]

Furthermore, fake news is sometimes used for propaganda's mean, taking the shape of organized campaign of disinformation. The phenomenon is commonly known as "troll factories":[44] people paid in order to be present on social networks and preach the official line. The "trolls" or sometimes bots not only massively publish disinformation, twisting and manipulating the public debate, but also, through comments and private message, may sometimes provoke fear and a chilling effect on the freedom of expression.[45]

7.1.3.2 Fake News As Criminal Offense

Overall, the perception that fake news does not present an immediate danger to the EU's core values, combined with the relative novelty of the "fake news epidemic", have contributed to the EU's non-existent reaction. Contrary to hate speech, no offense has been established at EU level.

---

[42] Renda (2018).

[43] Klonick (2019), p. 2418.

[44] Nicolas (2018), p. 36.

[45] Aro (2016), pp. 121–132.

Nevertheless, many State members have regulated fake news from a criminal law perspective and it is important to highlight the fact that this offense must be interpreted on the light of the ECtHR's jurisprudence. Specifically, the Court seems to consider that freedom of speech encompasses freedom to tell lies,[46] which means that any offense of fake news must be compatible with the triple test of legitimate restriction to freedom of speech (see Sect. 8.1.2). In the case of public dissemination of misinformation, it means that some principles must be respected.

First, the offense must only concern objective information (news), not opinion, and this information must be found false from a scientific point of view. The Court takes care to emphasize that the lie must be obvious, in the sense that a simple exaggeration should not be considered as a lie.[47] However, in other case, the Court had ruled that a defective presentation of information should be assimilated to no information at all (and possibly to a violation to the duty to provide access to information).[48]

Furthermore, it is possible to criminalize fake news only in case whereas the fake news has a real impact on the society. The Court imposes an in concreto analysis of the disruption of the public order.[49] For a message on Facebook, it means that the fact that the message is publicly accessible is not enough to consider its impact. In order to apply a sentence, the judge will have to estimate the number of views, likes, share, the number of followers, generally, etc.

Finally, criminalization of fake news would need the proof of a criminal intent, which presupposes that the perpetrator has knowledge, first of all, of the false nature of the information. Otherwise, the offense would potentially affect even parodies and thus be disproportionate as regards as the legitimate interest of the public order protection. This condition is, once again, posed by the European Court, which ruled that the condemnation of an individual for fake news without proof of its criminal intent violated the freedom of expression.[50]

7.1.3.3 Fake News from the EU Perspective

In any case, the appearance of large-scale disinformation campaigns with foreign powers supposedly involved, has considerably modified the perception of misinformation as a public threat. Furthermore, fake news related to public health issues during the pandemic stresses the fact that, even if fake news per se does not directly entail violence, it may still kill or destabilize entire societies by affecting elections and referendum.

---

[46] ECtHR, Salov V Ukraine, no 65518/01, 6 September 2005.

[47] ECtHR, Brzezinsk v Poland, 47542/07, 25 July 2019.

[48] Association Burestop et autres c. France, nos 56176/18 et 5 autres, 1st July 2021.

[49] ECtHR, Hertel v. Switzerland, 59/1997/843/1049, 25 August 1998.

[50] ECtHR, Salov V Ukraine, op.cit.

Until now, the EU Commission's answer has mainly been restricted to three actions: the creation of a Code of Practice on Disinformation,[51] the publication of a Communication entitled "Tackling online disinformation: a European approach",[52] and the development of an European Digital Media Observatory, which works as hub for EU fact-checkers.

As regards fake news on social networks, it should be noted that

> 2016 represents something of a political shift in the dynamics of public–private cooperation in the field of cybersecurity, centred around the apparent unwillingness and limited capacity of social media platforms to tackle the spread of disinformation using their systems.[53]

Facebook, in particular, is accused of negligence. In its communication, the EU Commission announces that

> [t]he online platforms that distribute content, particularly social media, video-sharing services and search engines, play a key role in the spread and amplification of online disinformation. These platforms have so far failed to act proportionately, falling short of the challenge posed by disinformation and the manipulative use of platforms' infrastructures.[54]

The main tool used by EU authorities in tackling misinformation is a Code of Practice created in 2018, which was completed by a "Srengthened Code of Practice on misinformation" proposed in 2021 (see Sect. 7.2.2). In case of misinformation, Facebook is invited to reduce the visibility of the content,to add some complementary information, and to demonetize any attempt at generating revenues from fake news, in cooperation with organizations called "trusted flaggers" (see Sect. 7.2.1). Facebook will delete a content or block an account only in case of immediate threat to life. Nonetheless, it could be argued that the technique of "shadowbanning" (the Facebook's algorithm automatically downgrades the visibility of fake news content) is de facto similar to censorship. Through the DSA proposal, the EU has therefore taken the initiative to impose more transparency in the moderation techniques used by Facebook (see Sect. 7.2.2).

While, in conclusion, hate speech has mainly been handled from a restriction perspective, fake news is mostly managed through a pedagogic perspective (the addition of information banners). As both phenomena continue to proliferate on social networks, it is difficult to appreciate which perspective is the best placed to protect EU democratic societies. Fake news criminalization, as long as it is implanted in a human rights' compatible manner, should not be completely opted out from the discussion, as a way to deal with the most violent organized campaigns of disinformation that aim to destabilize a country.

---

[51] Available at https://ec.europa.eu/newsroom/dae/document.cfm?doc_id=54454.

[52] EU Commission (2018) Tackling online disinformation: a European approach. Communication. COM/2018/236 final.

[53] Carrapico and Farrand (2021).

[54] EU Commission (2018) Tackling online disinformation: a European approach. Op.cit.

7.1.4   The Impact of the Audiovisual Media Services Directive

7.1.4.1   The Application of the Audiovisual Media Services Directive to Facebook

It could be surprising to discuss the impact of the revised Audiovisual Media Services Directive (AVMSD)[55] on Facebook's moderation policy. Indeed, the first AVMSD is to be understood as the foundation of an EU law of audiovisual media, focusing on classic media such as radio or Television. With the revision of the Directive in 2018, the EU legislator took note of the paradigm shift: "mainstream media" is not the television anymore, as it has lost its crown in profit to social media.

Specifically, the EU legislator considers that

> [v]ideo-sharing platform services provide audiovisual content which is increasingly accessed by the general public, in particular by young people. This is also true with regard to social media services, which have become an important medium to share information and to entertain and educate, including by providing access to programmes and user-generated videos. Those social media services need to be included in the scope of Directive 2010/13/ EU because they compete for the same audiences and revenues as audiovisual media services. Furthermore, they also have a considerable impact in that they facilitate the possibility for users to shape and influence the opinions of other users. Therefore, in order to protect minors from harmful content and all citizens from incitement to hatred, violence and terrorism, those services should be covered by Directive 2010/13/EU to the extent that they meet the definition of a video-sharing platform service.[56]

However, the legislator immediately clarifies that

> [w]hile the aim of Directive 2010/13/EU is not to regulate social media services as such, a social media service should be covered if the provision of programmes and user-generated videos constitutes an essential functionality of that service. The provision of programmes and user-generated videos could be considered to constitute an essential functionality of the social media service if the audiovisual content is not merely ancillary to, or does not constitute a minor part of, the activities of that social media service.[57]

Although Facebook has a lot of user-generated videos available, this is not its main purpose. It could be argued that the social network mainly offers a combination of texts and images. The Directive only covers audiovisual content and its application to Facebook is in this context an issue. As Facebook's main purpose is not to offer "programs" of user-generated videos to the public, it remains to be seen whether these videos constitute "an essential functionality" of the platform, and/or if the

---

[55] Directive (EU) 2018/1808 of the European Parliament and of the Council of 14 November 2018 amending Directive 2010/13/EU on the coordination of certain provisions laid down by law, regulation or administrative action in Member States concerning the provision of audiovisual media services (Audiovisual Media Services Directive) in view of changing market realities, OJ L 303, 28.11.2018, p. 69, ELI: http://data.europa.eu/eli/dir/2018/1808/oj.

[56] Recital 4 of the Directive.

[57] Recital 5 of the Directive.

platform dedicates a special section of the wider content to the videos.[58] Nevertheless, the "stories" section of the platform (short user-generated photo and video collections that can be viewed up to two times and disappear after 24 h) is a special section of the platform dedicated to video. But once again, the content is not purely video, as photos are allowed too. Furthermore, the platform provides a "Facebook Watch" tool, which focuses on the presentation of short videos.

Therefore, the main issue is to be determined is whether videos are "an essential functionality" of Facebook. The Directive does not provide any further explanation on this point, but, following the injunction of the EU legislator, the EU Commission has issued specific guidelines on this topic.[59] The guidelines remark that

> [a]udiovisual content can be considered as a 'minor part' of the activity of the service whenever, on the basis of quantitative and/or qualitative considerations, it appears that it plays an insignificant role in the overall economy of the service. From a quantitative perspective, for example, the fact that the platform hosts a significant number of videos may suggest that audiovisual content is a non-minor part of the service. At the same time, irrespective of quantitative considerations, videos may constitute a non-minor part of the platform service whenever they contribute in an important manner to the attractiveness, functionality or market success of the service itself. This can be inferred from a number of elements, such as for instance the fact that users consume significant amount of videos or programmes or that the platforms invests in, or gives prominence to, audiovisual content.

The guideline lists four categories of indicators in determining the nature of the activity of the service. In the first category, entitled "Relationship between the audiovisual content and the main economic activity or activities of the service", four factors are mentioned: the overall architecture and external layout of the platform, the stand-alone nature of the audiovisual content, the existence of specific functionalities of the service tailored for, or specific to, audiovisual content, and the way the service positions itself on the market and the market segment it addresses.

Facebook passes each of the four tests of this first category. As regards the first element, it is clear that "the platform is geared towards the sharing of content in view of informing, educating or entertaining users rather than, for example, facilitating economic transactions".[60] With respect to the second indicator, Facebook's videos constitute an autonomous source of entertainment. The third indicator provides that the existence of auto-play functionality, which is incorporated in the platform, is a critical point. The fourth indicator analyzes the position of video content in the company's public communications. The company certainly gives priority to video content, for instance, through the "Facebook Watch" functionality.

The second category of indicators refers to "Quantitative and qualitative relevance of audiovisual content for the activities of the service". This criterion is merely statistical: is there a large amount of video on the platform? The answer, as far as Facebook is concerned, is positive.

---

[58] See article 1(1)(aa) of the AVMSD.

[59] EU Commission (2020), pp. 3–9.

[60] EU Commission (2020) op.cit.

The third category concerns monetization. Monetization is a huge factor in determining whether videos are an essential service of the platform. In our case, Facebook offers an optional service of monetization provided that some eligibility criteria are met.

The last category discusses the availability of tools aimed at enhancing the visibility or attractiveness of the audiovisual content. Once again, through "Facebook Watch", tools are provided that specifically enhance the consumption of videos. It is possible to promote videos through advertising tools and to track their performance (views).

Consequently, the platform ticks the boxes for all four categories of indicators, meaning that video does constitute an essential functionality of Facebook, in the sense of the AVMSD.

7.1.4.2   Main Principles of the AVMSD Relevant to Facebook

The consolidated version of the AVMSD[61] establishes a strict legal framework for video-sharing platform services. Article 28(b) of the AVMSD regulates the question. It establishes a duty to take appropriate measures as regards three distinct types of content: videos that may impair the physical, mental or moral development of minors, videos that contain incitement to violence or hatred directed against a group of persons or a member of a group based on any of the grounds referred to in Article 21 of the Charter (sex, race, color, ethnic or social origin, genetic features, language, religion or belief, political or any other opinion, membership of a national minority, property, birth, disability, age or sexual orientation), and videos that contain content the dissemination of which constitutes an activity which is a criminal offense under Union law, namely public provocation to commit a terrorist offense, offenses concerning child pornography and offenses concerning racism and xenophobia.

Therefore, the AVMSD completes and reinforces the protection against hate speech. It does not mean that Facebook is automatically liable for hate speech videos on the platform, as its responsibility is limited to taking "appropriate measures". This duty does not undermine the safe harbor mechanism. The EU legislator clearly explains that the assessment of this duty should take into account "the limited control exercised by those video-sharing platforms over those audiovisual commercial communications"[62] and that "those measures shall not lead to any ex-ante control

---

[61] Directive 2010/13/EU of the European Parliament and of the Council of 10 March 2010 on the coordination of certain provisions laid down by law, regulation or administrative action in Member States concerning the provision of audiovisual media services (Audiovisual Media Services Directive) (codified version) ELI: http://data.europa.eu/eli/dir/2010/13/2018-12-18.

[62] Article 28b (3) of the Directive.

measures or upload-filtering of content which do not comply with Article 15 of Directive 2000/31/EC."[63]

Interestingly, this duty is limited through some procedural safeguards, identified in Article 28(b) (3). In broad terms, Facebook has to stipulate in its terms and conditions that uploading these videos constitutes a breach of contract. A reporting system for videos that allegedly violate the terms and conditions has to be installed and where a report has been submitted, the user has to be informed. In the specific case of content that could potentially harm minors, the duty to take measures of protection also embraces "the establishing and operating age verification systems for users of video-sharing platforms with respect to content which may impair the physical, mental or moral development of minors" and "providing for parental control systems that are under the control of the end-user with respect to content which may impair the physical, mental or moral development of minors".[64]

In conclusion, the AVMSD's impact in combating illegal content on Facebook is not to be underestimated. First, contrary to the EU legislation on hate speech, any kind of discrimination stated in Article 21 of the Charter, including language, sexual orientation, and disability, are covered. Second, the protection of minors is directly addressed. Finally, the duty to take appropriate measures in order to tackle massive dissemination is understood to be a legal incentive for Facebook to intensify its vigilance in this respect.

7.2   The Co-regulation Techniques Used in Combating Illegal Content

7.2.1   The Practical Importance of Trusted Flaggers Organizations

The Internet has replaced the traditional hierarchy of knowledge with a networking of competencies. Ideally, through networking, the best answer to a question would automatically emerge from the mass of information. In practice, however, many psychological biases influence the result, with the undesired consequence that disinformation flourishes on social media. Put otherwise, the question is how people can access quality information without experts, such as journalists and scientists, acting as an intermediary. To fill the void between user-generated information and professional journalism, a new category of journalists has appeared: fact-checkers. A fact-checking organization aims to monitor the social network, searching for content that manifestly contradicts the scientific consensus on a specific point. When such content is found, the fact-checking organization may choose to publish an article on

---

[63] Article 28b (3) of the Directive.

[64] Article 28b (3) points h and f of the Directive.

its page, explaining scientifically how and why the content does not reflect what is currently accepted as truth.

Fact-checking organizations are therefore not related to Facebook and their findings are not binding on the company. Both journalists and users are ambivalent as regards the role of fact-checkers.[65] The main issues with fact-checking are related to the lack of transparency of the service: both users and journalists find it difficult to rely on one service, as it is not always clear on what "competence" basis it would be "judging" the veracity of content posted on Facebook. Some notorious dysfunctions of fact-checking organizations have been noticed, where they have flagged serious investigation articles as misinformation.[66]

Nevertheless, the relative success of fact-checking organizations in tackling fake news has led the EU Commission to widen its reach to illegal content in general. The EU Commission refers to "trusted flaggers", as "specialised entities with specific expertise in identifying illegal content, and dedicated structures for detecting and identifying such content online."[67]

An example of trusted flagger can be found in the INHOPE network of hotlines for reporting child sexual abuse material. INHOPE began in 1999, as a forum for various national hotlines in Europe, run by concerned citizens and dedicated to reporting online child pornography. With the help of EU funding, the hotlines further consolidated their efforts, creating a single organization that, over time, has evolved into a global network (with hotlines in 43 countries).[68] The network works as an intermediary, ensuring the anonymity of the flagger, through a secure platform, and the efficiency of the complaint mechanism. Once the complaint is reviewed by an internal analyst, two mechanisms are set in motion: a notice and take down procedure, and a communication to the competent national law enforcement agency. All the data are sent to INTERPOL to be entered into the International Child Sexual Exploitation (ICSE) database for victim and perpetrator identification purposes. It should be noted that Facebook is relatively unaffected by INHOPE's activities. Indeed, only 1% of the complaints addressed to the trusted flagger concerned the social network.[69]

The trusted flaggers' involvement in tackling illegal online content has been institutionalized in Articles 19 to 21 of the DSA proposal (see Sect. 6.2.4). Article 19 is entitled "Trusted flaggers". It connects the trusted flaggers' activity to the notice and take down procedure. Article 19 (1) gives priority to notices from trusted flaggers, which must be processed without delay. In other words, a direct line of communication between Facebook and trusted flaggers must be established.

---

[65] Brandtzaeg et al. (2018), pp. 1109–1129.

[66] Coombes (2022), p. 376.

[67] EU Commission (2018) Tackling online disinformation: a European approach. Communication. COM/2018/236 final.

[68] See https://www.inhope.org/EN/articles/who-we-are.

[69] INHOPE (2020).

However, with the enhanced prerogatives of trusted flaggers comes greater accountability. The Committee of Ministers of the Council of Europe, in its 2021 guide on content moderation, warns against depending excessively on trusted flaggers.[70] There is a fear of creating entities that would monopolize the notion of scientific truth, at the cost of a democratic debate. It considers that

> [w]hen internet intermediaries use specialised organisations (variously referred to as "trusted flaggers" or "priority flaggers") as a filter through which to get more reliable reports of infringing content, specific transparency rules are needed for such initiatives, in order to ensure that no perverse incentives or conflicts of interest are accidentally created and that their level of effectiveness and trustworthiness remains consistently high. Use of trusted flaggers should not be mandatory and notices from trusted flaggers should not be considered "actual knowledge" of illegality of content. The status of "trusted flaggers" should be periodically, independently evaluated.[71]

The DSA proposal proposes an answer to this legitimate concern. Control over the status of trusted flaggers is to lie with the new position of the Member State's Digital Services Coordinator. The organization mainly has to prove its expertise, its independence from any online platform, and its objectivity (Article 19 (2)), or else the status may be revoked (Article 19(6)). This control is also carried out by Facebook, in the sense that if there is a significant number of false flags, the online platform has to inform the Digital Services Coordinator (Article 19 (5)).

7.2.2   E-governance Through Soft Law and Its Impact on Illegal Online Content

7.2.2.1   The Promotion of EU Codes of Conduct for Online Platforms

Trusted flagger organizations should be seen only as a complement to the main activities of the platform in fighting misinformation. The practical situation in this aspect shows mixed results. On the one hand, it cannot be denied that Meta massively invested in methods of protection against misinformation. On the other hand, most of this investment focused on the United States, even though daily active users in other countries make up the vast majority of the userbase.[72] It should also be noted that Facebook encounters a serious conflict of interest in moderating its content, as the most profitable content is also the most engaged, which effectively means the most hateful and dividing content. Whistleblowers have warned about the

---

[70] Steering Committee for Media and Information Society (2021).

[71] Par.26 of the Guidance note.

[72] Harbath K. (2022) I Worked at Facebook. It's Not Ready for This Year's Election Wave. The New York Times. https://www.nytimes.com/2022/01/29/opinion/facebook-2022-election.html.

lack of transparency and good faith of Meta as regards this aspect, saying that this conflict is usually resolved by reference to the company's interests only.[73]

Article 16 of the e-Commerce Directive indicates that the EU Commission shall encourage the drawing up of codes of conduct at Union level, by trade, professional and consumer associations or organizations designed to contribute to the implementation of the Directive. The EU Code of Conduct on countering hate speech online,[74] prepared by the EU Commission in 2016, has been described as "the most debated and perhaps the most influential European instrument"[75] in this field. Furthermore,

> [t]he impact of the Code of Conduct has been regularly monitored and the most recent results show a very positive trend. Two and a half years after signature of the Code, evaluations show that IT Companies respond to notices within 24h in the majority of cases and remove on average 72% of content notified to them, compared to 59% in 2017 and only 28% in 2016.[76]

Meta is one of the main targets of the Code of Conduct and one of its initial signatories, alongside Microsoft, Twitter, and YouTube. The code does not rely on articles and legal duties, but on a series of statements, each of them representing a voluntary commitment. These statements mainly concern the notice and take down procedures. It sets a principle that reaction should occur in less than 24 h, which should lead to the removal or disablement of access to illegal content. It imposes a set of core principles (which can also be found in the DSA proposal): objectivity of the treatment, transparency, partnerships and communications with law enforcement authorities and civil societies organizations, and emphasis on pedagogical actions.

Consequently, the Code of Conduct on online hate speech promotes a proactive approach that is not particularly revolutionary or original. It could be argued that the real impact of the Code of Conduct is psychological. First, it asks for a practical commitment from Facebook, which feels the pressure of showing more substantial results in its efforts to tackle online illegal content. Second, it also contains an invisible threat. By promoting the EU Code of Conduct, the Commission also delivers an implicit message: "we prefer to let you regulate the topic, but we will closely monitor your effort and in case of failure we will replace soft law by legislative and imperative actions".

---

[73] Pelley S. (2021) Whistleblower: Facebook is misleading the public on progress against hate speech, violence, misinformation. CBC News. https://www.cbsnews.com/news/facebook-whistleblower-frances-haugen-misinformation-public-60-minutes-2021-10-03/.

[74] See https://ec.europa.eu/info/policies/justice-and-fundamental-rights/combatting-discrimination/racism-and-xenophobia/eu-code-conduct-countering-illegal-hate-speech-online_en#theeucodeofconduct.

[75] Bayer and Bard (2020) Hate speech and hate crime in the EU and the evaluation of online content regulation approaches. Op.cit., 53.

[76] EU Commission (2019) Countering racism and xenophobia in the EU: fostering a society where pluralism, tolerance and non-discrimination prevail, Commission Staff Working Document, Brussels, SWD (2019) 110 final, 6.

The "Code of Practice on Disinformation" follows the same model. Published in 2018 and signed by Facebook,[77] the Code defines disinformation as

> verifiably false or misleading information' which, cumulatively, (a) 'Is created, presented and disseminated for economic gain or to intentionally deceive the public'; and (b) 'May cause public harm', intended as 'threats to democratic political and policymaking processes as well as public goods such as the protection of EU citizens' health, the environment or security.

This self-regulatory code focuses on political advertising, imposing enhanced monitoring.

Facebook specifies its policy on fake news in its Community Standards:

> Reducing the spread of false news on Facebook is a responsibility that we take seriously. We also recognise that this is a challenging and sensitive issue. We want to help people stay informed without stifling productive public discourse. There is also a fine line between false news and satire or opinion. For these reasons, we don't remove false news from Facebook, but instead significantly reduce its distribution by showing it lower in the News Feed.

Because of its pure self-regulatory nature, the Code of Practice on Disinformation does not include any compliance mechanism. The members have to publish self-assessments on their commitment. For 2019, Facebook announced an improvement of its machine learning capabilities, which will allegedly be more effective in finding and removing violating behavior, and also declared that it had doubled the number of participating independent fact-checkers. However, one look at the Community Standards Enforcement Report published twice a year by Facebook is enough to assess the issue. The Report refers to various categories of content infringing Facebook's Community Standards:

> adult nudity and sexual activity, bullying and harassment, child nudity and sexual exploitation of children, fake accounts, hate speech, regulated goods, spam, terrorist propaganda and violence and graphic content.

No mention is made of fake news. As the Community Standards explain, fake news is not removed; its visibility is only diminished.

While transposing most of the Code of Conduct's principles into legislation, the DSA proposal does not completely abandon this soft law perspective. However, it indicates a shift from self-regulation towards co-regulation. The codes of conduct need to be revised to comply with this new approach. Characteristically, in 2021, the EU Commission proposed a guidance text towards a "strengthened Code of Practice", which will revise the current Code of Conduct on Disinformation, attempting to correct the shortcomings of the text.[78]

The Guidance asks for further commitments. First, disinformation should be demonetized. Facebook's Content Monetization Policies do include two relevant

---

[77] See the document: https://ec.europa.eu/newsroom/dae/document.cfm?doc_id=54789.

[78] ECOPNET (2021) Commission Presents Guidance to Strengthen the Code of Practice on Disinformation. https://www.ecopnet.com/post/commission-presents-guidance-to-strengthen-the-code-of-practice-on-disinformation.

mechanisms: restricted content and prohibited content. Under the first mechanism, monetization of the content is reduced. An example of such content is "Debated social issues", defined as content that

> depicts or discusses the following subjects in a polarising or inflammatory manner: Race, Gender, National origin, Age, Political affiliation, Ethnicity, Disability, Sexual orientation, Socioeconomic class, Religion, Immigration, Legitimacy of elections.

Under the second mechanism, monetization of the content is deactivated. Two instances of prohibited content are set out: "Misinformation", defined as "Content that has been rated false by a third-party fact-checker", and "Misleading medical information", which is "Content that contains medical claims that have been disproven by an expert organisation. Including, but not limited to, anti-vaccination claims".

Second, the EU Commission aims through the strengthened Code to better cover emerging forms of manipulative behavior used to spread disinformation (such as bots, fake accounts, organized manipulation campaigns, account takeovers), and include tailored commitments to ensure transparency and accountability of measures taken to reduce its impact. Third, the EU Commission asks for the creation of more tools, thus allowing the user to better understand and handle misinformation. For instance, Facebook could offer an option for the user to not see any kind of content that has been flagged as misinformation.

Therefore, the DSA proposal will not mark the end of the codes of conduct—quite the opposite. The approach is institutionalized in Article 35, as it generalizes the use of codes of conduct to all kinds of online illegal content. However, this does not mean that the DSA proposal intends to enforce this self-regulation model as a general solution. This principle has to be read in conjunction with the other measures in the DSA proposal that specifically concern the GAFAM. In Article 56 it is stated that in case

> the very large online platform concerned offers commitments to ensure compliance with the relevant provisions of this Regulation, the Commission may by decision make those commitments binding.

In this case, if Facebook does honor its commitment, Article 59 gives the Commission the power to apply fines for "failing to comply with a voluntary measure made binding by a decision pursuant to Articles 56". These fines can amount to 6% of its total turnover in the preceding financial year. The EU Commission has the tools to exercise strict control over the compliance with the core e-governance principles it has set. As a consequence, e-governance—rather than self-regulation—tends to constitute a co-regulation system.

7.2.2.2   Facebook's Oversight Board

In the context of co-regulation, transparency becomes a core principle that affects all activities of the platform. The EU codes of conduct and the DSA regulation proposal promote transparency in the moderation techniques used, but transparency is also needed in the enforcement of these techniques. Anticipating the regulation, Meta innovated by instituting an "Oversight Board", which in practice plays the role of a "Facebook Supreme Court".[79] The Oversight Board works as a parallel organization that is independent from Facebook. This independence is relative, as Board members are selected by Facebook from civil society.[80] However, Facebook has ensured that both the Board and its administration are funded by an independent trust and supported by an independent company that is separate from Facebook.[81]

The Board intervenes as an "appeal" in case of Facebook's intervention: after a report, where a first decision on moderation has been taken, and after an internal review of this decision has already been carried out. The Board is then competent to discuss the pertinence of this internal review if it wishes to. Indeed, although Facebook may ask it to pronounce on a delicate issue it has encountered, the Board normally chooses the cases that it will handle, selecting cases that "are difficult, significant and globally relevant". Facebook has announced that it will treat all decisions from the Board as binding.

From this, it can be concluded that the Board is incorrectly called the "Facebook Supreme Court". Its role is clearly to assist the company into policing the content by using some rare and complicated cases as an alleged reason to publish improved guidelines. Nevertheless, these guidelines are extremely important as they shed light on the interpretation given by Facebook on its commitment to tackle online hate speech. For the first three years of the Board's existence, almost two dozen decisions were published, most of them relating directly or indirectly to hate speech. From these cases we can form the general idea that, from the Board's point of view, Facebook's moderation has two main shortcomings: it is too strict and it is defective.

As regards the first point, the Board clearly gives precedence to freedom of expression. The first case ever reviewed by the Board concerned hate speech in a comment. Since the post was ultimately deleted by its author, it was de facto impossible for the Board to request the reinstallation of the comment and the case was closed.[82] The second case discussed a post created in the context of the publication of the Muslim prophet caricatures. The author implied that France posed a problem to Muslims while at the same time they were oppressed in China and concluded that "[there is] something wrong with Muslims psychologically." Facebook had moderated the content, but the Board disagreed. It considered that "the text is better understood as a commentary on the apparent inconsistency between Muslims' reactions to events in France and in China."[83]

In the same way, in another case, the Board considered that a post stating that "if the tongue of the kafir (the non-Muslim) starts against the Prophet, then the sword should be taken out of the sheath.", referring to the French President as the devil and

---

[79] Dipayan (2019).

[80] From the 20 members of the board, 3 have a background related to the EU and 5 to the US.

[81] Source: https://oversightboard.com/.

[82] Case Report 2020-001-FB-UA.

[83] Case Decision 2020-002-FB-UA.

calling for the boycott of French products, is not characteristic of hate speech.[84] Consequently, the Board overturned the Facebook's decision to moderate.

In another case, again, the Board overturned the decision to moderate as hate speech a post in Turkish using the "Two buttons meme" (an image depicting a man hesitating between two buttons to push) with the following texts: "The Armenian Genocide is a lie" and "The Armenians were terrorists that deserved it." From the Board's perspective, the use of the "Two buttons meme" shows that the user's intent was to point out the contradiction between the two statements.[85]

The same liberal approach applies to fake news. In a case related to a post claiming that the French authorities refused to authorize hydroxychloroquine against COVID-19 while it was a harmless drug used everywhere else in the world, the Board overturned Facebook's decision to moderate. The Board found that Facebook's decision did not comply with international human rights standards on limiting the freedom of expression.

In the Board's opinion, given that Facebook had a range of tools to deal with misinformation, such as providing users with additional context, Facebook failed to demonstrate why it did not choose a less intrusive option than removing the content.[86] Furthermore, the Board highlighted the need to provide context to determine whether the misinformation is of a nature to cause harm. It also considered that this case raised important issues of distinguishing between opinion and fact. In other words, the Board did not consider that fake news, even when it put life in danger, should be removed. Similarly, the Board agreed with Facebook that a post from a medical authority which claimed that lockdowns are ineffective and had been condemned by the World Health Organization, did not create a risk of imminent harm and should not be deleted.[87] On the contrary, in cases where a heated and ongoing conflict is going on, the Board found that removing unverifiable rumors about ethnic conflict is consistent with Meta's human rights responsibilities as a business, in the sense that unverifiable rumors in a heated and ongoing conflict could lead to grave atrocities.[88]

As regards defective moderation, the Board has severely criticized Facebook in some cases. For instance, in an instance where an account had been wrongly restricted because of hate speech, without the possibility of human intervention due to the high moderation demands related to the pandemic, the Board requested that Facebook restore both human review of content moderation decisions and access to a human appeals process to pre-pandemic levels as soon as possible.[89] Another case of automatic moderation related to a situation of "counter speech". While the message was apparently hate speech and was moderated as such, it was

---

[84] Case Decision 2020-007-FB-FBR.

[85] Case decision 2021-005-FB-UA.

[86] Case Decision 2020-006-FB-FBR.

[87] Case decision 2021-008-FB-FBR.

[88] Case decision 2021-014-FB-UA.

[89] Case decision 2021-003-FB-UA.

only trying to raise awareness of historic crimes against indigenous people in North America.[90]

In another case,[91] a user had been moderated for using a quote (incorrectly) attributed to Goebbels. Facebook claimed that posts which share a quote attributed to a dangerous individual are treated as expressing support for them, unless the user provides additional context to make their intent explicit and it removed the post because the user did not make clear whether they had shared the quote to condemn Joseph Goebbels, to counter extremism or hate speech, or for academic or news purposes. The Board criticized this decision on two points: first, this rule for quotes from "dangerous individuals" is not part of the published Community Standards and denotes a dangerous lack of transparency as regards the rules regarding moderation. Second, the Board found that the quote did not support Nazi ideology or the regime's acts of hatred and violence. Comments on the post from the user's friends supported the user's claim that they sought to compare the presidency of Donald Trump to the Nazi regime.

Finally, in the famous case of Donald Trump's suspension,[92] while upholding the decision on suspension, the Board again pointed out some defects as regards the sanctions. Indeed, Facebook had first suspended the account for 24 h, but later changed its opinion and imposed an indefinite suspension. The Board considered that penalties have to be necessary and proportionate, as regards the gravity of the violation and the prospect of future harm. In other words, the infinite duration of the suspension may have been too severe, and Facebook was invited to review its decision after some time. Following the decision, Facebook modified the sanction and imposed a 2-year ban of services to the former president.

In conclusion, this very protective of the freedom of expression stance of the Board reflects its mainly Atlantic composition. It also stresses the growing ideological divide between Europe and the US on the notion of freedom of speech (see Chap. 8). For the Board, calls for violence against the French in the context of growing religious tensions were not deemed to be hate speech, while Trump's rally to protesters did constitute prohibited praise or support of people engaged in violence.

This bias of the Board is also visible in decisions on violations of the Community Standards. The Board upheld a decision to remove content flagged as hate speech, because a post from an Armenian, during the Nagorno-Karabakh conflict, used a slur to describe people from Azerbaijan.[93] In another case, the Oversight Board upheld Facebook's decision to remove specific content that violated the express prohibition on posting caricatures of black people in the form of blackface, contained in its Hate Speech Community Standard.[94] The Board did acknowledge that in the Netherlands,

---

[90] Case decision 2021-012-FB-UA.

[91] Case Decision 2020-005-FB-UA.

[92] Case decision 2021-001-FB-FBR.

[93] Case Decision 2020-003-FB-UA.

[94] Case decision 2021-002-FB-UA.

this was done without apparent racist intent and as a form of traditional cultural expression, but nevertheless considered that the use of blackface is widely recognized to be a harmful racial stereotype. However, it could be argued that the "Zwarte Piet" from the Netherlands is culturally and historically very different from the US "Mammy" blackface character that contained very strong racist elements.[95] In other words, while the American's blackface undeniably connotes racism, the issue is much more delicate regarding European blackface uses.

Overall, the "slur case", the "blackface" case, and Trump's case comprise, so far, the only situations where the Board endorsed Facebook's moderation. Furthermore, by virtue of its nature as an appellate body for Facebook's moderation, the Board does not hear cases where someone has complained of a lack of moderation. This situation further enhances the position of the Board as the guardian of a specific understanding of the freedom of expression as expressed, mainly, through US values and which is arguably not entirely compatible with the EU perspective on this matter (see Sect. 8.1.1).

7.2.3 The Cooperation with the Authorities

The proactive approach preferred by the EU authorities in matters of disinformation should not obscure the fact that the intentional public distribution of false information that causes trouble to society is traditionally an offense recognized by some Member States. For instance, in Italy, the law punishes the publication and dissemination of false, exaggerated or biased news which may undermine public order.[96] While a classic criminal procedure would fail to effectively prevent the damage done by the propagation of fake news, some Member States have matched the offenses to modern tools of enforcement. In Germany, the NetzDG (see Sect. 6.2.1) accomplishes exactly this purpose. In a similar vein, in France, the law "against manipulation of information"[97] enacted in 2018, provides the possibility of judicial control (within 48 h) of manifestly fake news during election campaigns, as well as a duty on social media to cooperate with the authorities.

The authorities' powers to intervene with the platform's management should not be without any safeguards, or else it could be seen as a disproportionate threat to freedom of expression. For instance, the French law that gave the executive the power to ask online service providers for moderation of hate speech content within 24 h, with criminal sanctions in case of violation of this duty, was ruled

---

[95]Lemmens (2017), pp. 120–141.

[96]Article 656 of the Italian Criminal Code.

[97]LOI n° 2018-1202 du 22 décembre 2018 relative à la lutte contre la manipulation de l'information, NOR: MICX1808389L, ELI: https://www.legifrance.gouv.fr/eli/loi/2018/12/22/MICX1808389L/jo/texte, JORF n°0297 du 23 décembre 2018.

unconstitutional by the French Constitutional Court.[98] When fundamental freedoms are at stake, only judicial control can guarantee the relative protection of all interests at stake.

The DSA proposal emphasizes the need for cooperation between the authorities and Meta. Specifically, in Article 21, a duty is placed on the social network to notify the national authorities about illegal content. The article states that

> [w]here an online platform becomes aware of any information giving rise to a suspicion that a serious criminal offence involving a threat to the life or safety of persons has taken place, is taking place or is likely to take place, it shall promptly inform the law enforcement or judicial authorities of the Member State or Member States concerned of its suspicion and provide all relevant information available.

In the case of Facebook, the concerned Member States should normally be the Member State where the suspected offender resides or is located, or the Member State where the victim of the suspected offense resides or is located. However, in case of illegal content derived from false accounts of uncertain national origin, Facebook may either contact the Irish law enforcement authorities (as the place where it is established) or inform Europol.

References

Aro J (2016) The cyberspace war: propaganda and trolling as warfare tools. Eur View 15(1): 121–132

Bayer J, Bard P (2020) Hate speech and hate crime in the EU and the evaluation of online content regulation approaches. Policy Department for Citizens' Rights and Constitutional Affairs Directorate-General for Internal Policies PE 655.135 - July 2020, p 27

Brandtzaeg PB, Følstad A, Chaparro Domínguez MÁ (2018) How journalists and social media users perceive online fact-checking and verification services. Journalism Practice 12(9): 1109–1129

Carrapico H, Farrand B (2021) When trust fades, Facebook is no longer a friend: shifting privatisation dynamics in the context of cybersecurity as a result of disinformation, populism and political uncertainty. JCMS J Common Market Stud. https://doi.org/10.1111/jcms.13175

Conway M, Scrivens R, Macnair L (2019) 'Right-Wing Extremists' persistent online presence: history and contemporary trends', ICCT Policy Brief, 25 November 2019, https://icct.nl/publication/right-wing-extremists-persistent-online-presence-history-and-contemporary-trends

Coombes R (2022) Facebook versus the BMJ: when fact checking goes wrong. BMJ 376. https://doi.org/10.1136/bmj.o95

Dikaiakos M, Pallis G, Markatos E (2016) Mandola: monitoring and detecting online hate speech. ERCIM News No. 107 (Special Theme: Machine Learning), p 49

Dipayan G (2019) Facebook's oversight board is not enough harvard business review

ECOPNET (2021) Commission presents guidance to strengthen the code of practice on disinformation. https://www.ecopnet.com/post/commission-presents-guidance-to-strengthen-the-code-of-practice-on-disinformation

---

[98] Décision n° 2020-801 DC du 18 juin 2020.

Ekathimerini.com (2018) Court clears author Soti Triantafyllou of 'racism' in her writing. Kathimerini, https://www.ekathimerini.com/news/228220/court-clears-author-soti-triantafyllou-of-racism-in-her-writing/

European Commission (2020) Lesbian, gay, bisexual, transgender and intersex+ equality strategy. Roadmap. Ref. Ares(2020)2793707 - 29/05/2020

INHOPE (2020) Annual Report. https://inhope.org/media/pages/the-facts/download-our-whitepapers/c16bc4d839-1620144551/inhope-annual-report-2020.pdf

Klonick K (2019) The Facebook oversight board: creating an independent institution to adjudicate online free expression. Yale Law J 129:2418

Lemmens K (2017) The dark side of 'Zwarte Piet': a misunderstood tradition or racism in disguise? A legal analysis. Int J Human Rights 21(2):120–141. https://doi.org/10.1080/13642987.2016.1276448

Levy N (2017) Am I a racist? Implicit bias and the ascription of racism. Philos Q 67(268):534–551

Mathew B, Dutt R, Goyal P, Mukherjee A (2019) Spread of hate speech in online social media. In Proceedings of the 10th ACM conference on web science, pp 173–182

Nicolas AC (2018) Taming the trolls: the need for an international legal framework to regulate State use of disinformation on social media. Geo Law J Online 107:36

Nurik C (2019) "Men Are Scum": self-regulation, hate speech, and gender-based censorship on Facebook. Int J Commun 13:21

OHCHR (2011) Rabat Plan of Action on the prohibition of advocacy of national, racial or religious hatred that constitutes incitement to discrimination, hostility or violence, A/HRC/22/17/Add.4

Renda A (2018) The legal framework to address "fake news": possible policy actions at the EU level. Policy Department for Economic, Scientific and Quality of Life Policies, European Parliament, http://www.europarl.europa.eu/supporting-analyses

Report from the Commission to the European Parliament and the Council on the implementation of Council Framework Decision 2008/913/JHA on combating certain forms and expressions of racism and xenophobia by means of criminal law, COM(2014)27 final

Steering Committee for Media and Information Society (2021) Content Moderation, Best practices towards effective legal and procedural frameworks for self-regulatory and co-regulatory mechanisms of content moderation. Guidance Note adopted by the Steering Committee for Media and Information Society (CDMSI) at its 19th plenary meeting, 19–21 May. Council of Europe

Temperman J (2008) Blasphemy, defamation of religions and human rights law. Netherlands Q Human Rights 26(4):517–545

Waseem Z (2016) Are you a racist or am I seeing things? annotator influence on hate speech detection on twitter. In: Proceedings of the first workshop on NLP and computational social science, 138–142

Chapter 8
Freedom of Expression and the Rise of AI

Although democracy is institutionally built on three pillars—the legislature, the executive and the judiciary—the media have for a long time been seen as the fourth, unofficial pillar. Without press, radio and television, no efficient control can be exercised by the population over the functioning of the first three pillars. Nowadays, the question is: what place do social networks occupy in this schema? Is Facebook the fifth pillar of democracy in the age of information? Mark Zuckerberg certainly believes so.[1]

The relationship between social media and classic media is to be characterized, at least, as ambiguous: ontologically, they are opposing sources of information, one based on decentralization, the other on expertise. Furthermore, while radio and television, in Europe at least, operate on the basis of objective pluralism, which obliges the media to carry out debates between various ideologies without taking a position, social media operate on the basis of bubbles of information that annihilate most debates.

However, both traditional media and social media operate in parallel to shape public opinion. Both nowadays exert an equally huge influence on the practical functioning of modern democracy. Facebook's position is paradoxical: it is criticized for its censorship, on the one hand, and its lack of action against illegal content, on the other. It would be easy to conclude that both critics cancel each other out and that the company has struck the difficult balance between protection of freedom of speech and protection of legitimate interests of democratic societies, but the situation is much more complex.

This paradox on Facebook's influence on freedoms can be resolved, as the real issues regarding protection of the freedom of expression are not those that one would expect at first sight. First, it is important to stress that freedom of expression, from the EU perspective, does not exclude censorship, as an exception and under strict scrutiny (Sect. 8.1). Second, although freedom of expression does not mean the

---

[1] Paul (2019).

absence of control over the expression, the issue remains of who exerts this control, and on what basis. It will be argued that Facebook's platform has de facto evolved into a new legal entity which could be called a "digital public space". In this context, the time has come to revisit the general non-horizontal application of freedom of expression (Sect. 8.2). Third, it should be highlighted that the main threat posed to freedom of expression by the platform is invisible, in the sense that the functioning of the platform itself (Facebook's algorithm), through its mechanism of "shadow moderation", constitutes a substantial risk to the right to be informed, which is an inherent part of the freedom of expression (Sect. 8.3).

8.1 The Notion of Freedom of Speech, Between Universalism and Cultural Particularism

8.1.1 The Three Generations of Freedom of Expression

8.1.1.1 Freedom of Expression As the "Right to Provoke"

Human rights have been classified, through the theory of the "three generations", into three categories: civil and political rights; economic, social and cultural rights; and collective or solidarity rights.[2] Although this theory is not unanimously accepted,[3] it has the advantage of clearly describing a fundamental element of human rights: their evolving nature. The theory also resonates as a legal endorsement of the famous "liberty, equality, fraternity" political slogan that fueled European revolutions. As freedom of expression is traditionally part of the first generation of human rights, it is commonly accepted that its protection is better ensured in the US than in Europe,[4] which is more accepting of some boundaries to its exercise. However, it can be argued that freedom of speech does not exclusively belong to the first category of human rights, but also has ramifications on the second and the third (see below on the protection of the pluralism and on the notion of the right to be informed). This argument highlights the most substantial difference between the US and the European perspectives on freedom of expression: while the US mainly defends a view of human rights as contained in the first category, the Europeans have embraced the multidimensional nature of human rights.

This divergence of position on freedom of expression has a huge impact on Facebook's position: by nature, the US company, its American founder, and even its advisory board (see Sect. 7.2.2) tend to adopt the US view on freedom of speech.

Nevertheless, as regards the core component of freedom of speech as a civil and political right, the US and Europe agree: both the US freedom of speech and the EU

---

[2] Vasak K. (1977) A 30 year struggle, UNESCO Courier, November 1977, 29.
[3] Jensen (2017).
[4] Gray (2016).

freedom of expression encompass the right to express diverging, provoking, non-consensual points of view. In a dissenting opinion in the landmark case Abrams v. United States,[5] Justice Oliver Wendell Holmes argued that the First Amendment protects the right to dissent from the government's viewpoints and objectives, advancing the famous theory of the "marketplace of ideas". By drawing an analogy with liberal economic ideas, the theory holds that the truth and, by extension, the general interest will naturally emerge from the free confrontation of ideas. In 1969, the US Supreme Court's decision in Brandenburg v. Ohio[6] enshrined this as the dominant public policy in US free speech law, explaining that the government cannot punish inflammatory speech unless that speech is "directed to inciting or producing imminent lawless action and is likely to incite or produce such action".

The marketplace of ideas doctrine remains the basis of Facebook's philosophy, which fuels some critics:

> the second century since Justice Holmes's proposed his influential marketplace of ideas concept would see it playing out in a technological environment where marketplace competition between falsity and truth is replaced algorithmically with endless bubbles, cocoons and silos creating for individuals and groups only the illusion of marketplaces.[7]

However, the marketplace of ideas presupposes that all ideas are equal in their influences and impact. It could be argued that this dogma is refuted through "Brandolini's law",[8] a known Internet adage that postulates that the amount of energy needed to refute misinformation is an order of magnitude larger than to produce it.

The European approach on the core component of freedom of speech, redefined as freedom of expression in Europe, does not differ much. Interpreting Article 10 of the ECHR, the ECtHR has assumed the mantle of the guardian of freedom of expression in Europe. The Court has repeatedly stated that "[f]reedom of expression constitutes one of the essential foundations of a democratic society, one of the basic conditions for its progress and for each individual's self-fulfilment".[9]

The "little red schoolbook" case[10] constitutes the landmark decision which characterizes the European approach to this matter. The case concerned the publication of a book that aimed to educate teenage readers about sex, containing detailed explanations on the topic. The British authorities had found part of the explanations obscene and censored the book. The ECtHR found that the intent to protect children was a legitimate interference to freedom of expression, but, overall, it established the famous principle that

---

[5] Abrams v. United States, 250 U.S. 616 (1919).

[6] Brandenburg v. Ohio, 395 U.S. 444 (1969).

[7] Kerr (2019), pp. 477–512.

[8] Williamson (2016), p. 171.

[9] ECtHR, Linges v. Austria, no. 9815/82, 8 July 1986.

[10] ECtHR, Handyside v. UK, no. 5493/72, 7 December 1976.

freedom of expression. . .is applicable not only to 'information' or 'ideas' that are favourably received or regarded as inoffensive or as a matter of indifference, but also to those that offend, shock or disturb the State or any sector of the population.

8.1.1.2   Freedom of Expression and Right to Pluralism

Freedom of expression is not limited to the state's negative obligations as regards citizens' freedom. States also have the duty to enforce an "equality" of the access to a medium of expression. Indeed, it has quickly become apparent in the age of mass media that the freedom of expression would be meaningless without equitable access to a proper medium of expression. For instance, in the context of radio and television broadcasted through specific frequencies attributed by the International Telecommunication Union (ITU) to its member States, the rarity of available frequencies resulted in a rarity of the available medium. In other words, there was not enough space for all opinions to be expressed separately.

Translated into legal terms, this situation provoked the development of a new aspect of freedom of expression: the protection of pluralism. This objective justifies for instance the specific duty in television broadcasting to recognize the right of reply. Article 28 of the revised AVMSD states that

any natural or legal person, regardless of nationality, whose legitimate interests, in particular reputation and good name, have been damaged by an assertion of incorrect facts in a television programme must have a right of reply or equivalent remedies.

Generally speaking, from the EU perspective, the freedom of expression's imperative of efficiency led to the imposition of various legal regimes for the protection of pluralism. For the press, it is possible to refer to "external pluralism" as the multiplicity of newspapers ensures the plurality of voices, while for radio-television it is necessary to enforce an "internal pluralism", that is an objectivity of the expression allied with a fair repartition of the airtime.

Nevertheless, while these ideas have been enshrined in Member States' constitutional laws, for instance in France or in Germany, and despite the multiple interventions of the EU Parliament on this topic[11] and the interest shown by the EU authorities,[12] it has to be underlined that the EU Commission has failed to adopt a general legislative act protecting media pluralism.[13]

The situation has paradoxically not evolved in the digital age. Although, apparently, the problem of the rarity of the medium is solved on social networks, as everybody may open an account, it has been noted, in fact, that

Internet users will have access to more and more information from more and more sources even as the media environment they navigate is increasingly dominated by a limited number of very large players and see consolidation and cost-cutting elsewhere in the media

---

[11] EU Parliament (2013).

[12] EU Commission (1992).

[13] Bard et al. (2016).

landscape which can over time reduce media pluralism by undermining the diversity of original, professional news production.[14]

Specifically, while the fight against media concentration in the field of television has led to the establishment of the principle of internal pluralism, the same conditions are developing for hosting online services, as Facebook benefits from a dominant position in the market of social media.

In this context, the ECtHR's position on this topic is extremely valuable. In the Grand Chamber's decision Centro Europa,[15] the Court stated that

> to ensure true pluralism in the audio-visual sector in a democratic society, it is not sufficient to provide for the existence of several channels or the theoretical possibility for potential operators to access the audio-visual market. It is necessary in addition to allow effective access to the market so as to guarantee diversity of overall programme content, reflecting as far as possible the variety of opinions encountered in the society at which the programmes are aimed.[16]

also adding that

> A situation whereby a powerful economic or political group in society is permitted to obtain a position of dominance over the audio-visual media and thereby exercise pressure on broadcasters and eventually curtail their editorial freedom undermines the fundamental role of freedom of expression in a democratic society as enshrined in Article 10 of the Convention, in particular where it serves to impart information and ideas of general interest, which the public is moreover entitled to receive.[17]

Consequently, from an EU perspective, the fundamental interest in protecting freedom of expression does not entail only the protection of the individual's right to express but also the necessary objectivity from the part of the entities that control the medium of expression, in order to ensure an effective equality between the various opinions expressed. By analogy, it could be argued that while the US perspective of the free marketplace of ideas is based on a neoliberal approach of autoregulation, the EU concept of freedom of expression enforces strict anti-competition rules to protect the plurality of voices.

8.1.1.3   Freedom of Expression and the Right to Be Informed

A third dimension of the freedom of expression is related to the quantity and quality of information available to citizens. In essence, through the protection of freedom of expression, the right of free public communication is protected. However, a communication needs a source, a channel, and a receiver. Freedom of speech stricto sensu protects the source, and the right to pluralism: the channel. Even with a protection of the right to express and a protection of pluralism, the freedom would

---

[14] Kleis Nielsen et al. (2016), p. 34.

[15] ECtHR, Centro Europa 7 S.R.L. and Di Stefano v. Italy, no. 38433/09, 7 June 2012.

[16] Par.130 of the decision.

[17] Par.133 of the decision.

be meaningless without effective protection of the receiver of the communication. It is therefore generally accepted that the freedom of expression also encompasses a right to be informed.

Characteristically, the Universal Declaration of Human Rights states that

> [e]veryone has the right to freedom of opinion and expression; this right includes freedom to hold opinions without interference and to seek, receive and impart information and ideas through any media and regardless of frontiers.[18]

The right to be informed is only partially recognized by the European Court of Human Rights. Although the court had ruled that Article 10 can justify the obligation for the state to provide access to information to the citizens that ask for them in some circumstances,[19] it was also noted in the Bureaustop case[20] that this obligation should not be extended to a duty to communicate information in general. Specifically, the relevance of a potential duty to inform should be examined according to the following criteria: the purpose of the request for information, the nature of the information sought, the role of the applicant, and whether or not the information is already available. Nevertheless, it is worth mentioning that in the same case, the court adds that "insincere, inaccurate or insufficient nature of information provided by a public authority pursuant to an obligation to inform" should be seen as equivalent to a refusal to inform.[21] This development is extremely important in the context of fake news, for instance, as it could mean that the regulation of fake news should not be seen (only) as a restriction to the freedom of speech but as an inherent concept of the freedom of expression, through the notion of a duty to inform.

Furthermore, access to the Internet itself is included in the protection of the freedom of expression through this aspect. In the same way, mechanisms to restrict the visibility of a message on the platform have to be dealt with as restrictions to the right to be informed, that should pass the relevant test as regards their legitimacy (see below, Sect. 8.1.2). Specifically, the Committee of Ministers of the Council of Europe formulates some basic recommendations on how content moderation must be compatible with the right to be informed. It declares that

> Internet intermediaries should respect the rights of users to receive, produce and impart information, opinions and ideas. Any measures taken to restrict access (including blocking or removing content) as a result of a State order or request should be implemented using the least restrictive means. When restricting access to content in line with their own content-restriction policies, intermediaries should do so in a transparent and non-discriminatory manner. Any restriction of content should be carried out using the least restrictive technical means and should be limited in scope and duration to what is strictly necessary to avoid the collateral restriction or removal of legal content.[22]

---

[18] Article 19 of the Universal Declaration of Human Rights (1948).

[19] ECtHR, Magyar Helsinki Bizottság c. Hongrie [GC], no 18030/11, 8 November 2016.

[20] ECtHR, Association BURESTOP 55 et autres c. France, nos 56176/18 et 5 autres, 1st July 2021.

[21] Par.85 of the Decision.

[22] Council of Europe's Committee of Ministers (2018).

Consequently, the right to be informed requires an objectivity of the publication process by social media. As such, it plays a fundamental role in regulating Facebook. The protection of this interest will justify various interventions and initiatives, for instance, the right to explanation in case of AI-based publishing activities (see Sect. 8.3.2) or the justification for the DSA proposal (see Sect. 9.2).

8.1.2 The Legitimate Restrictions on Freedom of Expression in Europe

8.1.2.1 The Three-Part Test

From the European perspective, only the right to life, freedom of thought, and the prohibitions on torture, inhuman treatment or punishment, and degrading treatment or punishment are seen as absolute rights. Freedom of expression, on the contrary, like many other human rights, has to be balanced with legitimate interests in order to shape the notion of illegal content. Article 10 (2) of the ECHR stipulates that

> [t]he exercise of these freedoms, since it carries with it duties and responsibilities, may be subject to such formalities, conditions, restrictions or penalties as are prescribed by law and are necessary in a democratic society, in the interests of national security, territorial integrity or public safety, for the prevention of disorder or crime, for the protection of health or morals, for the protection of the reputation or rights of others, for preventing the disclosure of information received in confidence, or for maintaining the authority and impartiality of the judiciary.

The test developed and used by the ECtHR to assess the legitimacy of an interference with the freedom of expression is well-settled in the Court's case-law. This test contains three steps, restated in Mouvement raëlien suisse v. Switzerland[23] and Animal Defenders International v. the United Kingdom.[24] Accordingly, the limitation must be provided by law, pursue a legitimate aim, and be necessary in a democratic society. This three-part test applies any time an action occurs that affects—even indirectly—the freedom of expression.

Whether the interference was "prescribed by law" and whether it "pursued one of the legitimate aims" are not, generally speaking, difficult questions to answer. In the context of Facebook and by analogy, the first test implies a degree of transparency and foreseeability (the limitation has to be set out in the Community Standards with sufficient precision), while the second test is related to a duty of objectivity (the Community Standards shall be applied uniformly and should be compatible with the EU legal framework). The third test, that is the necessity of the restriction in a democratic society, requires the application of the principle of proportionality. As

---

[23] ECtHR, Mouvement raëlien suisse v. Switzerland, Grand Chamber, no. 16354/06, 13 July 2012.
[24] ECtHR, Animal Defenders International v. the United Kingdom, Grand Chamber, no. 48876/08, 22 April 2013.

the existence of a legitimate aim has already been established in the second test, the issue is to determine how far this interest can justify a limitation. It is in practice the most substantial part of the legitimacy test for limitations and the one that often monopolizes the Court's attention.

This analysis of the proportionality of the limitation has been the subject of most scrutiny from the Court. The relevant criteria have been restated in Morice v. France[25] and Pentikäinen v. Finland.[26] The test, first, requires the existence of a "pressing social need". With regard to this requirement, it has to be noted that

> [a] pressing social need is not synonymous with "indispensable", but neither has it the flexibility of such expressions as "admissible", "ordinary", "useful", "reasonable" or "desirable".[27]

Second, the test asks for an assessment of the nature and severity of the sanctions. Mainly, it means the least restrictive measure is the only one acceptable. Also, as regards the nature of the sanction, the Court views "general measures" with suspicion. For instance, in a case where homosexual activists in Russia received an administrative fine for the offense of "public activities aimed at the promotion of homosexuality among minors", the Court found the offense did not correspond to a social need. Notably, it found that given the vagueness of the terminology used and the potentially unlimited scope of their application, these provisions are open to abuse in individual cases.[28] Third, the test of proportionality requires that relevant and sufficient reasons are explicated in order to justify the limitation to freedom of expression.

In conclusion, the three-part test proposes a general guideline as regards the limits of freedom of expression in the European perspective. The test represents the quintessence of the in concreto approach, as the legitimacy of a limitation to the freedom of speech will be examined in the light of the case as a whole. Furthermore, limitations on content related to political expression or on debate on questions of public interest are handled more strictly. From a European perspective, it is this test that should regulate any intervention and/or moderation activities on the platform.

8.1.2.2   The Chilling Effect Doctrine

The chilling effect doctrine has its roots in the US and originally derives from defamation law.[29] The doctrine highlights the potential deterrent effect of a restriction to future forms of expression. In other words, the doctrine attempts to handle the dangers of self-moderating or self-censoring due to fear of legal consequences.

---

[25] ECtHR, Morice v. France, Grand Chamber, no. 29369/10, 23 April 2015.
[26] ECtHR, Pentikäinen v. Finland, Grand Chamber, no. 11882/10, 20 October 2015.
[27] ECtHR (2020b).
[28] ECtHR Bayev v. Russia, no. 67667/09, 13 November 2017.
[29] Townend (2017).

It should be noted that self-censorship is very common with Facebook. Research shows 71% of users exhibit some level of last-minute self-censorship.[30] Not all self-censorship is bad (Plato allegedly said that "[w]ise men speak because they have something to say; fools because they have to say something") and not all self-censorship is dictated by concern about legal repercussions. Nevertheless, a limitation to freedom of expression, even if it is ruled legitimate, always has a secondary effect: the necessary margin of appreciation as regards the limitation's enforcement comes with a form of legal uncertainty, and eventually some individuals will refrain from expressing their thoughts for fear of legal consequences, even if their fears are not justified. The chilling effect doctrine refers to this specific secondary effect.

The chilling effect doctrine could be regarded as being incorporated in the three-part test, as the test includes an analysis on the severity of the restrictive measure. However, this is a restrictive approach that does not encompass the entire reality of the chilling effect. Another point of view would be to consider the chilling effect doctrine as another test of legitimacy of a restriction to free speech, independently of the three-part test. As the three-part test focuses on the circumstances of the case, a measure may be found to be legitimate on this basis. But at the same time, it is possible for a sanction to have the effect of hindering non-similar but conceptually close future expressions even if their restriction would have been retrospectively illegal.

Consequently, the chilling effect test has two practical effects. First, it mainly works as regards the severity of the sanction: even if a sanction is deemed to be proportionate under the case's circumstances, its imposition violates the freedom of speech if it is perceived by the public as a form of severe censorship. Second, it should be used as an interpretative rule, against the generalization of specific limitations to freedom of expression.

8.1.2.3 The Theory of Abuse of Rights

In order to reach a conclusion on the definition of the freedom of expression and to discuss its application to the platform, we need to define its scope. Indeed, the European approach is characterized by its specificity in this field, which is rooted in its modern history. It should not be forgotten that the rise of Nazism in Germany and their takeover of the government, until the Reichstag fire in 1933, followed a democratic process. Between other fundamental lessons from this disaster, came the realization that democracies should be equipped with the means to protect themselves against viral ideas aiming to harm them, and eventually to destroy them.

This fundamental shift in the ontological perception of freedom of expression has been transcribed in legal terms by the ECtHR, through the theory of abuse of rights. Simply put, some ideas and opinions are so extreme that their anti-democratic

---

[30] Das and Kramer (2013).

content deprives them of their privilege of being protected under Article 10 of the Convention. Invoking Article 17, which states that

> [n]othing in [the] Convention may be interpreted as implying for any State, group or person any right to engage in any activity or perform any act aimed at the destruction of any of the rights and freedoms set forth herein or at their limitation to a greater extent than is provided for in the Convention,

the Court finds that it is abusive of the applicant to call for the protection of the freedom of expression.

This concept is deeply ingrained in many legal systems: from the idea of "fraus omnia corrumpit" ("fraud corrupts everything", which means that a right should not be used with malicious intent to ask for the enforcement of an act) used for instance in France or "ex turpi causa non oritur actio" ("an action does not arise from a dishonorable cause") in common law countries, a common philosophy emerges: the legal system should defend itself against malicious actions that would profit from it foro unjust ends.

Indeed, if Article 17 is successfully invoked, the three-part test implied in Article 10 is circumvented in its totality. In this case, the restriction to freedom of expression is not scrutinized as such, but as a measure of protection of core democratic values. Put otherwise,

> In prohibiting the 'abuse of rights' Article 17 is geared to providing democracies with the means of combating acts and activities which destroy or unduly restrict fundamental rights and freedoms, whether those acts or activities are carried out by a 'State', a 'group' or an 'individual'.[31]

Arguably, Article 17 is an extreme measure that should be reserved for situations of manifest conflict between the litigious content and the core values of democracy. This mainly refers to serious cases of hate speech. This limited application of Article 17 is certainly justified, as it should remain an exceptional measure. However, it entails a certain degree of legal uncertainty that is clearly present in the ECtHR's case-law.

Indeed, the Court may choose to discard this approach and to apply the "classic" road of the three-part test of the Article 10. For instance, the legitimacy of a restriction on hate speech restriction was analyzed under Article 10 in the cases Altıntaş v. Turkey,[32] Sürek (no.1) v. Turkey,[33] Özgür Gündem v. Turkey,[34] Gündüz v. Turkey,[35] Vejdeland and Others v. Sweden,[36] and Balsytė-Lideikienė v. Lithuania.[37]

---

[31] ECtHR (2020a), p. 6.

[32] ECtHR, Altıntaş v. Turkey, no.: 50495/08, 10 March 2020.

[33] ECtHR, Sürek (no.1) v. Turkey, no.: 26682/95. 8 July 1999.

[34] ECtHR, Özgür Gündem v. Turkey, no.: 23144/93, 16 March 2000.

[35] ECtHR, Gündüz v. Turkey, no.: 59745/00, 13 November 2003.

[36] ECtHR, Vejdeland and Others v. Sweden, no.: 1813/07, 9 February 2012.

[37] ECtHR, Balsytė-Lideikienė v. Lithuania, no.:72596/01, 4 November 2008.

Alternatively, the Court sometimes chooses to directly use Article 17, thus sidestepping the protection of Article 10. It happened, for instance, for content in Russia portraying Jews as the source of evil and calling for their exclusion from social life,[38] for an offensively racist article written by a teacher for a college newspaper,[39] for a message promoting a terrorist organization on television broadcast,[40] for denying facts of the Holocaust,[41] for promoting negationism through a controversial comedy,[42] as well as for promoting white supremacy[43] or religious hate.[44]

These two alternative approaches require a case-by-case approach for more flexibility.[45] It should be highlighted that, while the three-part test, enshrined in international law, is familiar to Facebook's Oversight Board (see Sect. 7.2.2), the concept of abuse of rights is, on the contrary, absent from its decisions.

Characteristically, Facebook had created an exception for public figures (for instance the US President) that are (in principle) not bound by the hate speech regulation on the social network, although the exception was removed in 2021 in the wave of the Trump scandal. On the contrary, the ECtHR considers that—to paraphrase a famous quote from pop culture—"the greater the power, the greater the responsibility". Indeed,

> the Court has employed the argument that persons of influence – politicians, party leaders, teachers or simply famous figures like a football player – owe a particular responsibility due to their enhanced influence on their followers.[46]

8.1.3 Moderation and Account Suspension

8.1.3.1 Facebook's Restrictions to Freedom of Expression

The ECtHR has often underlined that online information is protected by the freedom of expression. The protection is granted whatever the type of message being conveyed and even when the purpose is profit-making in nature.[47] The Court also had the opportunity to explain that freedom of expression also covers social

---

[38] ECtHR, Pavel Ivanov v. Russia, no. 35222/04, 20 February 2007.

[39] ECtHR, Seurot v. France, no 57383/00, 18 May 2004.

[40] ECtHR, Roj TV A/S v. Denmark, no. 24683/14, 17 April 2018.

[41] ECtHR, Garaudy v. France, Application no. 65831/01, 25 Mach 2003.

[42] ECtHR, M'Bala M'Bala v. France, Application no.: 25239/13, 20 October 2015.

[43] ECtHR, Glimmerveen and Haqenbeek v. the Netherlands, Application nos.: 8348/78 & 8406/78, 11 October 1979.

[44] ECtHR, Belkacem v. Belgium, Application no.: 34367/14, 20 July 2017.

[45] McGonagle (2013), p. 10.

[46] Bayer and Bard (2020). Op.cit., p. 38.

[47] ECtHR, Ashby Donald and Others v. France, no. 36769/08, 10 January 2013.

networks in general. In particular, the situations of YouTube[48] and Google Blogspot[49] were discussed.

In the YouTube judgment, the Court reiterated its position expressed in the Google Blogspot case that it did not authorize the blocking of access to an entire Internet site on account of just some of its contents. It also acknowledged the unique characteristic of social media, noting that

> political content ignored by the traditional media is often shared via YouTube, thus fostering the emergence of citizen journalism. From that perspective, the Court accepts that YouTube is a unique platform on account of its characteristics, its accessibility and above all its potential impact, and that no alternatives were available to the applicants.[50]

In this context, access to the social network, the possibility to write posts and stories, and to comment and share, are protected as free expressions, assuming that freedom of expression is recognized as having a horizontal effect, which is highly debated (see Sect. 8.2). The general direction of case-law is to distinguish social media from traditional media. While freedom of expression is protected in both cases, assessing the legitimacy of a restriction must differ. In other words, it is not possible to apply by analogy all previous findings on traditional media to the Internet.

The main reason for this differentiation is to be found in the impact of online communication. While for radio, television and press the impact is constant and the media is classified as local or national, generalist or specialized, it is impossible to proceed with an a priori assessment of the impact of a post on Facebook. It does not mean that the impact of information on the platform is greater or less important than on traditional media—merely that it depends on the context. In some cases, the Court

> has acknowledged that the electronic network, serving billions of users worldwide, is not and potentially will never be subject to the same regulations and control, and that the policies governing reproduction of material from the printed media and the Internet may differ,

while in other cases, it considers that

> the choices inherent in the use of the Internet and social media mean that the information emerging therefrom does not have the same synchronicity or impact as broadcasted information (...), and that a telephone interview broadcast in a programme available on an Internet site had a less direct impact on viewers than a television programme.[51]

Therefore, assuming that any user-generated content has a distinct but relative impact on society and is protected under the umbrella of freedom of expression, Facebook's tools of moderation should be scrutinized. Moderation must comply with the policy set up in the Community Standards. However, this does not protect the user against arbitrariness, as the Community Standards may be incomplete, uncertain or lack the necessary safeguards for freedom of expression. Characteristically, applying the Community Standards on nudity, Facebook moderated the

---

[48] ECtHR, Cengiz and Others v. Turkey, nos 48226/10 and 14027/11, 12 December 2015.

[49] ECtHR, Ahmet Yıldırım v. Turkey, no 3111/10, 18 December 2012.

[50] Par.52 of the Judgment.

[51] ECtHR (2020b), par. 595.

famous and iconic photograph of a young girl fleeing a Napalm bombing during the Vietnam War. This moderation provoked a wild wave of reactions, as Norway's Prime Minister even accused Facebook of editing history by erasing images.[52] The company finally reinstated the picture.

As a hosting service provider, Facebook is required to provide a reporting option (see Sect. 6.1). In fact, a large panel of reactions is available to the social network: informing the author, reducing the visibility of specific content or attaching a warning to the content, demonetizing (a video), labelling a page as an untrusted source, placing a notice on the content before it is shared, removing the content, suspending the account for a limited period, or banishing the user from the platform.

Following the recommendations of the Advisory Board (see Sect. 7.2.2), Facebook does not remove fake news content but only labels it as misinformation, unless there is an immediate threat to life. In the first two months of the pandemic, while 98 million posts were labelled as misinformation, only seven million posts were removed as such in comparison.[53] The company revised its policy as regards sanctions in 2021, making it more severe.[54] First, "Pages That Repeatedly Share False Claims" will be labelled as such, with links to fact-checkers' articles that debunk these claims. Second, if a user repeatedly shares content that has been rated by a fact-checking partner, the distribution of all his or her posts in friends' news feeds will be reduced. Third, a notification will be shown to the user who wishes to share content marked as misinformation.

The principle of the less restrictive measure implied in the three-part test does not mean that simple reduction of visibility (shadow moderation) should automatically prevail as the less severe sanction. Ultimately, it is the degree of the content's illegality that determines the adequate sanction. Nevertheless, to simply let the platform decide on the sanction without any safeguards potentially constitutes a huge threat to the freedom of expression. The EU legislator intervenes through the DSA proposal, which, if adopted, will lead to a further tightening of Facebook's policy stance on this matter.

Specifically, Article 20, entitled "Measures and protection against misuse" regulates in detail the adequacy of penalties decided by the social network. Article 20 (1) specifies that

> [o]nline platforms shall suspend, for a reasonable period of time and after having issued a prior warning, the provision of their services to recipients of the service that frequently provide manifestly illegal content.

The reference to a prior warning indicates that suspension is only available as a penalty in case of recidivism. The notion of manifestly illegal content is certainly subject to discussion, but Article 20 (3) indicates that Facebook should be

---

[52] Solsvik and Abutaleb (2016).

[53] Lerman (2020).

[54] Facebook (2021).

taking into account all relevant facts and circumstances apparent from the information available to the online platform. Those circumstances shall include at least the following: (a)the absolute numbers of items of manifestly illegal content or manifestly unfounded notices or complaints, submitted in the past year; (b)the relative proportion thereof in relation to the total number of items of information provided or notices submitted in the past year; (c)the gravity of the misuses and its consequences; (d)the intention of the recipient, individual, entity or complainant.

Article 20 (4), finally, creates a duty of enhanced transparency for Facebook. The platform shall

set out, in a clear and detailed manner, their policy in respect of the misuse referred to in paragraphs 1 and 2 in their terms and conditions, including as regards the facts and circumstances that they take into account when assessing whether certain behaviour constitutes misuse and the duration of the suspension.

8.1.3.2   The Accountability of the Moderation

It could be concluded from the above that moderation is not a right, but a duty. In this sense, moderation should be impartial, transparent and predicable. The DSA proposal introduces a safeguard against abuse of the notification system. According to Article 20 (2) of the proposal, a user, individual or entity that frequently submits notices or complaints that are manifestly unfounded could have its right to complain through the notice process be temporarily suspended (after a prior warning).

Furthermore, the DSA proposal also imposes transparency. Hiding problematic speech without users being aware of it "has serious ramifications for public debates".[55] The proposed regulation aims to impose transparency at each step of the process (see Sect. 6.2.4). Transparency should also be provided to society in general. In Article 13, it is stated that

[p]roviders of intermediary services shall publish, at least once a year, clear, easily comprehensible and detailed reports on any content moderation they engaged in during the relevant period.

A list of information follows that should be included in the report, such as the number and type of orders from the authorities, of notices submitted, and of content moderation engaged in at the providers' own initiative.

---

[55] Kalsnes and Ihlebæk (2021), pp. 326–342.

8.2   The Rise of Digital Public Spaces

8.2.1   The "Facebook Friend": A Friend Like No Other

Every user of the platform instinctively distinguishes between the traditional concept of "friend" and the notion of "Facebook friend" which refers to a connection that has a privileged access to the user's content, depending on the settings of the account and of the content. While competitors prefer to use more neutral terms, such as "contact" for LinkedIn or "follower" for Twitter, the idea of friends conveys a specific meaning in a legal context. The close friend for instance is not part of the public from a copyright law perspective.

In his book "Facebook Nation",[56] Newton Lee describes an experience in a US high school. A group of students created a fake profile and sent friend requests to 200 pupils in their school. Only two messaged to ask for more information, while nearly 60% accepted the invitation, and an additional 55 Facebook users sent friend requests to the profile.

This autonomous concept of the "Facebook friend" that could cover requests from "friends", but also from co-workers, parents, teachers, neighbors, or students, has already been analyzed by the courts. In the US, some decisions have discussed the potential conflicts of interest in "Facebook friendship" between a judge and an attorney, between a judge and a party, between an attorney and the opposite party, etc. The general trend emerging from these decisions and opinions is that that merely being friends on Facebook does not, per se, establish a close relationship.[57]

The main difficulty from a legal point of view is not to determine if a Facebook friend is a friend, but whether the limitation of a communication to "friends only" has the consequence of confining a communication to the realm of private messages. The line between public and private ways of communication is extremely blurred on social networks. However, most media regulations are based on a distinction between private and public communications. The criminal offenses of child pornography or grooming may occur through private messages. Defamation, depending on the national system, may also occur through a private channel. However, hate speech, misinformation, denial of genocide, provocation to commit suicide, or support of terrorism need a public channel. For instance, in the EU Regulation against online terrorist content, the legal framework requires a "dissemination to the public", defined as "the making available of information, at the request of a content provider, to a potentially unlimited number of persons".[58]

As a consequence, the social network generates a gray zone between private and public communications, presenting difficulties to the EU legislator who presently fails to acknowledge its existence. A communication to Facebook friends does not

---

[56]Lee (2014), p. 31.

[57]Hudson (2019).

[58]Article 2 (3) of the Regulation (EU) 2021/784 of the European Parliament and of the Council of 29 April 2021 on addressing the dissemination of terrorist content online (see Sect. 6.2.1).

constitute a private communication in the sense that the content is not addressed to persons belonging to the immediate social environment of the author; but neither it is a public communication defined as a communication "to a potentially unlimited number of persons". Depending on the context and the publication's settings, the courts will therefore have to exercise their discretion as to whether the publication belongs in the public sphere or not.

8.2.2   Social Networks As a Digital Public Space, Between Utopia and Dystopia

8.2.2.1   In Search of the Horizontal Effect

Under the so-called "state action doctrine",[59] freedom of speech is primarily seen in the US as a negative obligation of non-intervention. In other words, it is recognized as having a vertical effect, obliging the state to respect the citizen's freedom. In the context of Facebook, this approach becomes irrelevant: to ask Facebook to respect a content and not arbitrarily moderate it is to ask for a horizontal enforcement of the freedom of speech: from one private actor towards another.

Under the umbrella of horizontal effect, it is possible to distinguish various "correlative private duties".[60] If we picture these duties as a pyramid, at the lowest level there is the positive duty of the state to restrict intervention on human rights from an individual to another. One level above, there are established specific positive duties of the state in this field (for instance, the duty to protect pluralism in media). True horizontal effect occurs, however, only at the higher level of the pyramid: when human rights law enforces a private duty at national level, or even more absolutely, at international level.

Article 11 of the Charter of the Fundamental Rights of the EU[61] enshrines the freedom of expression and information into primary EU law. It states that

> 1. Everyone has the right to freedom of expression. This right shall include freedom to hold opinions and to receive and impart information and ideas without interference by public authority and regardless of frontiers. 2. The freedom and pluralism of the media shall be respected.

The word "include" here is of tremendous importance, as it implies that the right exceeds the simple negative obligation of the state not to interfere with individual rights.

Nevertheless, all primary EU law has, as a rule, a horizontal effect, assuming the specific rule fulfils the conditions set by the ECJ for direct effect. However, the

---

[59] Huhn (2005), p. 1379.

[60] Knox (2008), p. 1.

[61] Charter of Fundamental Rights of the European Union, OJ C 326, 26.10.2012, p. 391–407, ELI: http://data.europa.eu/eli/treaty/char_2012/oj.

Charter also specifies in Article 51 (1) that it is addressed to the EU institutions and to the Member States, and in Article 52 (5) that

> [t]he provisions of this Charter which contain principles may be implemented by legislative and executive acts taken by institutions, bodies, offices and agencies of the Union, and by acts of Member States when they are implementing Union law, in the exercise of their respective powers. They shall be judicially cognisable only in the interpretation of such acts and in the ruling on their legality.

It could be then deduced that horizontal effect is excluded from the application of the Charter. However, it is also important to highlight that horizontal effect is not explicitly excluded from the wording of Article 51 and, on the contrary, it is arguable that the Charter does have a horizontal effect.[62] Furthermore, the ECJ has in some landmark decisions noted that the fact certain provisions are addressed to the Member States does not prevent rights from being conferred at the same time on any individual who has an interest in the performance of the duties thus laid down.[63]

The idea of the horizontal effect of human rights has particularly been developed in Germany. The German theory of "third party effect" or "Drittwirkung", which promotes indirect horizontal effect of human rights, has become a model in Europe.[64] Direct effect was established by the German Federal Labour Court in a case concerning the prohibition of political speech at a workplace.[65] The Court considered that freedom of expression would be rendered largely ineffective if individuals with large economic power were in position by virtue of this power to restrict this right at will. Furthermore, in the famous Blinkfüer case,[66] the giant periodicals distributor Springer-Verlag instructed newspaper stands to boycott the pro-socialist magazine Blinkfüer. The distributor combined the call to boycott with threats of economic sanctions. Under the doctrine of indirect horizontal effect of freedom of expression, the freedom of expression of the socialist magazine were under threat from the freedom of expression of the distributor and the court may intervene here as arbitrator between the two legitimate interests.[67] In this case, the distributor's behavior was found to be unlawful under civil jurisdiction.

The ECJ concurs with the German courts on this point. In the Viking Line judgment,[68] the question is directly asked about the direct horizontal effect of a provision of EU primary law. The Court answered that

> the abolition, as between Member States, of obstacles to freedom of movement for persons and freedom to provide services would be compromised if the abolition of State barriers

---

[62] Frantziou (2015), pp. 657–679.

[63] ECJ, C-43/75, Defrenne v. Sabena (No 2), 08/04/1976, ECLI:EU:C:1976:56.

[64] Krzeminska-Vamvaka (2009).

[65] BAGE 1, 185 (1954).

[66] 25 BVerfGE 256 (1969).

[67] Oster (2015), p. 107.

[68] ECJ, C-438/05, International Transport Workers' Federation and Finnish Seamen's Union v. Viking Line ABP and OÜ Viking Line Eesti, 11/12/2007, ECLI:EU:C:2007:772.

could be neutralised by obstacles resulting from the exercise, by associations or organisa-
tions not governed by public law, of their legal autonomy.[69]

In conclusion, it would be greatly exaggerated to consider the doctrine of horizontal
effect an absolute obstacle to the enforcement of freedom of expression against
Facebook. In the European tradition, indirect and sometimes even direct horizontal
effect is conditionally recognized. Paradoxically, it is possible to find a basis for the
horizontal effect of freedom of expression against Facebook in the anti-terrorist
content Regulation (see Sect. 6.2.1). Indeed, Article 5 (1) of the Regulation specifies
that the hosting service provider exposed to terrorist content shall moderate

> in a diligent, proportionate and non-discriminatory manner, with due regard, in all circum-
> stances, to the fundamental rights of the users and taking into account, in particular, the
> fundamental importance of the freedom of expression and information in an open and
> democratic society, with a view to avoiding the removal of material which is not terrorist
> content.

Simply put, the EU legislator explains that non-terrorist online content should be
dealt with through principles of the freedom of expression.

8.2.2.2   The Rising Notion of Digital Public Space

Not only should the horizontal effect of freedom of expression be acknowledged
with respect to Facebook's unique technical, economic, or even political power (see
above), but the conditions are also met for the emergence of new theories in this
field. It is proposed here that by its importance, in terms of user numbers or of time
spent on the social network, Facebook occupies a distinct position in the digital
world. A study in Asia showed that millions of Facebook users had no idea they were
using the Internet.[70] These findings may be somehow funny, but also revealing:
Facebook's user activity on the platform is perceived as independent from using the
Internet, because the platform has occupied a specific and monopolistic function on
the Internet as non-media specific, non-topic specific social network.

Facebook is identified as the modern counterpart of the Athens Agora in Greek
antiquity: a public place of free discussions and debates. However, unlike the ancient
Agora, Facebook does not merely provide "chairs" (see Chap. 6). Not only does
Facebook formulate the boundaries of lawful expression through its Community
Standards, enforcing it through its moderation, but it also, through applying its
algorithm, influences what content is seen and what comment appears as more
relevant. The format and the design of the platform also favor short and simple
answers to long messages and structured debates.

Despite its flaws, this analogy with the ancient Agora remains relevant. It has
been noted that "[a]s intermediaries between politics and the people, platforms are

---

[69] Par.57 of the decision.

[70] Mirani (2015).

restructuring the public sphere."[71] In other words, although the owner and administrator of the platform are private entities, the platform itself de facto enters into the realm of public space. By drawing an analogy with the concept of public service under French administrative law, it could be said that the private character of the entities does not matter as much as its function in society. Facebook's mutation to a digital public place requires some specific regulations. Besides, multiplying legislation in the EU is clearly distinguishing a specific legal framework for the GAFAM, using their economic power as a criterion in order to distinguish them.

A digital public space must provide the conditions of an Agora. This means that four basic principles need to be implemented: obligation of transparency on the algorithm, obligation of transparency on the moderation's policy and practices, compliance of the Community Standards with EU media law, and duty of care towards its users.

While the DSA proposal incorporates most of these principles, it is worth mentioning that Facebook had also taken the initiative, during the Trump era, to implement some of them. The platform's efforts have been remarked upon and for instance a French mission to the government notes that

> t]he speed of deployment and progress made during the last 12 months by an operator such as Facebook show the benefits of capitalising on this self-regulatory approach already being used by the platforms, by expanding and legitimising it.[72]

Nevertheless, no legislation or case-law explicitly consecrates this notion of public digital space, which could clarify the platform's status and the company's duties.

8.2.3   Contract Law: The Surprising Defender of Freedom of Speech

As shown above, freedom of expression's impact as a legally binding norm against Facebook is still unclear: although the concept itself, continually enriched with new case-laws, is sufficiently detailed to handle all legal issues related to the moderation of the platform, its enforcement against a private entity still raises some issues. In this context, contract law provides an alternative way of protecting the user against potential moderation abuses.

The case of the painting "The Origin of the World" perfectly illustrates this situation. In 2011, a French school teacher tried to upload on the platform Courbet's well-known painting called "The Origin of the World" (1866) and famously representing a realistic, closely cropped depiction of the genitals of a woman lying on a bed with her legs spread. Facebook had shut down his account for violating the

---

[71] Busch et al. (2021), p. 21. https://platformobservatory.eu/app/uploads/2021/03/05Platformpower.pdf.

[72] Desmaris et al. (2019).

Community Standards relating to nudity. From its conception, this painting was a flag bearer: its audacity and virtuosity represented a victory of the freedom of artistic expression against the prudishness of pornography regulations. Its place in the history of art was briefly disputed as the work remained in private collections for a long time before becoming an iconic representation of the realism of the period. Therefore, it was perhaps fate that the painting would become the center of the thorny relationship between Facebook's policies and users' freedom of expression.

The Paris Civil Court first discarded the jurisdiction clause stipulating that all litigation had to be tried in the courts of California.[73] It followed previous case-law that considered that this kind of clause in Facebook's Terms of Service is null and void in the relationship between the consumer and the business.[74] Nevertheless, under EU law, this provision would have been held to be abusive, with the same consequences.

On the merits of the case, in 2018,[75] the Court reiterated the findings regarding the abusive character of some clauses in Facebook's contract. This time, the choice of law clause that stipulated Californian law as the relevant legal framework, was declared null and void. Moreover, the user had used two accounts and the banned account had been opened under a pseudonym. As no explanation was provided by Facebook for his banishment from the platform, it was uncertain whether the revocation of the contract was due to the painting or the violation of the contractual duty to use one's real name. The court did note that in any case the contractual obligations of the parties had to be read together with the general duty of good faith imposed by the Civil Code. However, the Court avoided taking a position on the merits regarding the violation of the Community Standards, referring once again to EU consumer protection law. The power given to Facebook in the terms of service to unilaterally revoke the contract, immediately and without justification, is interpreted as an abusive clause (see Sect. 9.1.1). In conclusion, the unilateral revocation of the contract without justification or delay constitutes a faulty execution of the contract, contrary to the principle of good faith.

Therefore, Facebook was held to be liable for moderating the painting. However, no damages were awarded to the user, as he owned another account which remained active. Whilst interesting, the case does not deal with the most pressing issues: could contract law be invoked in order to avoid the potential difficulties related to the arguable lack of horizontal effect of the freedom of expression? The combination of contract law general principles (such as good faith in the execution of a contract) with the EU principle of non-discrimination would indicate a strict responsibility of the social network. Moreover, it could be said that all of Facebook's policies are de facto binding the company into behaving more objectively with respect to the unfair commercial practice legislation (see Sect. 9.1.2). In consequence, not only

---

[73] Civil Court Paris, Frédéric X/Facebook, 05/03/2015.

[74] French Court of Appeal of Pau, Sebastien R/Facebook RG, 12/1373, 23/03/2012.

[75] Civil Court Paris, Frédéric X/Facebook, 15/03/2018, n° 12/12401.

moderation principles and enforcement but also the content presentation would be subject to a principle of objectivity.

The DSA proposal, while being a huge step towards the completion of the social media's legal framework, does not regulate this specific issue. Nevertheless, Article 12 of the proposal plays an important role in this context. According to this article,

> [p]roviders of intermediary services shall include information on any restrictions that they impose in relation to the use of their service in respect of information provided by the recipients of the service, in their terms and conditions. That information shall include information on any policies, procedures, measures and tools used for the purpose of content moderation, including algorithmic decision-making and human review. It shall be set out in clear and unambiguous language and shall be publicly available in an easily accessible format.

Article 12 (2) adds that

> [p]roviders of intermediary services shall act in a diligent, objective and proportionate manner in applying and enforcing the restrictions referred to in paragraph 1, with due regard to the rights and legitimate interests of all parties involved, including the applicable fundamental rights of the recipients of the service as enshrined in the Charter.

In conclusion, through judicial control, the mechanism of abusive clauses, and the DSA proposal, Facebook's moderation policy is under scrutiny. The first and immediate consequence of this intervention is to impose more transparency. However, these binding rules regarding the content of Facebook's Community Standards could also be a preliminary step towards a more compelling legal framework based on contract law and aiming at protecting users' freedom of expression.

8.3 The Black Box of Facebook's Algorithm

8.3.1 The Algorithm: Myths and Reality

The research on AI and algorithms is surrounded by a mythical aureole and by mythical thinking.[76] After all, it is through an algorithm's invisible action that the chaos of data is converted to the information presented. First of all, it has to be stated that, regardless of whether Facebook closely collaborates with powerful internal AI to analyze and evaluate the content, the "algorithm" itself is not AI. It just executes a predeterminate series of settings, classified under four main ranking signals: recency, popularity, content type, and relationship. Its fundamental purpose is simple and unique: maximize profit by capturing the user's attention as long and/or as frequently as possible.

The algorithm will be the judge who decides what appears on the users' news feeds and in what order. Giving the limited extent of the average user's attention, the competition to appear in the news feed is significant. It was estimated that on

---

[76] Kreft (2017), pp. 146–166.

average, an "organic post" (a non-paid publication) in 2020 had a reach of around 5.20%.[77]

The algorithm appeared on the platform in 2009 but it is not a static tool. It responds to changes of policy and is constantly evolving. For instance, in 2018, it was modified to give priority to content with meaningful discussions (lots of comments), or in 2019, to put forward original videos of high quality (that is, that the user watches for a long time). Nevertheless, humans working for the company constantly assess and refine the results of the algorithm's function. It has even been concluded that this demonstrates that the algorithm cannot be neutral, with the result being that Facebook is not a hosting service but an editor.[78] It could be argued that Facebook occupies a unique and hybrid position, paradoxically undertaking the roles of both hosting service, protected by the safe harbor (see Chap. 6) and editor, responsible for its editorial choices.

The influence of the algorithm is not restricted to the mere experience on the platform. This hierarchization of information impacts the users in their daily life. For the sake of a research project, the platform influenced for a week the content published on users' walls. The scope of the research was to determine if it was enough to change the mood of the users and the results were positive.[79] In other words, the algorithm has the power to manipulate the feelings of its users, positively or negatively, in a specific geographic area. It should be recalled that through the huge collection of personal data at its disposal, the platform is in a position to proceed to microtargeting operations, that is to exploit the feelings of a user precisely. These feelings are identified, or even predicted, based on personality analysis. It is argued that by examining only 300 "likes" and other reactions from the users, Facebook is in a position to accurately determine their personality.[80]

Furthermore, the algorithm has some obvious repercussions on democratic societies. While the link between the algorithm's filtering effect and the worldwide rise of populism has not been established, suspicions of a possible correlation continue to grow, and more and more research is highlighting this. For instance, a relationship has been spotted between the number of anti-refugee posts in Germany on far-right Facebook pages and the number of hate crimes in the same period.[81] Moreover, it has also been said that the algorithm, as a filter bubble (or as a polarization amplifier), intrinsically undermines our ability to collectively think about our problem.[82]

In 2020, a report requested by the EU took a behavioral science approach to investigate the impact of online platforms on political behavior.[83] It identified

---

[77]Cooper (2021).

[78]Helberger and Trilling (2016).

[79]Wilson et al. (2012), pp. 203–220.

[80]Youyou et al. (2015), pp. 1036–1040.

[81]Müller and Schwarz (2020).

[82]Vaidhyanathan (2018), p. 10.

[83]Lewandowsky et al. (2020).

"algorithmic content curation" as one of the fundamental key "pressure points" that affect our modern democracy. The report notes that

> [a]lgorithms make decisions without public oversight, regulation or a widespread under-standing of the mechanisms underlying the resulting decisions. Most algorithms are consid-ered proprietary trade secrets and therefore operate as black boxes where neither individual users nor society in general knows why information in search engines or social media feeds is ordered in a particular way.[84]

The report also underlines the risk posed by the automatic biases that the algorithm creates without being accountable.

While an "algorithm awareness" develops amongst Facebook's users, which can be defined as the knowledge of the consequences of the algorithm's function on a certain action or lack of action, a complex interrelationship develops where the reality of the algorithm or sometimes only an imaginary algorithm, does alter the user's experience.[85]

8.3.2   Facebook's Algorithm and the Ambiguous Right to Explanation

The algorithm's protection depends on its secrecy (see Sect. 4.1.2) and traditionally the GAFAM do not communicate on the details of the functioning of their tools. Although, as a rule, online algorithms are similar to black boxes, in the sense that it is not easy to immediately identify the reasons for their specific output, Meta had understood the growing concern from civil society and the authorities on this point. The company has taken some initiatives to add more transparency to its algorithm's practical operation. In 2019, the company introduced the "why I am seeing this post" tool that gives detailed information to the user on the algorithm's reasoning.[86] The tool completes for all posts the "Why am I seeing this ad?" tool launched in 2014. In parallel, the company has started to communicate at great length about its algo-rithms. For instance, the details of Instagram's algorithm were published in 2021 on the company's blog.[87]

Although it is not intended to do so, the algorithm operates de facto as a form of moderation: by choosing what type of content appears first and assuming that most of users do not check half of their feed, it actually determines what content will be visible and what content will be "shadow banned".[88] To use an analogy, a shadow banned content would be like being on the second page Google's search results (it was famously said that "[t]he best place to hide a dead body is page 2 of Google").

---

[84]Lewandowsky et al. (2020), op.cit. p. 45.

[85]Bucher (2017), pp. 30–44.

[86]Sethuraman (2019).

[87]Mosseri (2021).

[88]Horten (2021).

In this context, Facebook's new strategy of communication on its "black box" is welcome. However, is it or should it be a legal duty? To answer this question, it is necessary to return to an analysis of the core components of the GDPR (see Chap. 2) and how it arguably introduced a much discussed "right to explanation".[89]

The GDPR provides a specific regime for "Automated individual decision-making, including profiling". Article 22 states as principle that

> [t]he data subject shall have the right not to be subject to a decision based solely on automated processing, including profiling, which produces legal effects concerning him or her or similarly significantly affects him or her.[90]

It is undeniable that Facebook's algorithm constitutes automated individual decision-making, but does it produce legal effect or similarly significantly affect the users? Article 29 notes on this point that

> [i]n many typical cases the decision to present targeted advertising based on profiling will not have a similarly significant effect on individuals (. . .) However it is possible that it may do, depending upon the particular characteristics of the case, including: the intrusiveness of the profiling process, including the tracking of individua ls across different websites, devices and services; the expectations and wishes of the individuals concerned; the way the advert is delivered; or using knowledge of the vulnerabilities of the data subjects targeted.[91]

Facebook's access certainly does not produce legal effect, in the sense that the order of presentation of a news feed or even, generally speaking, Facebook's myriad AI (see below, Sect. 8.3.3) aimed at profiling and content management, exercises an influence on statutory or contractual users' rights. However, in the light of the algorithm's profound influence on the effective protection of the freedom of expression of Facebook's users, it could be reasonable to consider the possibility that it falls within the definition of automated individual decision-making. In this case, it does not mean that the algorithm is illegal (at least for adults). Article 22 (2) authorizes it when it is needed for the performance of a contract, which is the case here.

Nevertheless, classifying the algorithm as automated individual decision-making has to be linked to Articles 13(2) (f) and 14(2) (g) about the data subject's right to be informed and Article 15(1) (h) about the data subject's right of access. These articles allow for the use of a "right to explanation", as they mainly impose on the controller a duty to provide meaningful information about the logic involved and explain the significance and envisaged consequences of the processing.

The Article 29 Working Party remarks on this duty that

> [t]he controller should find simple ways to tell the data subject about the rationale behind, or the criteria relied on in reaching the decision. The GDPR requires the controller to provide meaningful information about the logic involved, not necessarily a complex explanation of the algorithms used or disclosure of the full algorithm. The information provided should,

---

[89] Wachter et al. (2017), pp. 79–90.

[90] Article 22(1) of the GDPR.

[91] Article 29 Data Protection Working Party (2018) Guidelines on Automated individual decision-making and Profiling for the purposes of Regulation 2016/679. wp251rev01, p. 22.

however, be sufficiently comprehensive for the data subject to understand the reasons for the decision.[92]

Indeed, much uncertainty exists as regards the binding duty to explanation in the GDPR with respect to AI-based data processing. It has been argued that in this context, specific attention should be given to the GDPR's recitals (mainly, Recital 71) that more explicitly refer to a right to explanation.[93]

Nevertheless, a right to explanation can be found outside of the scope of GDPR, in the Regulation 2019/1150 that regulates the interactions between online platforms and business users (see Sect. 9.1.2). Indeed, Article 5 (1) of the Regulation states that

> [p]roviders of online intermediation services shall set out in their terms and conditions the main parameters determining ranking and the reasons for the relative importance of those main parameters as opposed to other parameters.

However, this new obligation is not identical to a right to explanation. Contrary to an ex-post right to explanation, it does not specify the reasons for a specific ranking but gives ex-ante the general parameters on which the ranking will be based. Nevertheless, where the ranking is affected by a notification (for instance, a third user makes a complaint on intellectual property infringement), the business user has, according to the proposal, the right to be informed and to inspect the content of the notification.[94] Ironically, the proposal imposes the exact opposite of the right to explanation, imposing that the online platform should refrain to

> disclose algorithms or any information that, with reasonable certainty, would result in the enabling of deception of consumers or consumer harm through the manipulation of search results.[95]

8.3.3 Through a Regulation of AI

8.3.3.1 The Mystery Surrounding AI

A large panel of moderation tools (see Sect. 8.1.3) are available to Facebook. Some of them imply a human intervention, but most of them can also automatically work through AI decision-making. This situation challenges the status quo with the protection of freedom of expression. The Oversight Board had to consider a case where Facebook's automated systems originally removed the post for violating the company's Community Standards on Adult Nudity and Sexual Activity. The Board found that the post was allowed under a policy exception for "breast cancer

---

[92] Article 29 Data Protection Working Party (2018) Guidelines on Automated individual decision-making and Profiling for the purposes of Regulation 2016/679, op.cit. p. 25.

[93] Vorras and Mitrou (2021), pp. 247–264.

[94] Article 5 (4) of the Regulation.

[95] Article 5 (6) of the Regulation.

awareness" and considered that Facebook's automated moderation in this case raised important human rights concerns.[96]

Use of AI is not limited to moderation. AI is everywhere on the platform. Image recognition, ad targeting, video originality analysis, text translation or the notification system (its content and its frequency) are also ruled by Facebook's AI. Facebook's algorithm, in combination with formidable profiling AI, achieves an unparalleled level of intrusion into users' intimacy. On the one hand, the frightening degree of precision of targeted ads contributes to the creation of a chilling effect on freedom of expression, but, mainly, the content selection answering to the perceived desires of the user deeply affects the right to information. The Cambridge Analytica scandal (see Sect. 2.2.3) helped the public and Meta itself (as the company started a civil rights audit)[97] to understand that the functioning of the platform was undermining democracy. On the other hand, turning one's back to this technology because of its destructive potential would be inconceivable. Simply put, "[w]hat is at stake is therefore less to preserve liberal democracy as we know it, than to be able to reinvent new forms of democracy fit for the age of AI."[98]

Therefore, calls for the regulation of AI are growing. However, it should be noted that the notion of "artificial intelligence" is still evolving and is still as mysterious as it is popular. Historically, AI was a purpose: to create and teach machines to acquire intelligence similar to biological intelligence. This approach was flawed for multiple reasons. It was mainly because the concept of intelligence itself is wrapped in uncertainty. The philosopher George Santayana famously wrote that "[i]ntelligence is quickness in seeing things as they are".[99] Intelligence is not to be confused with self-awareness. It is a cognitive ability turned on in the individual's environment, attempting to perceive its complexity and interpreting it.

Meanwhile, computer science has seen a paradigm shift with the development of "machine learning" technologies, which revolutionize the development of AI. Nowadays, a more technical and realistic definition of AI predominates. Multiple AI techniques form an ecosystem and instead of the previous homogeneous approach, a classification of AI is preferred.[100] Generally speaking, AI could still be referred to as

> any machine or algorithm that is capable of observing its environment, learning, and based on the knowledge and experience gained, taking intelligent action or proposing decisions.[101]

[96] Case Decision 2020-004-IG-UA.

[97] Sandberg (2018).

[98] Šucha and Gammel (2021), p. 26.

[99] Santayana (1980).

[100] Samoili et al. (2020).

[101] Craglia et al. (2018), p. 19.

8.3.3.2   The Artificial Intelligence Act

While a demand exists for the regulation of AI, experts have also pointed out that maybe co-regulation and soft law schemes are preferable so as not to stifle innovation.[102] Nevertheless, the EU has decided to invest in a robust legal framework relating to AI, probably wishing to send a strong signal to the implicated stakeholders and to civil society. It is clear that Meta has been aware for some years of the side effect of its AI function. As it has been noted, "the models that maximize engagement also favor controversy, misinformation, and extremism: put simply, people just like outrageous stuff."[103] However, maximizing engagement is the core concept that defines the service. It is doubtful that Facebook would voluntarily restrain the power of its AI. In this context, the EU Commission's decision to impose a hard law regulation mechanism makes sense.

Three initiatives are scheduled by the EU Commission. Their purpose is to build trust in technology in order to help it thrive in society. The Commission therefore considers that it is necessary to address liability issues related to new technologies, including AI systems, directly through a sui generis regulation (for instance, the legal issues related to self-drive vehicles), and indirectly through modernization of the existing sectoral safety legislation (e.g. through Machinery Regulation, the General Product Safety Directive etc.)

Most importantly, the Commission has already proposed a regulation on the risks posed by AI. The Artificial Intelligence Act proposal[104] assumes a technical and precise definition of AI, targeting specific technologies, instead of its normal technology-neutral approach. This approach is explained in Recital 6, which notes that

> the notion of AI system should be clearly defined to ensure legal certainty, while providing the flexibility to accommodate future technological developments. The definition should be based on the key functional characteristics of the software, in particular the ability, for a given set of human-defined objectives, to generate outputs such as content, predictions, recommendations, or decisions which influence the environment with which the system interacts, be it in a physical or digital dimension. AI systems can be designed to operate with varying levels of autonomy and be used on a stand-alone basis or as a component of a product, irrespective of whether the system is physically integrated into the product (embedded) or serve the functionality of the product without being integrated therein (non-embedded). The definition of AI system should be complemented by a list of specific techniques and approaches used for its development, which should be kept up-to-date in the light of market and technological developments through the adoption of delegated acts by the Commission to amend that list.

---

[102] Craglia et al. (2018) op.cit, p. 68.

[103] Hao (2021).

[104] Proposal for a Regulation of the European Parliament and of the Council laying down harmonized rules on Artificial Intelligence (Artificial Intelligence Act) and amending certain Union Legislative acts COM/2021/206 final.

Social media are far from monopolizing the use of AI and, on the contrary, AI emerges in every aspect of society. Therefore, a horizontal definition of AI is preferred here by the EU legislator, and the proposal does not refer even once to the specific use of AI by social media. Nevertheless, the proposal is of crucial importance for Facebook.

The Artificial Intelligence Act is underpinned by a risk-based approach, distinguishing between three levels of risks induced by the AI, from the most dangerous to the safest. In the first level, the proposal excludes absolutely some noxious uses of this technology. Article 5 (1) (a) of the proposal prohibits

> the placing on the market, putting into service or use of an AI system that deploys subliminal techniques beyond a person's consciousness in order to materially distort a person's behaviour in a manner that causes or is likely to cause that person or another person physical or psychological harm

and Article 5 (1) (b) prohibits

> the placing on the market, putting into service or use of an AI system that exploits any of the vulnerabilities of a specific group of persons due to their age, physical or mental disability, in order to materially distort the behaviour of a person pertaining to that group in a manner that causes or is likely to cause that person or another person physical or psychological harm.

As explained above, Facebook's AI has the potential to manipulate its users' behavior. It is also possible that it may result in physical harm. For instance, United Nations investigators revealed that Facebook played a "determining role" in the ethnic cleansing of the Rohingya in Myanmar.[105] Investigators reported that

> [t]he role of social media is significant. Facebook has been a useful instrument for those seeking to spread hate, in a context where, for most users, Facebook is the Internet. Although improved in recent months, the response of Facebook has been slow and ineffective. The extent to which Facebook posts and messages have led to real-world discrimination and violence must be independently and thoroughly examined. The mission regrets that Facebook is unable to provide country-specific data about the spread of hate speech on its platform, which is imperative to assess the adequacy of its response.[106]

The platform's implication in the genocide is certainly the most tragic misuse of the network to date. It is, incidentally, a strong reminder that the dangerousness of the platform should not be underestimated.

Do the prohibitions enshrined in Article 5 (1) (a) and (b) comprise a duty for Facebook to correct the most-documented filter bubble effect created by its algorithm? Unfortunately, the article does not specify whether the prohibition only concerns AI intended to manipulate individuals with harmful consequences or if negligent AI is also concerned. While the wording of Article 5 (1) (a) suggests that an intent must be proven, Article 5 (1) (b) only requires that the motive be the manipulation of specific group of persons due to their age, physical or mental disability.

---

[105] Human Rights Council (2018).

[106] Par.74 of the report.

However, it is however highly uncertain that a court would regard persons susceptible to hate speech as a group with mental disability, although, from a psychological point of view, a racist is an individual having a psychopathological defect/narcissistic personality disorder which allows for the dehumanization of others.[107]

Consequently, Facebook's AI avoids a general prohibition. Overall, as insidiously destructive as its AI can be characterized, it would be a very audacious and probably unconstitutional (as regards freedom of commerce) step to say that Facebook's AI is similar to a weapon.

However, does it belong to the second level of the legal framework, the "High-Risk AI Systems"? At first sight, it is not disputable that it falls within the definition of AI posing a serious threat to fundamental rights provided for in Article 7 (1) (b) of the proposal. However, the specific and closed list of concerned sectors considered as "High-Risk AI" in the proposal's Annex III does not mention social media anywhere. The list only concerns situations such as using AI for critical infrastructure management. Nevertheless, the list also contains a reference to

> [b]iometric identification and categorisation of natural persons: (a)AI systems intended to be used for the 'real-time' and 'post' remote biometric identification of natural persons.

In conclusion, it is reasonable to assume that the most important AI-controlled features of Facebook elude the heavy legal framework required for High-Risk AI, except for potential future uses of biometric identification models by the platform.[108] For instance, since ID cards contain biometric data, it is a matter of discussion whether Facebook's ID card verification tool (available for instance for people who cannot log in for some reasons) falls within this classification.

---

[107] Bell (1978), pp. 89–92.

[108] The notion of biometric identification here should be interpreted on the light of the Recital 8 of the proposal:

> The notion of remote biometric identification system as used in this Regulation should be defined functionally, as an AI system intended for the identification of natural persons at a distance through the comparison of a person's biometric data with the biometric data contained in a reference database, and without prior knowledge whether the targeted person will be present and can be identified, irrespectively of the particular technology, processes or types of biometric data used. Considering their different characteristics and manners in which they are used, as well as the different risks involved, a distinction should be made between 'real-time' and 'post' remote biometric identification systems. In the case of 'real-time' systems, the capturing of the biometric data, the comparison and the identification occur all instantaneously, near-instantaneously or in any event without a significant delay. In this regard, there should be no scope for circumventing the rules of this Regulation on the 'real-time' use of the AI systems in question by providing for minor delays. 'Real-time' systems involve the use of 'live' or 'near-'live' material, such as video footage, generated by a camera or other device with similar functionality. In the case of 'post' systems, in contrast, the biometric data have already been captured and the comparison and identification occur only after a significant delay. This involves material, such as pictures or video footage generated by closed circuit television cameras or private devices, which has been generated before the use of the system in respect of the natural persons concerned.

Finally, a third level of classification is included in the proposal, which imposes an arguably light legal framework in certain specific cases. Article 52, entitled "Transparency obligations for certain AI systems" establishes a duty of transparency in three situations, which are relevant to Facebook.

First, Article 52 (1) states that

> [p]roviders shall ensure that AI systems intended to interact with natural persons are designed and developed in such a way that natural persons are informed that they are interacting with an AI system, unless this is obvious from the circumstances and the context of use.

This rule concerns interactions with AI and aims at avoiding any kind of deception related to this form of communication. For instance, "chatbots" are nowadays extensively used and, due to their growing effectiveness, it has even been proposed that empathic chatbot could be therapeutic in combating adverse effects of social exclusion.[109] According to this article, this tool should be flagged as communication with AI to avoid any misunderstanding.

Second, Article 52 (2) stipulates that "[u]sers of an emotion recognition system or a biometric categorisation system shall inform of the operation of the system the natural persons exposed thereto". Facebook is directly affected by this article, as, for instance, its face recognition system falls within the category of a biometric categorization system. As regards the "emotion recognition system", Facebook does not officially automatically process its users' mood through AI analysis of their behavior. It could be argued that it does not have to, as most users already reveal their emotional state through the various reaction buttons. However, it has patented various tools to do so and has acquired an arsenal of "emotional tech".[110] For instance, in 2017, Facebook was granted a patent on a system of detection of emotions based on typing speed, which would automatically add emotion stickers to text messages, and a patent on a system of detection of emotions through capturing the picture of a face, in order to automatically add "emoji" to the photo.

Third, Article 52 (3) of the proposal states that

> [u]sers of an AI system that generates or manipulates image, audio or video content that appreciably resembles existing persons, objects, places or other entities or events and would falsely appear to a person to be authentic or truthful ('deep fake'), shall disclose that the content has been artificially generated or manipulated.

This disposition concerns the Facebook users who would post videos on the platform using deepfake technology. This technology, which allows a face to be inserted in a video, has dramatically grown in popularity and accuracy, with the consequence that the resulting video may be confused with a real one under some circumstances. While this practice is certainly not illegal by itself (respecting, however, copyright law provisions for the use of video, data privacy legislation, and the right to publicity/protection of personality for the use of the face), it has also been used in

---

[109] De Gennaro et al. (2020), p. 3061.

[110] CB Insights (2017).

the context of misinformation (see Sect. 7.1.3). The duty of transparency would therefore oblige the author to flag the content as "produced through AI" when uploaded on the platform.

In conclusion, this duty of transparency is a positive step towards better regulation of AI. However, the practical implications of the Artificial Intelligence Act, if adopted, would be minimal for Facebook. The proposal fails to meet the need for a complete legal framework for AI that is not "high risk", which would encompass not only a right to transparency, but also the right to explanation already suggested by the GDPR and a right against discriminative bias of the AI. However, the Artificial Intelligence Act does not close the door to further regulation of this topic. In Article 69, it suggests a co-regulation approach, through the adoption of codes of conduct in this field, under the supervision of the EU Commission.

References

Bard P, Bayer J, Carrera S (2016) A comparative analysis of media freedom and pluralism in the EU Member States. Research paper by the European Parliament's Committee on Civil Liberties, Justice and Home Affairs (LIBE). PE 571.376

Bayer J, Bard P (2020) Hate speech and hate crime in the EU and the evaluation of online content regulation approaches. Op.cit., p 38

Bell CC (1978) Racism, narcissism, and integrity. J Natl Med Assoc 70(2):89–92

Bucher T (2017) The algorithmic imaginary: exploring the ordinary affects of Facebook algorithms. Inf Communication Soc 20(1):30–44. https://doi.org/10.1080/1369118X.2016.1154086

Busch C, Graef I, Hofmann J, Gawer A (2021) Uncovering blindspots in the policy debate on platformpower: Final report. European Commission. https://platformobservatory.eu/app/uploads/2021/03/05Platformpower.pdf

CB Insights (2017) Facebook's emotion tech: patents show new ways for detecting and responding to users' feelings. CB Insights, research briefs. https://www.cbinsights.com/research/facebook-emotion-patents-analysis/

Cooper P (2021) How the Facebook algorithm works in 2021 and how to make it work for you. Hootsuite. https://blog.hootsuite.com/facebook-algorithm/

Council of Europe's Committee of Ministers (2018) Recommendation CM/Rec(2018)2 to member States on the roles and responsibilities of internet intermediaries, 7 March, par.2.3

Craglia M, Annoni A, Benczur P, Bertoldi P, Delipetrev P, De Prato G, Feijoo C, Fernandez Macias E, Gomez E, Iglesias M, Junklewitz H, Lopez Cobo M, Martens B, Nascimento S, Nativi SM, Polvora A, Sanchez I, Tuomi I, Vesnic Alujevic L (2018) Artificial intelligence - A European perspective. EUR 29425. Publications Office, Luxembourg, p 19. https://doi.org/10.2760/936974

Das S, Kramer A (2013) Self-censorship on Facebook. In: Proceedings of the International AAAI Conference on Web and Social Media, vol 7, no 1

De Gennaro M, Krumhuber E, Gale L (2020) Effectiveness of an empathic chatbot in combating adverse effects of social exclusion on mood. Front Psychol 10:3061. https://doi.org/10.3389/fpsyg.2019.03061

Desmaris S, Dubreuil P, Loutrel B (2019) Creating a French framework to make social media platforms more accountable: Acting in France with a European vision. Mission report "Regulation of social networks – Facebook experiment". https://www.numerique.gouv.fr/uploads/Regulation-of-social-networks_Mission-report_ENG.pdf

ECtHR (2020a) Guide on Article 17 of the European Convention on Human Rights. Council of Europe, Strasbourg, p 6

ECtHR (2020b) Guide to Article 10 of the Convention – Freedom of expression. Council of Europe, Strasbourg

EU Commission (1992) Pluralism and media concentration in the internal market. An assessment of the need for community action. Green Paper. Annexes. COM (92) 480 final/annex, 23 December 1992

EU Parliament (2013) Resolution on the EU Charter: standard settings for media freedom across the EU. 2011/2246(INI), 21 May 2013

Facebook (2021) Taking action against people who repeatedly share misinformation, Facebook app, https://about.fb.com/news/2021/05/taking-action-against-people-who-repeatedly-share-misinformation/

Frantziou E (2015) The horizontal effect of the charter of fundamental rights of the EU: rediscovering the reasons for horizontality. Eur Law J 21(5):657–679

Gray A (2016) Freedom of speech: which country has the most? World Economic Forum. https://www.weforum.org/agenda/2016/11/freedom-of-speech-country-comparison/

Hao K (2021) How Facebook got addicted to spreading misinformation. MIT Technology Review. https://www.technologyreview.com/2021/03/11/1020600/facebook-responsible-ai-misinformation

Helberger N, Trilling D (2016) Facebook is a news editor: the real issues to be concerned about. Media Policy Blog

Horten M (2021) Algorithms patrolling content: where's the harm?. Available at SSRN 3792097

Hudson D (2019) If your judge is your Facebook friend, should that be disqualifying? ABA Journal. https://www.abajournal.com/magazine/article/judge-facebook-friend-florida

Huhn WR (2005) The State action doctrine and the principle of democratic choice. Hofstra Law Rev 34:1379

Human Rights Council (2018) Report of the independent international fact-finding mission on Myanmar, A/HRC/39/64, https://www.ohchr.org/Documents/HRBodies/HRCouncil/FFM-Myanmar/A_HRC_39_64.pdf

Jensen S (2017) Putting to rest the three generations theory of human rights. Open Global Rights. https://www.openglobalrights.org/putting-to-rest-the-three-generations-theory-of-human-rights/

Kalsnes B, Ihlebæk KA (2021) Hiding hate speech: political moderation on Facebook. Media Culture Soc 43(2):326–342

Kerr R (2019) From Holmes to Zuckerberg: keeping marketplace-of-ideas theory viable in the age of algorithms. Communication Law Policy 24(4):477–512. https://doi.org/10.1080/10811680.2019.1660543

Kleis Nielsen R, Cornia A, Kalogeropoulos A (2016) Report on Challenges and opportunities for news media and journalism in an increasingly digital, mobile, and social media environment, Council of Europe Report, Ref DGI(2016)18, p 34

Knox JH (2008) Horizontal human rights law. Am J Int Law 102:1

Kreft J (2017) Algorithm as demiurge: a complex myth of new media. In: Batłko R, Szopa A (eds) Strategic imperatives and core competencies in the era of robotics and artificial intelligence. IGI Global, Pennsylvania, pp 146–166

Krzeminska-Vamvaka J (2009) Horizontal effect of fundamental rights and freedoms – much ado about nothing? German, Polish and EU theories compared after Viking Line. Jean Monnet Working Paper 11/09. https://jeanmonnetprogram.org/wp-content/uploads/2014/12/091101.pdf

Lee N (2014) Facebook Nation, 2nd edn. Springer, Cham

Lerman R (2020) Facebook says it has taken down 7 million posts for spreading coronavirus misinformation. The Washington Post. https://www.washingtonpost.com/technology/2020/08/11/facebook-covid-misinformation-takedowns/

Lewandowsky S, Smillie L, Garcia D, Hertwig R, Weatherall J, Egidy S, Robertson RE, O'connor C, Kozyreva A, Lorenz-Spreen P, Blaschke Y, Leiser M (2020) Technology and democracy: understanding the influence of online technologies on political behaviour and decision-making, EUR 30422 EN. Publications Office of the European Union, Luxembourg, ISBN 978-92-76-24089-1, JRC122023. https://doi.org/10.2760/593478

McGonagle T (2013) The Council of Europe against online hate speech: conundrums and challenges. IViR. https://rm.coe.int/16800c170f, p 10

Mirani L (2015) Millions of Facebook users have no idea they're using the internet. Quartz. https://qz.com/333313/milliions-of-facebook-users-have-no-idea-theyre-using-the-internet/

Mosseri A (2021) Shedding more light on how Instagram works

Müller K, Schwarz C (2020) Fanning the flames of hate: social media and hate crime. SSRN: https://ssrn.com/abstract=3082972

Oster J (2015) Media freedom as fundamental right. Cambridge University Press, Cambridge, p 107

Paul K (2019) Zuckerberg defends Facebook as bastion of 'free expression' in speech. The Guardian. https://www.theguardian.com/technology/2019/oct/17/mark-zuckerberg-facebook-free-expression-speech

Samoili S, López CM, Gómez E, De Prato G, Martínez-Plumed F, Delipetrev B (2020) AI watch, defining artificial intelligence. EUR 30117 EN. Publications Office of the European Union, Luxembourg. https://doi.org/10.2760/382730

Sandberg S (2018) An update on the Civil Rights Audit. Facebook blog. https://about.fb.com/news/2018/12/civil-rights-audit/

Santayana G (1980) Reason in common sense: the life of reason Volume 1. Unabridged Dover Press, Mineola

Sethuraman R (2019) Why am I seeing this? We have an answer for you. Facebook Newsroom. https://about.fb.com/news/2019/03/why-am-i-seeing-this/

Solsvik T, Abutaleb Y (2016) Facebook reinstates Vietnam photo after outcry over censorship. Reuters. https://www.reuters.com/article/us-facebook-norway-primeminister-idUSKCN11F194

Šucha V, Gammel J-P (2021) Humans and societies in the age of artificial intelligence. Publications Office of the European Union, Luxembourg, p 26. https://doi.org/10.2766/61164

Townend J (2017) Freedom of expression and the chilling effect. In: Tumber H, Waisbord S (eds) The Routledge companion to media and human rights. Routledge, Abingdon

Vaidhyanathan S (2018) Anti-social media: how Facebook disconnects us and undermines democracy. Oxford University Press, Oxford, p 10

Vorras A, Mitrou L (2021) Unboxing the black box of artificial intelligence: algorithmic transparency and/or a right to functional explainability. In: Synodinou TE, Jougleux P, Markou C, Prastitou-Merdi T (eds) EU internet law in the digital single market. Springer, Cham, pp 247–264

Wachter S, Mittelstadt B, Floridi L (2017) Why a right to explanation of automated decision-making does not exist in the general data protection regulation. Int Law Data Privacy 76:79–90

Williamson P (2016) Take the time and effort to correct misinformation. Nature News 540(7632): 171

Wilson R, Gosling S, Graham L (2012) A review of Facebook research in the social sciences. Perspect Psychol Sci 7(3):203–220

Youyou W, Kosinski M, Stillwell D (2015) Computer-based personality judgments are more accurate than those made by humans. Proc Natl Acad Sci 112:1036–1040

Chapter 9
E-commerce, Consumer Protection and Advertising Rules

It is estimated that

> [o]ver 80% of social referrals to e-commerce sites come through the most used social platforms some of which having more than 2 billion monthly active users and 7 million active advertisers.[1]

The platform has come a long way since the time it was only a virtual place for posting selfies. Facebook enjoys a remarkably unique position: it already has, by definition, contact with billions of potential consumers. This giant marketplace is characterized by a paradox: while myriads of e-commerce shops are flourishing, and although e-commerce was a lifeline for many companies during the pandemic, the biggest share of the overall value generated is attributed to the GAFAM.[2]

The EU, through pursuing its ideal of a single market, has much experience in regulating this field, both through competition law policies and consumer protection principles. These regulations, however, are not enough to address the gigantic gap created by the platform. Furthermore, new legal issues emerge, such as the rise of cryptocurrencies, which deeply interest Meta. Consequently, this field of law is characterized by constant reforms and updates, at the risk, sometimes, of coherence issues.[3]

One of the most substantial reforms was the adoption of the "omnibus Directive"[4] in 2019, which modifies all four basic EU instruments of consumer protection: the Consumer Rights Directive (2011/83/EU), the Price Indications Directive (98/6/

---

[1] European Commission (2020b), p. 24.

[2] See European Commission (2020a).

[3] Cauffman and Goanta (2021), pp. 758–774.

[4] Directive (EU) 2019/2161 of the European Parliament and of the Council of 27 November 2019 amending Council Directive 93/13/EEC and Directives 98/6/EC, 2005/29/EC and 2011/83/EU of the European Parliament and of the Council as regards the better enforcement and modernisation of Union consumer protection rules, OJ L 328, 18.12.2019, p. 7–28, ELI: http://data.europa.eu/eli/dir/2019/2161/oj.

EU), the Unfair Contract Terms Directive (93/13/EEC), and the Unfair Commercial Practices Directive (2005/29/EC). Even more recently, the EU Commission has intervened again with new regulation proposals. The EU's intervention is mainly through the "digital services package", composed of the DSA proposal (see Sect. 6. 2.4) and the Proposal for a Regulation on Contestable and Fair markets in the Digital Sector (the Digital Markets Act) (DMA).[5]

This chapter will first present the existing legal arsenal on e-commerce and consumer protection (Sect. 9.1) and then focus on the new rules emerging from the digital services packages in this field (Sect. 9.2). Finally, it will discuss the legal repercussions of Facebook's cryptocurrency project, called "Diem" which should be closely examined as example of how EU regulations forced the company to withdraw a project despite being one of its core strategies (Sect. 9.3).

9.1 The Existing Legal Arsenal on e-Commerce and Consumer Protection

9.1.1 Consumer Protection and Facebook Marketplace

9.1.1.1 Abusive Clauses and Duty of Conformity

Facebook's contractual relationships with its users are governed by a constellation of policies. Other than the basic provisions in the Terms of Service, Community Standards, and data policy, a multitude of other policies may apply depending on the situation, such as commercial terms, advertising policies, music guidelines or "live policy" (for live streaming events). It is impressive that these various policies are construed as applying worldwide, ignoring for instance the specificities of EU contract law. However, many clauses contained in these policies may not pass the fairness test introduced by the EU legislator.[6] Already some national courts have considered that the California courts jurisdiction clause is abusive (see Sect. 8.2.3). It should be reminded that any abusive clause in a contract between consumer and business is deemed to be void under EU law. Furthermore, although the concept of consent is far less strict in contract law than in data privacy legislation, EU consumer protection law entails a duty to provide clear and accessible information related to the contractual obligations induced by the creation of an account on the platform.

The philosophy of the law relating to abusive clauses is to ensure that a business does not unfairly exploit an imbalance in the overall economics of the contract. Since access to the platform is free, the users' economic burden could be seen as inexistent.

---

[5]Proposal for a Regulation of the European Parliament and of the Council on contestable and fair markets in the digital sector (Digital Markets Act), 2020/0374(COD).

[6]Council Directive 93/13/EEC of 5 April 1993 on unfair terms in consumer contracts. ELI: http:// data.europa.eu/eli/dir/1993/13/2011-12-12.

However, this perspective overlooks the fact that users' data is collected as a means of payment in lieu of monetary compensation in the so-called "data economy". The EU legislator adopted this point of view in the Directive on certain aspects concerning contracts for the supply of digital content and digital services.[7] Indeed, the Directive does not only apply where a monetary price is given as consideration but also when "the consumer provides or undertakes to provide personal data to the trader".[8] The omnibus Directive has generalized this position to all EU instruments concerning consumer protection.[9]

One recurrent theme on Facebook is that the creation of multiple legal burdens will eventually lead the company to have to charge for access. This shift towards another business model will necessitate a huge update to the contractual obligations. However, the Directive on supply of digital services does mention that modification of this kind of contract is legal only if "made without additional cost to the consumer".[10] It has to be concluded that the shift towards paid access would simply not be legal from an EU law perspective.

Furthermore, the Directive states in Article 8 that the digital service shall

be fit for the purposes for which digital content or digital services of the same type would normally be used, taking into account, where applicable, any existing Union and national law, technical standards or, in the absence of such technical standards, applicable sector-specific industry codes of conduct.[11]

It is therefore possible to conclude that, in case of negligent enforcement of technical moderation standards, and generally speaking of the users' account management, the company's liability is triggered. Interestingly, the ECJ explicitly legitimates the role of consumer associations as watchdogs in these matters. Specifically, the Court has validated the compatibility with EU law of the German legislation which allows a consumer protection association to bring legal proceedings against the person

---

[7] Directive (EU) 2019/770 of the European Parliament and of the Council of 20 May 2019 on certain aspects concerning contracts for the supply of digital content and digital services. OJ L 136, 22.5.2019, p. 1–27, ELI: http://data.europa.eu/eli/dir/2019/770/oj.

[8] Article 3 (1) of the Directive.

[9] See recital 31 of Directive 2019/2161:

Digital content and digital services are often supplied online under contracts under which the consumer does not pay a price but provides personal data to the trader. Directive 2011/83/EU already applies to contracts for the supply of digital content which is not supplied on a tangible medium (i.e. supply of online digital content) regardless of whether the consumer pays a price in money or provides personal data. However, that Directive only applies to service contracts, including contracts for digital services, under which the consumer pays or undertakes to pay a price. Consequently, that Directive does not apply to contracts for digital services under which the consumer provides personal data to the trader without paying a price. Given their similarities and the interchangeability of paid digital services and digital services provided in exchange for personal data, they should be subject to the same rules under that Directive.

[10] Article 19 (1) (b) of the Directive.

[11] Article 8 (1) (a) of the Directive.

allegedly responsible for an infringement of the laws protecting personal data, on the basis of the infringement of the prohibition of unfair commercial practices, a breach of a consumer protection law or the prohibition of the use of invalid general terms and conditions. Proof of a mandate from concerned consumers is not even required.[12]

9.1.1.2 Concerns Over Meta's Growing Market Power

It has been noted by the EU Commission that

> [a]lthough their impact depends on the types of platform concerned and their market power, some platforms can control access to online markets and can exercise significant influence over how various players in the market are remunerated. This has led to a number of concerns over the growing market power of some platforms. These include a lack of transparency as to how they use the information they acquire, their strong bargaining power compared to that of their clients, which may be reflected in their terms and conditions (particularly for SMEs), promotion of their own services to the disadvantage of competitors, and non-transparent pricing policies, or restrictions on pricing and sale conditions.[13]

The issue is that the abuses by Meta of its dominant position on the social media market are not restricted to acts of merging (see Sect. 2.2.5), as Article 102 of the TFEU also refers to exploitative conduct as being characteristic of a dominant position. Specifically, three kinds of exploitative abuse by Facebook that could directly harm consumers can be listed: excessive pricing, that is, in marketplace of data, the collection of 'excessive' amounts of personal data, discriminatory pricing (use of profiling tools to vary prices such as those for advertising), and unfair trading conditions, through the imposition of unfair policy for instance.[14]

Therefore, the collection of excessive amounts of personal data become an issue at the frontier between data privacy legislation and competition law. The cumulative application of principles of competition law on issues related to personal data presents some conceptual difficulties, as some conflicts may arise between the GDPR's principles and competition law. It could be said that the GDPR, as lex specialis, already incorporates all EU law principles, including competition law rules, and exclusively applies in this matter. The German courts had therefore asked the ECJ to take an explicit position on this matter, asking whether

> the rules in Chapter VIII, in particular in Article 80(1) and (2) and Article 84(1), of Regulation (EU) 2016/679 1 preclude national rules which – alongside the powers of intervention of the supervisory authorities responsible for monitoring and enforcing the Regulation and the options for legal redress for data subjects – empower, on the one hand, competitors and, on the other, associations, entities and chambers entitled under national

---

[12]ECJ, C-319/20, Meta Platforms Ireland Limited, formerly Facebook Ireland Limited, v Bundesverband der Verbraucherzentralen und Verbraucherverbände – Verbraucherzentrale Bundesverband e.V., 28 April 2022, ECLI: ECLI:EU:C:2022:322.

[13]EU Commission (2015).

[14]Botta and Wiedemann (2019), pp. 465–478.

law, to bring proceedings for breaches of Regulation (EU) 2016/679, independently of the infringement of specific rights of individual data subjects and without being mandated to do so by a data subject, against the infringer before the civil courts on the basis of the prohibition of unfair commercial practices or breach of a consumer protection law or the prohibition of the use of invalid general terms and conditions.[15]

The case will hopefully cast more light on this thorny issue.

In parallel, the revelation that Meta had participated in a secret agreement called "Jedie Blue" with Alphabet for online display advertising services did not go unnoticed by the EU Commission. The EU Commission opened a formal antitrust investigation into this matter.[16] With the participation of Meta's Audience Network in Google's Open Bidding program, it is a credible possibility that any other competitors in the market of online advertisement would have been de facto excluded from the market, thereby breaching EU competition rules on anticompetitive agreements between companies. Through header biddings such as Google Open Bidding, advertisement publishers offer their space to multiple networks of announcers at once. Although advertisements on the Facebook platform work differently from a technical perspective, it is easy to argue that both companies directly compete in the market of online advertisement, generally speaking. A deal between then would constitute an illegal cartel under EU competition law.

9.1.1.3 Dark Patterns Again and Other Unfair Commercial Practices

Dark patterns (see Sect. 2.4.4 for an analysis from the perspective of data privacy legislation) are part of a general deception scheme that is potentially present on social media, the responsibility for which lies with both the platform as a trader, but also with third parties profiting from the deceptions. Various social media practices fall within the scope of unfair commercial practices, as defined by the EU Directive.[17] The EU Commission remarked in 2016 that

[s]ome social media have become platforms for advertising, product placement and consumer reviews. Therefore, they can present increased risks for hidden and misleading advertising, given that commercial elements are often mixed with social and cultural user-generated content. Furthermore, consumers could experience social media just as services

---

[15] ECJ, C-319/20, Facebook Ireland Limited v. Bundesverband der Verbraucherzentralen und Verbraucherverbände – Verbraucherzentrale Bundesverband e.V., logged on 15 July 2020.

[16] European Commission (2022) Antitrust: Commission opens investigation into possible anticompetitive conduct by Google and Meta, in online display advertising. Press Release. IP/22/1703.

[17] Directive 2005/29/EC of the European Parliament and of the Council of 11 May 2005 concerning unfair business-to-consumer commercial practices in the internal market and amending Council Directive 84/450/EEC, Directives 97/7/EC, 98/27/EC and 2002/65/EC of the European Parliament and of the Council and Regulation (EC) No 2006/2004 of the European Parliament and of the Council ('Unfair Commercial Practices Directive'). OJ L 149, 11.6.2005, p. 22–39. ELI: http://data.europa.eu/eli/dir/2005/29/oj.

for the exchange of information between consumers and may not be aware that traders use social media for marketing purposes.[18]

The regulation applies to Facebook and prohibit it from facilitating and selling paid "likes" and sponsored comments, from deceptively using the term "free" while presenting services that receive personal data as consideration, and from directly exhortation to children (Article 5 (3) of the Directive). Article 6 of the Directive prevents Facebook from misleading users in relation to commercial practices involving the use of mechanisms such as "likes". Recital 49 of the omnibus Directive characteristically considers that

> Traders should also be prohibited from submitting fake consumer reviews and endorsements, such as 'likes' on social media, or commissioning others to do so in order to promote their products, as well as from manipulating consumer reviews and endorsements, such as publishing only positive reviews and deleting the negative ones. Such practice could also occur through the extrapolation of social endorsements, where a user's positive interaction with certain online content is linked or transferred to different but related content, creating the appearance that that user also takes a positive stance towards the related content.[19]

It also applies to third-party traders and prohibits hidden marketing, spam and subscription traps. According to point 22 of Annex I of the Directive, it is prohibited to be "falsely representing oneself as a consumer", which includes the emerging phenomenon of false "likes" and comments.

More generally, the Directive plays an essential normative role, as its intervention transforms Facebook's various policies into a binding instrument. Indeed, it has been asserted that

> [n]otwithstanding their possible incorporation into the user agreement, these unilateral instruments also have a legally binding effect on Facebook to the extent that they make public representations about the firm's business practice. If the actual practice departs from these representations, this would constitute an infringement of the rules on fair competition.[20]

Some legal actions are emerging on this matter that will eventually lead to jurisprudential clarification. Notably, the European Consumer Organization (BEUC), that comprises a great number of national consumer protection organizations, filed a complaint against WhatsApp for multiple breaches of EU consumer rights in July 2021. The group considered that the company exercised unfair pressure, in the sense of the Unfair Commercial Practices Directive, on its users to accept the updates of its terms of service, though persistent notifications, using obscure new terms and failing to explain in plain and intelligible language the nature of the changes induced by the terms' update.[21] Following this complaint, the European Commission and the network of national consumer authorities (CPC) sent a letter to WhatsApp, asking

---

[18] EU Commission (2016).
[19] Recital 49 of the Directive 2019/2161.
[20] Wielsch (2019), pp. 197–220.
[21] BEUC (2021).

the company to clarify the changes it made in 2021 to its terms of service and privacy policy and ensure their compliance with EU consumer protection law.[22]

Overall, it should be noted that the EU omnibus Directive has considerably improved the consumer protection within the framework of Facebook's marketplace. First, it adds to Directive 2011/83 on consumers' rights an article 6a that concerns "Additional specific information requirements for contracts concluded on online marketplaces". Too often the marketplace gives users the illusion of a "garage sale" while it is used by business to gain new opportunities. Article 6a aims to correct this situation. It obliges Facebook to identify the seller, that is to declare whether the third party offering the goods, services or digital content is a trader or not, and to explain to the consumer that, in case the seller is a private individual, consumer protection laws do not apply to the contract. Second, it improves the protection against price alteration practices. Specifically, false discounts[23] are prohibited. Automatic price alterations based on individual consumer data are not strictly prohibited (use of personal data in order to proceed to real-time pricing of the goods or services), but a strict duty of information that the price is personalized is added.[24]

9.1.2   Advertising on Facebook

9.1.2.1   General EU Rules on Advertising

Advertising is, by far, Facebook's principal source of revenue. However, advertising is traditionally heavy regulated in the EU. For audiovisual content, it is necessary to refer to the Audiovisual Media Directive (see Sect. 7.1.4). The Directive on Unfair Commercial Practices also applies (see above, Sect. 9.1.1).

Moreover, the Directive concerning misleading and comparative advertising should be mentioned.[25] This Directive proposes a horizontal legal framework for all advertisements, independently of their medium, that regulates misleading and unlawful comparative advertising. Under this directive, comparative advertising per se is not illegal, but associated with a very strict set of conditions that seriously hinder its use. The Directive also adds the possibility of indirect collective action,

---

[22] European Commission (2022) Consumer Protection: WhatsApp has to inform consumers better about the use of their personal data. Press Corner. https://ec.europa.eu/commission/presscorner/detail/en/mex_22_642.

[23] Article 6a of Directive 98/6/EC.

[24] See recital 45 of the omnibus Directive.

[25] Directive 2006/114/EC of the European Parliament and of the Council of 12 December 2006 concerning misleading and comparative advertising (codified version), OJ L 376, 27.12.2006, p. 21–27. ELI: http://data.europa.eu/eli/dir/2006/114/oj.

actions by organizations "regarded under national law as having a legitimate interest in combating misleading advertising or regulating comparative advertising".[26]

Finally, some sector-specific regulations also interfere with the freedom to advertise, partially or totally banning certain advertisements for some products or containing some deceiving information. A general ban applies to advertisements for prescription medicines[27] and to tobacco advertisements.[28] Specific legal frameworks also apply for nutrition and health Claims,[29] regulating when indications such as "low fat" or "helps lower cholesterol" can be mentioned, for food information to consumers,[30] and for food supplements.[31]

Together with the EU relevant legal framework regulating online advertising, Facebook has also, in the search of "authentic" content, developed a series of specific contractual obligations applying to advertisers on Facebook. The company aims to fight "click-baiting". According to the company,

> [c]lick-baiting is when a publisher posts a link with a headline or body text that encourages people to click to see more, without telling them much information about what they will see. Clickbait intentionally omits crucial information or exaggerates the details of a story to make it seem like a bigger deal than it really is.

The risk of click-baiting is one of shadow moderation: the company which multiplies click-baiting practices, if found by the AI, would see its visibility reduced on the platform.

However, this self-regulation approach had already resulted in many failures. One major concern is whether Facebook adopts efficient enough measures to protect its users against "scam" (fraudulent and misleading) advertisements. Given the strategic importance of advertising for the company and the huge economic influence of some

---

[26] Article 5 (1) of the Directive.

[27] Directive 2001/83/EC of the European Parliament and of the Council of 6 November 2001 on the Community code relating to medicinal products for human use, ELI: http://data.europa.eu/eli/dir/2001/83/2019-07-26.

[28] Directive 2003/33/EC of the European Parliament and of the Council of 26 May 2003 on the approximation of the laws, regulations and administrative provisions of the Member States relating to the advertising and sponsorship of tobacco products, ELI: http://data.europa.eu/eli/dir/2003/33/2003-06-20.

[29] Regulation (EC) No 1924/2006 of the European Parliament and of the Council of 20 December 2006 on nutrition and health claims made on foods, ELI: http://data.europa.eu/eli/reg/2006/1924/2014-12-13.

[30] Regulation (EU) No 1169/2011 of the European Parliament and of the Council of 25 October 2011 on the provision of food information to consumers, amending Regulations (EC) No 1924/2006 and (EC) No 1925/2006 of the European Parliament and of the Council, and repealing Commission Directive 87/250/EEC, Council Directive 90/496/EEC, Commission Directive 1999/10/EC, Directive 2000/13/EC of the European Parliament and of the Council, Commission Directives 2002/67/EC and 2008/5/EC and Commission Regulation (EC) No 608/2004, ELI: http://data.europa.eu/eli/reg/2011/1169/2018-01-01.

[31] Directive 2002/46/EC of the European Parliament and of the Council of 10 June 2002 on the approximation of the laws of the Member States relating to food supplements, ELI: http://data.europa.eu/eli/dir/2002/46/2021-03-20.

advertisers, it could be argued that Facebook has a conflict of interest and would naturally place the interests of the advertisers over those of its users. For instance, it has been reported that TikTok advertisements featuring young girls' provocative dancing videos appeared for a while on news feeds of middle-aged men. Facebook's AI had automatically targeted the most common and profitable audience for this content,[32] without any consideration for the potentially perverse effects of such activity.

Specifically, the recent years have seen a huge outbreak of fraudulent advertisements related to cryptocurrency investments. As a result, Facebook has been forced to take some targeted measures, through an "Ads policy on cryptocurrency products and services".[33] From now on, advertisers planning to run ads promoting cryptocurrency, cryptocurrency exchanges, cryptocurrency mining software and hardware, and cryptocurrency investment advice must first receive confirmation that they are eligible to do so.

9.1.2.2 The Regulation 2019/1150 and the Protection of Business Users

In 2019, the EU adopted the Regulation on promoting fairness and transparency for business users of online intermediation services.[34] The regulation aims to reshapes the rules for doing business online, by regulating the conduct of online platforms. However, it is stated that

> [t]his Regulation shall not apply to online payment services or to online advertising tools or online advertising exchanges, which are not provided with the aim of the facilitating the initiation of direct transactions and which do not involve a contractual relationship with consumers.[35]

This exception casts a shadow over the application of the regulation to Facebook. However, it is also explained that

> [e]xamples of online intermediation services covered by this Regulation should consequently include online e-commerce market places, including collaborative ones on which business users are active, online software applications services, such as application stores, and online social media services, irrespective of the technology used to provide such services. In this sense, online intermediation services could also be provided by means of voice assistant technology. It should also not be relevant whether those transactions between business users and consumers involve any monetary payment or whether they are concluded in part offline. However, this Regulation should not apply to peer-to-peer online intermediation services without the presence of business users, pure business-to-business online intermediation services which are not offered to consumers, online advertising tools and

---

[32] Silverman and Mac (2020).

[33] See https://www.facebook.com/business/help/438252513416690.

[34] Regulation (EU) 2019/1150 of the European Parliament and of the Council of 20 June 2019 on promoting fairness and transparency for business users of online intermediation services, OJ L 186, 11.7.2019, p. 57. ELI: http://data.europa.eu/eli/reg/2019/1150/oj.

[35] Article 1 (3) of the Regulation.

online advertising exchanges which are not provided with the aim of facilitating the initiation of direct transactions and which do not involve a contractual relationship with consumers.[36]

In conclusion, it is clear that the EU legislator intended that the platform should be subject to this regulation. Anyway, Facebook had already incorporated the regulation in its contractual ecosystem, adding a specific "Platform to Business Notice" that deals with the impact of the regulation.[37]

In the context of this regulation, Facebook is considered to be a "provider of online intermediation services", defined as legal entity "which provides, or which offers to provide, online intermediation services to business users".[38] Generally speaking, the protection of business users against the market power of the online platform here is dealt with by emphasizing the transparency of the decision process. This transparency is achieved here through imposing various formalities. Therefore, the Regulation has been described as mostly "procedural",[39] at the expense of a more substantial duty of fairness. For instance, Article 3 of the Regulation concerns the "terms and conditions" and imposes transparency on the proposed services and on the terms' potential updates. Also, Article 8 does not actually prohibit differential treatment of business users. It only imposes transparency (that is information) on the various criteria used for differential treatment.

Article 11 merits specific attention, as it establishes an internal complaint-handling system, which Facebook has implemented in this notice.[40] The Regulation requires the online platform provider to identify in their terms and conditions at least two mediators whom they are willing to engage with to attempt to reach an agreement with business users on the settlement, out of court, of any disputes (Article 12). However, at the time of publishing, the platform had yet to choose relevant organizations.

9.1.3 Facebook Competitions

Facebook's algorithm reacts to popularity, which is one of its four major signals (see Sect. 8.3.1). To gain visibility, a brand needs to gain in popularity, which is measured in reactions such as "likes", and in comments. The marketing idea of many companies worldwide is simply to artificially boost the post's popularity, by giving some incentives to react to and/or comment on it. This scheme normally implies a lottery for some specific products of the brand or for some popular gadgets. Participating in the lottery requires various interactions. It could be a simple "Like to

---

[36]Recital 11 of the Regulation.

[37]See https://www.facebook.com/legal/PlatformtoBusinessNotice.

[38]Article 2 (3) of the Regulation.

[39]Busch (2020).

[40]See https://www.facebook.com/commerce_manager/p2b/support/.

win" prize, a "Tag to enter" giveaway, a "like and share" gift, or a "like and comment" contest.

Before discussing the legality of these practices (see below), it should be underlined that even from a practical point of view these competitions are flawed. Indeed, if the user has set his or her settings to private, it would not be possible to trace whether he or she has really shared the content. In the same way, tagging a friend or a family member may not be possible based on the person's settings.

Facebook classifies any content that incentivizes people to click a link or respond to a post through likes, comments or shares under the general term of "engagement bait". All of Facebook's contests fall within this category, together with other similar behaviors such as "vote baiting" content (posts that ask the users to vote using the reaction buttons) or "tag baiting" content (requesting users to "tag" a friend in the comments).

Facebook has trained an AI mechanism to detect engagement bait.[41] This content is "shadow moderated" in the sense that it is shown less in the users' news feed. Furthermore, according to the Content Monetization Policies,[42] such content cannot be monetized. However, shadow moderating has a certain effect on freedom of expression, which means that rules governing its enforcement should be clearly set out. In the case of engagement bait, no clear and general prohibition appears in Facebook's various policies. Indeed, the prohibition appears under Principle 2 of the News Feed Publisher Guidelines, relating to authenticity of content, but no explicit reference to the Publisher Guidelines can be found in the Terms of Service and whether this policy has been incorporated in the contract between Facebook and its users is debatable.

Finally, it must be underlined that not only do Facebook's competitions that are based on "likes" (potentially) violate the contract with the platform, but the organization of a lottery is also, from a legal point of view, a dangerous activity, regardless of contract law. In most EU Member States, a strict legal framework applies to gambling activities in general, from state monopolies to administrative authorizations. Organizing a "clandestine" lottery would expose the company to severe administrative and/or criminal fines. Moreover, a lottery requires specific procedures to guarantee the independence and the neutrality of the draw, most commonly with the participation of notaries public. Any competition that deviates from this procedure would expose the company to criminal and/or civil litigation based on fraud.

---

[41] Silverman and Huang (2017).

[42] See https://www.facebook.com/business/help/1348682518563619.

9.2   The Novelties of the DSA Package Proposal

9.2.1   The DSA Proposal's Impact on e-Commerce

Although it cannot be said the existing legal framework on e-commerce, consumer protection, and advertising practices is non-existent, social media pose new legal issues that needed to be addressed. In intervening, the EU regulator's main purpose is to impose more transparency with respect to the identity of the various actors the services offered.

First, in Article 22 of the DSA proposal, the EU Commission requires the traceability of traders. In case the trader is not located in the Union, it is the duty of the online platform to collect certain information as a condition for pursuing economic activity with the trader. The information collected is listed in the article, which refers for instance to identification documents, bank accounts, and "a self-certification by the trader committing to only offer products or services that comply with the applicable rules of Union law".[43] Facebook has also a related duty to make reasonable efforts to assess whether the collected information is reliable.[44] Finally, the online platform is obliged to make this information available to the recipients of the service, in a clear, easily accessible and comprehensible manner.[45]

Moreover, Article 24 of the DSA proposal, entitled "Online advertising transparency", states that

> [o]nline platforms that display advertising on their online interfaces shall ensure that the recipients of the service can identify, for each specific advertisement displayed to each individual recipient, in a clear and unambiguous manner and in real time: (a)that the information displayed is an advertisement; (b)the natural or legal person on whose behalf the advertisement is displayed; (c)meaningful information about the main parameters used to determine the recipient to whom the advertisement is displayed.

This way, covert marketing is clearly declared illegal. It is not only Facebook that is obliged to adhere to its policy to publish "sponsored content" above the advertisement; traders should also avoid organizing stealth marketing campaigns, such as viral videos presented as authentic.

As part of the category of "very large online platform", Facebook is additionally obliged to follow additional online advertising transparency rules. According to Article 30 of the DSA proposal, it shall "compile and make publicly available through application programming interfaces" a set of information concerning the advertisement, even for one year after the end of the campaign. The information includes the content of the advertisement, the natural or legal person on whose behalf the advertisement is displayed, and

> whether the advertisement was intended to be displayed specifically to one or more particular groups of recipients of the service and if so, the main parameters used for that purpose.[46]

---

[43] Article 22 (1) (f) of the DSA Proposal.

[44] Article 22 (2) of the DSA Proposal.

[45] Article 22 (6) of the DSA Proposal.

[46] Article 30 (2) (d) of the DSA Proposal.

The shadow of Cambridge Analytica here is clearly visible: the EU regulator keeps in mind the possibility of mass manipulation of the electorate through targeted advertisements. This enhanced duty of transparency offers a way to track and eventually restrict this kind of attack on democracy, on the condition, obviously, that this information is used and analyzed accordingly.

Furthermore, both the Council and the Parliament had added new concepts to the original proposal submitted by the Commission. For instance, the compromise DSA proposal also regulates the practice of "dark patterns" (see Sect. 2.4.4 on uses of dark patterns by Facebook and how they relate to the GDPR). Although it is extremely difficult to give a precise legal definition of dark patterns, it should be accepted that any attempt to deceive the platform's user or to impede them from using their rights under the GDPR (for instance, to delete their Facebook account) falls within that definition.

9.2.2 The DMA's Impact on e-Commerce

The DMA proposal works together with its twin, the DSA proposal, to achieve the same purpose: to regulate the GAFAM. It is explicitly stated by the EU Commission:

> A few large platforms increasingly act as gateways or gatekeepers between business users and end users and enjoy an entrenched and durable position, often as a result of the creation of conglomerate ecosystems around their core platform services, which reinforces existing entry barriers. As such, these gatekeepers have a major impact on, have substantial control over the access to, and are entrenched in digital markets, leading to significant dependencies of many business users on these gatekeepers, which leads, in certain cases, to unfair behaviour vis-à-vis these business users. It also leads to negative effects on the contestability of the core platform services concerned.[47]

Indeed, the notion of gatekeeping applies to companies which have at least 45 million monthly end users in the EU and 10 000 annual business users. This obviously makes Facebook a "gatekeeper".[48]

The EU is concerned first of all by the impact that Facebook's enormous economic power has on business users and end-users. Recital 7 of the Proposal indicates that

> business users and end-users of core platform services provided by gatekeepers should be afforded appropriate regulatory safeguards throughout the Union against the unfair behaviour of gatekeepers in order to facilitate cross-border business within the Union and thereby improve the proper functioning of the internal market.

But it is not its only concern. More fundamentally, it is recognized that the GAFAM possess a pan-European economic power that could rival the national institutions, and which is able to distort the single market by itself. Recital 7 continues with this observation:

---

[47] EU Commission (2020a).

[48] Article 2 (2) (c) of the DMA Proposal.

while gatekeepers tend to adopt global or at least pan-European business models and algorithmic structures, they can adopt, and in some cases have adopted, different business conditions and practices in different Member States, which is liable to create disparities between the competitive conditions for the users of core platform services provided by gatekeepers, to the detriment of integration within the internal market.

Consequently, the DMA proposal sets out some new principles to regulate the GAFAM. Overall, 18 rules are in the DMA proposal and in theory all of the principles apply to all gatekeepers. However, some of the rules are not relevant to Facebook in practice, as they seem to have been specifically established in order to fight against Google and Apple's dominant position in the smartphone interface market.

One of the most important principles for Facebook is that of non-discrimination enshrined in Article 5, that states that gatekeepers should

allow business users to offer the same products or services to end users through third party online intermediation services at prices or conditions that are different from those offered through the online intermediation services of the gatekeeper.[49]

In addition, the proposal includes more legal principles, some of which could potentially be relevant for Facebook. However, the principles in Article 6 of the DMA proposal are not mandatory per se. The EU Commission has the prerogative to activate them against a specific gatekeeper, taking a case-by-case approach.

The proposal also adds a principle of fairness, specifying that the gatekeeper should

refrain from using, in competition with business users, any data not publicly available, which is generated through activities by those business users, including by the end users of these business users, of its core platform services or provided by those business users of its core platform services or by the end users of these business users.[50]

Moreover, the proposal inserts an obligation of interoperability. The EU Commission's original proposal mentioned that the gatekeeper should

allow the installation and effective use of third party software applications or software application stores using, or interoperating with, operating systems of that gatekeeper and allow these software applications or software application stores to be accessed by means other than the core platform services of that gatekeeper. The gatekeeper shall not be prevented from taking proportionate measures to ensure that third party software applications or software application stores do not endanger the integrity of the hardware or operating system provided by the gatekeeper.[51]

It should be noted that Facebook already authorizes third-party developers to integrate their solution into their platform. Nevertheless, in the final agreement reached with the Parliament and the Council in 2022,[52] this duty of portability has

---

[49] Article 5 (b) of the DMA Proposal.

[50] Article 6 (1) (b) of the DMA Proposal.

[51] Article 6 (1) (c) of the DMA Proposal.

[52] European Parliament (2022) Deal on Digital Markets Act: EU rules to ensure fair competition and more choice for users. Press Release. https://www.europarl.europa.eu/news/en/press-

been extended and now also covers instant messaging, which would have huge consequences for Meta's Facebook messenger and WhatsApp services.

Furthermore, the principle of portability of personal data present in the GDPR (see Sect. 2.2.4) is largely extended: it covers all kind of data and its effective exercise is ensured. The proposal states that the gatekeeper should

> provide effective portability of data generated through the activity of a business user or end user and shall, in particular, provide tools for end users to facilitate the exercise of data portability, in line with Regulation EU 2016/679, including by the provision of continuous and real-time access.[53]

The possibility to use combined personal data (for instance personal data from both the Facebook platform and the WhatsApp service) is restricted and only the lawful basis of explicit consent is retained as legitimate.

In conclusion, the DMA proposes very specific rules, targeted with precision at some GAFAM activities that are regarded threatening the free market. It could be said that the digital market and the GAFAM's influence have forced the EU legislator to adapt its classic approach on competition law. In this sense,

> [i]t breaks in a radical way with the long-term evolution towards a standard-based rule of reason approach in competition law (with its focus on the effects on consumer welfare), which is widely seen as ineffective for digital markets.[54]

Nevertheless, even if this selection of "18 commandments" by the EU legislator in the DMA proposal is certainly backward-looking,[55] the regime's flexibility is preserved through a mechanism that provides the Commission with the power to add new obligations. Indeed, the Commission may intervene through ensuing delegated acts, in order to ensure market contestability and B2B fairness.[56]

9.3 Diem: Facebook's Cryptocurrency

9.3.1 Facebook's History with Digital Currencies: From Libra to Diem

The major shortcoming of Facebook's marketplace from an economic point of view is that it does not support online payments. Generally speaking, the lack of micro-transaction tool manifestly hinders the economic potential of the platform. In this context, Meta's interest in developing an internal form of payment should not be seen just as a way to keep in touch with the technological developments of the

---

room/20220315IPR25504/deal-on-digital-markets-act-ensuring-fair-competition-and-more-choice-for-users.

[53] Article 6 (1) (h) of the DMA Proposal.

[54] Kerber (2021).

[55] de Streel and Larouche (2021), pp. 46–63.

[56] Article 10 of the DMA Proposal.

famous blockchain technology that gave birth to the iconic Bitcoin, but mainly as a vital strategic axis for the platform. To enable a payment feature is key for the development of social commerce.[57] However, as much as Facebook wanted its payment system, its initiative encountered fierce opposition from various actors (see below) which ultimately led to the cancellation of the project.

In 2019, Facebook announced that it had prepared a digital currency called "Libra". However, multiple court actions were filed with respect to this name, on the ground that it potentially infringes various trade marks. In Europe, the attempt to protect Libra failed, as Facebook finally withdrew its EU trade mark application after receiving five oppositions.[58] Eventually, Meta announced that it had changed its project name and called it "Diem" ("Day", in Latin). In 2022, the company announced that it had sold its Diem assets to a third party, officially closing all relationship with the cryptocurrency.[59] It is the first time Meta has abandoned one of its major strategic investments. As it appears that the EU's efforts to regulate the matter had heavily influenced Meta's decision to shut the project down, the Diem experience provides valuable lessons on the interactions between the company and EU regulators.

The essence of the project was to create a payment feature using blockchain technology but in a restricted environment and with safeguards that assure its stability. Indeed, the volatility of most "first wave" cryptocurrencies such as Bitcoin had neutralized any attempts to use them as anything other than a risk investment project (and arguably a Ponzi pyramid scheme).[60] The Diem cryptocurrency was to be managed by a not-for-profit association, formally independent from Facebook, called the "Diem Association".[61] Unlike Bitcoin, Diem tokens will not be created by mining. They will be created when purchased ("minted") and destroyed ("burned") when spent. Their value is pegged to real currencies (mainly US dollars) in order to preserve its stability, on the model, generally, of a new generation of cryptocurrencies called "stablecoins". Only members of the Diem Association have access to the blockchain, so as to preserve its stability and security. Diem tokens are backed by a reserve of assets made up of cash or cash equivalents and very short-term government securities.

In 2019, the EU saw this initiative as a threat to financial stability, as Facebook would become a "shadow bank", that is a financial service similar to traditional commercial banks but unregulated. In a joint statement, the EU Ministers of Finance declared that

> [n]o global stablecoin arrangement should begin operation in the European Union until the legal, regulatory and oversight challenges and risks have been adequately identified and addressed.[62]

---

[57] Riefa (2020).

[58] See https://euipo.europa.eu/eSearch/#details/trademarks/018083389.

[59] Rudegeair and Hoffman (2022).

[60] Chiluwa (2019), pp. 439–458.

[61] https://www.diem.com/en-us/white-paper/#cover-letter.

[62] Council of the EU (2019).

It could be argued that this project was in part the cause of the EU Commission's new legislative proposal on this matter (see Sect. 9.3.3), which probably marked the end of the project.

9.3.2 Smart Contracts

It has been announced that Diem supports "smart contracts" technology. A smart contract is a code programmed into a blockchain and attached to a specific cryptocurrency transaction. The transaction will execute upon receiving the right trigger programmed in the smart contract. This way, the code mimics the "term" of a contract. A simple term, such as the payment of a sum each month, will be encoded without difficulty into smart contracts. In the same way, any trigger from the digital world (e.g. the account has achieved certain value or the date of creation was before a certain date) would serve as an automatic term. This solution can extend to triggers from the real world, too. For instance, a transaction is carried out once a death certificate of the account's owner is uploaded onto the blockchain by a trusted agent.

Smart contracts technology has received an enthusiastic reception from the tech world and some legal scholars. It is noted that "[b]y virtue of their tamper-proof, time-stamped and immutable character, smart contracts offer a viable option to create and strengthen trade relationships".[63] It is argued that smart contracts could enhance consumer protection, by inscribing the reimbursement of the consumer into the smart contract in case of non-execution of the contract.

Other legal scholars are more reserved. The automatic logic of a smart contract is by nature incompatible with the notion of interpretation of the contractual intent, which is fundamental in contract law. Smart contracts in this sense cannot reflect the relational contractual theory, where rights and obligations laid down in a written contract are just a part of the broader relationship between two transacting parties.[64] Moreover, smart contracts cannot encompass the notions of good faith or force majeure.[65] The fact that an agreement is in part codified in the shape of a smart contract does not protect the parties from defective titles or informational defects for instance.[66] Finally, as shown in the example above with the death certificate, smart contracts cannot replace the mechanisms of contract law: what if the death certificate is falsified, or unreadable by the machine, or for some legal reason (missing person) no death certificate is available? Consequently, "smart contracts" are not contracts in the legal sense of the term, but automatic means of execution of some parts of the contract (conditional transactions).

---

[63] Borgogno (2019), pp. 885–902.

[64] Levy (2017), pp. 1–15.

[65] Gianscaspro (2017), pp. 825–835.

[66] Muka Tshibende (2019), pp. 871–884.

9.3.3 The EU Regulation on Cryptocurrency and Its Impact on Diem

The EU officially acknowledged the existence of cryptocurrencies in 2019, through a modification of its criminal law protection against fraud. Indeed, the Directive on combating fraud and counterfeiting of non-cash means of payment[67] states that

> 'virtual currency' means a digital representation of value that is not issued or guaranteed by a central bank or a public authority, is not necessarily attached to a legally established currency and does not possess a legal status of a currency or money, but is accepted by natural or legal persons as a means of exchange, and which can be transferred, stored and traded electronically.[68]

The Directive ensures that any kind of fraud related to cryptocurrencies is efficiently assessed by criminal law.

As shown above (Sect. 9.3.1), Diem is to be regarded as a "stablecoin" and its stability presents an even bigger threat to the EU institutions than a classic volatile cryptocurrency such as Bitcoin. While the EU institutions were opposed to the Diem project in the absence of a relevant legal framework, the 2020 regulation proposal by the EU Commission on "markets in Crypto-assets",[69] takes an all-new dimension. Diem is certainly implicitly targeted by this initiative. Characteristically, the EU Commission notes that

> [a] relatively new subset of crypto-assets – the so-called 'stablecoins' – has recently emerged and attracted the attention of both the public and regulators around the world. While the crypto-asset market remains modest in size and does not currently pose a threat to financial stability, this may change with the advent of 'global stablecoins', which seek wider adoption by incorporating features aimed at stabilising their value and by exploiting the network effects stemming from the firms promoting these assets.[70]

In the proposal, stablecoins such as Diem are described by two concurrent notions, the "asset-referenced token" on the one hand, and the "e-money token" on the other hand. While an "asset-referenced token" is defined as

> a type of crypto-asset that purports to maintain a stable value by referring to the value of several fiat currencies that are legal tender, one or several commodities or one or several crypto-assets, or a combination of such assets,[71]

the "e-money token" means

---

[67]Directive (EU) 2019/713 of the European Parliament and of the Council of 17 April 2019 on combating fraud and counterfeiting of non-cash means of payment and replacing Council Framework Decision 2001/413/JHA, OJ L 123, 10.5.2019, p. 18–29, ELI: http://data.europa.eu/eli/dir/2019/713/oj.

[68]Article 2 (d) of the Directive.

[69]Proposal for a Regulation of the European Parliament and of the Council on Markets in Crypto-assets, and amending Directive (EU) 2019/1937, COM/2020/593 final.

[70]EU Commission (2020a).

[71]Article 3 (1) (3) of the Proposal.

a type of crypto-asset the main purpose of which is to be used as a means of exchange and that purports to maintain a stable value by referring to the value of a fiat currency that is legal tender.[72]

In other words, Diem is definitely an "asset-referenced token", but it may be an "e-money token" if it mainly focuses on cross-border exchanges of values.

First, the Regulation proposal imposes several substantial formalities on the "asset-referenced token issuer", which must be established in the EU and publish a white paper that must be approved by its competent authority. It should be noted that the Diem Association has indeed published its "white paper",[73] but for now, has elected Switzerland for its headquarters. It is most probable that Diem will belong to the subcategory of "significant asset-referenced tokens" because of the cross-border activities involved.[74] Consequently, as another formality, a decision from the European Banking Authority (EBA) is needed before the authorization is given (Article 39).

Then, a regime of responsibility of the issuer of asset-referenced tokens is proposed. They are to act honestly, fairly and professionally (Article 23), their marketing communications are to be controlled (Article 24), some transparency requisites are set (information obligations in Article 26, rules on conflicts of interest in Article 28, notification of changes to its management body in Article 29, publication of various policies regarding the token owners' rights in Article 35) and they are required to establish a complaint handling procedure (Article 27).

Subsequently, rules are established for the stability of the scheme. Rules are set on the reserve of assets backing the asset-referenced tokens (Article 32), requirements are enacted for the custody of the reserve assets (Article 33), and the reserve of assets must be invested in very secure and short-term investments only (Article 34). The proposal institutes an obligation of an own fund (Article 31) "equal to an amount of at least the higher of the following: (a)EUR 350 000; (b) 2% of the average amount of the reserve assets referred to in Article 32." This threshold could be regarded as very low, due to the possibility of massive and unpredictable movements in the digital environment, and, specifically, due to the disinformation campaigns that plague the platform. However, Article 31 (2) provides for an adjustment mechanism, giving national authorities the competence to increase this threshold up to 20% depending on the risks involved.

Most importantly, Article 36 blocks the road towards financial services, stating that

[i]ssuers of asset-referenced tokens or crypto-asset service providers shall not provide for interest or any other benefit related to the length of time during which a holder of asset-referenced tokens holds asset-referenced assets.

---

[72] Article 3 (1) (4) of the Proposal.

[73] DIEM (2019).

[74] Article 39 (1) (e) of the Proposal.

Furthermore, assuming that Diem would be classified as a significant asset-referenced token, an obligation of interoperability is set that could have potentially been problematic for Meta. Article 41 (2) states that

> [i]ssuers of significant asset-referenced tokens shall ensure that such tokens can be held in custody by different crypto-asset service providers authorised for the service referred to in Article 3(1) point (10), including by crypto-asset service providers that do not belong to the same group, as defined in Article 2(11) of Directive 2013/34/EU of the European Parliament and of the Council, on a fair, reasonable and non-discriminatory basis.

Alternatively, in cases where Diem is recognized not as an asset-referenced token but as e-money, a similar regime applies as regards the formalities, responsibilities, etc. Like the asset-referenced token, an e-money token can be regarded as "significant" with enhanced obligations. However, the matter becomes even more complicated for the Diem Association. Indeed, in this case, no activity would be legal unless the Diem Association received the statute of credit institution or of "electronic money institution" within the meaning of Article 2(1) of Directive 2009/110/EC. Article 43 also states that "e-money tokens" are deemed to be electronic money for the purpose of the electronic money institution Directive.[75]

Nevertheless, Diem could avoid the classification of Diem as "e-money" because its value is not based on a single fiat money but on a basket of various fiat moneys. However, Diem's white paper refers to a project to create subcategories of the token that would be based on a single fiat currency.[76] This project would trigger the most restrictive "e-money" regime, which certainly had a substantial impact on the company's decision to withdraw from the project.

References

BEUC (2021) Consumer groups file complaint against WhatsApp for unfairly pressuring users to accept its new policies. Press release, 12.07, https://www.beuc.eu/publications/consumer-groups-file-complaint-against-whatsapp-unfairly-pressuring-users-accept-its/html

---

[75] Directive 2009/110/EC of the European Parliament and of the Council of 16 September 2009 on the taking up, pursuit and prudential supervision of the business of electronic money institutions amending Directives 2005/60/EC and 2006/48/EC and repealing Directive 2000/46/EC, OJ L 267, 10.10.2009, p. 7–17, ELI: http://data.europa.eu/eli/dir/2009/110/oj.

[76] The White paper mentions that

> We are therefore augmenting the Libra network by including single-currency stablecoins in addition to ≈LBR, initially starting with some of the currencies in the proposed ≈LBR basket (e.g., LibraUSD or ≈USD, LibraEUR or ≈EUR, LibraGBP or ≈GBP, LibraSGD or ≈SGD). This will allow people and businesses in the regions whose local currencies have single-currency stablecoins on the Libra network to directly access a stablecoin in their currency.

Source: https://www.diem.com/en-us/white-paper/#cover-letter.

Borgogno O (2019) Smart contracts as the (new) power of the powerless? The stakes for consumers. Eur Rev Private Law 6:885–902

Botta M, Wiedemann K (2019) Exploitative conducts in digital markets: time for a discussion after the facebook decision. J Eur Compet Law Practice 10(8):465–478. https://doi.org/10.1093/jeclap/lpz064

Busch C (2020) The P2B Regulation (EU) 2019/1150: towards a "procedural turn" in EU platform regulation? J Eur Consumer Market Law 9(4)

Cauffman C, Goanta C (2021) A new order: the digital services act and consumer protection. Eur J Risk Regul 12(4):758–774. https://doi.org/10.1017/err.2021.8

Chiluwa IM (2019) "Truth," Lies, and Deception in Ponzi and Pyramid Schemes. In: Handbook of research on deception, fake news, and misinformation online. IGI Global, Hershey, pp 439–458

Council of the EU (2019) Joint statement by the Council and the Commission on "stablecoins". Press release. https://www.consilium.europa.eu/en/press/press-releases/2019/12/05/joint-statement-by-the-council-and-the-commission-on-stablecoins/

de Streel A, Larouche P (2021) The European Digital Markets Act proposal: how to improve a regulatory revolution. Concurrences N° 2-2021, 46–63

DIEM (2019) White paper 2.0. Diem association. See https://www.diem.com/en-us/white-paper/

EU Commission (2015) A digital single market strategy for Europe. Communication to the EU Parliament and the Council. COM(2015) 192 final

EU Commission (2016) Guidance on the implementation/application of Directive 2005/29 on unfair commercial practices, Working Document accompanying the document Communication from the Commission "A comprehensive approach to stimulating cross-border e-Commerce for Europe's citizens and businesses". SWD/2016/0163 final

EU Commission (2020a) Explanatory memorandum to the proposal for a regulation on markets in crypto-assets, and amending directive. SEC(2020) 306 final

EU Commission (2020b) Impact Assessment Report accompanying the Digital Markets Act proposal. Commission Staff Working Document. SWD(2020) 364 final, p 24

Gianscaspro M (2017) Is a "Smart Contract" really a smart idea? Insights from a legal perspective. Comp Law Secur Rev 33:825–835

Kerber W (2021) Taming tech giants with a per-se rules approach? The digital markets act from the "Rules vs. Standard" Perspective. Available at SSRN: https://ssrn.com/abstract=3861706 or https://doi.org/10.2139/ssrn.3861706

Levy K (2017) Book-smart, not street-smart: blockchain-based smart contracts and the social workings of law, 3. Engaging science. Technol Soc:1–15. https://doi.org/10.17351/ests2017

Muka Tshibende L-D (2019) Contract law and smart contracts: property and security rights issues. Eur Rev Private Law 6:871–884

Riefa C (2020) Consumer protection on social media platforms: tackling the challenges of social commerce. In: Synodinou TE, Jougleux P, Markou C, Prastitou T (eds) EU internet law in the digital era. Springer, Cham. https://doi.org/10.1007/978-3-030-25579-4_15

Rudegeair P, Hoffman L (2022) Facebook's cryptocurrency venture to wind down, sell assets. Wall Street Journal. https://www.wsj.com/articles/facebooks-cryptocurrency-venture-to-wind-down-sell-assets-11643248799

Silverman H, Huang L (2017) Fighting engagement bait on Facebook. About Facebook (fb.com)

Silverman C, Mac R (2020) Facebook profits as users are ripped off by scam ads. BuzzFeed News. https://www.buzzfeednews.com/article/craigsilverman/facebook-ad-scams-revenue-china-tiktok-vietnam

Wielsch D (2019) Private law regulation of digital intermediaries. Eur Rev Private Law 2:197–220

Chapter 10
Conclusion

In physics, the famous "Irresistible force paradox" asks this question: What happens when an unstoppable force meets an immovable object? The social media revolution is certainly unstoppable, and, at the same time, the EU is also certainly not willing to give up its sovereignty. But the premise of the question is flawed: neither an irresistible force, nor an immovable object exists in the universe. The real question is therefore one of interaction: how the EU can influence and accompany the societal changes induced by the platform, and how the new online activities push for an adaptation of existing legal principles and for an evolution of the institutions.

For the first aspect of this question, the answer needs to take into account the complex web of legal issues surrounding the activities of social media: rules on personal data, protected by IP law data, raw data, defamation, hate speech, and misinformation laws, interpreted in the light of freedom of expression, and, finally, e-commerce law. It has been decided to individually discuss each of them here, presenting an ever-changing map of EU regulations and case-law from the ECJ. This way, the legal challenges and the interests at stake for each field of law are easily accessible and understandable. However, this presentation should not hide the general picture of the scale of the EU interventions that are relevant to Facebook. These interventions indicates a growing and certainly justified fear: "[m]any fear Google, Amazon, and Facebook, and their power over not just commerce, but over politics, the news, and our private information."[1] Consequently, a "Facebook EU law" is currently emerging.

On the second aspect of this question, it would be superficial to only retain from this work the multiplicity of EU regulations. While this long and patient construction of a social media legal framework is itself worth mentioning, Facebook's influence is far deeper. By forcing the EU institutions to intervene to protect the single digital market, the platform unconsciously participates in a deepening of the EU's integration. This evolution is clearly present for instance in the DMA proposal, which

---

[1] Wu (2018).

P. Jougleux, *Facebook and the (EU) Law*, Law, Governance and Technology Series 48, https://doi.org/10.1007/978-3-031-06596-5_10

transforms the EU Commission into a digital regulator. Overall, the need to adapt had consequences on the EU institutions' philosophy. It has been said that

> laissez-faire politics and decades of deregulation have reduced the capacity and willingness of lawmakers to address these systemic concerns. Antitrust action provides a ready framework for intervening in the platform economy.[2]

This double evolution does not occur without friction. From the Schrems decisions we can see a concrete danger to the fragmentation Facebook's network. The Cambridge Analytica scandal has damaged citizens' and the institutions' confidence in the company. At the same time, it is undeniable that social media has considerably enhanced the right of billions of persons to express and to be informed, during a time when the level of citizens' mistrust towards traditional media is on the rise.[3]

This book started with a metaphor between the current GAFAM and the East India Companies. For two centuries, the Companies enjoyed a monopoly over Europe's dealings with Asia. At the risk of oversimplifying a complex historic reality, it could be asserted that the fall of the British East India Company was provoked by two main events: the enforcement of sanctions against illegal activities and a democratic surge. The first event refers to the "Opium Wars", when the Chinese government asked the company to hand over all its opium stock. The second event describes the locals' rebellion and insurgence from its Indian territories. Likewise, the EU institutions have recently, through multiple new regulations and proposals, explicitly clarified their intent to enforce the "EU way" against social media and to protect democratic values in the digital world.

This does not have to mean the fall of Facebook. The EU institutions, through a model of co-regulation in some fields such as copyright law, hate speech, or misinformation, are ready to acknowledge the privileged position of partner to the company. Future developments will show whether the parties are ready to progress this way.

References

Ardèvol-Abreu A, Gil de Zúñiga H (2017) Effects of editorial media bias perception and media trust on the use of traditional, citizen, and social media news. Journalism Mass Commun Q 94(3): 703–724
Rochefort A (2020) Regulating social media platforms: a comparative policy analysis. Commun Law Policy 25(2):225–260. https://doi.org/10.1080/10811680.2020.1735194
Wu T (2018) The curse of bigness: antitrust in the new gilded age. Columb Global Reports, 15

---

[2]Rochefort (2020), pp. 225–260.
[3]Ardèvol-Abreu and Gil de Zúñiga (2017), pp. 703–724.

Printed in the United States
by Baker & Taylor Publisher Services